Elevator and Escalator Accident Reconstruction and Litigation

Fourth Edition

James Filippone, P.E.
Joel D. Feldman, Esq.
Ronald D. Schloss
David A. Cooper
Joseph L. Stabler
Gabriel F. Zambrano

Lawyers & Judges Publishing Company, Inc.
Tucson, Arizona

Lawyers & Judges Publishing Company, Inc.

P.O. Box 30040 • Tucson, AZ 85751-0040
(520) 323-1500 • FAX (520) 323-0055
e-mail: sales@lawyersandjudges.com
www.lawyersandjudges.com

Library of Congress Cataloging-in-Publication Data

Names: Filippone, James, editor.
Title: Elevator and escalator accident reconstruction and litigation / James Filippone, P.E., Joel D. Feldman, Esq., Ronald D. Schloss, David A. Cooper, Joseph L. Stabler, Gabriel F. Zambrano [editors].
Description: Fourth edition. | Tucson, Arizona : Lawyers & Judges Publishing Company, Inc., [2018] | Includes bibliographical references and index.
Identifiers: LCCN 2018043708| ISBN 9781936360727 (hardcover : alk. paper) | ISBN 1936360721 (hardcover : alk. paper)
Subjects: LCSH: Liability for elevator accidents--United States. | Liability for escalator accidents--United States.
Classification: LCC KF1287.5.E45 E43 2018 | DDC 346.7303/22--dc23
LC record available at https://lccn.loc.gov/2018043708

ISBN-13: 978-1-936360-72-7
ISBN-10: 1-936360-72-1

Printed in the United States of America
10 9 8 7 6 5 4 3 2 1

Dedications

I dedicate this book to my wife Deanna, daughter Alyssa and grandson Jericho.

—James Filippone

I dedicate my portion of this book to my wife Dianne L. Anderson, and my children, Casey and Brett. I gratefully acknowledge the assistance of Sarah Martine and Cathy Lundy in the preparation of this book.

—Joel D. Feldman

I dedicate my portion of this book to my father for introducing me to elevators and to my entire family, thirteen and growing, but especially to my wife Rosalie (Campbell) Schloss, who gave me immense support throughout the last fifty plus years.

—Ronald D. Schloss

I dedicate this book to Lynda, my partner and friend, who has provided endless support in the preparation of this book.

—David A. Cooper

I dedicate my portion of this book to my mother and father who introduced me to the elevator industry and served as my role models and mentors; my family who are my business partners; my wife and executive administrative assistant, Donna, for her continued love, patience and support over the past 36 years; my two creative and perceptive sons, Jay and Ben; and Ben's safe return following his service and sacrifice as a U.S. Army Combat Infantryman, Baghdad, Iraq (2006-2008). Hooah!

—Joseph L. Stabler

Contents

Photographs and Illustrations

Preface

The primary purpose of this book is dedicated to public safety. The authors hope that this book will assist those who strive to protect the public. The authors also hope that this book will spur changes that will reduce the frequency and severity of accidents.

This book is intended to provide guidance for accident reconstruction and litigation related to devices such as elevators and escalators. The points of view of the attorney, defendant, plaintiff, engineer, manufacturer, building owner or manager, inspector, risk manager, maintainer, and even the users are explored. It is intended to provide the reader with a basic understanding of the operation of this type of equipment, the potential dangers, typical accident scenarios and variables, the process of determining the causes of an accident, and successful litigation procedures. Our intent is not to make the reader an expert in these areas, but rather to outline a general process. It is also hoped that this book can help bring some common sense into the investigation and litigation of elevator and escalator accidents.

In addition, elevator and escalator components vary from manufacturer to manufacturer and vintage. Each installation also presents its own unique variables and conditions. Therefore, it is not feasible, nor is it intended, for this book to describe all the possible hazards that exist, all the possible causes of accidents, or all the potential cures. While the book is primarily directed toward users in the U.S., the information offered can be very useful elsewhere, particularly in Canada and the U.K. Because of the similar elevator and escalator code requirements in the U.S. and Canada, the vast majority of the issues that arise in the U.S. will also arise in Canada. We have also included in Chapter 10 issues germane to the U.K.

Because of the differing and constantly changing laws and regulations in the various jurisdictions it is not feasible, nor intended, for this book to be an all-inclusive treatise on the law and regulatory requirements, even in the U.S.

Most of the technical sections of the first edition of this book were completed with the ASME A17.1d-2000 Safety Code for Elevators and Escalators (which is an addendum to the ASME A17.1-1996 Edition) as the latest published code in the U.S. Subsequently, the ASME A17.1-2000 Edition (not to be confused with the ASME A17.1-d-2000 addenda) was published. This code contained many significant changes (e.g., new safety devices, maintenance requirements) from previous versions of the ASME A17 code, not the least of which was how the code was organized and numbered. Many of the technical changes introduced should improve the safety of new elevators and escalators and likely will significantly affect accident analyses. The 2000 edition also "harmonized" the U.S. and Canadian elevator and escalator code provisions, so that they were almost identical. However, the scope of the changes was so extensive that it was issued with an extended phase-in period and had an effective date of March 23, 2002. Most jurisdictions have since adopted it or later editions.

The second edition of this book was written with the ASME A17.1-2004 Safety Code for Elevators and Escalators as the latest published code in the U.S. Also, a supplement ASME A17.1S-2005 was approved but not yet published. This supplement covered the inclusion of "machine room-less" technology. Elevators using this technology are new to the U.S., but have been deployed widely in Europe and Asia. The impact on accidents of this technology will bear watching, especially for maintainability issues and worker safety.

The third edition of this book was written with the ASME A17.1-2010/CSA B44-10 Safety Code for Elevators and Escalators (an addenda to the ASME A17.1-2007/CSA B44-07 Edition) as the latest published code in the U.S. This is a bi-national code, applicable in both the U.S. and Canada. In addition, the ASME A17.6-2000 Standard for Elevator Suspension, Compensation and Governor Systems was published. This was the first edition of a new standard to codify requirements for traditional steel wire ropes and novel technologies, such as aramid fiber ropes (nonmetallic) and elastomeric coated steel belts (small diameter steel cords with a flat elastomeric covering). Also, the ASME A17.7-2007/CSA B44.7-2007 Performance-Based Safety Code for Elevators and Escalators was published. This was the first edition of a new standard to codify a process for approving alternative designs for the prescriptive requirements contained in the ASME A17.1/B44 standards that traditionally were addressed ad hoc in each jurisdiction via a variance process. In effect, accredited third party organizations approve designs that vary from the consensus ASME A17.1/B44 standards for monetary compensation. The impact on accidents of this will bear watching.

The prevailing elevator and escalator safety codes when this Fourth Edition was being written are described in Chapter 1.

As can be seen, the elevator and escalator industry is presently in a relatively high state of flux due to a dynamic technological, economic, and regulatory environment. Although it is likely that these new developments will affect the accident rate, only time will tell to what extent. The impact on safety bears watching.

A very disturbing development in the elevator industry is the corporate management decision to focus on profits at the expense of providing adequate maintenance. The effect on the accident rate will be predictable.

It is a sad fact of life that accidents occur. However, the key question to ask is what caused the accident and what were the contributory factors. Some accidents have an element of "in the wrong place at the wrong time" about them, and others have an element of disregard for the equipment involved. Sadly others fall into the category of sheer negligence or incompetence.

The authors have had the unpleasant task of investigating numerous accidents that have included deaths and disfigurements. They hope that this book will be a catalyst for change so that these incidents may be avoided in the future.

The authors have seen escalators that were placed in service with a step missing (imagine the potential injuries and pain that could have resulted), and people who have somehow managed to bypass barriers and walk up an escalator on the step axles, after all of the steps were removed! Clearly the potential for abuse exists on all sides involved.

Most people have an inordinate fear of elevators, and a cavalier attitude toward escalators. To the contrary, the potential dangers to a passenger are far greater on an escalator than an elevator. This is because the elevator passenger is enclosed in the cab, which for the most part isolates the passenger from the moving components. The escalator passenger is constantly exposed to moving components.

The most common fear on elevators is free fall, which is a rare occurrence. The most frequent elevator accidents are trips and falls and being hit by the doors. While significant injuries can result from these types of accidents, death and disfigurement seldom occur. Probably, the most serious potential danger to elevator passengers is falling down the hoistway (shaft). The potential for serious injury and death is probably greater for elevator mechanics than for passengers because the mechanics are often in inherently hazardous locations that the general public never enters (e.g., pits, top of car, machine room).

Escalator entrapment-type injuries (such as side-of-step entrapments, combplate entrapments, handrail) have resulted in disfigurements, strangulations, scalpings, and even death. Unfortunately, the victims are frequently small children.

It is claimed that the total number of escalator accidents is small compared to the large number of users. However, this is of little comfort to the victims and their families, especially considering that the injuries are severe and the risks are well known. Despite the basic fact that the passenger will always be close to the moving components on escalators, efforts can be made to minimize the risks.

Passengers on an elevator or escalator place their trust in inspectors for ensuring that the equipment is in a safe operating condition. However, the lack of funding in the inspecting agencies has created a disturbing trend toward "self-inspections" by maintenance companies (talk about the fox watching the chicken coop). In addition, many jurisdictions give inspectors immunity from lawsuits, which can lead to lax enforcement. Also, even the best inspector cannot discover changes made to the equipment after it has been inspected.

This book will commonly use the term *elevators and escalators* to include not only elevators and escalators, but also other vertical transportation equipment such as dumbwaiters, material lifts and moving walks. In addition, the term A17.1 will be used interchangeably for ASME A17.1 and ASME A17.1/CSA B44.

Chapter 1

Codes, Regulations and Related Issues

Synopsis

1.1 The AHJ and the Governing Code

There is an old saying among inspectors: "*Codes are written in blood*". This recognizes that most codes include requirements to prevent known hazards from occurring based on actual accidents.

The codes that govern the design, construction, operation, inspection, testing, maintenance, alteration and repair of vertical transportation equipment (elevators, escalators, moving walks, dumbwaiters, material lifts, stairway chairlifts and platform, or wheelchair, lifts) are in a virtual state of Balkanization. This is due to the large number of organizations responsible for adopting and enforcing the applicable code requirements. These organizations are known as authorities having jurisdictions (AHJs).

There are hundreds, if not thousands, of AHJs in the U.S. alone. This includes various federal government agencies (U.S. Postal Service, General Services Administration, Department of Defense, etc.), various state governments and agencies, and various local governments and agencies. The governing code for the vertical transportation equipment in a building will be determined by which AHJ has jurisdiction over the building. Therefore, it is not uncommon to have several buildings adjacent to each other, especially in large cities, each under the domain of a different AHJ.

To further complicate this situation is the fact that some AHJs have not adopted any code to govern vertical transportation equipment. For example, Texas did not have an elevator code for many years. In addition, each AHJ may interpret the same code requirements differently.

Another complication arises because vertical transportation equipment is governed by the code that was in effect when the equipment was approved for installation or alteration by the AHJ. Therefore, even within the same AHJ, different codes may apply and be enforced. This means that two elevators side by side in the same building may be governed by different codes.

Most code requirements are not retroactive. Notable exceptions are inspections and tests, alterations, and maintenance, repairs and replacements. However, a number of jurisdictions have retroactive requirements. These can be contained in the local building code or by adoption of the ASME A17.3 *Safety Code for Existing Elevators and Escalators*.[1]

In general, a jurisdiction adopts and enforces a code through the process of passing laws and issuing regulations. Usually one of the model building codes will be used, which in turn will specify the applicable elevator and escalator code. However, many AHJs have or have had their own building codes, and many may have had their own elevator codes at one time.

Until 2000, three major competing model building codes were being used in the U.S., mostly on a regional basis. These were the *National Building Code,*[2] the *Uniform Building Code,*[3] and the *Standard Building Code*.[4] As model codes, they were published with the intent for them to be adopted by jurisdictions nationally and internationally. They cover the requirements for various building systems, including vertical transportation equipment. These three codes were harmonized and published in 2000 as the *International Building Code*.[5] However, many jurisdictions have adopted their own building codes. For example, New York City had its own building code for many years until it recently adopted the International Building Code (with many exceptions).

The ASME A17.1 *Safety Code for Elevators and Escalators*[6] (ASME A17.1) is the most universally used model elevator and escalator code in the U.S. As of 2011, every state in the U.S. with an elevator and escalator code has adopted the ASME A17.1 Code (some with and some without exceptions or changes).

This apparent uniformity is deceiving. For instance, when the 1999 version of ASME A17.1 was the latest version many jurisdictions had only adopted earlier versions. For example, New York City had only adopted the 1989 version and Chicago had only adopted the 1971 version (plus most but not all of the addenda through 1975). However, both have now adopted a more current version. In addition, as mentioned previously, existing equipment is still for the most part governed by earlier or different codes than is new equipment.

Other jurisdictions had their own outdated codes in effect until recently. For example, until about 2004 when it adopted ASME A17.1-2000 with the A17.1a-2002 addenda, Pennsylvania had its own code, which was basically a 1938 code with amendments up to 1981.

Enforcement of the governing code can be through the use of government workers, contract workers, or third parties. However, some jurisdictions are allowing elevator and escalator maintenance contractors to inspect their own work or building owners hiring their own inspectors, even with the obvious conflict of interest that this raises.

New Jersey is used to illustrate the hierarchy of these codes and regulations. The New Jersey Administrative Code (NJAC) is a set of regulations that establishes which codes are adopted and establishes enforcement mechanisms. The NJAC adopts, in part, the International Building Code (IBC), with certain changes. The IBC in turn adopts for vertical transportation equipment the ASME A17.1 Code and establishes certain additional requirements. Enforcement is overseen by a state agency, either directly or through local jurisdictions. These local jurisdictions may directly employ their enforcement officials; they may contract with private companies to perform the inspections; or they may use state inspectors.

The code situation for vertical transportation equipment mirrors the situation for other codes related to various building systems (such as fire protection and electrical). However, a strong movement is under way both nationally and internationally to harmonize these various codes. For example, harmonization of ASME A17.1 *Safety Code for Elevators and Escalators* and CAN/CSA B44 *Safety Code for Elevators, Escalators, Dumbwaiters, Moving Walks and Freight Platform Lifts*[7] (the elevator and escalator code effective in most of Canada) was approved in 2000 and became effective in 2002. The outcome was two almost identical codes, with a few deviations. Although these two model codes were very similar (identical in many sections), numerous differences existed before this harmonization. The ASME A17.1-2007/CSA B44-07 Safety Code for Elevators and Escalators was approved/issued in 2007 as the first fully bi-national (US and Canada) code.

As can be seen from the previous discussion, the codes that govern vertical transportation equipment are, paradoxically, in states of both constant flux and stagnation. The model codes are constantly being updated to address new technology and enhance safety, but there is usually a delay of years before an AHJ adopts these revisions.

Determining which code applies in a jurisdiction can be frustrating. The best course of action is to rely on your elevator and escalator expert. If the situation requires otherwise, the best local sources are the local building code enforcement agency and the state code enforcement agency. Be aware that erroneous information can easily be given. It is best to get the pertinent information in writing.

Another good source is the Internet. Two good sites are www.eadai.com and www.elevator-world.com. The first, www.eadai.com, provides extensive information on how to locate codes and standards, and provides a directory of AHJs in the U.S. and Canada with links to the appropriate regulations. The second website, www.elevator-world.com, is an excellent source for information related to elevators and escalators. Again, remember that codes are in a constant state of flux, so always check that the information shown is current.

It is important to note that no matter what code applies, it represents the *minimum level of safety* that is required. Every manufacturer exceeds the requirements of the code simply by the fact that many details of the standard features of an elevator are not even addressed in the code. These details have been considered by some as commercial issues and not safety issues, though in practice they can and do affect safety.

1.2 Elevator and Escalator Codes, Standards, and Publications

A. ASME A17.1/CSA B44—Safety Code for Elevators and Escalators

The ASME A17.1/CSA B44[26] Safety Code for Elevators and Escalators currently covers the requirements for the design, construction, operation, inspection, testing, maintenance, alteration and repair of elevators, escalators, dumbwaiters, material lifts with automatic transfer devices, and moving walks. It primarily covers newly installed equipment, but does have retroactive provisions for existing equipment, primarily those for tests and inspections, alterations, maintenance, repairs and replacements.

The fourth edition of this book was written with the A17.1-2016/CSA B44 2016 Edition Safety Code for Elevators and Escalators as the latest published code in the U.S and Canada. This is a bi-national code, applicable in both the U.S. and Canada. In effect, this code contains the complete ASME A17.1 code with additional CSA B44 requirements. Previously they were published as very similar separate standards—ASME A17.1 *Safety Code for Elevators and Escalators* and CSA B44 *Safety Code for Elevators, Escalators, Dumbwaiters, Moving*

Walks and Freight Platform Lifts. These two standards were "harmonized" in their 2000 editions, which made them almost identical and they were published as a bi-national standard for the first time with the A17.1-2007/CSA B44-07 edition. This book will use the term A17.1 interchangeable for ASME A17.1 and ASME A17.1/CSA B44.

The A17.1 Code is approved as an ANSI (American National Standards Institute) standard, which means it is a national consensus standard. This designation recognizes that the Code was developed under procedures that meet the criteria established by ANSI.

Some earlier versions of A17.1 covered the requirements for wheelchair lifts and stairway chairlifts. However, ASME A18 *Safety Standard for Platform Lifts and Stairway Chairlifts*[8] now covers those devices.

A17.1-2013/CSA B44-13 included a detailed section on wind turbine elevators, which applies to elevators permanently installed inside a wind turbine tower to provide vertical transportation of authorized personnel and their tools and equipment for servicing, maintaining and inspecting wind turbine equipment. However, detailed requirements for wind turbine elevators were no longer included in A17.1-2016/CSA B44-16 but instead refer to the newly published ASME A17.8-2016/CSA B44.8-16 *Standard for Wind Turbine Tower Elevators*[30].

The first edition of the ASME A17.1 Code was approved and issued in 1921. The 1925 and 1931 editions contained some retroactive provisions for existing equipment to be altered to meet new requirements.

Many of these code editions have supplements (updates), formally known as addenda (or supplements for special cases), which were approved and issued in between editions. Each code addendum is given a sequential letter designation (to denote the supplement sequence), in addition to a year designation. For example, the sixth addendum to the 1971 A17.1 code (approved in 1975) is designated as A17.1f-1975 and the second addendum to the 1996 Code (approved in 1998) is designated A17.1b-1998.

Currently, each edition and addendum has an effective date, which typically is later than the issue date in order to allow users of the Code to make the transition to the new requirements. For many years the code cycle was for an edition to be issued every three years, with annual supplements. However, a three-year cycle with no addenda has been recently adopted. A full history of the A17.1 Code can be found in its Foreword.

The 1955 edition of ASME A17.1 is considered the base for all of the subsequent editions that have been issued up until A17.1-2000, and it significantly differs from the earlier editions. The 2000 edition of A17.1 was significantly revised in both technical content and format. Therefore, elevators are frequently differentiated into "pre-1955," "1955 through 2000" and "2000 and later" categories for code purposes.

As stated earlier, the A17.1/B44 Code is a model code intended to be adopted by various jurisdictions in the U.S. and Canada. Therefore, it in itself does not have any legal standing until it is adopted by the AHJs. **However, it does represent the *minimum* standard for industry practice.**

The ASME Foreword of A17.1 currently provides a summary of the history of the code. The ASME Preface of A17.1 currently covers the intent of the code, the form and arrangement of the document, the use of metric units, the application of requirements to new technology, ASME elevator publications, correspondence with the A17 Committee, abbreviations used in the code and attending Committee meetings. The CSA Preface contains information applicable to Canadian issues. In addition, a roster of all the various A17 and B44 committees and a summary of the changes in each new edition/addendum is also provided in A17.1/B44. Part 1 of A17.1 (the Introduction in previous editions) currently lists what equipment is specifically covered and what equipment is specifically not covered within its scope, covers the retroactive application of its requirements, explains the effective date, explains the purpose of the code, explains the use of alternative methods and exceptions, and provides definitions of terms used in the code. Appendices at the end of the book provide explanatory information.

Most of the A17.1 Codes (A17.1-1921 through A17.1d-2000) were divided into a number of parts (designated with upper case Roman numerals). These parts were further divided into sections (designated with Arabic numerals). For example, Part I is divided into Sections 100, 101, 102, etc., and Part II is divided into Sections 200, 201, 202, etc. Each of these Sections is further broken down into Rules. For example Rule 100.1a, 100.1b, 100.1c, etc.

As an example, A17.1c-1999 is broken down into the following parts:

Part I—Hoistways, Hoistway Enclosures, and Related Structures for Electric Elevators
Part II—Machinery and Equipment for Electric Elevators
Part III —Hydraulic Elevators
Part IV—Power Sidewalk Elevators
Part V —Private Residence Elevators
Part VI—Hand Elevators
Part VII—Hand and Power Dumbwaiters
Part VIII—Escalators
Part IX—Moving Walks
Part X—Routine, Periodic and Acceptance Inspections and Tests
Part XI—Engineering and Type Tests

Part XII—Alterations, Repairs, Replacements and Maintenance
Part XIII—Design Data and Formulas
Part XIV—Material Lifts and Dumbwaiters with Automatic Transfer Devices
Part XV—Special Purpose Personnel Elevators
Part XVI—Rack and Pinion Elevators
Part XVII—Inclined Elevators
Part XVIII—Screw Column Elevators
Part XIX—Elevators Used for Construction
Part XX—Not used; formerly Inclined Stairway Chairlifts and Inclined and Vertical Wheelchair Lifts
Part XXI—Not used; formerly Private Residence Inclined Stairway Chairlifts and Inclined and Vertical Wheelchair Lifts
Part XXII—Shipboard Elevators
Part XXIII—Rooftop Elevators
Part XIV—Elevator Safety Requirements for Seismic Risk Zone 2 or Greater
Part XXV—Limited-Use/Limited-Application Elevators
Appendices

The 2000 edition of A17.1 was significantly revised in both technical content and format from the earlier editions. Some of the significant technical changes that were introduced are:

- Establishing significantly enhanced maintenance requirements (reduces the probability of injuries in general)
- Requiring ascending car overspeed protection (reduces the probability of the car striking the overhead structure)
- Requiring protection against unintended car motion away from the landing under certain failure modes (reduces the probability of falls down the hoistway and shear/crushing injuries)
- Permitting plunger grippers (reduces the probability of the car free falling upon a loss of hydraulic pressure)
- Significantly increasing the overhead clearance requirements (reduces the probability of the car striking the overhead structure)
- Enhancing requirement for temperature and humidity control in machine rooms (reduces the probability of control malfunction)
- Requiring a railing on top of the car for certain conditions (reduces the probability of workers falling)
- Doubling the required illumination at landing sills and in machine rooms (reduces the probability of trips/falls and worker injuries)

- Specifying the maximum kinetic energy of closing doors in addition to the average kinetic energy (reduces the probability and severity of injuries for door strikes)
- Prohibiting side emergency exits (reduces the probability of people falling down the hoistway)
- Requiring a car door interlock for certain conditions (reduces the probability of people falling down the hoistway)
- Eliminating machine room inspection operation when the car door or hoistway door bypass switches are enabled (reduces the probability of falls down the hoistway and shear/crushing injuries)
- Establishing permissive requirements for lowering the car of a hydraulic elevator in the case of main power supply failure (reduces the probability of entrapments)
- Establishing security levels for keys used for the operation or access to equipment (reduces the probability of injuries in general)

As can be seen, many safety enhancements were incorporated into A17.1-2000. While it does contain certain requirements that the authors feel could diminish the level of safety (e.g., not automatically requiring conformance with ASME A17.3 for alterations), overall it overwhelmingly enhances the level of safety for vertical transportation equipment.

The A17.1-2000 and later editions are divided into a number of parts (designated by an Arabic numeral—e.g., Part 2). These parts are further divided into sections (designated with Arabic numerals in a decimal format—e.g., Section 2.1). These sections are further divided into requirements (designated with Arabic numerals in a decimal format—e.g., Requirement 2.1.6.2).

A17.1-2016 is broken down into the following parts:

Part 1—General
Part 2—Electric Elevators
Part 3—Hydraulic Elevators
Part 4—Elevators With Other Types of Driving Machines
    4.1- Rack-and-Pinion Elevators
    4.2- Screw Column Elevators
    4.3- Hand Elevators
Part 5—Special Application Elevators
    5.1- Inclined Elevators
    5.2- Limited-Use/Limited-Application Elevators
    5.3- Private Residence Elevators
    5.4- Private Residence Incline Elevators

5.5- Power Sidewalk Elevators
5.6- Rooftop Elevators
5.7- Special Purpose Personnel Elevators
5.8- Marine Elevators
5.9- Mine Elevators
5.10- Elevators Used for Construction
5.11- Wind Turbine Tower Elevators
5.12- Outside Emergency Elevators

Part 6—Escalators and Moving Walks

Part 7—Dumbwaiters and Material Lifts

7.1- Power and Hand Dumbwaiers Without Automatic Transfer Devices
7.2- Electric and Hand Dumbwaiers Without Automatic Transfer Devices
7.3- Hydraulic Dumbwaiters Without Automatic Transfer Devices
7.4- Material Lifts Without Automatic Transfer Devices
7.5- Electric Material Lifts Without Automatic Transfer Devices
7.6- Hydraulic Material Lifts Without Automatic Transfer Devices
7.7- Automatc Transfer Devices
7.8 Power Dumbwaiters with Automatic Transfer Devices
7.9- Electric Material Lifts with Automatic Transfer Devices
7.10- Hydraulic Material Lifts with Automatic Transfer Devices

Part 8—General Requirements

8.1- Security
8.2- Design and Data Fomulas
8.3- Engineering Tests, Type Tests and Certification
8.4- Elevator Seismic Requirements
8.5- Escalator and Moving Walk Seismic Requirements
8.6- Maintenance, Repair, Replacement and Testing.
8.7- Alterations
8.8- Welding
8.9- Code Data Plate
8.10- Acceptance Inspections and Tests
8.11- Periodic Inspections and Witnessing of Tests
8.11- Flood Resistances

Part 9—Reference Codes, Standards and Specifications

Non-Mandatory Appendices

B. ASME A17.2—Inspectors' Manual/Guide for Inspection of Elevators, Escalators and Moving Walks

This standard contains detailed recommended "how-to" procedures, guidelines and cautionary notes for the inspection and testing of elevators, escalators and moving walks to verify compliance with the ASME A17.1 Code. Many AHJs specifically require that inspections and tests be performed in accordance with A17.2.

Historically, the ASME A17.2 *Inspectors' Manual for Elevators and Escalators*[9] has been published as one book. The first edition of ASME A17.2 was approved in 1937. The eighth edition was approved and issued in 1988. After the A17.2b-1990 addendum (second supplement to A17.2-1998) the book was split into three separate volumes: the ASME A17.2.1 *Inspectors' Manual for Electric Elevators,*[10] the ASME A17.2.2 *Inspectors' Manual for Hydraulic Elevators*[11] and the ASME A17.2.3 *Inspectors' Manual for Escalators and Moving Walks.*[12]

It was again combined into one book with the issue of A17.2-2001 and renamed the *Guide for Inspection of Elevators, Escalators and Moving Walks.*[13] The latest edition as of 2016 was published in 2014 and is scheduled to be published again in 2017. A full history of the Inspectors' Manuals can be found in its Foreword.

Currently a new edition is issued every three years, without any supplements (addenda). Many previous editions had supplements (addenda). Until the Inspectors' Manual was split into separate volumes, the same numbering system was used as in the pre-2000 ASME A17.1 Code (100.1, 100.2, ...). Therefore, the clauses in the Inspectors' Manuals are known as "Items" to help differentiate them from the A17.1 rules. The numbering system subsequently adopted is similar to an ISO numbering system (1.1.1, 1.1.2, etc.).

The Inspectors' Manuals contain a preface, introduction and appendices similar to that used in ASME A17.1. Notable appendices include checklists that are recommended for use when documenting inspections and tests.

An important aspect of the Inspectors' Manuals is that they are designed to address the requirements for A17.1-1955 and later editions and the ASME A17.3 *Safety Code for Existing Escalators.* A limited number of certain requirements of earlier editions have also been included when deemed appropriate. Since the requirements of the earlier A17.1 (pre-1955) codes are significantly different, they are addressed by the earlier versions of the Inspectors' Manuals.

ASME A17.2-2014 includes procedures for the inspection and testing of electric and hydraulic elevators, limited-use limited-application elevators, escalators, moving walks, machine room-less elevators, private residence electric and hydraulic elevators, inclined elevators, and private residence inclined elevators.

ASME A17.2 has been approved by ANSI.

C. ASME A17.3—Safety Code for Existing Elevators and Escalators

The ASME A17.3 *Safety Code for Existing Elevators and Escalators* contains the minimum requirements that were deemed necessary for a ***"reasonable degree of safety for the general public."*** It is intended to be adopted by the AHJs and its provisions are explicitly intended to be retroactive.

Currently, A17.3 contains provisions for electric elevators, hydraulic elevators, dumbwaiters, escalators, moving walks, hand elevators, sidewalk elevators, and private residence elevators. The A17.3 Code has been approved by ANSI.

Unless an AHJ adopts A17.3, it is usually not enforceable. However, it does represent the industry standard for the minimum level of safety. A number of jurisdictions have adopted ASME A17.3 or portions of it. As indicated earlier, AHJs may have their own retroactive requirements in addition to or in lieu of ASME A17.3.

For many versions of A17.1, whenever an alteration is made to existing elevators or escalators it is required that all the requirements of ASME A17.3 must be met regardless of the type of alteration. This is in addition to the specific changes needed for each particular alteration. This is required even if the jurisdiction did not adopt A17.3. This provision was intended to force building owners to bring the level of safety of their vertical transportation equipment to the minimal level of safety when they made a financial commitment to alter the equipment. Some say that it has had the opposite effect by discouraging building owners from upgrading their equipment, because they must then meet certain additional requirements of ASME A17.3 that can become financially significant. Subsequently, A17.1 was revised to only require conformance with A17.3 if the AHJ adopted it.

The first edition of A17.3 (A17.3-1986) was issued in 1986. A17.3-2015 was the latest edition published as this fourth edition was being written. Currently a new edition is published every three years without addenda, or if it is not revised it must be reaffirmed in five years. A full history of A17.3 is contained in its Foreword.

D. ASME A17 Interpretations

ASME publishes interpretations of Code rules/requirements rendered by the A17 Committee as guidance to users of the Code. These interpretations are in response to written requests for answers to specific questions. Anyone can submit an inquiry to the A17 Committee. However it could take years for ASME to give an answer as to the intent of the code rule. Therefore review the interpretations to see if it has already been asked and answered.

The published interpretations are grouped together by time periods. For A17.1 the first set covers the years 1972 to 1979. The 33rd set, the latest published as of 2016, covers the period from July 2012 to October 2015. Similar though much less extensive interpretations have been issued for A17.2 and A17.3. Approved interpretations that have not yet been published are available on the A17 website.

E. Other ASME Elevator Publications

ASME A17.4 *Guide for Emergency Personnel*[14] provides recommended procedures for the safe evacuation of passengers from stalled elevators and firefighters' service operating procedures. It was previously titled the Guide for Emergency Evacuation of Passengers from Elevators. The latest published edition was ASME A17.4-2015 when this book was being written.

CSA B44.1/ASME A17.5 *Elevator and Escalator Electrical Equipment*[15] contains requirements for obtaining the listing and labeling of drive machine controllers, logic controllers, and operating devices that start, stop, regulate, control and protect electrical equipment in the scope of A17.1. The latest published edition was CSA B44.1-14/ASME A17.5-2014 when this book was being written.

ASME A17.6 *Standard for Elevator Suspension, Compensation and Governor Systems*[24] was published in 2007. This was the first edition of a new standard to codify requirements for traditional steel wire ropes and novel technologies, such as aramid fiber ropes (nonmetallic) and elastomeric coated steel belts (small diameter steel cords with a flat elastomeric covering). The latest edition as this book was being written was was ASME A17.6-2010.

ASME A17.7/CSA B44.7 *Performance-Based Safety Code for Elevators and Escalators*[25] was published in 2007. This was the first edition of a new standard to codify a process for approving alternative designs for the prescriptive requirements contained in the A17.1/B44 standards that traditionally were addressed ad hoc in each jurisdiction via a variance process. In effect, accredited third party organizations approve designs that vary from the consensus A17.1/B44 standards for monetary compensation. The latest editions was ASME A17.7-2007/CSA B44.1- 07 when this book was being written.

ASME A17.8-2016/CSA B44.8-16 *Standard for Wind Turbine Tower Elevators* was the first published edition, although previous requirements were contained in ASME A17.1-2013/CSA B44-13.

The Handbook A17.1 *Safety Code for Elevators and Escalators*[16] contains commentary, illustrations and diagrams intended to explain the A17.1 Code requirements. Although published by ASME, the contents of that book are the opinions of its authors and have not been approved by the A17 Committee. The latest edition as this book was being written was ASME A17.1-2013/CSA B44-13.

The QEI-1 *Standard for the Qualification of Elevator Inspectors*[17] covers the recommended procedures for the qualification and duties of inspectors of equipment within the scope of A17.1 and their supervisors. It also contains the requirements for accreditation of organizations that certify QEI inspectors. Currently, two organizations are accredited to certify QEI inspectors and supervisors. The latest edition as this book was being published was ASME QEI-1-2013.

F. Other Elevator and Escalator Publications

The *Elevator Industry Field Employees' Safety Handbook*[18] is the foremost publication devoted to delineating the proper safety practices that should be used when working around elevators and escalators. While this document is intended for use by mechanics, it has many parts that are applicable to others (e.g., inspectors). The latest edition when this book was being written was the 2015 edition.

In the past, revisions were held until sufficient material was available to justify the cost of publishing a supplement. However, now revisions will be published electronically as soon as they are approved. Printed supplements will also be published periodically.

The National Electric Code (NFPA 70),[19] commonly referred to as the NEC, contains the specific electrical requirements related to elevators and escalators in Article 620 and other general electrical requirements. The *National Electric Code Handbook*[20] contains useful commentary and explanations of the requirements of the NEC. The latest edition when this book was being written was the 2017 edition.

1.3 Inspections and Tests

Enforcement of the governing code is accomplished through inspections and tests of the elevators and escalators. Each AHJ establishes the scope and frequency of these inspections and tests through regulations and laws. If an AHJ has no governing regulation regarding elevators and escalators, no inspections or tests may be conducted other than those that might be performed voluntarily by the equipment owner or its maintenance service company.

ASME A17.1 traditionally recognized the following types of inspections and tests:

- acceptance inspection and tests—comprehensive procedures that are performed after the elevator or escalator is installed or altered, but before it is placed in service for use by the public. Included are all the procedures contained in the routine/periodic inspections and periodic tests plus certain additional ones.

- periodic tests—extensive procedures performed by the equipment owner's agent, usually the maintenance company, while the inspector witnesses it. Typically, these are performed annually, every three years and/or every five years depending on the equipment. Typically, they are conducted in conjuntion with one of the periodic inspections.
- periodic inspections (formerly called routine inspections prior to A17.1-2000)—limited in nature such that it can be performed by an inspector by themselves. Typically, these are performed semi-annually, one concurrently with a periodic test.

Starting with A17.1-2000, the inspection and test frequencies became nonmandatory (i.e., recommended frequencies which requires AHJs to specifically mandate the inspection frequency instead of relying on A17.1).

Inspectors may be government workers, contract workers or independent third-party workers, depending on the AHJ. However, some jurisdictions are beginning to allow elevator and escalator maintenance contractors to inspect their own work, even with the obvious conflict of interest that this raises.

It is natural to conclude that the inspection was faulty if something goes wrong with the elevator or escalator after it was inspected or tested. This is not always the case. Certain deficiencies take time to develop. If these types of deficiencies played a part in the accident, then they likely should have been found during the inspection and test procedure. However, once an inspector walks away from an elevator or escalator, the equipment can be easily compromised (e.g., safety switches bypassed). In addition, not all components or systems are required to be inspected or tested. Certainly, an inspector cannot be held at fault in these cases.

Conversely, if the equipment subsequently becomes involved in an accident, it is natural to conclude that if an inspector cited no deficiencies after inspecting or testing the equipment, then there must have been nothing wrong with it. Again, this is not always the case. Although inspections and tests are performed to ensure safety, they are only designed to check for code compliance. In fact, most AHJs will prohibit an inspector from citing a violation that exceeds the applicable code requirements. A component may be in poor condition and on the verge of failure, but if there is no code violation then the inspector is in most cases powerless to cite a violation. In addition, not all components or systems are required to be inspected or tested. In fact, the inspector may be penalized for citing a non-violation. In many cases a creative inspector will find a way to force the issue and have the deficiency corrected. While many inspectors are competent professionals, they are human and do make mistakes, and sadly some are incompetent or corrupt.

Through its regulations or laws, each AHJ establishes the requirements for an individual to qualify to perform inspections and tests on elevators and escalators. The AHJs may have their own certification processes, or they may rely on the certification process of another organization.

ASME A17.1 requires that an elevator and escalator inspector be QEI-certified. Many AHJs have adopted this requirement, but many have not. This certification is obtained by passing a comprehensive written test on the ASME A17.1 Code and related codes. Certain experience requirements must be met in order to take the test. Supervisors of elevator inspectors are also required to be QEI-certified and must meet additional requirements. There are currently two QEI accreditation organizations.

As noted above, A17.2 contains detailed recommended "how-to" procedures, guidelines and cautionary notes for the inspection and testing of electric and hydraulic elevators, limited-use limited-application elevators, escalators, moving walks, machine room-less elevators, private residence electric and hydraulic elevators, inclined elevators and private residence inclined elevators to verify compliance with the ASME A17.1 Code; and many AHJs specifically require that inspections and tests be performed in accordance with A17.2.

1.4 Accessibility Requirements

The topic of elevator accessibility is complicated and too complex to cover adequately in this limited treatise. The reader is directed to *ADA & Building Transportation* for a thorough discussion on the subject of elevator accessibility.[23] The following is a brief discussion of some pertinent issues.

The Americans with Disabilities Act (ADA) of 1990 is the foremost familiar requirement regarding elevator accessibility for the disabled. Its precursor, the Rehabilitation Act, Section 504 (1973), prohibited discrimination against disabled persons for organizations receiving federal financial assistance and set forth requirements for accessibility among other things. However, it must be recognized that the ADA is a federal statute and not a code or regulation. Therefore, it cannot be enforced by local jurisdictions, but must be enforced by the courts and the Department of Justice.

The ICC/ANSI A117.1 Accessible and Usable Buildings and Facilities[21] (not to be confused with ASME A17.1) is a national standard that provides accessibility requirements, including those for elevators. This standard is the basis of many local building code requirements for elevator accessibility by the disabled. By adopting this standard, local jurisdictions can enforce requirements for accessibility, which is not possible with the ADA. For the most part, the requirements of A117.1 and the ADA are very similar. The first version of A117.1 was issued in 1961 and the 2009 version was the most recent as of 2016. Earlier versions were known as ANSI 117.1 or CABO/ANSI A117.1 *Making Buildings and Facilities Accessible to and Usable by the Physically Handicapped.* Some jurisdictions have their own accessibility regulations.

Title II of ADA applies to state and local government facilities and Title III applies to public accommodations and commercial facilities. The scope of ADA indicates when an elevator must be installed as a component of an accessible route in multi-story buildings and gives a number of exceptions. If a building or facility is permitted to use the elevator exception then a limited use-limited application elevator (LULA) conforming to the requirements of ADA and ASME A17.1 can be used. In multi-story residential dwelling units, either a private residence elevator (conforming to ADA and ASME A17.1) or a LULA may be used. Private residence elevators are permitted by ASME A17.1 only in private residential dwelling units or for access to private residences in buildings if they are not accessible to the general public or other building occupants. LULAs are power passenger elevators in which the use and application are limited by size, capacity, speed and rise. Of note is when platform (wheelchair) lifts can be used as a component of an accessible route in multi-story buildings. Platform (wheelchair) lifts are permitted as a component of an accessible route new construction only where permitted by ADA. They are permitted as a component of an accessible route in an existing building.

The *ADA Accessibility Guidelines for Buildings and Facilities* (ADAAG) provided the pertinent elevator guidelines related to the ADA for many years. The United States Architectural and Transportation Barriers Compliance Board, also known as the "Access Board" in Washington, D.C., developed and maintained ADAAG, which was adopted by the Departments of Justice and Transportation (DOJ and DOT) as the design standards for new construction and alteration under the Americans with Disabilities Act. These standards were applicable in all 50 states as the minimum standard, but AHJs can enforce a standard that is stricter. These guidelines were first published in 1991 and subsequently amended.

On September 15, 2010 the Department of Justice published in the federal register the 2010 ADA Standards for Accessible Design (2010 Standards). This standard represents the new requirements for newly designed, constructed or altered state and local government buildings and facilities, public accommodations and commercial facilities to be readily accessible to and usable by individuals with disabilities. Between September 10, 2010 and March 15, 2012 a phase-in period was permitted. State and local government buildings and facilities could have used the 1991 ADA standards (without the elevator exemption), UFAS (see below), or the new 2010 ADA standards; and public accommodations and commercial facilities could have used either the 1991 or 2010 ADA standards. On and after March 15, 2012 the new 2010 ADA standards were required to be used.

The *Uniform Federal Accessibility Standards* (UFAS) contains requirements for elevator accessibility in buildings designed, constructed or leased by federal agencies. This standard was developed to minimize the differences between the standards used previously by four federal agencies (the General Services Administration, the Departments of Housing and Urban Development and Defense, and the United States Postal Service) that are authorized to issue standards under the Architectural Barriers Act of 1968, and between those standards and the access standards recommended for facilities that are not federally funded or constructed.

The NEII *Minimum Passenger Elevator Requirements for the Handicapped*[22] was a set of requirements first published in 1976. It was the elevator industry's response to standardizing the accessibility requirements for elevators. It was subsequently withdrawn because it was not consistent with the ADA.

Both ICC/ANSI A117.1 and the 2010 ADA Standards recognize automatic operation passenger elevators conforming to ASME A17.1, including private residence elevators and limited-use/limited-application elevators (LULAs), and platform (wheelchair) lifts conforming to ASME A18.1 (previously covered by ASME A17.1) as components of accessible routes.

Stairway chairlifts covered by ASME A18.1 (previously covered by ASME A17.1) are not recognized by ICC/ANSI A117.1 and the 2010 ADA standards as components of accessible routes in multiple story buildings. They are usually installed in private residences.

1.5 Existing Equipment

A. ASME A17.3 and Other Retroactive Requirements

As discussed earlier in this chapter, existing equipment generally must only meet the requirements of the code in effect when it was originally installed. Notable exceptions are inspections and tests, alterations, and maintenance, repairs and replacements.

However, a number of jurisdictions have retroactive requirements. These can be contained in the local building code or by adoption of the ASME A17.3. See Section 1.2C above for a discussion of ASME A17.3. Also, the 1925 and 1933 editions of A17.1 contained some retroactive provisions for existing equipment. In addition, jurisdictions may have their own retroactive requirements.

The standard of care for the industry necessitates that the requirements of ASME A17.3, new codes and new technology be addressed and evaluated by the building owner and the maintenance service company.

B. Alterations, Maintenance, Repairs, Replacements and Modernization

A17.1-2000 and later editions established significantly enhanced maintenance requirements. The previous requirements were minimal. See Section 1.2A above and Chapter 4 (especially Section 4.2B) for additional discussion on maintenance issues.

It is important to distinguish between maintenance, repair, replacement, alterations, and modernization. While the various codes may define these terms, the following is a general discussion of the terms.

Maintenance is the process of cleaning, lubrication, examination, adjustment, replacement or repair of parts and testing. Replacement is the process of substituting components with other components that are basically the same. Repair is the process of rehabilitating components. An alteration is a modification to the equipment, such that there is some fundamental change (e.g., increase in rated speed). ASME A17.1 contains a detailed list of alterations and defines each of these terms.

The term "modernization" is commonly heard in the elevator and escalator industry, but there is no universal definition of this term. It could be as simple as aesthetic changes to the interior of the cab, or as extensive as entirely new controls and machinery. Instead of defining it, ASME A17.1 merely refers the reader to the definition of maintenance, repair, replacement and alteration. In many cases, a modernization will be considered an "alteration" by code, and therefore may trigger the retroactive requirements of A17.3.

1.6 Other Devices

There are a number of devices that can easily be confused with those that are governed by ASME A17.1.

Material lifts and dumbwaiters are governed by the requirements of ASME A17.1. Therefore, they share many of the same characteristics as elevators. Material lifts in the U.S. have traditionally been essentially very large dumbwaiters and therefore were not permitted to carry any riders. When ASME A17 was "harmonized" with CSA B44 in 2000, these devices were designated as Type A material lifts; and Type B material lifts that were already included in CSA B44 were added to ASME A17.1. Type B material lifts are permitted to carry only one operator with a number of restrictions such as: access and usage limited to authorized personnel, limited speed and travel, restrictions on penetrating floors and limited to continuous pressure type controls. Type B material lifts are not prevalent in the U.S. All material lifts are required to be inspected and tested by the AHJ by ASME A17.1.

There are devices known as vertical reciprocating conveyors (VRCs), which could be confused with material lifts. VRCs are covered by the significantly less stringent, less prescriptive and less costly requirements of ASME B20.1 Safety Standard for Conveyors and Related Equipment.[27] VRCs are typically not inspected or tested by AHJs and are located in industrial settings. They are supposed to be installed, maintained and operated by trained personnel, but often are not. VRCs are not permitted to carry riders, but sometimes are ridden. The combination of the preceding has resulted in serious injuries, including fatalities. These devices are beyond the scope of this book.

There are devices known as material hoists, which could be confused with material lifts. Material hoists are covered by ANSI/ASSE A10.5 Safety Requirements for Material Hoists.[28] This standard applies to material hoists used to raise or lower materials during construction, alteration or demolition. It is not applicable to the temporary use of permanently installed personnel elevators as material hoists. These devices are beyond the scope of this book.

Elevators used for construction are governed by ASME A17.1. This classification applies to elevators temporarily used for construction or demolition to provide transportation for construction personnel, tools and materials only. In effect, it is a special application of a regular elevator. Inspections by the AHJ are required by ASME A17.1 on a more frequent basis than when the elevator is in normal use and testing as for other elevators.

There are devices known as personnel hoists and employee elevators which are covered by ANSI/ASSE A10.4 Safety Requirements for Personnel Hoists and Employee Elevators on Construction and Demolition Sites.[29] This standard applies to the design, construction, installation, operation, inspection, testing, maintenance, alterations and repair of hoists and elevators that are not an integral part of buildings, are installed inside or outside buildings or structures during construction, alteration, demolition operations and are used to raise and lower workers and other personnel connected with or related to the structure. They may also be used for transporting materials under specific circumstances defined in the standard. These devices are beyond the scope of this book.

Endnotes

1. ASME A17.3 *Safety Code for Existing Elevators and Escalators*. American Society of Mechanical Engineers (ASME)

2. *National Building Code*. Building Officials and Code Administrator (BOCA)

3. *Uniform Building Code*. International Conference of Building Officials (ICBO)

4. *Standard Building Code*. Southern Building Code Congress International (SBCCI)

5. *International Building Code*. International Code Council (ICC)

6. ASME A17.1 *Safety Code for Elevators and Escalators*. American Society of Mechanical Engineers (ASME)

7. CAN/CSA B44 *Safety Code for Elevators, Escalators, Dumbwaiters, Moving Walks and Freight Platform Lifts*. Canadian Standard Association (CSA)

8. ASME A18.1 *Safety Standard for Platform Lifts and Stairway Chairlifts*. American Society of Mechanical Engineers (ASME)

9. ASME A17.2 *Inspectors' Manual for Elevators and Escalators*. American Society of Mechanical Engineers (ASME)

10. ASME A17.2.1 *Inspectors' Manual for Electric Elevators*. American Society of Mechanical Engineers (ASME)

11. ASME A17.2.2 *Inspectors' Manual for Hydraulic Elevators*. American Society of Mechanical Engineers (ASME)

12. ASME A17.2.3 *Inspectors' Manual for Escalators and Moving Walks*. American Society of Mechanical Engineers (ASME)

13. *Guide for Inspections of Elevators, Escalators and Moving Walks*. American Society of Mechanical Engineers (ASME)

14. ASME A17.4 *Guide for Emergency Personnel*. American Society of Mechanical Engineers (ASME).

15. ASME A17.5 *Elevator and Escalator Electrical Equipment*. American Society of Mechanical Engineers (ASME)

16. Handbook A17.1 *Safety Code for Elevators and Escalators*. Edward A. Donoghue. American Society of Mechanical Engineers (ASME).

17. QEI-1 *Standard for the Qualification of Elevator Inspectors*. American Society of Mechanical Engineers (ASME).

18. *Elevator Industry Field Employees' Safety Handbook.* Elevator World.

19. *National Electric Code* (NFPA 70). National Fire Protection Association (NFPA)

20. *National Electric Code Handbook.* National Fire Protection Association (NFPA)

21. ICC/ANSI A117.1 *Accessible and Useable Buildings and Facilities*. International Code Council (ICC)

22. NEII *Minimum Passenger Elevator Requirements for the Handicapped.* National Elevator Industry, Inc. (NEII)

23. *ADA and Building Transportation. Edward A. Donoghue. Elevator World.*

24. ASME A17.6 *Standard for Elevator Suspension, Compensation and Governor Systems* American Society of Mechanical Engineers (ASME)

25. ASME A17.7/CSA B44.7 *Performance-Based Safety Code for Elevators and Escalators* American Society of Mechanical Engineers (ASME) and Canadian Standard Association (CSA)

26. ASME A17.1/ CSA B44 *Safety Code for Elevators and Escalators*. American Society of Mechanical Engineers (ASME) and Canadian Standard Association (CSA)

27. ASME B20.1 *Safety Standard for Conveyors and Related Equipment*, American Society of Mechanical Engineers.

28. ANSI/ASSE A10.5 *Safety Requirements for Material Hoists*, American Society of Safety Engineers.

29. ANSI/ASSE A10.4 *Safety Requirements for Personnel Hoists and Employee Elevators on Construction and Demolition Sites*, American Society of Safety Engineers.

30. A17.8-2016/CSA B44.8-16 *Standard for Wind Turbine Tower Elevators*

Chapter 2

Description of the Equipment and Illustrations

Synopsis

2.1 Terminology
- A. Glossary
- B. Equipment Term Usage

2.2 Types of Equipment
- A. Electric Elevators
- B. Hydraulic Elevators
- C. Elevator Doors
- D. Escalators
- E. Moving Walk
- F. Other Equipment

2.3 Photographs and Illustrations
- A. Electric Elevators
- B. Hydraulic Elevators
- C. Elevator Doors
- D. Escalators
- E. Moving Walks
- F. Miscellaneous

2.1 Terminology

A. Glossary

Having a clear understanding of the terminology of any specialized field is critical for success in that field. This includes the elevator and legal vocations. In recognition of this, the nomenclature shown in the glossary at the end of this book is provided for general guidance. The terms are intended to be understandable for the layperson, but also to be useful for those with more in-depth knowledge. Therefore, enough information is provided to ensure accuracy without being too technical.

These terms are not definitions. It is important to distinguish this nomenclature from definitions. Many codes and regulations define these terms differently. Terms may also be defined differently in different editions of the same code or standard. It is imperative to ascertain the definitions of these terms in each jurisdiction, in order to determine the appropriate meaning. Different terms may be used for the same situation in different jurisdictions, whether they are different countries or different locations within the same country. Different terms may be used in the same jurisdiction for the same thing as a result of slang or jargon. In some cases, terms may have different meanings to different people because no formal definition has been established. Technical changes can also create new definitions and can require revisions to existing definitions. In addition, terms can vary between manufacturers and based on vintage. In general, the terms are those used in the U.S., unless otherwise noted.

The globalization that so pervades our world today has also affected the elevator/escalator codes and industry standards. The ASME A17.1 and CAN/CSA B44 codes were published as a single bi-national code in 2007. Some of the authors were involved in this effort. Similar efforts are in progress with some of the other standards and codes listed in the glossary, and are possible in the future. This could affect the meanings of a number of terms listed in the glossary.

Accident reconstruction is as much an art as it is science. In some cases, the analysis of the cause of an accident can be significantly altered depending on how a device is classified: a personnel hoist used for construction or an elevator used for construction, a vertical reciprocating conveyor or a material lift, a material hoist or a material lift, and so on. Although this chapter or the glossary will not make you an expert in the elevator and escalator field or the legal field, we hope they will give you a "feel" for the significance of certain key terms and issues.

Some words of caution. Heed the old adage: *A little bit of knowledge can be dangerous.* Rely on the appropriate expert (legal or technical), not your knowledge of some buzzwords.

When searching for a term, remember it could be listed differently than you might expect. The terms were listed in a manner we thought to be the most appropriate and the most helpful to the user.

The glossary was designed to serve as a self-contained reference document, but not as a replacement for a good dictionary. Although the glossary is quite extensive, it by no means covers all of the terms that apply to vertical transportation equipment.

The reader is encouraged to suggest additional terms and other desirable changes for possible inclusion in future editions.

B. Equipment Term Usage

The vertical transportation equipment covered in this book is primarily elevators and escalators. However, where appropriate other similar equipment is covered. This includes, but is not limited to, moving walks, dumbwaiters and material lifts. Although they primarily involve horizontal movement, moving walks are included since they can be very similar to escalators and can be used for limited vertical movement. Material lifts and dumbwaiters are included because they share many of the same characteristics as elevators but are limited to carrying goods.

Hence, the term vertical transportation is used to cover all these types of equipment. Similarly, the use of the term "elevator and escalator" is intended to be all-inclusive. When the term elevator is used, it is primarily intended to apply to elevators only, but it may also apply to the other equipment. When the term escalator is used, it is primarily intended to apply only to escalators, although in many cases it will also be applicable to moving walks.

2.2 Types of Equipment

The main purpose of this section is to familiarize the reader with the various types of equipment and to provide a very brief and basic description of their operation. Keep in mind that there are hundreds, if not thousands, of variations that have been produced over the years by various manufacturers.

A. Electric Elevators

Electric elevators consist of two main types: *traction* and *winding drum.*

A typical traction elevator has a car that is connected by a set of suspension wire ropes to a counterweight. Typically, the counterweight weighs as much as the empty car plus 40 to 50 percent of its rated load. The ropes are routed over the driving machine sheave (grooved wheel), known as a *drive sheave*. The driving machine usually is located above the hoistway (*overhead machine*), but may be located below the lowest landing (basement machine) or elsewhere. The car is propelled by the friction developed between the suspension ropes and the drive sheave as the sheave rotates. Traction elevators are used mainly in mid and high rise buildings.

The drive sheave is rotated by a motor. The motor can rotate the drive sheave directly (*gearless traction*) or indirectly (*geared traction*) through gearing. Geared elevators are usually limited to speeds of approximately 350 fpm and typically used in mid rise buildings, while gearless elevators are used in high rise buildings and can achieve speeds of 1800 fpm or more. One of the Shanghai Towers elevators can obtain speeds of over 4000 FPM (42.8 miles/hour or 69 kilometres/hour) and has been named the fastest in the world by the Guiness World

Records when this edition was being written, but even faster ones are expected. In comparison, Usain Bolt—the fastest man in the world—runs at approximately 2,500 FPM (27.44 miles/hour or 44 km/hour) or a cheetah runs approximately 5,700 FPM (64.8 miles/hour).

The motor will be either a DC (*direct current*) or an AC (*alternating current*) type. The DC motors will have electrically conductive brushes that electrically connect the stationary wiring to the rotating *commutator*. There have been various methods used to control DC motors. For many years, *motor-generator* (*mg*) sets were the standard method for converting AC power into DC power for the motor and generator field (Ward-Leonard) control circuits. This technology has been supplanted by solid state SCR technology eliminating the motor/generator. There have been various methods used to control AC motors. For many years, AC motors were limited in their application due to poor control features. However, modern *VVVF* (*variable voltage, variable frequency*) technology has provided AC motors with the means to provide good controllability.

The driving machine will have a mechanically applied and electrically released brake. The brake is not used to stop the car for DC motors in normal operation. Instead, the car is stopped electrically and the brake is used to hold the car stationary. However, *with single-speed AC* and *two-speed AC* motors the brake is used to stop the car, which accounts for their poor stopping accuracy. This limitation has been eliminated with VVVF AC motor control.

There are many variations to the basic roping arrangement. The ropes commonly are diverted by a *deflector sheave* to provide sufficient separation of the car and counterweight. In some arrangements, multiple deflector sheaves are utilized to achieve the desired results. Sometimes after the ropes pass over the drive sheave, then pass over a *secondary sheave* and then pass back over the drive sheave. This is known as a *double wrap* arrangement, and is used to increase the available traction. In *two-to-one (2:1)* roping arrangements both ends of the suspension ropes are fixed (*dead-ended*) to the overhead structure and multiple sheaves are used to route the suspension ropes to the car and counterweight. For 2:1 arrangements, the car moves at half the speed of the driving machine and the tension on the ropes is one-half the total it would be otherwise.

The car and counterweight are usually guided along T-shaped rails (*guide rails*) that are provided on both sides of car and counterweight using either *roller guides* (the most common) or sliding guide shoes (limited to slow speeds). These guides limit both side-to-side and front-to-back movement.

A number of different safety devices are provided on electric elevators that remove power from the driving machine and set its brake upon the detection of an unsafe condition (e.g., stop switches, limit switches to protect against over travel at the terminal landings, hoistway door interlocks).

A *speed governor* is used to continuously monitor the speed of the car through a *governor rope* that is attached to the car. When the speed exceeds a predetermined amount, then an overspeed switch will remove power to the driving machine and its brake to stop it. Sometimes a speed reducing switch will also be used. If the speed continues to increase in the down direction, then the governor will trip (i.e., actuate) and retard the movement of the governor rope. This causes the governor rope to set (i.e., actuate) the car *safeties*. The safeties are mechanical devices attached to the car that engage the guide rails to stop the car. There are various types of governors and safeties. Car safeties are prohibited from stopping the car in the up direction by the A17.1 code. For many years the only method available to prevent an overspeed condition in the up direction for the car was the governor overspeed switch and the use of counterweight safeties. More recently, other methods, such as *rope brakes* and *emergency brakes*, have been introduced to stop cars that overspeed in the up direction, and can also prevent unintended motion with the elevator doors open.

In case of over-travel at the bottom landing, *buffers* are provided to prevent the cars or counterweight from striking the pit floor. Both spring buffers and oil buffers are used, with spring buffers limited to slower speeds. Resilient *bumpers* are permitted to be used for very slow speeds.

Many different devices have been used to control the stopping accuracy and leveling accuracy of the car. Some examples are mechanical selectors, magnetic inductors, electronic car top readers, and limit switches. Leveling and stopping accuracy will depend on which types of devices are used and on the type of elevator control.

A recent introduction into the U.S. and Canada is the *machine room-less (MRL)* elevator, although they have been installed for a number of years elsewhere (e.g., Europe, Asia). The machines for these elevators are installed inside the hoistway instead of in a traditional machine room. The controller may be installed inside the hoistway, in a panel at one of the landings or in a control room. Some manufacturers use non-metallic suspension ropes (made of *aramid* fibers) and plastic sheaves and others use *elastomeric coated steel belts* instead of wire suspension ropes.

The application of winding drum machines is very limited by both code restrictions and practical considerations. Suspension ropes are wound on a drum that supports both the car and counterweight. When the car descends, its ropes wind off the drum and the counterweight ropes wind on the drum. The opposite happens when the car ascends.

B. Hydraulic Elevators

The car for a hydraulic elevator is connected to a *jack* consisting of a *cylinder* and a *plunger* or *piston*.

By far the most common type of hydraulic elevator is the *direct acting* type, which has an underground cylinder and a plunger that is attached to the bottom of the car. The cylinder resides in the ground to a depth approximately the same as the travel of the car. An electric motor and pump, using hydraulic oil, propels the plunger and car in the up direction. The pump and motor do not operate when the car travels in the down direction. Instead, gravity causes the car and plunger to descend. The acceleration, speed and deceleration are controlled by a valve, known as a *control valve,* in both the up and down directions. A check valve that typically is integral to the control valve is used to hold the car stationary.

Variations include types that have the jack entirely above ground (known as *hole-less hydraulic* elevators). This includes *telescoping jacks* that have plungers that typically are attached to the top of the car on two sides (which operates very similar to direct acting hydraulic elevators) and *roped hydraulic* elevators (where the car is connected to the plunger by suspension ropes).

Guide rails, car guides, spring buffers, doors and gates are normally identical for hydraulic elevators as for electric elevators. A number of different safety devices are provided on hydraulic elevators to stop the driving machine upon the detection of an unsafe condition (e.g., low oil protection).

Hydraulic elevators are limited by practical considerations to low rise applications (approximately 60-75 feet or 6-8 floors), and travel at slow speeds (typically 100-200 fpm). However, they currently dominate the low rise applications in the U.S. and Canada. Hence, hydraulic elevators are very prevalent, since many buildings with elevators are low rise. They also dominate when heavy capacities are required (e.g. truck elevators).

Only roped hydraulic elevators are required to have governors and car safeties. The vast majority of existing hydraulic elevators have no means to protect against a free fall condition caused by a loss of hydraulic pressure. Some newer elevators are provided with *overspeed (rupture) valves,* which prevent downward movement if a loss of hydraulic pressure was caused by the failure of the piping between the hydraulic driving machine and the jack. However, this does not protect against a loss of pressure in the cylinder due to a leak caused by corrosion. *Plunger grippers* have been introduced to address this potentially catastrophic occurrence. Elevators with older jacks, especially single bottom jacks, should be replaced with cylinders having a double bottom (safety bulkhead) or fitted with added plunger grippers, which may be required by code in some jurisdictions.

MRL (machine room-less) type hydraulic elevators are also a recent introduction into the U.S. and Canada, although they have been installed for a number of years elsewhere (e.g., Europe, Asia). Similar to electric elevators, the driving machine is located in the hoistway and the controller may be installed inside the hoistway, in a panel at one of the landings or in a control room.

C. Elevator Doors

Elevators are provided with two sets of doors or gates. One set (*hoistway doors* or *gates*) is located at the landings at every entrance. The other set (*car door* or *gate*) is located on and travels with the car.

Only very old elevators have hoistway gates, and the rest have hoistway doors. Car gates are typically only provided on freight *elevators* (a *vertically sliding gate*) or very old passenger elevators (a horizontally sliding collapsible *gate*), and the rest have car doors.

There are three basic types of elevator doors: *swinging*, *horizontally sliding* and *vertically sliding*. Swinging doors typically must be manually opened and are primarily limited to older elevator hoistway doors. An exception would be residential elevators. Passenger elevators are primarily provided with power-operated, horizontally sliding car and hoistway doors. Freight elevators are primarily provided with *vertically biparting* (one panel moves up and the other down to open) hoistway doors and car gates that slide up to open, which can be either manually or power operated.

Elevator doors can consist of a single door panel or have multiple panels. Horizontally sliding doors are either *center opening* or *side opening types*. Center opening doors have two or more panels that open in opposite directions, while side opening doors have all panels that open in the same direction. If only one panel is provided that moves in the same direction then it is known as a *single speed door*, if two panels that move in the same direction are provided then it known as a two-speed door, and in some cases three panels are provided which are known as *three-speed doors*.

These doors can be of various widths. Door heights are typically a standard 7 feet for passenger elevators, but vary for freight elevators. All passenger elevators are provided with *door closers* to automatically close the hoistway doors if the elevator is not at the landing, while freight elevators do not.

Horizontally sliding doors will be guided and supported by rollers on a track located above the door panels. Door panels are also provided with bottom guides (*gibs*) that move in a slot in the *sill*. Newer elevators will be provided with *safety retainers*, which provide significantly enhanced protection against displacement of the door panels if the primary guiding means fails.

All elevators will have devices that lock the doors when the elevator is not at the landing and prevent the elevator from moving away from the landing when the doors are open. Most hoistway doors are provided with *interlocks*, but very old elevators and freight elevators that meet certain conditions may have *combination mechanical locks* and electric contacts. An interlock will achieve both these functions in an interdependent manner, while combination mechanical locks and electric contacts will achieve these functions in an entirely independent manner.

Most car doors are provided with an electric contact (commonly known as a gate switch) to prevent movement of the car with the door not in the closed position. Newer elevators will have devices (*door restrictors*), which prevent the car door from opening when the car is not at the landing. Recently some car doors have been provided with interlocks for elevators in unenclosed hoistways.

Power-operated doors typically are moved by a *door operator* mounted on the car top. Both sets of doors (car and hoistway) are moved at the same time, except for many freight elevators (where separate door operators are provided for the car gate and the hoistway doors) and where manually operated hoistway doors are provided. For many years, a *door clutch* has been used to open/close the hoistway and car doors as a unit, and to unlock the landing doors. Older elevators and freight elevators typically use a *retiring cam* to unlock the hoistway doors, which is independent of the door operator.

Most power-operated car doors and gates are provided with automatic reopening devices that will stop and reopen doors if the door is obstructed while closing or if there is an obstruction in the path of the closing door. These reopening devices generally are either mechanical (e.g., *safety edge*), photoelectric (e.g., *light curtain*), or proximity types or some combination thereof. For a number of years, automatic reopening devices have been provided that detect approaching objects.

D. Escalators

An escalator is a power driven device that carries passengers on steps whose treads remain horizontal while the direction of motion is typically at an angle of 30 degrees above the horizontal.

Most escalators have the driving machine located in the upper pit area (located under the landing plate), while others have the driving machine located under the exposed steps. Most escalators have a single driving machine, but others have two or more driving machines. Most escalators have a geared driving machine that is driven by an AC motor. The motor can be connected to the gearing through a continuous shaft, mechanical coupling, toothed gear or sometimes belts. Most older escalators travel at 90 fpm, while most newer escalators travel at 100 fpm.

Most escalators have steps that have one end connected to axles that are part of a specially engineered set of chains known as *step chains*. The steps are moved as the driving machine rotates a sprocket that in turn propels the step chains, which are supported by integral rollers that are supported on a track. The other end of the steps is supported by attached rollers that ride on a track. On older *modular* escalators, a *rack* made up of *step links* is propelled by roller chains.

Two *handrails* are provided that must move substantially at the same speed as the steps. These handrails are supported on *balustrades*. Almost all escalators have stationary *skirt* panels adjacent to the steps, although one manufacturer has introduced an escalator that has skirt panels attached to the steps.

A number of different safety devices (e.g., emergency stop switches, broken step chain devices, broken drive chain devices) are provided to stop the driving machine and set its brake upon the detection of an unsafe condition. Most newer escalators are provided with significantly more safety devices (e.g., handrail speed monitors, missing step devices, comb-step impact devices) than existing escalators.

E. Moving Walk

A moving walk is a power driven device that carries passengers on an uninterrupted surface that remains parallel to the direction of motion, which can vary up to 12 to 15 degrees from the horizontal.

There are two main types of moving walks, which differ mainly by their *treadway.* Most use *pallets,* which are basically flat escalator steps, while others use a rubber belt.

Moving walks share many of the same characteristics as escalators. However, their use is usually limited to airports and amusement parks.

F. Other Equipment

Elevators can vary based on the driving machine used to move the car and for special applications.

Some elevators are provided with rack and pinion driving machines. A motor rotates one or more *pinion gears* that engage a stationary *rack*. The driving machine is located on top of the car. These elevators are typically located on exterior structures, such as bridges, towers or gantry cranes. Rack and pinion driving machines are also commonly used on *personnel hoists* and *material hoists* used during construction of a building. Believe it or not, elevators are still permitted to be manually moved (hand-operated), although the authors are not aware of any installed for many years. While elevators (*screw column*) are permitted to be raised and lowered by screw threads, the authors are not aware of any that have been installed in the U.S. However, this type of driving machine has been used for *wheelchair lifts*.

Limited-Use/Limited-Application (LULA) elevators are limited in their use by size, capacity, speed and rise. They typically are intended to be alternatives to wheelchair lifts. *Private residence elevators* are elevators with limited size, capacity, speed and rise that are installed in a private residence or in a multiple dwelling as a means of access to a private residence. *Inclined elevators* travel at an angle of inclination of 70 degrees or less from the horizontal. Although the car is traveling on an incline, the car platform remains horizontal. *Sidewalk elevators* are freight elevators that operate between a landing on a sidewalk or other exterior area and floors below that landing through a moveable cover. *Rooftop elevators* operate between a landing at the roof level of a building and landings below through a moveable cover. *Special purpose elevators* are permanently installed in structures such as grain elevators, bridge towers and radio antennas that are used to transport authorized personnel and their tools/equipment only. *Shipboard elevators* are installed on ships, offshore drilling rigs or offshore oil production platforms for transporting personnel, maintenance equipment and ship stores. *Mine elevators* are used to transport personnel, materials, equipment and supplies in mines. When a permanently installed elevator is temporarily used during construction or demolition for transporting only personnel, tools and materials, it is classified as an *elevator used for construction*. This is different than a personnel hoist or material hoist, which are not an integral part of a building but are used during construction or demolition operations. Wind turbine elevators are used to transport authorized workers and their tools only, on wind turbine towers.

Dumbwaiters and *material lifts* are permitted only to transport materials. Dumbwaiters are typically very limited in size and capacity, while material lifts are very similar to an elevator.

Platform (wheelchair) lifts have platforms that are not fully enclosed, do not penetrate a floor and have limited speed, rise and platform area that are intended to transport the mobility impaired. *Stairway chair lifts* are devices with a seat that is guided up a stairway.

2.3 Photographs and Illustrations

A. Electric Elevators

Machine Room
Driving (hoist) machine
Governor
MG set
Controller
Selector
Disconnect switches

Car Top
Crosshead
Emergency exit
Door operator
Guides (roller/slide)
Car top reader
Rope fastenings

Hoistway (Shaft)
Guide rails
Limit switches
Suspension ropes
Governor rope
Counterweight
Deflector sheaves
Compensation ropes/chains
Door closers
Door interlocks
Door hangers/tracks/guides
Traveling cable(s)
Cams/vanes/steel tapes
Fascia
Pit equipment

Inside Car (Cab)
Lighting
Drop ceiling
Car doors/gates
Door reopening device
COP w/call buttons
Position indicators
Directional indicators
Phone/intercom
Alarm button
Stop switch
Car sill

Landings
Hoistway door
Call buttons
Position indicators
Directional indicators
Landing sill

Car Bottom
Safeties
Toe guard
Guides (roller/slide)
Buffer strike plates

Pit
Buffers
Governor tension sheave
Bottom limit switches
Pit ladder or door
Stop switch
Light

Figure A.1 *General locations of typical components of electric traction elevators. Photographs of selected components follow.*

Figure A.2 *Gearless traction driving (hoist) machine (1) brake; (2) suspension ropes and drive sheave; (3) motor*

Figure A.3 *Geared traction driving (hoist) machine*

Figure A.4 *Traction hoist machine—speed monitor*

Figure A.5 *Winding drum driving (hoist) machine*

Figure A.6 *Drive (hoist) machine (1) fields; (2) brushes; (3) commutator*

Figure A.7 *Drive (hoist) machine (1) traction (drive) sheave and ropes; (2) brake drum*

Figure A.8 *Motor-generator set (1) DC generator; (2) AC motor*

Figure A.9 *Brushes, brush holder, and commutator*

Figure A.10 *Brushes and commutator on driving (hoist) machine*

Figure A.11 *Worn brush and new brush*

Figure A.12 *Brush seating stones*

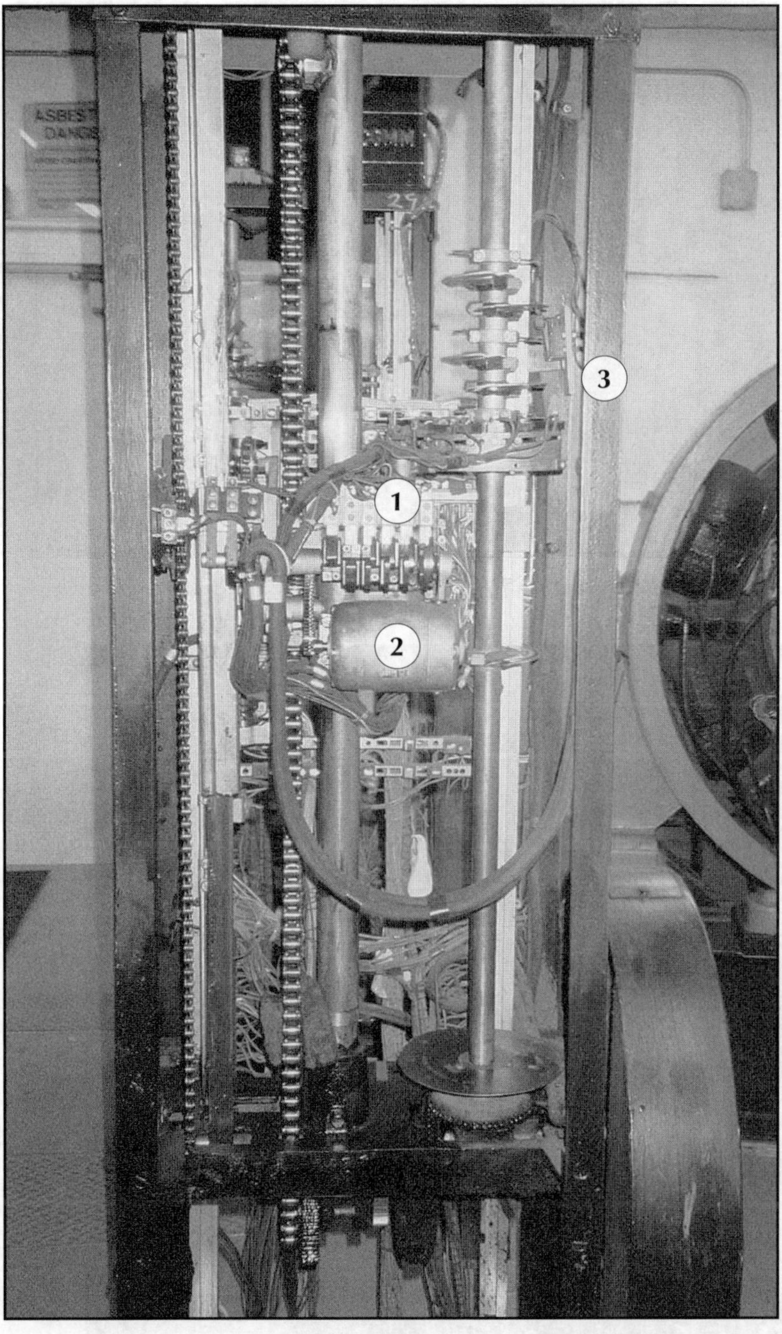

Figure A.13 *Selector (1) floor stops; (2) moving carriage; (3) leveling plates*

Figure A.14 *Selector (close-up)*

Figure A.15 *Speed governor—flyball type*

Figure A.16 *Speed governor—centrifugal type*

Figure A.17 *Jawless governor and cable tension switch*

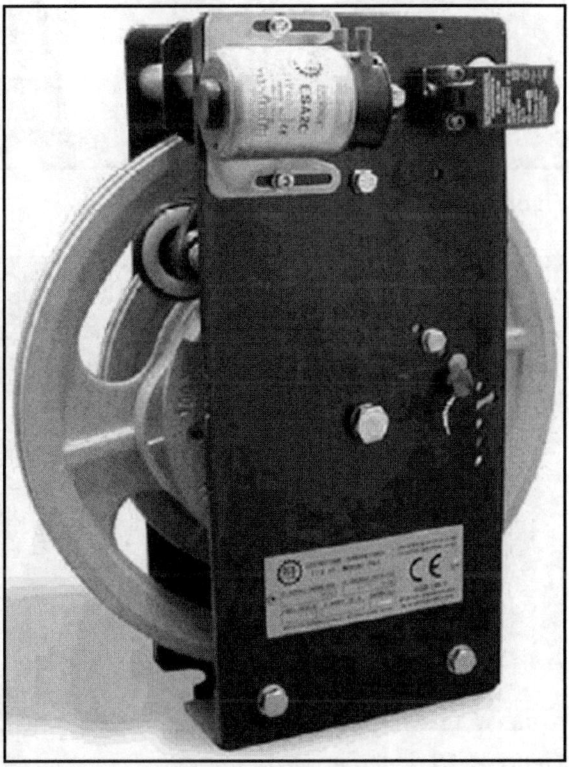

Figure A.18 *Governor cable tension sheave*

Figure A.19 *Speed governor monitor*

Figure A.20 Car safety mechanism

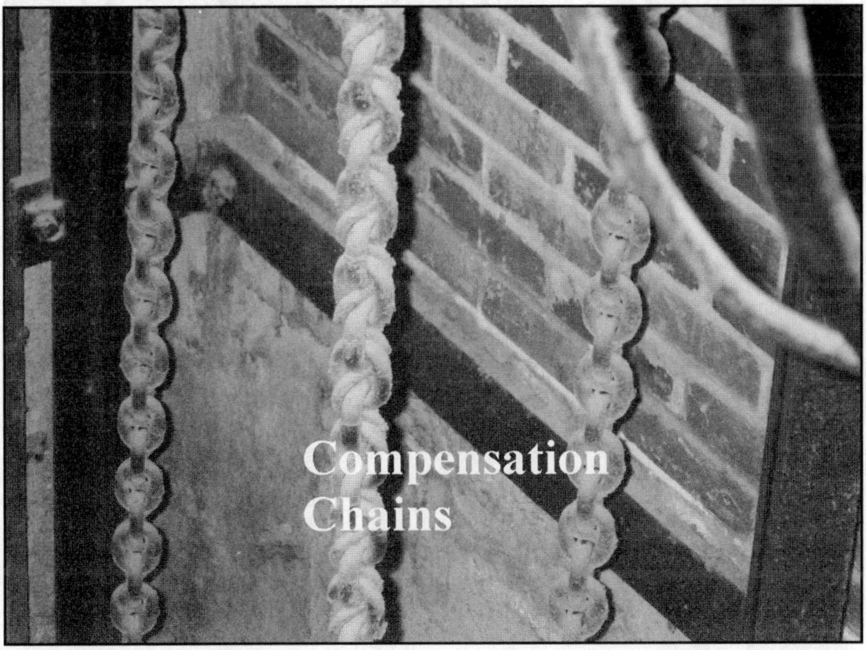

Figure A.21 Compensation chains

Figure A.22 *Compensation ropes and sheave*

Figure A.23 *Shackles (fastenings)—babbitted type suspension rope*

Figure A.24 *Testing procedure for determining total suspended load of car and counterweight*

Figure A.25 *Elastomeric coated steel belts driving a machine room less (MRL) elevator.*

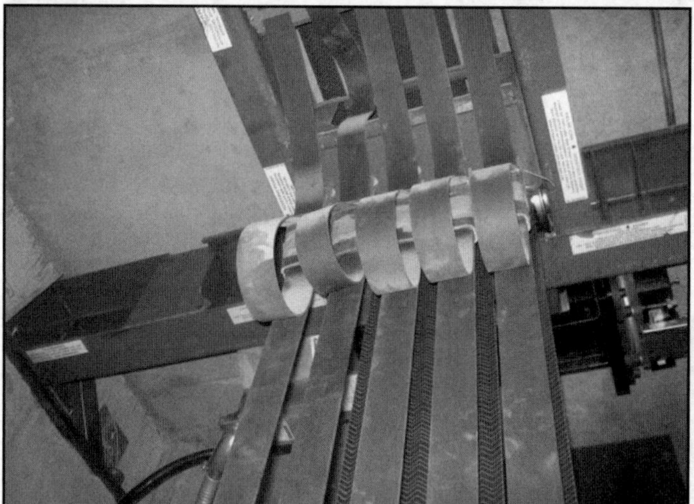

Figure A.26 *Elastomeric coated steel belts close-up*

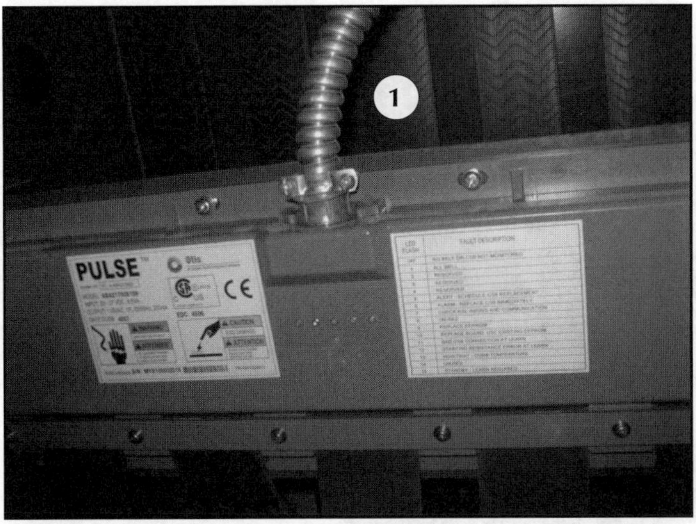

Figure A.27A *Elastomeric coated steel belt monitoring device (1) belts*

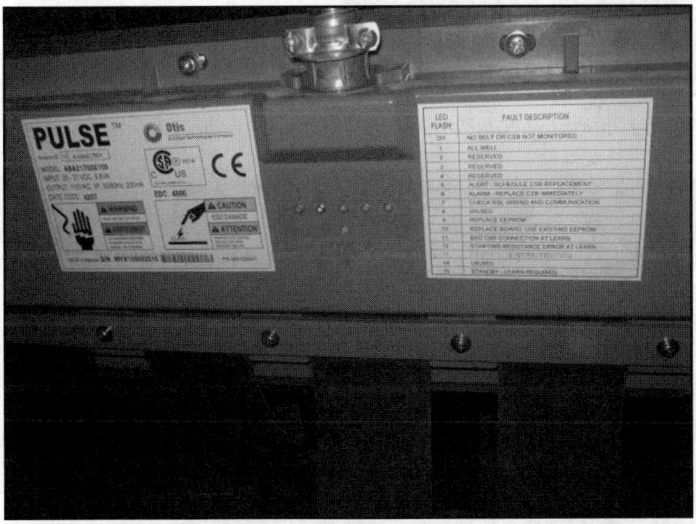

Figure A.27B *Monitor nameplate for elastomeric coated steel belt monitoring device*

Figure A.28 *Counterweight displacement detector (ring and string)*

Figure A.29 *Counterweight guide roller and retention means*

Figure A.30 *Counterweight*

Figure A.31 *Counterweight blocking (remove to account for hoist rope stretching over time)*

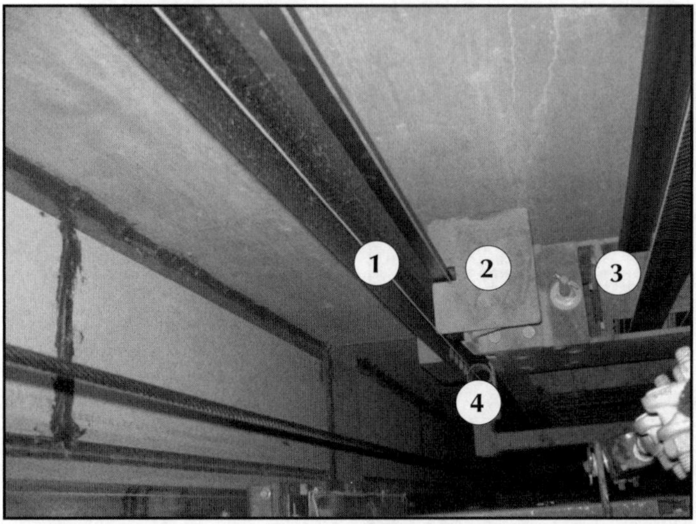

Figure A.32 *Counterweight (1) displacement detection wire; (2) retention means; (3) suspension means; (4) displacement detector tube; (5) guide-rail*

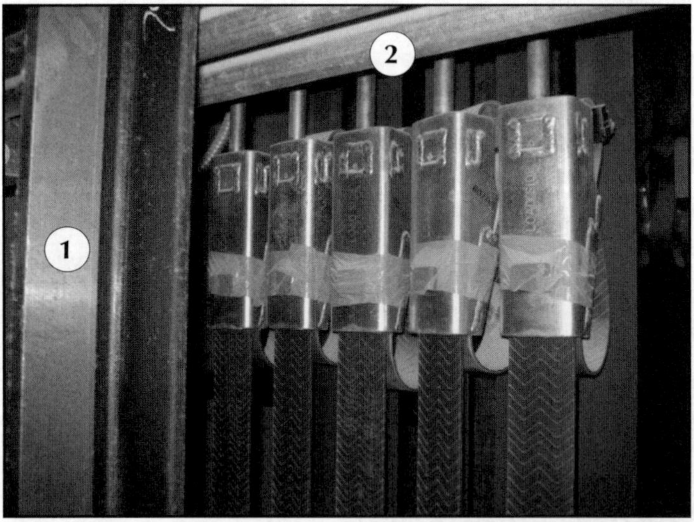

Figure A.33 *Elasomeric coated steel belts (1) guide rail; (2) terminating shackles*

Figure A.34 *Machine room less (MRL) elevator driving machine with elastomeric coated steel belt suspension means (side view)*

Figure A.35 *Machine room less (MRL) elevator driving machine with elastomeric coated steel belt suspension means (top view)*

Figure A.36A *Counterweight guard*

Figure A.36B *Counterweight guard (1) counterweight guide rails; (2) counterweight buffer*

Figure A.37 *Oil buffer with spring return*

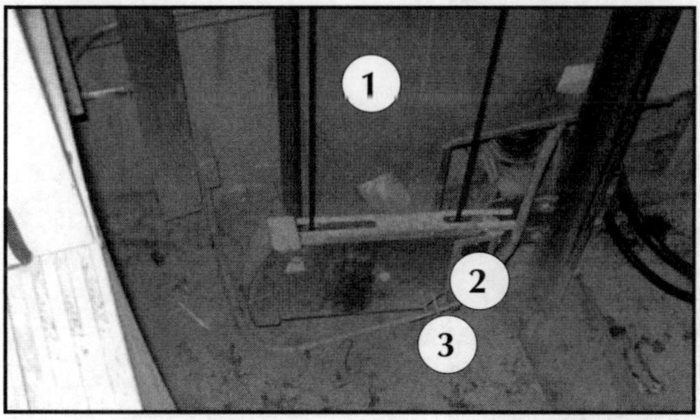

Figure A.38 *Governor tension sheave (1) governor rope; (2) switch; (3) trip lever*

Figure A.39 *Governor tension sheave*

Figure A.40 *Oil buffer (1) piston; (2) switch*

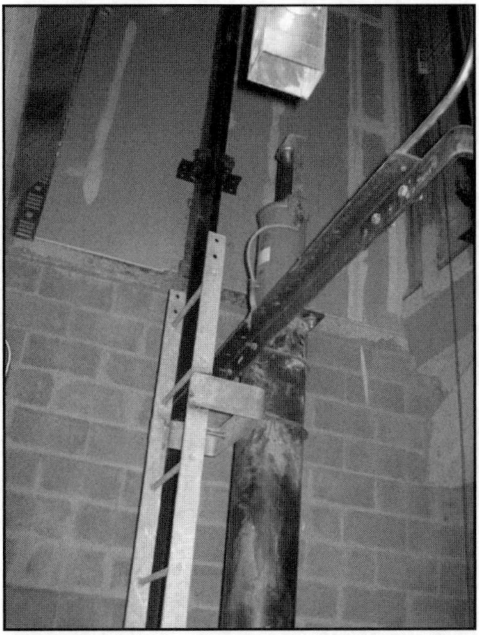

Figure A.41 *Oil buffer—car*

Figure A.42 *Geared traction driving machine*

Figure A.43 *Deflector sheave (1) shaft; (2) sheave with grooves*

Figure A.44 *Deflector sheave*

Figure A.45 *Driving machine geared type (1) gear box; (2) brake; (3) motor; (4) speed tachometer*

Figure A.46 *Speed governor (1) protective cover*

Figure A.47 *Aramid fiber rope (an alternate to steel ropes)*

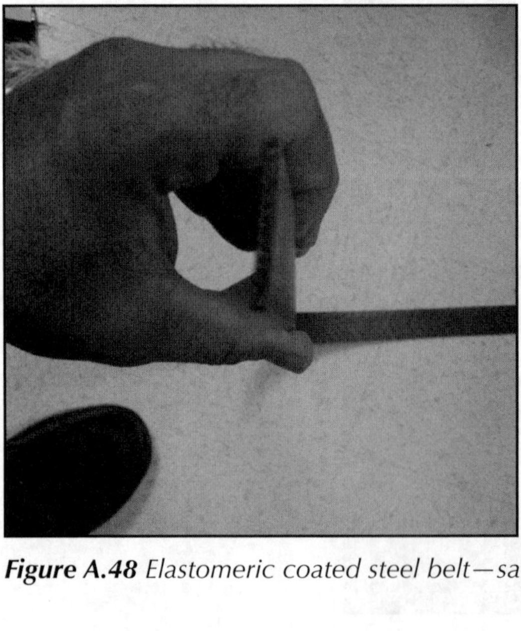

Figure A.48 *Elastomeric coated steel belt—sample*

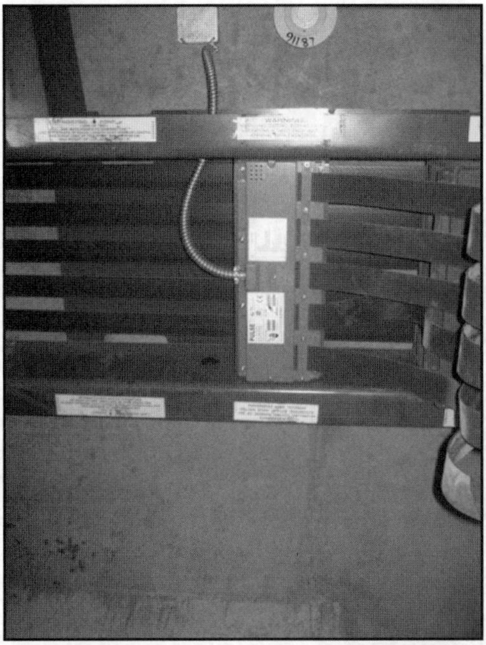

Figure A.49 *Elastomeric coated steel belts and monitor*

Figure A.50 *Wedge sockets*

Figure A.51 *Wedge sockets*

B. Hydraulic Elevators

Hoistway (Shaft)	Car Top	Landings
Guide rails	Emergency exit	Hoistway door
Limit switches	Door operator	Call buttons
Door closers	Guides (roller/slide)	Position indicators
Door interlocks	Car top reader	Directional indicators
Door hangers/tracks/guides	Landing sill	
Plunger		
Traveling cable(s)	**Inside Car (Cab)**	
Cams/vanes/steel tapes	Lighting	**Machine Room**
Fascia	Drop ceiling	Controller
Pit equipment	Car doors/gates	Disconnect switches
	Door reopening device	Selector
Pit	COP w/call buttons	Oil tank
Buffers	Position indicators	Control valve
Cylinder	Directional indicators	Motor and pump
Bottom limit switches	Phone/intercom	Piping
Pit ladder or door	Alarm button	
Stop switch	Stop switch	
Light	Car sill	
Piping		
	Car Bottom	
	Toe guard	
	Guides (roller/slide)	
	Buffer strike plates	
	Platen plate	

Figure B.1 *General locations of typical components of hydraulic (direct acting) elevators. Photographs of selected components follow.*

Figure B.2 *Plunger connection to bottom of car*

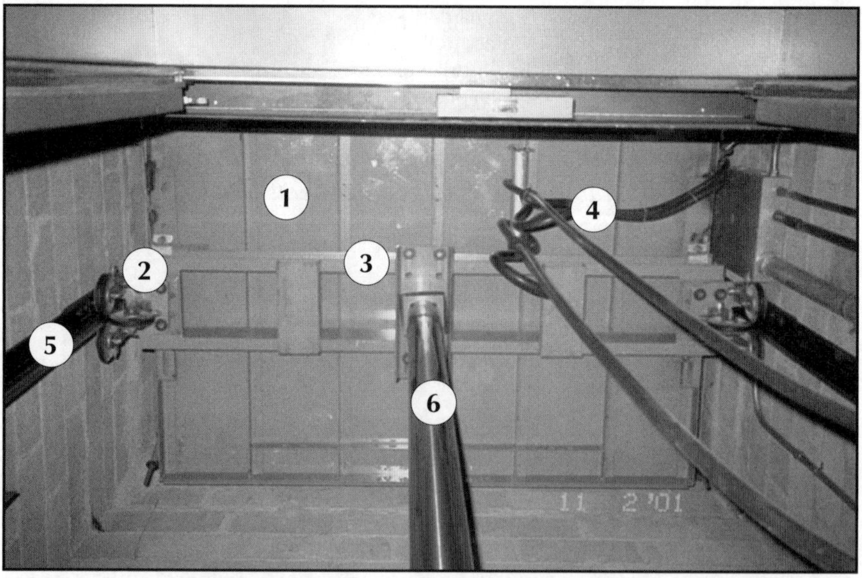

Figure B.3 *Car (bottom view) (1) car platform (bottom); (2) roller guides; (3) bolster channel; (4) traveling cables; (5) rails; (6) plunger*

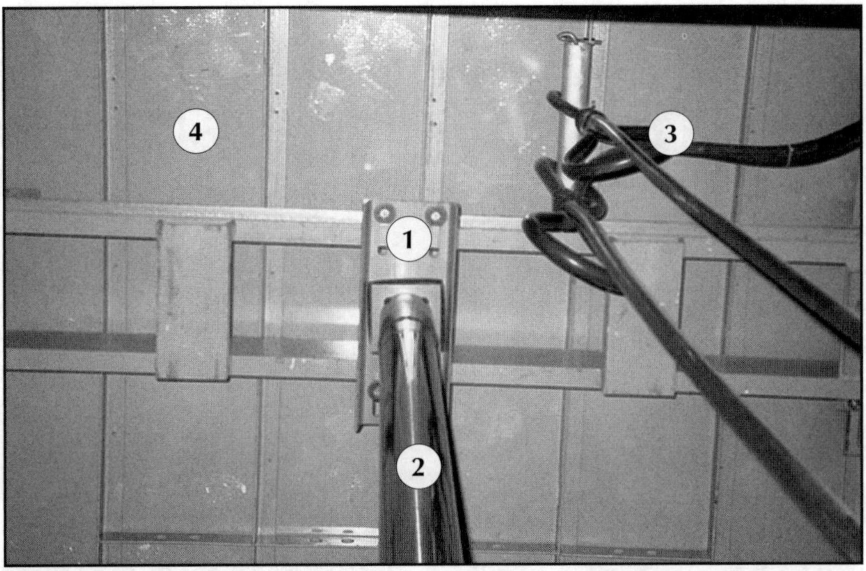

Figure B.4 *Car (bottom view, close up) (1) platen plate; (2) plunger; (3) traveling cables; (4) car platform (bottom)*

Figure B.5 *Typical inground cylinder type (1) jack (plunger and cylinder); (2) spring buffers*

Figure B.6 *Roller guides (close-up)*

Figure B.7 Roller guides (1) roller guides; (2) guide rail

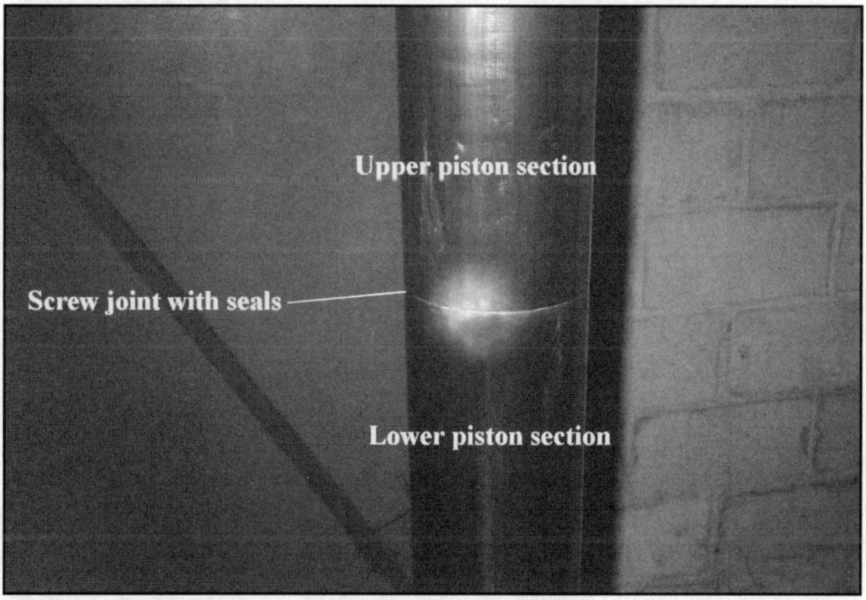

Figure B.8 Piston joint—multiple-section piston

Figure B.9 *Cylinder coupling (leaking)*

Figure B.10 *Hydraulic system (1) storage tank; (2) motor; (3) pump; (4) control valve; (5) muffler; (6) controller*

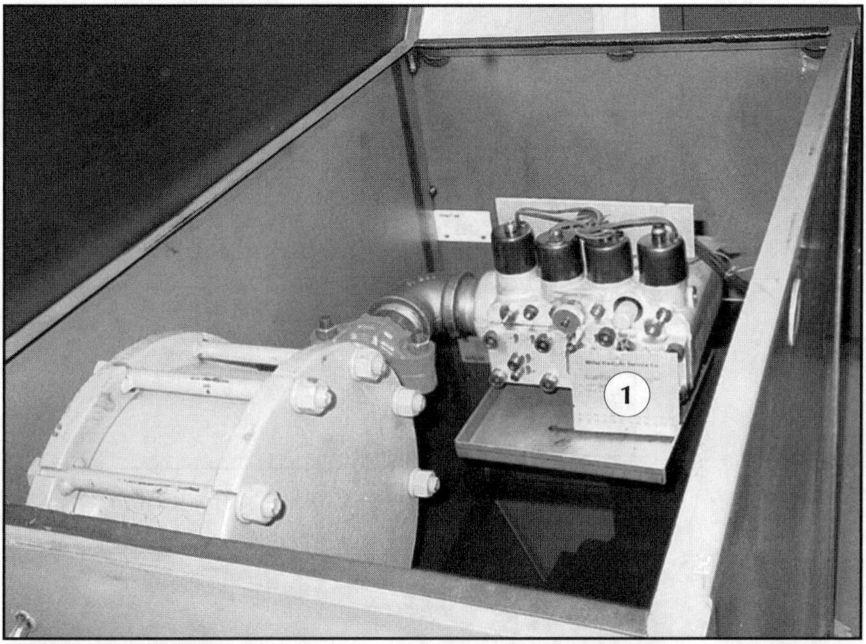

Figure B.11 *(1) Submersible control valve*

Figure B.12 *Hydraulic oil tank—cooling fan*

Figure B.13 *Hydraulic oil tank—heater switch*

Figure B.14 *(1) Hydraulic elevator—hole-less jack type*

Figure B.15 *(1) Hydraulic elevator—hole-less jack type*

Figure B.16 *(1) Hydraulic elevator—hole-less jack type*

Figure B.17 *(1) Hydraulic elevator—hole-less jack type*

Figure B.18 *(1) Hydraulic elevator—hole-less jack type*

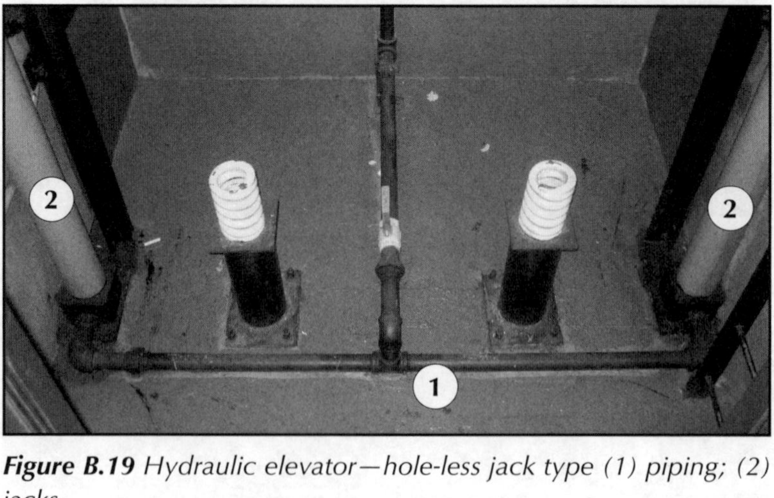

Figure B.19 *Hydraulic elevator—hole-less jack type (1) piping; (2) jacks*

Figure B.20 *Roped hydraulic elevator (1) traveling sheave with suspension ropes; (2) jack; (3) cartop*

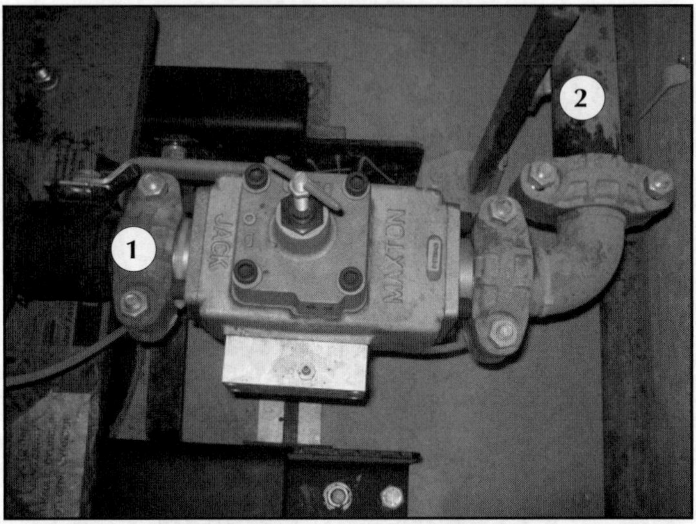

Figure B.21 *Overspeed valve (1) pipe to jack; (2) pipe to oil tank*

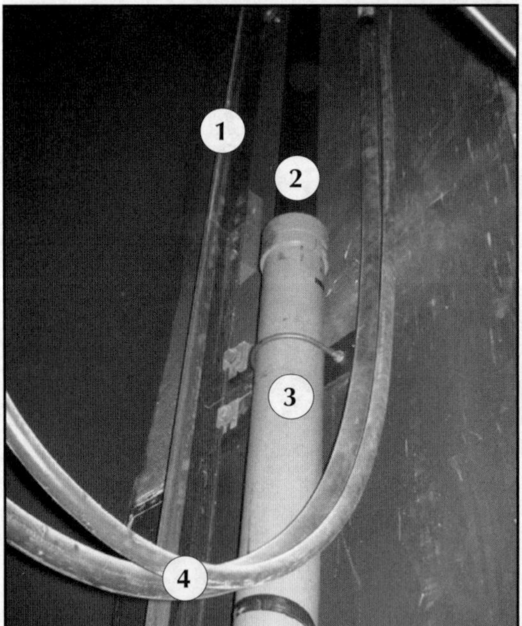

Figure B.22 *Holeless hydraulic jack (1) guide rail; (2) plunger; (3) cylinder; (4) traveling cables*

C. Elevator Doors

Figure C.1 *Freight elevator hoistway (landing) entrance doors open*

Figure C.2 *Freight elevator hoistway door interlock and retiring cam*

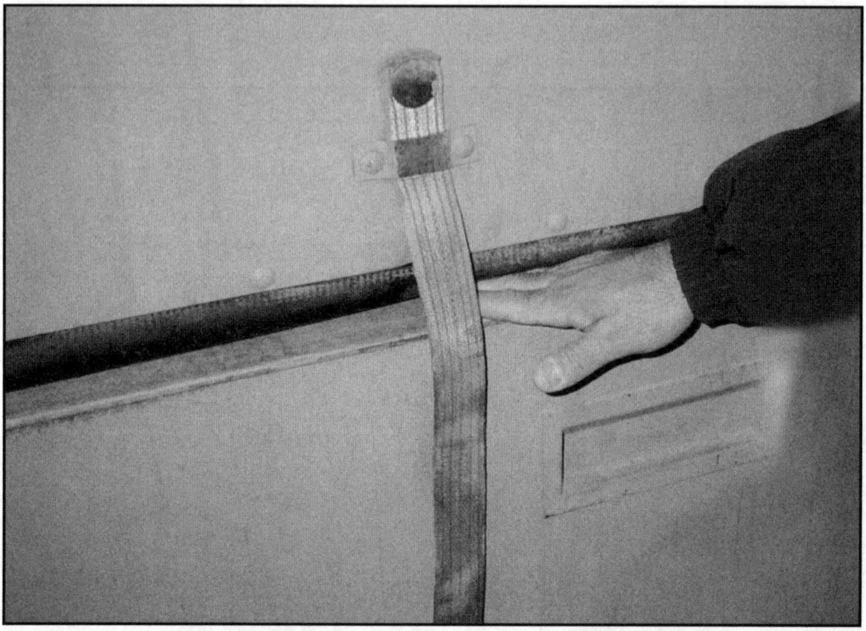

Figure C.3 *Entrapment area between biparting door panels (freight doors)*

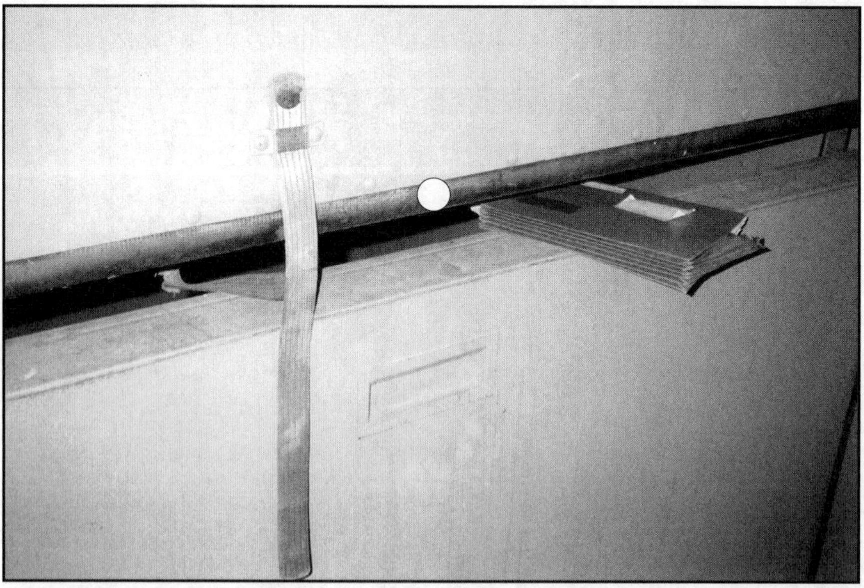

Figure C.4 *(1) Non-crushing, non-shearing freight elevator door astragal*

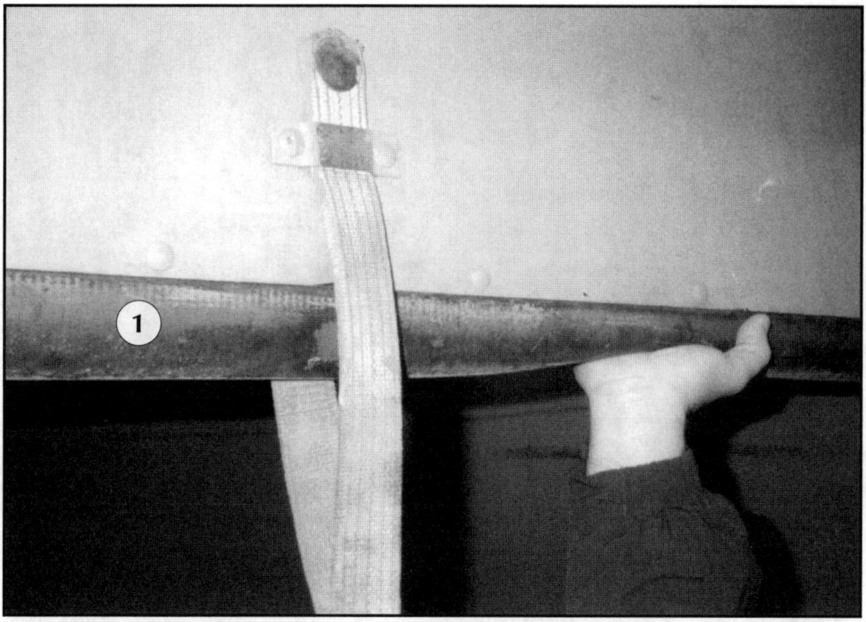

Figure C.5 *(1) Non-crushing, non-shearing freight elevator door edge*

Figure C.6 *Freight elevator hoistway door interlocks*

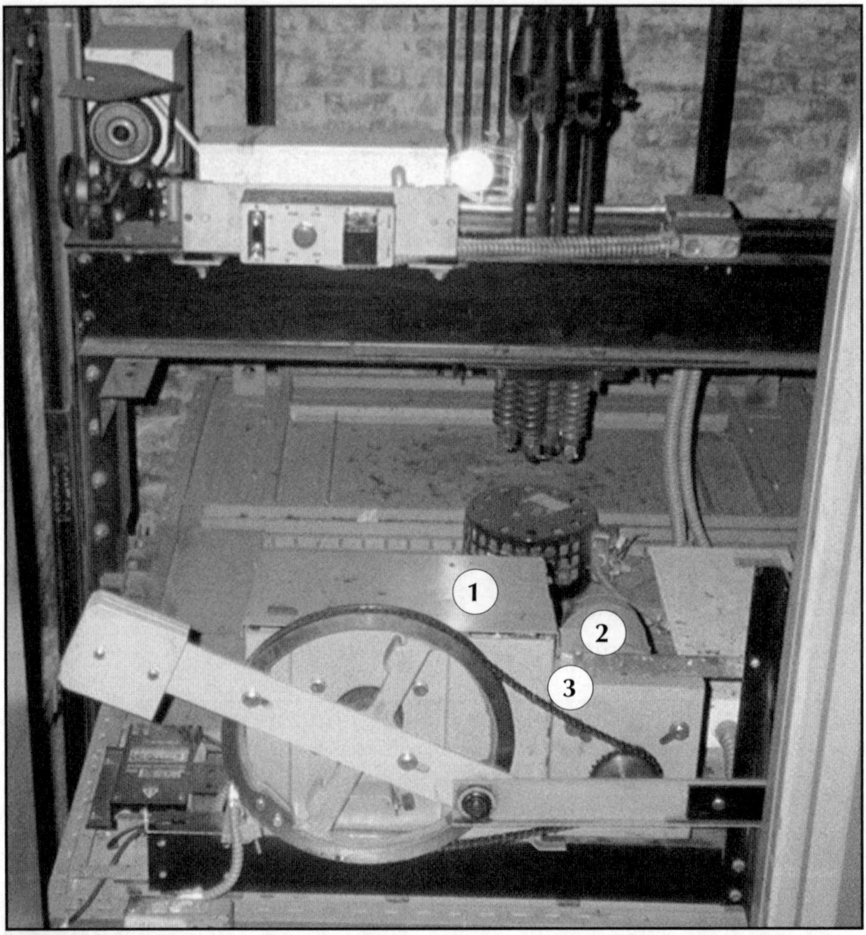

Figure C.7 *Car door operator (1) limit switch box (2) motor (3) chain*

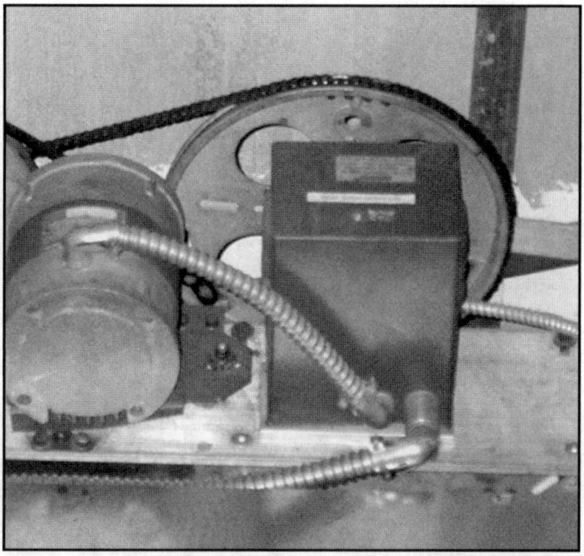

Figure C.8 *Car door operator (close-up)*

Figure C.9 *Car door equipment*

Figure C.10 *Car door equipment*

Figure C.11 *Car door equipment with retractable door re-opening device*

Figure C.12 *Hoistway door interlock and hangers*

Figure C.13 *Hoistway door interlock (close-up)*

Figure C.14 *Hoistway door upper track*

Figure C.15 *Hoistway door sill track with gibs (guides)*

Figure C.16 *Car and hoistway door sills (lower track)*

Figure C.17 *Hoistway door closer—lever arm type*

Figure C.18 *Hoistway door closer—spirator type*

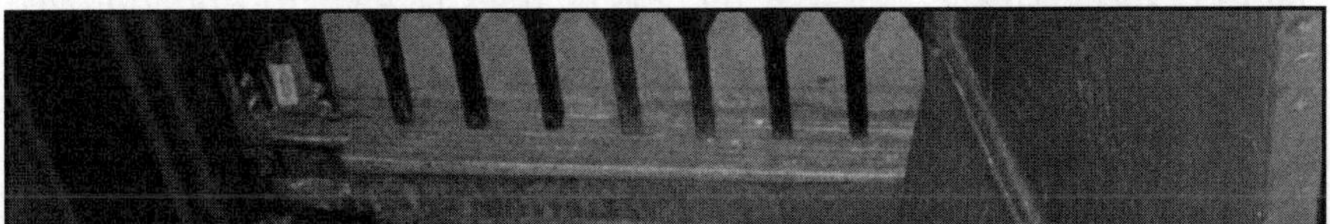

Figure C.19 *Hoistway door—swing type with a space guard—unapproved type in most jurisdictions*

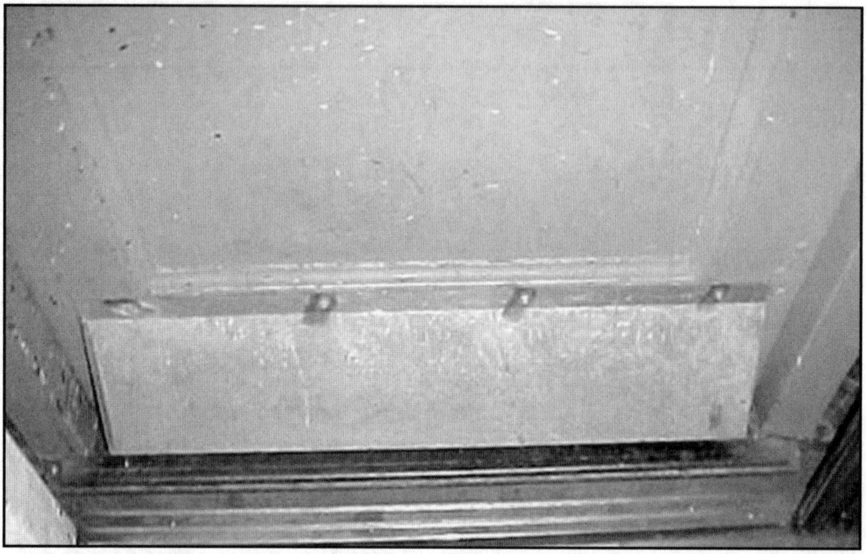

Figure C.20 *Hoistway door—swing type with a space guard—unapproved type in most jurisdictions (close-up)*

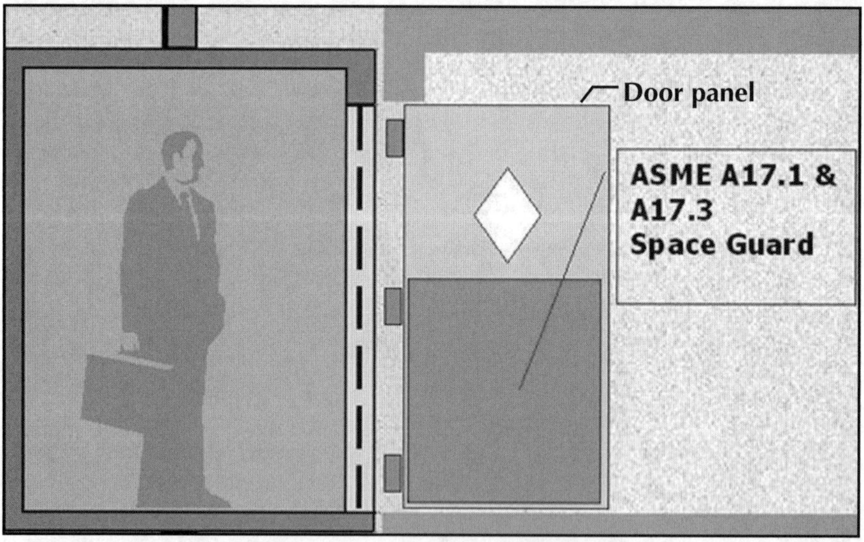

Figure C.21 *Hoistway door—swing type with space guard (illustration)—approved type currently required in most jurisdictions*

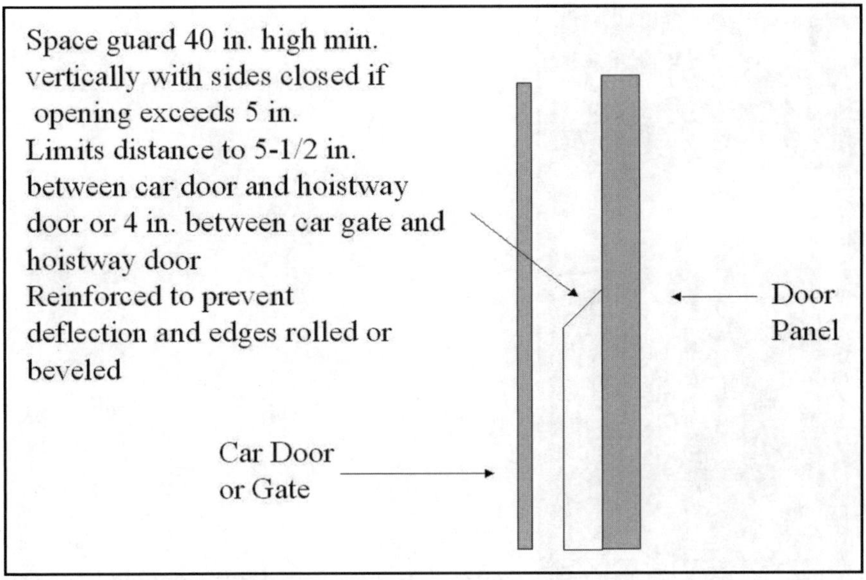

Figure C.22 *Hoistway door—swing type space guard—approved type currently required in most jurisdictions*

Figure C.23 *Single-speed side-opening hoistway type door*

Figure C.24 *Single-speed center-opening hoistway door (1) hall lantern; (2) elevator number; (3) escutcheon hole for drop key access; (4) floor number; (5) corridor call button; (6) moving panel; (7) sill or saddle*

Figure C.25 *Two-speed side-opening hoistway type door*

Figure C.26 *Two-speed center-opening hoistway type door*

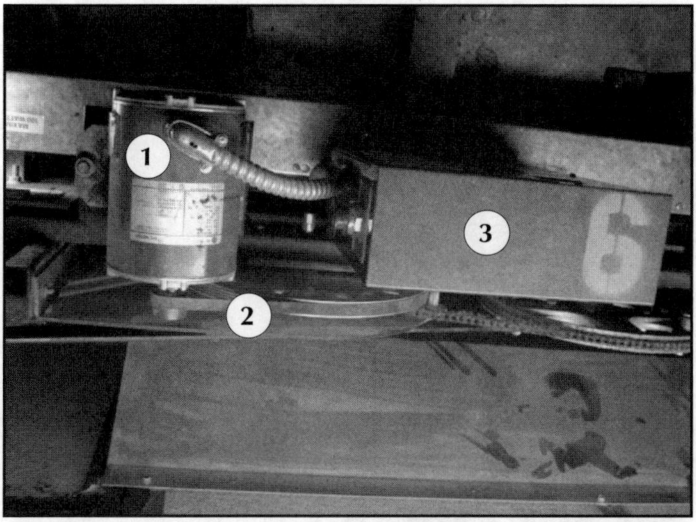

Figure C.27 *Car door operator (1) motor; (2) belt and pulleys; (3) door control box*

Figure C.28 *Hoistway door interlock (1) non-moving box; (2) clutch rollers and release lever*

Figure C.29 *Car door restrictor bracket—top*

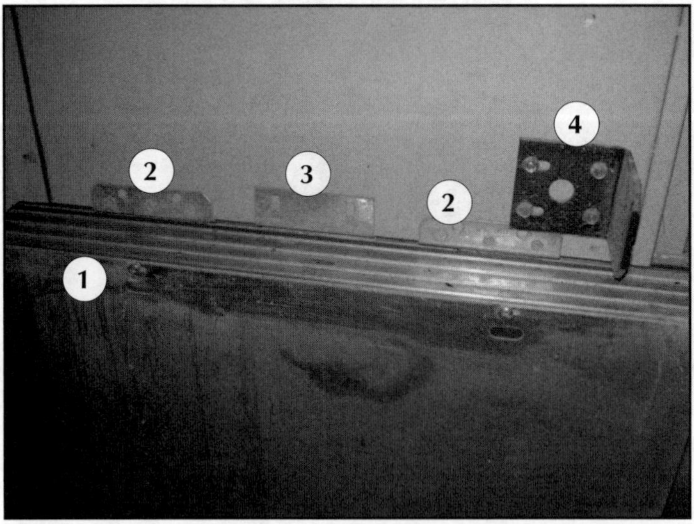

Figure C.30 *Hoistway door—bottom (1) fascia plate; (2) gib; (3) retainer or fire stop; (4) restrictor bracket*

Figure C.31 *Hoistway door—top (1) restrictor; (2) hanger*

Figure C.32 *Car door operator—top view*

Figure C.33A *Hoistway door*

Figure C.33B *Hoistway door unlocking device escutcheon*

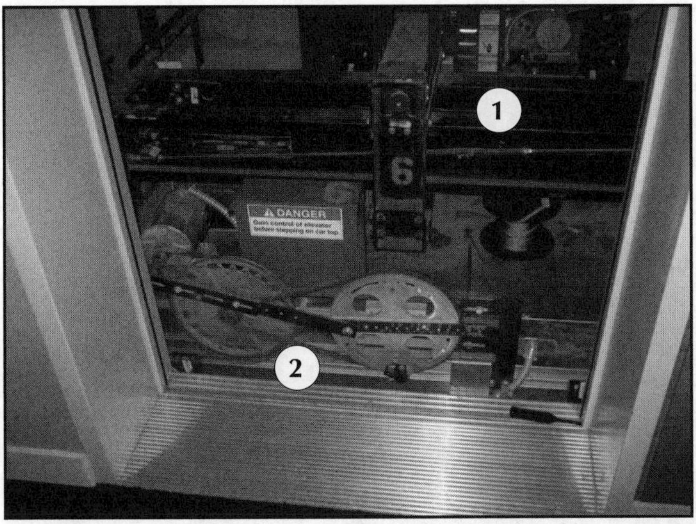

Figure C.34 Front and rear door operators and car top components (1) Rear car door operator; (2) Front car door operator

Figure C.35 Hoistway door access switch (1) tamper proof screw; (2) switch

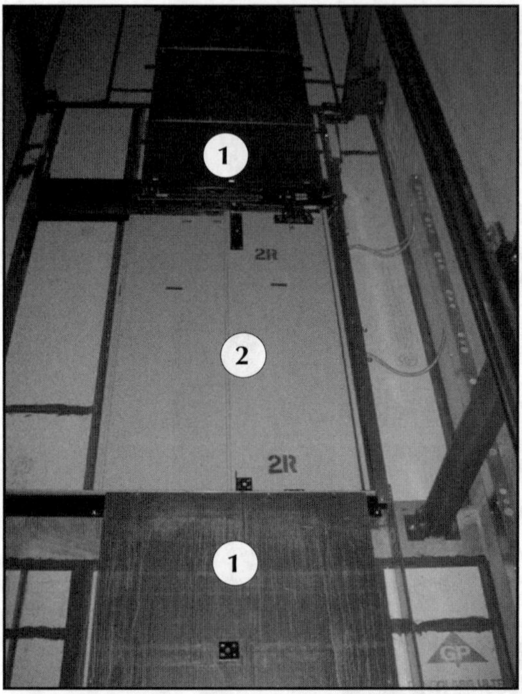

Figure C.36 *Hoistway (1) fascia; (2) door*

Figure C.37 *Hoistway door (inside hoistway)*

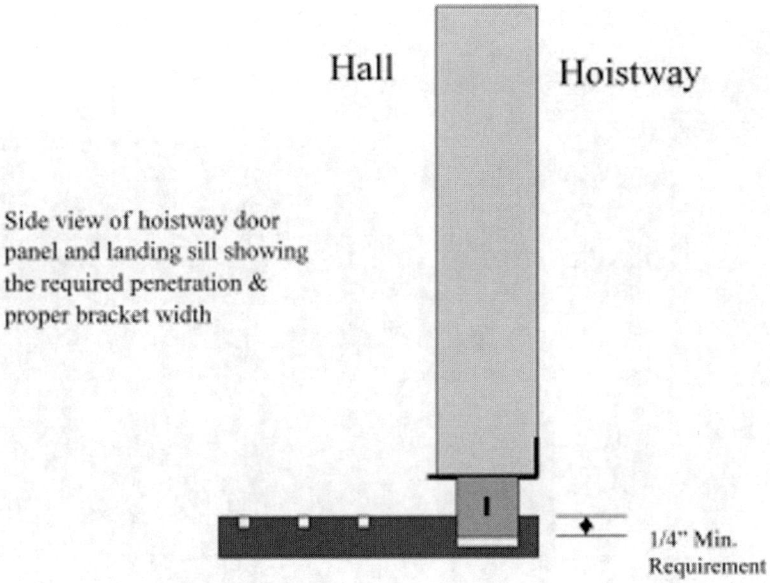

Figure C.38 *Lower penetration of gibs and safety retainer/fire stop.*

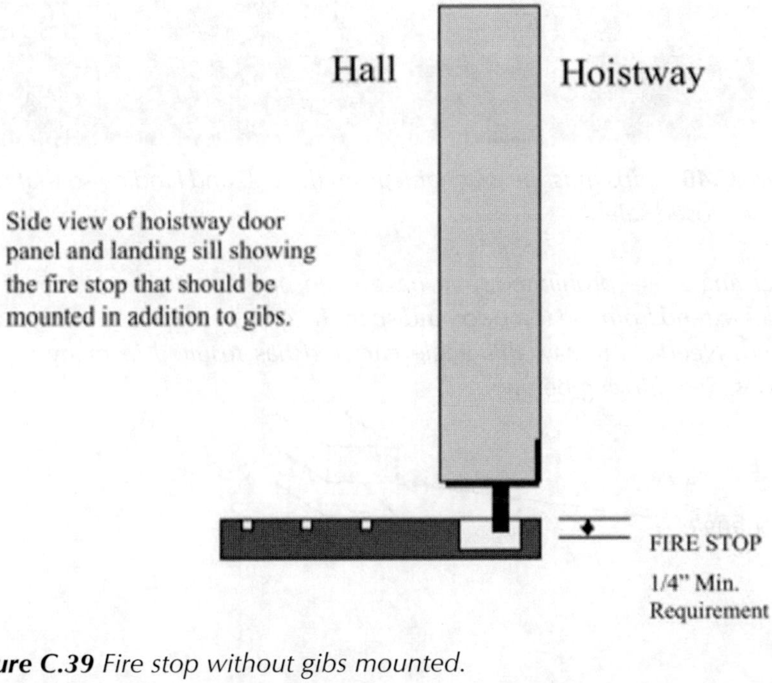

Figure C.39 *Fire stop without gibs mounted.*

Figure C.40 *Straps must be reachable from the cab and landing so that door can be closed safely.*

Shear angles are prohibited, and have been prohibited since 1955. These angles extend from the top door and span the gap, between the doors when closed. Needless to say, this angle can and has resulted in many serious injuries. See drawing below:

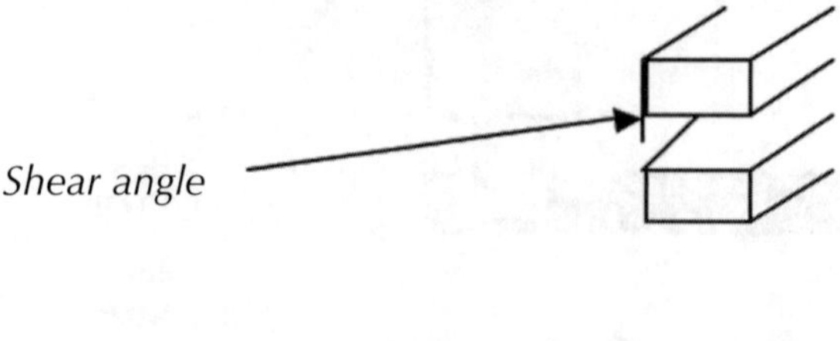

D. Escalators

Top Landing and Machinery Pit
Landing plate
Combplate and combs
Caution signs
Emergency stop switch
Start switch
Controller
Driving machine and brake
Main drive chain
Mainline disconnect switch
Handrail drive
Handrail entry/exit
Reversal stop device
Step-comb impact device or combplate stop switch
Speed sensor or governor

Riding Area and Underneath Steps
Steps (flat, transition, incline)
Handrails
Balustrades
Skirt panels
Decking
Ceiling intersection guards
Handrail tension device
Step chain
Step-skirt clearance
Skirt obstruction device
Step upthrust device
Step level device
Missing step device

Bottom Landing and Pit
Landing plate
Combplate and combs
Caution signs
Emergency stop switch
Handrail entry/exit
Start switch
Step-comb impact device or combplate stop switch
Turn around sprocket
Broken step chain device
Step chain carriage

Figure D.1 *General locations of typical components of escalators. Photographs of selected components follow.*

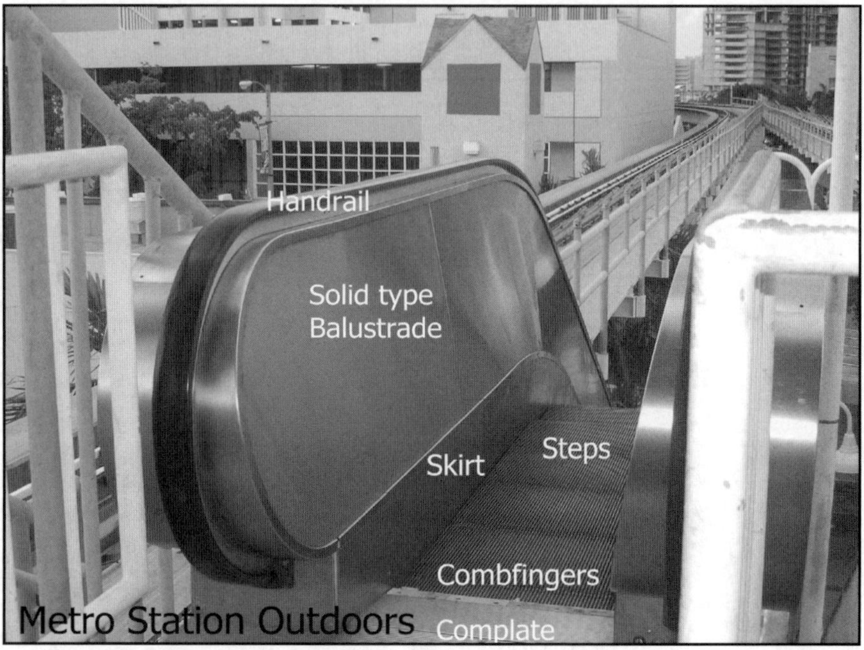

Figure D.2A *Escalator components—outdoor*

Figure D.2B *Control station on solid balustrade newel*

Figure D.3 *Caution sign*

Figure D.4 *Handrail inlet*

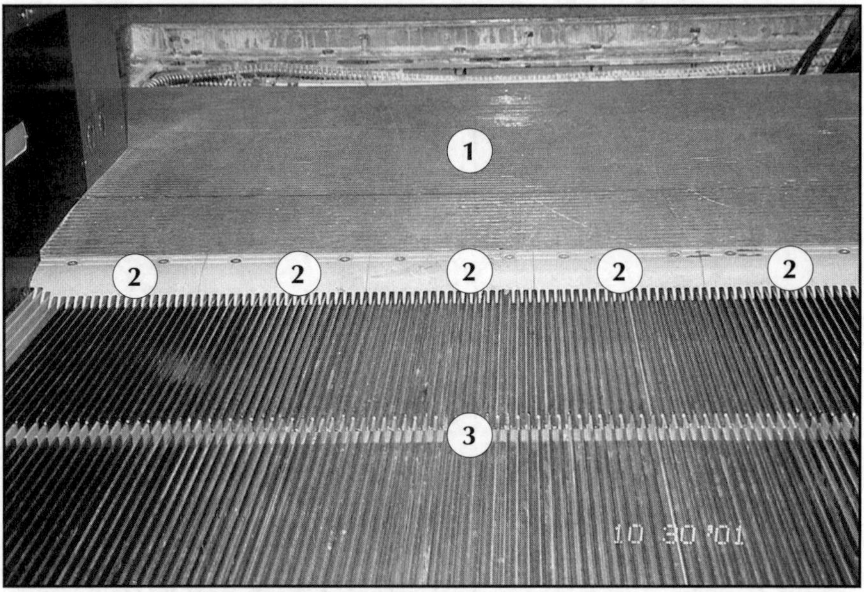

Figure D.5 *Escalator entrance/exit (1) landing/floor plate; (2) comb sections, attached to the combplate; (3) steps*

Figure D.6 *Missing step*

Figure D.7 *Steps at combs*

Figure D.8A *Combplate missing comb section*

Figure D.8B *Code violation: combfinger tips not penetrating into step tread slots*

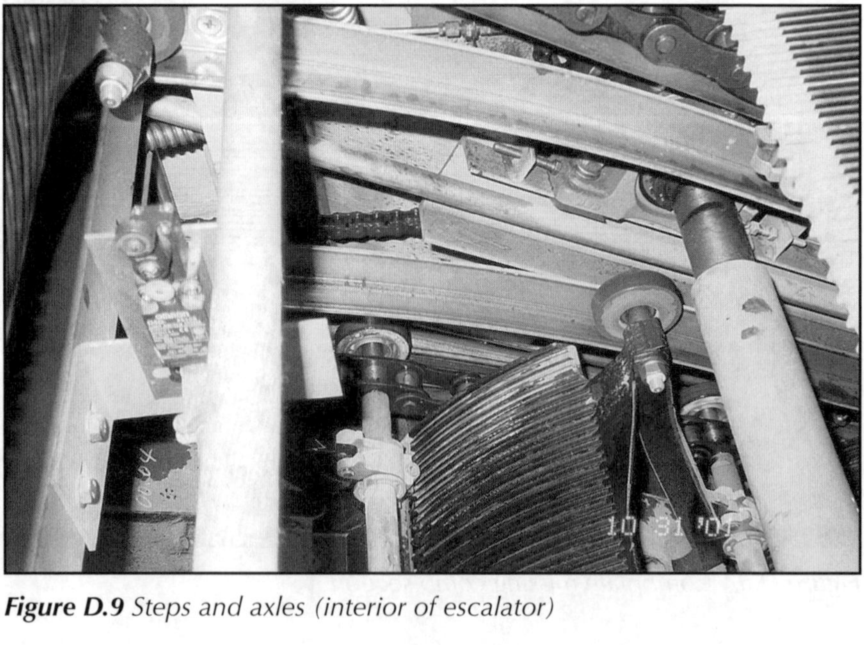

Figure D.9 *Steps and axles (interior of escalator)*

Figure D.10 *Step—side view (1) step roller; (2) step a-frame; (3) axle clamp*

Figure D.11A *Handrail drive system (1) handrail drive sheave; (2) drive chain; (3) handrail return side*

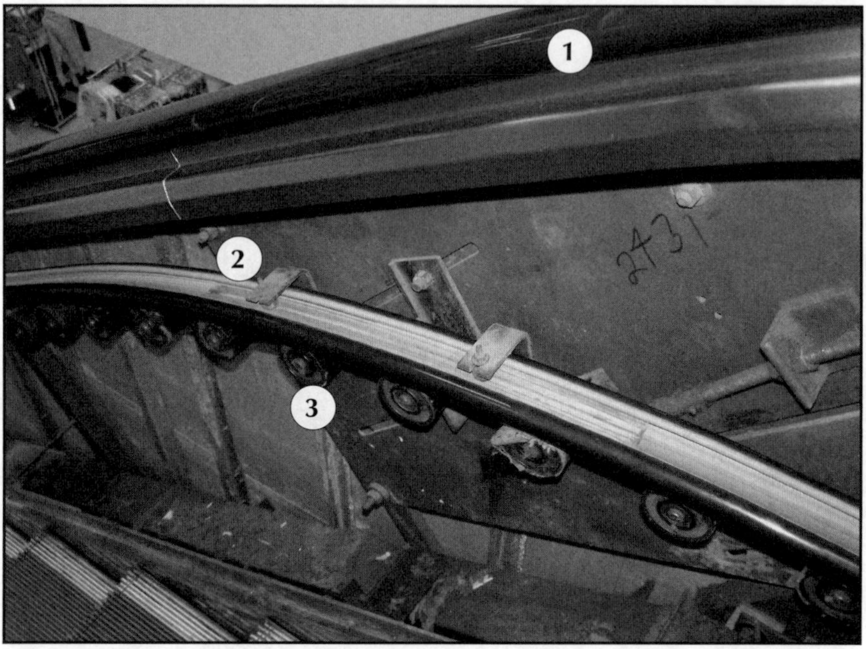

Figure D.11B *Handrail system (1) handrail passenger side; (2) handrail return side; (3) support rollers*

Figure D.11C *(1) Handrail newel wheel*

Figure D.11D *Step turnaround and step chain carriage at lower end (pit cover removed)*

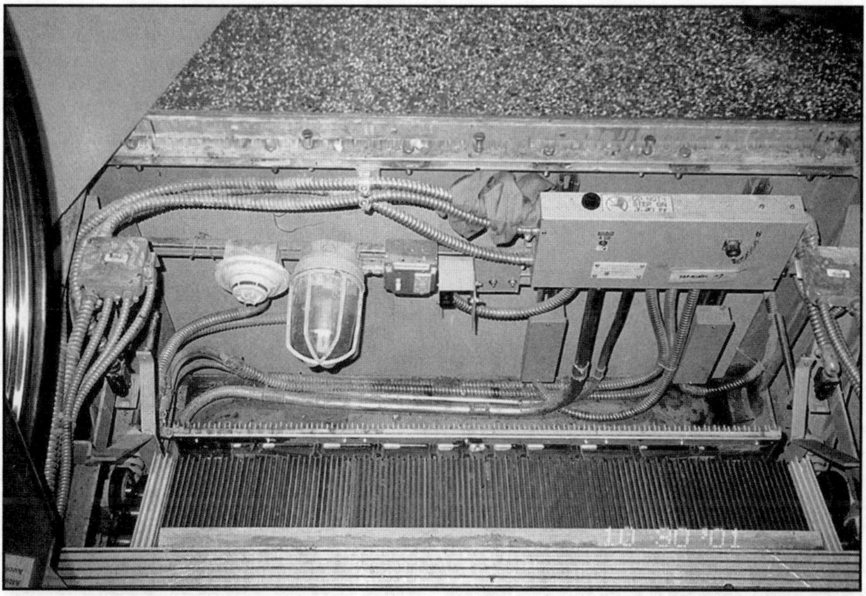

Figure D.12 *Bottom pit*

Figure D.13 *Barricaded end*

Figure D.14 *Drive machine (upper pit)*

Figure D.15 *Machinery space (upper pit)*

Figure D.16 *Drive unit—belt type*

Figure D.17 *One type of escalator reversal stop device*

Figure D.18 *Modular type drive machine (under steps)*

Figure D.19 *Modular drive brake*

Figure D.20 *Demarcation light fixtures (under steps at ingress/egress area)*

Figure D.21 *Escalator skirt brush—sample*

Figure D.22 *Escalator step showing screws that can damage entrapped objects or limbs*

Figure D.23 *Stanchions mounted above handrail to discourage handrail "surfing."*

E. Moving Walks

"Bottom" Landing and Pit	Riding Area and Underneath Pallets/Belt	"Top" Landing and Pit
Landing plate	Treadway (pallets/belt)	Landing plate
Combplate and combs	Handrails	Combplate and combs
Caution signs	Balustrades	Caution signs
Emergency stop switch	Decking	Start switch
Start switch	Pallet chain	Emergency stop switch
Handrail entry/exit comb impact device or combplate stop switch	Pallet level device	Handrail entry/exit
Turn around sprocket	Missing pallet device	Controller
Broken step chain device	Handrail tension device	Handrail drive
Carriage		Driving machine and brake
Broken treadway device		Main drive chain
		Mainline disconnect switch
		Comb impact device or combplate stop switch

Figure E.1 *General locations of typical components of moving walks. Photographs of selected components follow.*

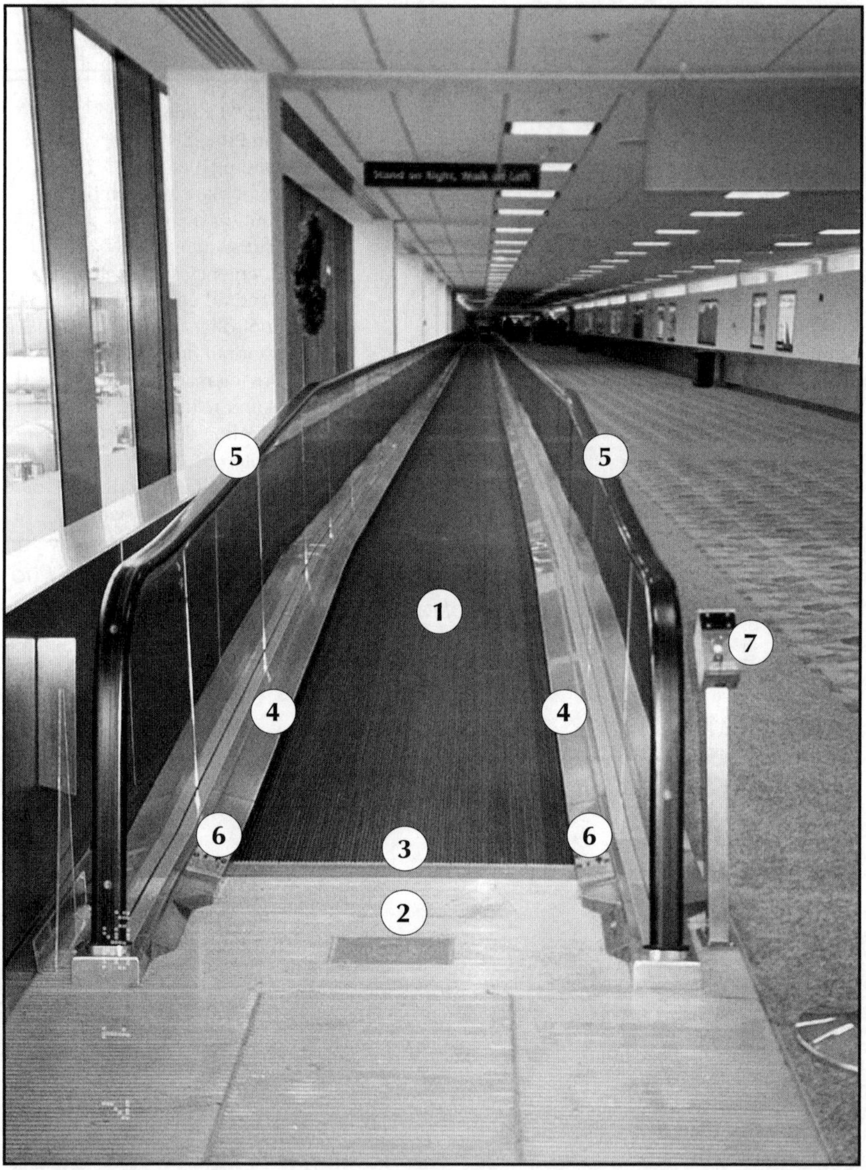

Figure E.2 *Belt type (1) belt treadway; (2) floor/landing plate; (3) comb plate with comb sections; (4) inner deck; (5) handrail; (6) caution sign; (7) stop switch*

Figure E.3 *Pallet type (1) pallet treadway*

Figure E.4 *Machinery space (pit)*

Figure E.5 *Driving machine components*

Figure E.6 *Pit (non-driving end)*

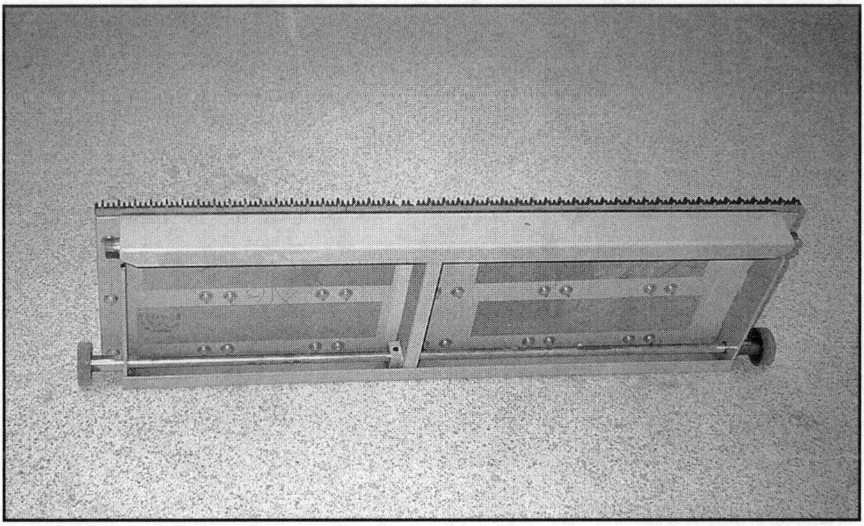

Figure E.7 *Pallet (underside)*

F. Miscellaneous

Figure F.1 *Driving (hoist) machine—rack and pinion type*

Figure F.2 *Controller—2000 vintage*

Figure F.3 *Linestarter*

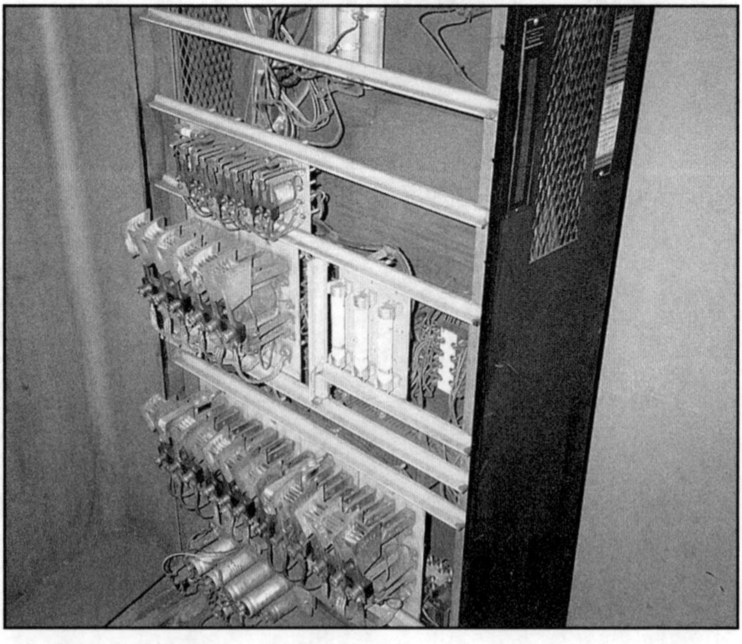

Figure F.4 *Controller with relays*

Figure F.5 *Contractors (high-current type)*

Figure F.6 *Printed-circuit control board*

Figure F.7 *Tools—left to right: torque wrench; comb-impact device force measuring gauge; pressure gauges and adapters*

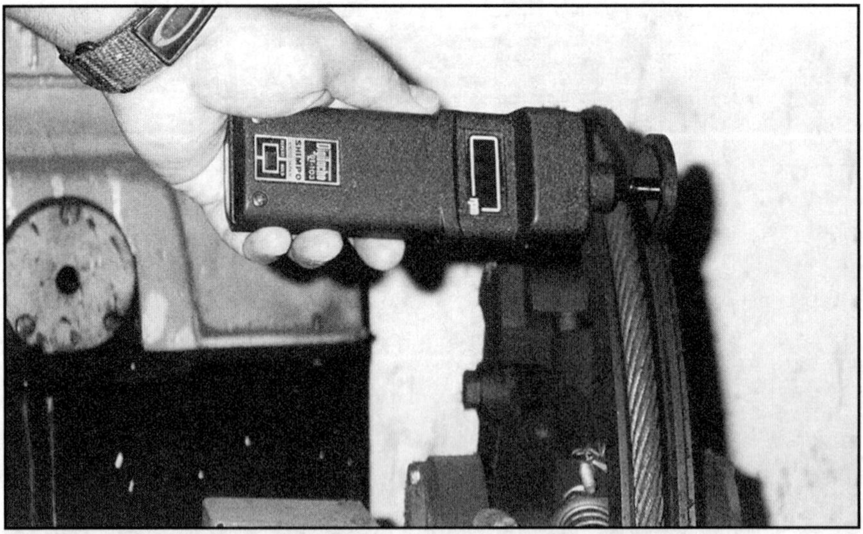

Figure F.8 *Elevator speed measured at governor with tachometer*

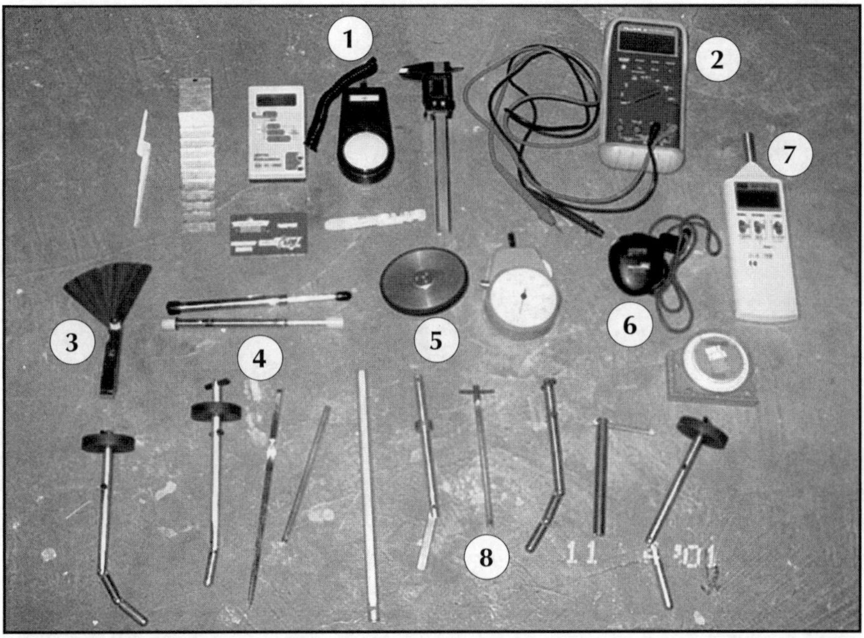

Figure F.9 *Examination instruments and tools (1) light meter; (2) multi- meter; (3) feeler gauge; (4) door force gauge; (5) tachometer; (6) stopwatch; (7) sound meter; (8) hoistway door unlocking tools*

Figure F.10 *Meter to measure light intensity*

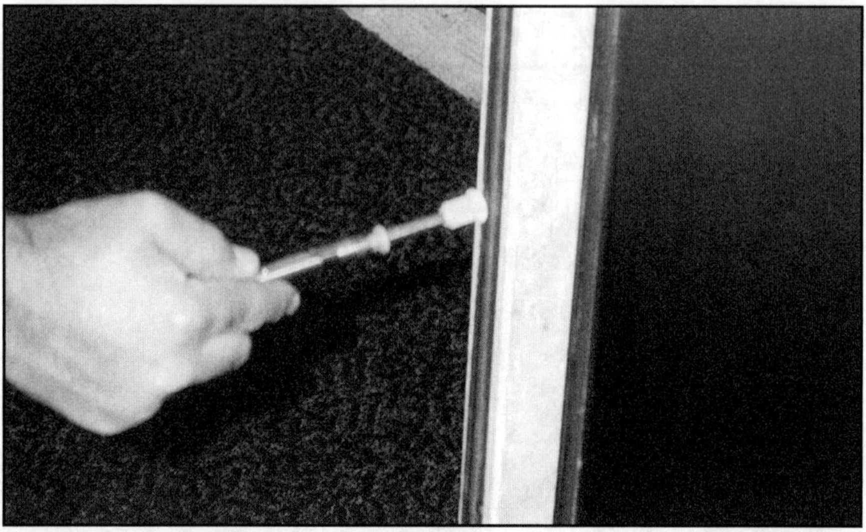

Figure F.11 *Checking door closing force*

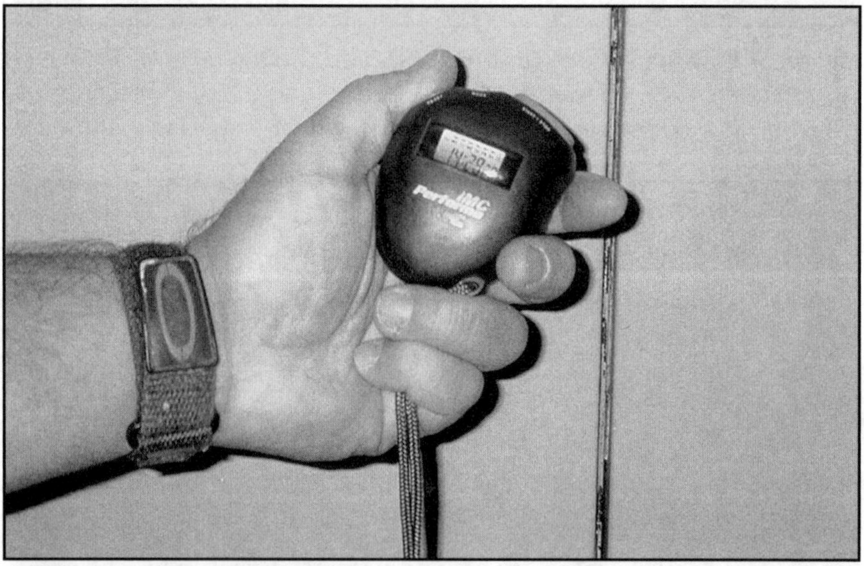

Figure F.12 *Checking door speed*

Figure F.13A *Position indicator inside car*

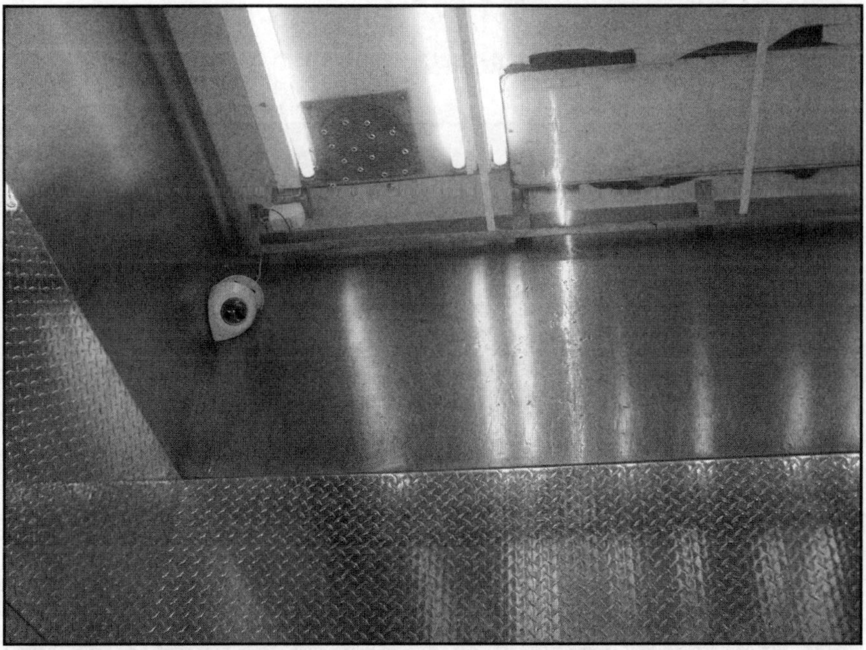

Figure F.13B *Video surveillance camera—top corner*

Figure F.14 *Car operating panel (COP)*

Figure F.15 *Car top equipment*

Figure F.16 *Car toe guard (apron)*

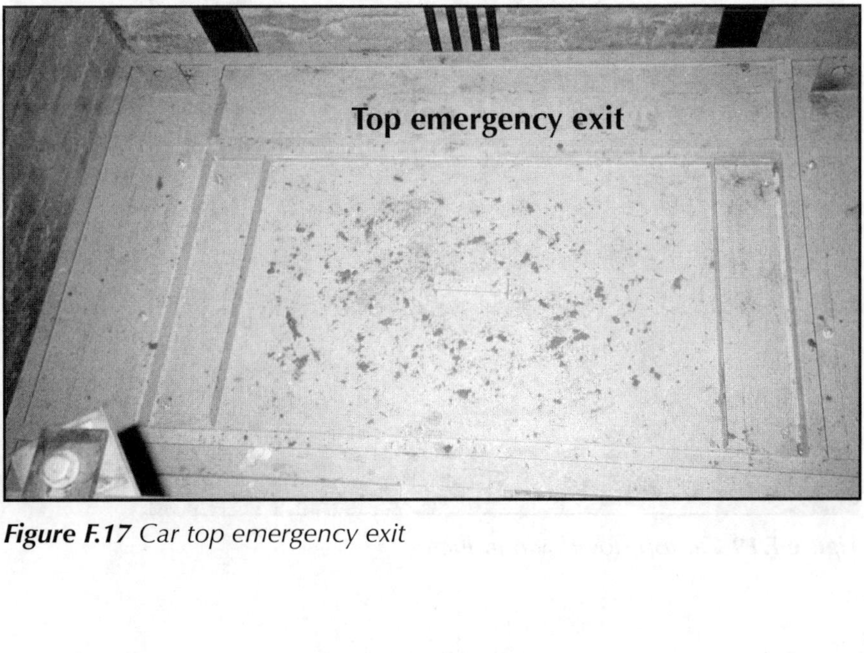

Figure F.17 *Car top emergency exit*

Figure F.18 *Car top crosshead data plate*

Figure F.19 *Car top slowdown inductor*

Figure F.20 *Measuring illumination level at landing and car sills*

Figure F.21 *Measuring illumination level—machine room*

Figure F.22 *Mainline power disconnect switches*

Figure F.23 *Standby power generator*

Figure F.24 *Standby power generator transfer switch*

Figure F.25 *Door to elevator pit*

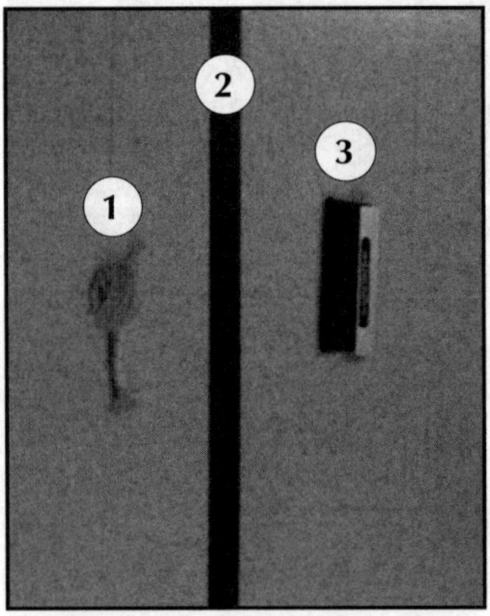

Figure F.26 *Miscellanous. (1) aramid fiber rope; (2) elastomeric coated steel belt; (3) escalator skirt brush for entrapment protections*

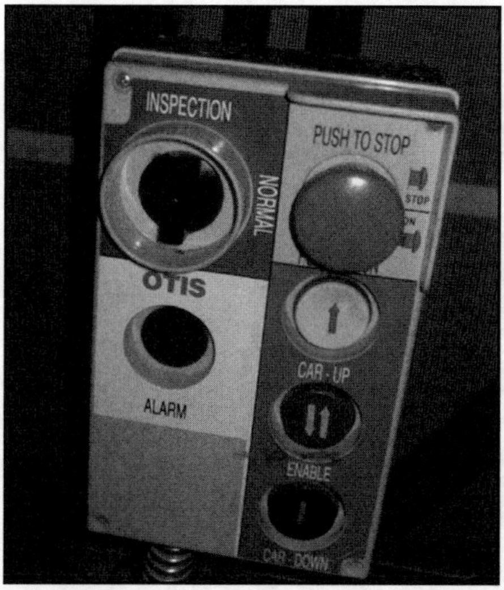

Figure F.27 *Car top operating device*

Figure F.28 *Fascia in hoistway*

***Figure F.29** Car top leveling and landing inductors*

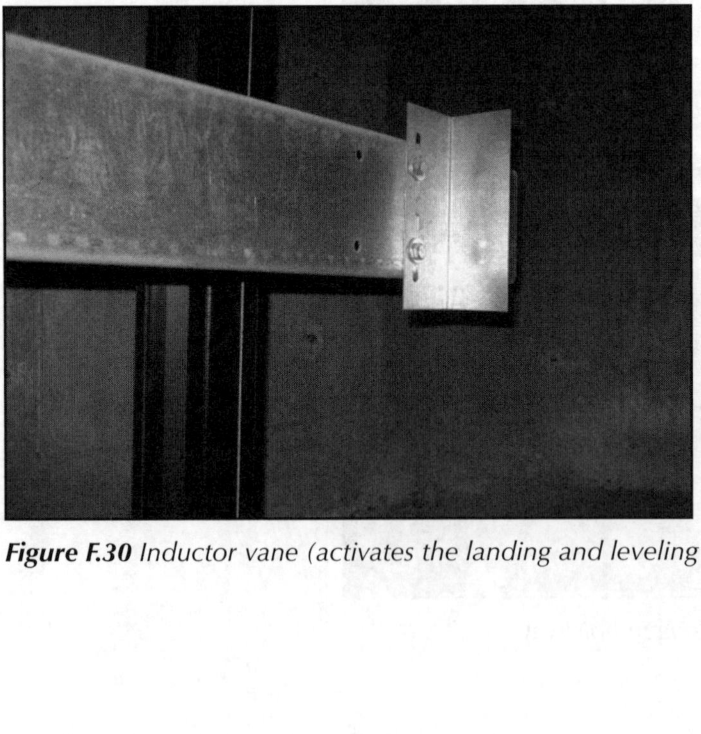

***Figure F.30** Inductor vane (activates the landing and leveling inductors)*

Figure F.31 *Car operating panel (1) floor buttons; (2) alarm bell; (3) door buttons; (4) telephone box*

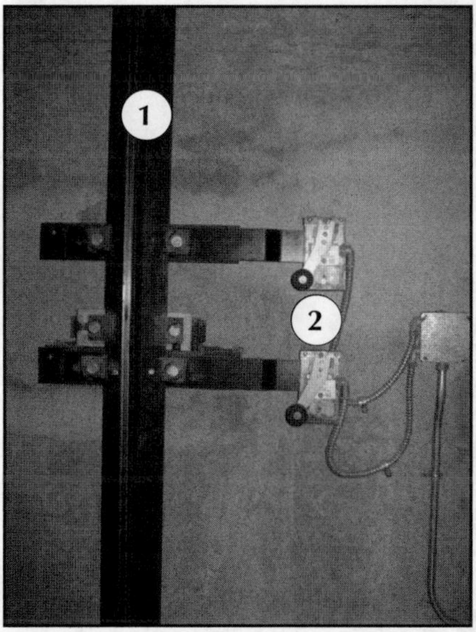

Figure F.32 *Hoistway limit switches at either top or bottom (1) car guide rail; (2) directional and final limits*

Figure F.33 *(1) Traveling cable*

Figure F.34 *Emergency power selector switch panel*

Figure F.35 *Firefighter's recall station—corridor*

Figure F.36 *Platform (wheelchair) lift*

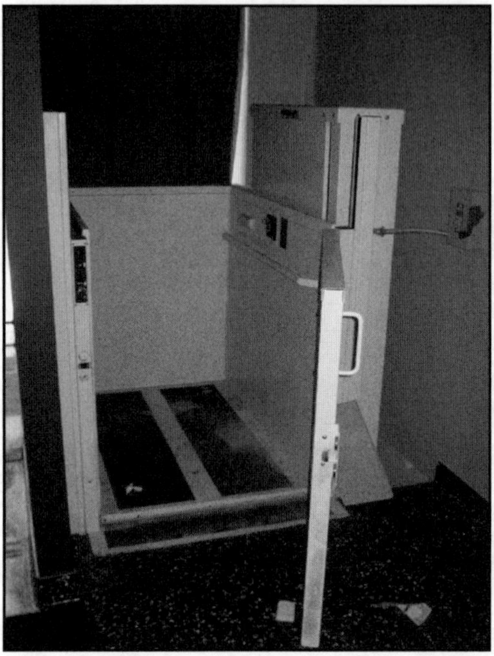

Figure F.37 *Wheelchair lift door opened*

Figure F.38 *Fall prevention (1) Protective railing on cartop*

Figure F.39–44 *The following are photos of Private Residence Elevator that contains a winding drum with two cables that subbport the load.*

Figure F.39 *Typical residential cab interior showing the car operating buttons and the emergency cab lighting fixture.*

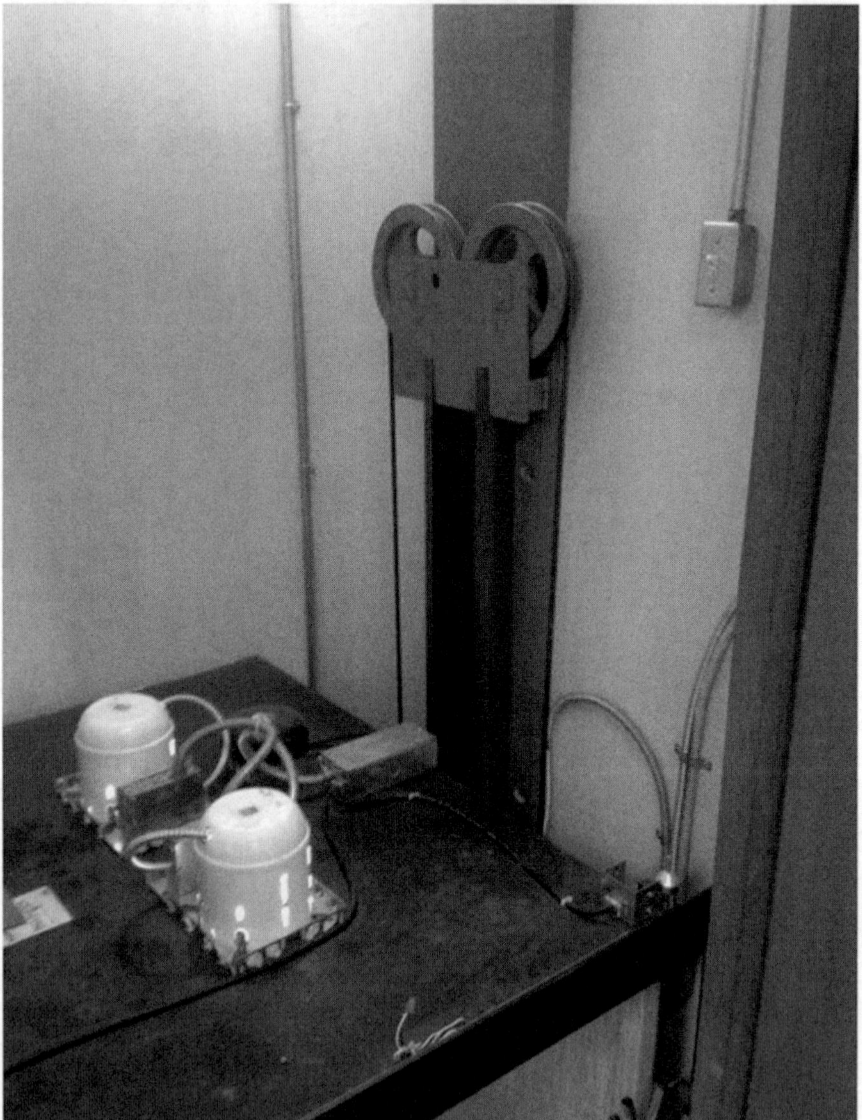

Figure F.40 *Residential elevator cab-top showing the sheaves for the two wire rope hoisting cables.*

Figure F.41 *Various hoistway components on a typical residential elevator.*

Figure F.42 *Residential elevator deflector sheaves that route the hoisting cables.*

Figure F.43 *Residential elevator power disconnecting switches that will stop the elevator when a broken cable(s) is detected.*

Figure F.44 *Residential elevator winding driven hoist machine.*

Chapter 3

Accident Statistics

Synopsis

3.1 Introduction

Most people have an inordinate fear of elevators, and a cavalier attitude towards escalators. However, the potential dangers to passengers are far greater on an escalator than in an elevator. This is because the elevator passenger is enclosed in the cab, which for the most part isolates the passenger from the moving components. On the other hand, the escalator passenger is continuously exposed to moving components.

The most common fear of passengers on elevators is free fall, which is an uncommon occurrence. The vast majority (estimated 75%) of passenger elevator accidents are trips or falls and being hit by the elevator doors. While significant injury can occur from these types of accidents, they are seldom in the realm of death and disfigurement. Probably, the biggest potential dangers to elevator passengers are falling down the hoistway (shaft) or being in the entranceway when the elevator moves. The potential for serious injury and death is probably greater for elevator mechanics than for passengers because the mechanics are often in inherently hazardous locations that the public never enters (e.g., pits, top of cars, hoistways).

The most frequent passenger escalator accidents are trips and falls, which is not surprising given their frequency on stationary stairs. However, escalator entrapment-type injuries (side-of-step, comb plate, handrail, etc.) have resulted in disfigurements, strangulations, degloving and avulsion injuries, scalpings, and even death. Tragically, the victims frequently are small children.

It is claimed that the total number of escalator accidents is small compared to the large number of users. However, this is of little comfort to the victims and their families, especially when considering the severity of the injuries, the ages of the victims, and the notoriety of the risks. Although it is unavoidable that passengers will usually be close to the moving components on escalators, remedial efforts can be made to minimize the risks.

It is a sad fact of life that accidents occur. However, the key questions to ask are what caused the accident and what were the contributory factors. Some accidents have an element of "in the wrong place at the wrong time" about them; some have an element of disregard for the equipment involved; and some fall into the category of negligence or incompetence.

Accident statistics related to elevators and escalators are usually not comprehensive, abundant or readily available. The statistics that do exist are usually limited in scope, parochial, and vary in their methodology. The elevator and escalator manufacturers and maintenance companies probably have the most extensive statistics of these accidents, but they do not voluntarily provide access to this information for obvious reasons. However, the causes and reasons for most of the accidents that occur are well-known in the industry, based on experience and accepted common knowledge.

While news reports of elevator and escalator accidents can be obtained, in many cases they are anecdotal and dramatized.

This chapter reviews the statistics for a few significant studies of elevator and escalator accidents. It is important to note that these are statistics of recorded accidents. Many of the accidents that generate lawsuits probably are not represented in these statistics. In fact, one of these studies determined that between 79 and 91 percent of the accidents that led to claims against New York City were not recorded.

3.2 Recorded Accidents

A. Consumer Product Safety Commission

1. Statistics: 2000 and Later

Per the National Elevator Industry Inc. (NEII), a total of 900,000 elevators and 35,000 escalators are in operation in the United States as of 2016.. However, the number of annual escalator injuries exceeds those for elevators although there are approximately six times more elevators than escalators (see Table 3.1). Of course, escalators are capable of transporting many more passengers than elevators in the same amount of time.

The Consumer Product Safety Commission (CPSC) estimated that in the three years from the beginning of 2013 to the end of 2015, there were 33,670 elevator injuries requiring hospitalization and 36,636 injuries on escalators in the U.S. (see Table 3.1). When compared to the figures in Section 3.2A.2 **the number of escalator injuries requiring hospital treatment has increased by almost 71.2% while similar elevator injuries have increased by only about 11.7% since the late 1990s.**

The statistics used by the CPSC are based on the statistical surveillance and follow-back system known as the National Electronic Injury Surveillance System (NEISS). This system records patients' accounts of their accidents at a sampling of hospital emergency rooms that are statistically representative of hospital emergency rooms nationwide. Currently this encompasses 100 hospitals out of more than 5,000 hospitals nationwide with emergency rooms. For more information about the CPSC and NEISS consult the website www.cpsc.gov.

Table 3.1
Elevator vs. Escalator Injuries Reported Requiring Hospital Treatment, 2013–2015

YEAR	ELEVATOR	ESCALATOR	TOTAL	% ESCALATOR
2013	11172	12260	**23432**	**52.32%**
2014	10969	12774	**23743**	**53.80%**
2015	11529	11602	**23131**	**50.16%**
TOTAL	*33670*	*36636*	***70306***	***52.11%***

Table 3.2
Elevator vs. Escalator Injuries by Age Group, 2015

AGE	ELEVATOR	ESCALATOR	TOTAL	% TOTAL
<18	1146	1549	**2695**	**11.65%**
18–34	1504	2140	**3644**	**15.75%**
35–64	3555	3962	**7517**	**32.50%**
>65	5324	3951	**9275**	**40.10%**
TOTAL	*11529*	*11602*	***23131***	***100.00%***

Table 3.3
Elevator vs. Escalator Injuries by Age Group, 2014

AGE	ELEVATOR	ESCALATOR	TOTAL	% TOTAL
<18	1773	1694	**3467**	**14.60%**
18–34	2121	2051	**4172**	**17.57%**
35–64	4033	4120	**8153**	**34.34%**
>65	3042	4909	**7951**	**33.49%**
TOTAL	*10969*	*12774*	***23743***	***100.00%***

Table 3.4
Elevator vs. Escalator Injuries by Age Group, 2013

AGE	ELEVATOR	ESCALATOR	TOTAL	% TOTAL
<18	1361	1690	**3051**	**13.02%**
18–34	2305	2497	**4802**	**20.49%**
35–64	3281	3590	**6871**	**29.32%**
>65	4225	4483	**8708**	**37.16%**
TOTAL	*11172*	*12260*	***23432***	***100.00%***

Tables 3.2 through 3.4 above show that older people are more likely to be injured on elevators and escalators. Senior citizens are more susceptible to injury caused by tripping on misleveled elevators, contact by closing elevator doors, and falling on escalators.

What was not available was data showing the increased danger for preschool children that is presented by riding on an escalator. The exposure of small body parts and footwear to moving parts and pinch/shear/crush points combined with a natural lack of awareness of the danger present on an escalator results in a substantial number of serious injuries. See Table 3.5 for older statistics for young children.

The following are some examples of elevator and escalator injuries and deaths compiled by the CPSC.

- A 4-year-old girl was killed when caught between floors in an elevator in a residential building. Her mother had gotten off before her and other children pressed the call button.
- An 88-year-old woman was exiting the elevator when she tripped and fell at a medical clinic. The floor and the elevator were not level. Cause of death were complications of pelvic fracture due to fall.

- An 8-year-old boy was deceased when he was crushed by a hotel elevator. He had become wedged between the elevator doors and a folding metal gate.
- A 35-year-old man was hospitalized in critical condition after he apparently pried open elevator doors and fell four floors.
- Two sisters, ages 6 and 7, were killed in a moving residential elevator. The elevator's safety feature was disabled, allowing it to ascend while the girls' heads stuck out past the gate.
- A 54-year-old man fell from an elevator that stopped 5 inches short of level floor, contusing both knees.
- A 37-year-old man died from asphyxiation when his clothing became entrapped in the downward moving steps and stationary bottom comb plate of an escalator at a subway station. He was found, on his back, with the coat wrapped tightly around his chest, because part of the coat was dragged into the comb plate. There were no witnesses as to how the coat became entangled.
- An 85-year-old woman lost her balance and fell onto the escalator at a store. Cause of death was blunt impact to head, trunk and extremities sustained in the fall.
- A 12-year-old boy was riding an escalator down (egress) from a baseball game when his right shoe got stuck between the moving step and the stationary left side of the escalator. The victim sustained injury to his right big toe. The extent of the injury was not determined.
- A 5-year-old girl was on the bottom step of a down escalator when her shoe got caught in the comb plate. She reached down to get her shoe when her hand also got caught in the comb plate. Her three middle fingers and part of her hand were amputated.
- An escalator incident at a theatre caused 71 children to suffer minor injuries. The escalator was heading up when it abruptly stopped and shifted slightly backwards causing the kids to fall.
- A 16-month-old girl was injured when her hand slipped between the moving stairs and the escalator wall and she became lodged. She may have been in a stroller when the incident happened. She was flown to the hospital for surgery.

2. Statistics: Prior to 2000

Statistics for accidents, by age of victim, from 1997 through 1999 are shown in Tables 3.5 and 3.6. Table 3.7 summarizes escalator accidents by year (from 1990 through 1994) and age of the victims. Table 3.8 provides average annual injuries on escalators by age of victim and type of accident (1990-1994), and Table 3.9 shows injuries on escalators by age of victim and type of accidents (1995).

Table 3.5
Accidents Involving Elevators, by Age of Victim, 1997–1999

Year	Total	Under Age 5	Age 5-14	Age 15-24	Age 25-64	Age 65 and Up
1997	10,331	11.3%	12.2%	14.8%	32.2%	29.4%
1998	9,403	10.1%	6.2%	9.9%	47.3%	26.4%
1999	10,421	9.0%	10.2%	9.2%	46.9%	24.7%
Total	**30.155**					

Table 3.6
Accidents Involving Escalators, by Age of Victim, 1997–1999

Year	Total	Under Age 5	Age 5-14	Age 15-24	Age 25-64	Age 65 and Up
1997	6,464	13.8%	12.5%	9.1%	31.7%	32.6%
1998	7,035	13.2%	12.3%	10.5%	35.0%	29.0%
1999	7,907	10.9%	10.8%	5.5%	36.6%	36.0%
Total	**21,406**					

Table 3.7
Escalator Accidents, by Age of Victim, 1990–1994

Year	Total	Under 5	5-14	15-64	Over 65
1990	4,900	800	600	2,100	1,400
1991	5,500	1,200	700	2,200	1,400
1992	5,000	1,000	700	1,500	1,800
1993	6,700	1,400	900	2,700	1,700
1994	7,300	1,300	1,200	2,900	1,600
Average	5,900	1,100	800	2,300	1,600

Table 3.8
Average Annual Injuries on Escalators, by Age of Victim, 1990–1994 (rounded to nearest hundred)

Age of Injured	Total Injuries	Falls	Body Part/ shoe caught	Other
All Ages	5,900	4,400	1,000	500
Under 5	1,200	700	500	-
5-14	800	400	300	100
15-64	2,200	1,700	200	300
Over 64	1,700	1,600	*	*

*Less than 100

Table 3.9
Injuries on Escalators, by Age of Victim and Type of Accident. 1995

Age of Injured	Total Injuries	Falls	Body Part/shoe caught
All Ages	6,000	5,200	1,000
Under 5	1,100	800 (15%)	300 (37,5%)
5-14	900	600 (11.5%)	300 (37.5%)
15-64	2,200	2,000 (38.5%)	200 (20%)
Over 64	1,800	1,800 (34.5%)	-

Table 3.10
Estimated Escalator Number of Emergency Room Treatment Injuries by Age of Victim and Type of Hazard (1998)

Age of Injured	Total	Falls	Hazard Pattern: Body Part, Clothing, or Shoe caught	Hazard Pattern: Other
Total	7,000*	5,000	1,200	900
< 5	900	400	400	100
5-14	900	300	400	100
15-64	3,200	2,500	300	400
64+	2,000	1,800	<100	200

- Note: Numbers may not add up to totals due to rounding

An analysis of these accident statistics for escalators is instructive:

- Table 3.10 indicates that 5,000 of the 7,000 (approximately 70%) injuries on escalators occurred due to falls. While only 1,200 (approximately 17%) of the injuries were caused by a body part, clothing or shoes being caught in escalators; these injuries included serious ones to young children such as dislocations, fractures, avulsions and degloving, crushing and disfigurements. For children younger that age 15 approximately 45% of all injuries resulted from a body part, clothing or shoes being caught in escalators. Almost 54% of all victims in 1998 on escalators were children under age 15 or persons age 65 or older, although they represent only approximately 20% of the U.S. Population..
- **Between 1990 and 1994, 60 percent of the injuries occurred to either children under 14 years of age or seniors 65 or older.** The injuries to children under five years of age accounted for 19 percent of the total; children between the ages of 6 to 14 years old accounted for 14 percent of the total; and the elderly accounted for 27 percent of the total.
- **Between 1985 and 1994, 21 deaths associated with escalators were reported to the CPSC. Of these 21 individuals, one was a child under five years of age, ten were between the ages of 24 and 64 and the remaining ten were over 65 years old.** The causes of these deaths were falls in 18 cases, clothing entanglement in two cases and electric shock in one.
- **Based on the annual averages shown in Table 3.8 (Escalator Injuries 1990-1994), falls accounted for 75 percent of the accidents; getting body parts or shoes caught in the escalators accounted for 17 percent of the accidents; and the remaining 8 percent were made up of lacerations and twisted ankles. Almost 20 percent of the injuries were to children under five years of age, and approximately 30 percent of the injuries were to people over 65 years of age.** The most frequently reported locations were malls, department stores and airports.

The following are examples of escalator accidents that the CPSC investigated:

- 1994—In Aurora, Colorado, a four-year-old girl injured her hand while sitting on an escalator step in a department store. She was riding on a down escalator with her mother, who was holding one of her hands. The girl's other hand was on the middle part of the step she was sitting on. At the bottom landing her hand got caught under the stationary comb plate at the landing. Fire personnel extricated her hand.

- 1994—In San Francisco, California, a six-year-old boy wearing tennis shoes got his right foot caught between a moving escalator step and a stationary skirt panel. He was holding onto the handrail with his right hand. The top of his shoe became lodged in the corner of the step where the riser of one step met the tread of an adjacent step. Part of his shoe was torn when his mother pulled him loose, slightly injuring his big toe.
- 1987—In St. Paul, Minnesota, an eight-year-old boy suffered crushed toes when his foot became caught between a moving escalator step and a stationary skirt panel. The boy was standing next to his mother, with most of his weight on one foot. The escalator shut off before they reached the landing. Paramedics extricated the boy's foot from the escalator.
- 1985—In St. Louis, Missouri, a five-year-old girl had two of her toes severed when her right foot became caught between a moving escalator step and a stationary skirt panel. The girl had one hand on the handrail and was holding her mother's hand with the other. Her parents were unable to free her foot. Her toes were reattached at a hospital, but she later lost one because of infection.

B. State of Florida

The following statistics were recorded by the State of Florida for the years 2003 through 2016[1]:

Table 3.11A
Number of Accidents Recorded (Florida 2003–2006) by Type of Device

	2003	2004	2005	2006	2007	2008	2009
Dumbwaiter	0	1	1	0	0	2	1
Escalator	286	328	397	368	430	413	214
Hydraulic Freight	2	6	14	14	3	11	1
Hydraulic Pass	42	82	63	33	28	36	28
Incline Stair	0	0	0	0	0	0	0
Incline Wheel	1	0	2	0	0	0	1
LULA	0	0	0	0	0	0	0
Moving Walk	15	28	44	63	45	38	46
Special Purp	0	0	2	0	1	0	0
Traction Freight	0	1	0	1	0	2	0
Traction Pass	42	58	49	33	44	46	57
Total	**388**	**504**	**572**	**512**	**551**	**548**	**348**

Table 3.11A (cont.)
Number of Accidents Recorded (Florida 2003–2006) by Type of Device

	2010	2011	2012	2013	2014	2015	2016	Total
Dumbwaiter	0	0	1	0	0	0	0	**6**
Escalator	224	240	242	227	233	315	236	**4153**
Hydraulic Freight	7	0	1	3	1	3	2	**68**
Hydraulic Pass	56	37	26	32	17	21	15	**516**
Incline Stair	0	0	0	0	1	0	0	**1**
Incline Wheel	2	0	1	0	0	0	1	**8**
LULA	0	0	1	2	0	0	0	**3**
Moving Walk	65	96	105	94	91	204	93	**1027**
Special Purp	0	0	0	0	0	0	0	**3**
Traction Freight	0	0	1	0	0	0	0	**5**
Traction Pass	40	35	50	45	27	35	31	**592**
Total	**394**	**408**	**428**	**403**	**370**	**578**	**378**	**6382**

Table 3.11B
Number of Accidents Recorded (Florida 2003–2006) by location

	2003	**2004**	**2005**	**2006**	**2007**	**2008**	**2009**
	59	67	72	70	71	69	58
Church	0	1	0	0	0	0	0
City Building	7	8	14	12	1	5	9
Commercial	249	354	421	393	440	426	244
Community College	0	2	0	0	0	0	0
Condo	19	24	28	7	8	13	6
County Bldg.	18	17	3	9	9	4	1
Food Service	0	0	1	0	0	0	0
Hospital	22	11	22	16	14	20	22
Industrial	0	2	0	0	2	2	1
Public Lodging	6	14	7	5	3	4	4
School K-12	0	0	0	0	0	4	2
State Agency	2	0	0	0	2	0	0
University	6	4	4	0	1	1	1
Total	**388**	**504**	**572**	**512**	**551**	**548**	**348**

Table 3.11B (cont.)
Number of Accidents Recorded (Florida 2003–2006) by location

	2010	2011	2012	2013	2014	2015	2016	Total
	44	75	52	66	49	74	43	**869**
Church	0	0	0	0	0	0	0	**1**
City Building	0	11	5	5	8	5	3	**93**
Commercial	310	284	324	283	295	465	304	**4792**
Community College	1	1	0	2	0	1	1	**8**
Condo	6	17	8	8	5	2	7	**158**
County Bldg.	2	1	8	1	2	7	3	**85**
Food Service	0	0	1	0	0	0	0	**2**
Hospital	18	18	25	30	10	17	16	**266**
Industrial	0	0	1	0	0	0	0	**8**
Public Lodg-ing	1	1	3	5	1	3	1	**64**
School K-12	0	0	0	1	0	0	0	**8**
State Agency	0	0	0	0	0	0	0	**4**
University	1	0	1	2	0	4	0	**25**
Total	**394**	**408**	**428**	**403**	**370**	**578**	**378**	**6382**

Several significant inferences can be drawn from these statistics:

- **From 2003 to 2016 escalators were involved with 4,158 out of 6,382 total injuries (over 65%) and moving walks were involved with 1,027 out of 6,382 total injuries (approx. 16%). This represents a combined approximately 81% of all injuries.**
- **Commercial buildings were involved with 4,792 out of 6,382 total injuries (75%).** This is surprising due to likelihood that these types of buildings are most likely to have greater financial resources that other types of buildings. However, depending how they classified buildings as commercial, those buildings may have had many more escalators than the other buildings.

C. Council of the City of New York City report

In April 1999 the City Council of New York issued a report[2] that painted a very disturbing picture of the elevator inspection and test program in New York City.[1] The main purpose of the report was to chronicle the long-standing and widespread corruption and what was described as gross mismanagement of the Department of Building's (DOB) Elevator Division. This section focuses on the pertinent statistics contained in that report.

A significant finding of the report was that the CPSC accident statistics might drastically understate accidents at the local level. For the period between January 1, 1994, and December 31, 1996, the CPSC reported five elevator-related fatalities in New York City. For this same period, the DOB's records documented 18 elevator-related fatalities—a 260 percent difference.

Another significant finding of the report was that between 79 and 91 percent of the accidents that led to claims against New York City were not recorded. This indicates that recorded accident statistics may grossly underestimate the number of actual accidents.

Also, the report indicated that 65 percent of all elevator complaints were not resolved. Perhaps this explains some of the unusual accident causes that were reported.

The following was reported as the total number of elevators in the ten most-populated U.S. cities:

New York City—63,138
Los Angeles—19,600
Chicago—17,500
Dallas—10,000
San Antonio—9,000
Philadelphia—8,000
Houston—7,000
San Diego—4,500
Detroit—4,000
Phoenix—2,842

The elevator accident statistics, based on DOB records between 1992 and 1996, are given in Table 3.12. There was a close correlation between the number of accidents and the number of elevators located in each of the city's five boroughs (Table 3.13).

Table 3.12
Elevator Accidents, by Type of Danger, 1992–1996

Danger	Total	Percent
Person fell down shaft	49	23%
Injury to elevator maintenance worker	32	15%
Elevator fell down shaft	24	11%
Other cause	24	11%
Elevator moved up or down abruptly	19	9%
Door Injury	12	6%
Elevator abruptly stopped or stalled	11	5%
Parking garage or automobile involved	10	5%
Attempting to exit stalled elevator	9	4%
Elevator surfing or trespassing	9	4%
Loose elevator part fell	8	4%
Elevator not level with landing (trip)	7	3%

There was a close correlation between the number of accidents and the number of elevators located in each of the city's five boroughs (see Table 3.13).

Table 3.13
Accident Statistics for New York City Boroughs, 1994-1996

Borough	Percent of Elevators	Percent of Accidents
Manhattan	65%	62%
Bronx	9%	10%
Brooklyn	14%	21%
Queens	11%	5%
Staten Island	1%	1%

Several significant inferences can be drawn from these statistics:

- The two most common dangers (being hit by the doors and trips or falls) together accounted for only 9 percent of the recorded injuries. However, the report did indicate that the DOB did not record 91 percent of all elevator accidents referenced in claims against the city and 79 percent of all NYC Housing Authority elevator accidents.

- People falling down the shaft was the most common danger, which should rarely occur for properly maintained elevators because of the protection provided at the landings (e.g., doors with interlocks and automatic closers).
- The second highest percentage of injuries occurred to elevator maintenance workers.
- The third highest percentage of injuries was related to elevators falling down the shaft. Again, this should be relatively rare for properly maintained elevators.

The report indicated that the Council's staff developed the following statistics by compiling the records of numerous government agencies (since no single entity had comprehensive records) and newspaper articles:

Elevator accidents (1992–1996)
Accidents—369, one every five days on average
Injuries—379
Fatalities—30

Elevator Emergency Responses (fiscal 1993–1996)
(Note that some overlap is possible.)
Fire department—13,750 "911" calls
Emergency service unit—4,355

Not surprisingly, the following statistics for the period between 1992 and 1996 indicate that an inordinately large number of accidents occurred in the city's public housing:

Percent of city's total elevators—5 percent
Percent of accidents—27 percent
Average number of complaints—87,035 a year or 238 a day
Passengers trapped in elevators:

- 1992—883
- 1993—847
- 1994—2,315
- 1995—3,747
- 1996—3,335 (277 percent increase from 1992)

The following are some short descriptions of the serious accidents mentioned in the report:

- Automobiles falling down the hoistway at parking garages because interlocks were deliberately bypassed by workers to save time opening and closing the landing doors. Disturbingly, in one case some of the building's workers and elevator maintenance mechanics deliberately altered the evidence to try to make it seem like the victims drove the automobile through the doors. In another, the elevator was repaired before an accident investigation could be conducted.
- A woman opened a landing door on the thirteenth floor and walked into the hoistway assuming the elevator was there with the lights out. She grabbed the ropes as she fell and landed on top of the car, which was on the first floor.
- A freight elevator plunged 25 floors, hit a girder and stopped. Two persons were injured.
- A man was crushed to death when a freight elevator he was unloading malfunctioned.
- A hospital patient on a gurney fell to his death in an elevator shaft.
- A 50-year-old female was crushed to death in an elevator shaft.
- A 94-year-old woman died when she fell getting off an elevator.
- A 33-year-old man died of head and torso injuries from falling down an elevator shaft.
- A 13-year-old boy died of head injuries sustained while "elevator surfing." He jumped from the top of one car toward another car, but missed and was pinned between the two cars.
- A man died of a skull fracture and subdural hemorrhage from falling down an elevator shaft as he was trying to assist people stuck in an elevator.

As mentioned above, the NYC Council report indicated that an inordinately large number of accidents occurred in the city's public housing for the period between 1992 and 1996. In December 2015, a resident of a public housing project for senior citizens in the Bronx reported that an elevator was *"going up and down by itself"* while the doors remained open to the New York City Housing Authority's (NYCHA) customer center. Despite this warning NYCHA did not respond and take the elevator out of service. An hour and a half later, an 84-year-old male resident attempted to enter the elevator, which drifted upwards by several feet catching the man's leg and hand. He ultimately fell out of the raised elevator into the hallway and died three days later from his injuries.

The New York City Department of Investigation (DOI) discovered that the housing authority did not take immediate action to put the elevator out of service after receiving the complaint, which could have prevented the accident. NYCHA senior management did not learn of and investigate the incident until four days later. Less than a month earlier, per DOI's investigation, a similar accident, also in the Bronx, trapped a resident's foot in the elevator door for over an hour resulting is a fractured leg.

The DOI report[3] released in March 2016 that followed its investigation revealed that the elevators involved in the accidents at both locations were equipped with fail-safe devices known as "brake monitors," which identify when an elevator's brakes are malfunctioning, and safely shut down the elevator, a function that might have prevented the incidents in the Bronx. However, in both cases the brake monitors were not operational. In fact, a post incident inspection of the elevator involved with the 84 year old man revealed that the electrical wiring had been disconnected and wrapped in electrical tape.

DOI also found that NYCHA was not in compliance with a 2014 revision to the New York City Building Code that requires property owners to install physical tags to document annual inspection and maintenance of elevator braking systems – established a full year earlier. Staff later admitted that they had "missed the boat" concerning this tagging and documentation of annual elevator brake inspections.

A post-incident review of the 1,080 NYCHA elevators that are equipped with brake monitors revealed that 80 brake monitors, or 7.4%, were not functioning properly. Though brake monitors were not required by NYC Building Code at that time for existing elevators, the policy of the DOB is that if a component is installed on an elevator, it must be functioning.

This probe led to NYCHA improving its protocols for inspecting elevators and brake monitors and ensuring prompt compliance with city building code changes. It also led to NYCHA retraining its staff who intake complaints and to a review and improvement of NYCHA's priority codes regarding elevator complaints. In addition to technical failures, DOI identified numerous communication lapses and missteps by NYCHA staff that contributed to the fatal accident, including that NYCHA's computerized complaint intake system did not provide an accurate problem code to describe and prioritize the elevator problem. The condition was designated a "Priority 5," requiring correction within 48 hours, as compared to various emergency elevator codes that are assigned "Priority 9," requiring response within 1 hour. Also, several NYCHA staff failed to appropriately communicate about and respond to the elevator malfunction and subsequent accident.

In January 2015 the NYC Building Code was amended to require that elevators must be equipped with emergency braking systems such as "rope grippers" to prevent unintended motion by 2027 in existing elevators. The March 2016 DOI report recommended that NYCHA perform a feasibility study to accelerate implementation of these devices as far in advance of the deadline as possible.

D. Center to Protect Workers' Rights study

The Center to Protect Workers' Rights analyzed the injuries and fatalities to workers in general (building workers, construction workers, freight handlers, etc.) and to workers installing, repairing, and maintaining elevators and escalators. An initial report was issued in 2006 and updated in September of 2013.[4] The updated study uses the most recent data available from the U.S. Bureau of Labor Statistics (BLS) from 2007–2009 and the Consumer Product Safety Commission (CPSC) from 2006–2010.

Incidents involving elevators and escalators each year kill about 31 people and seriously injure about 17,000 others in the United States, per CPWR analysis of data provided by the BLS (1992–2009) and the CPSC (1997–2010). Elevators are the prime culprit, causing about 90% of the deaths and 60% of the serious injuries. Half of the annual deaths are to people working in or near elevators—including those installing, repairing, and maintaining elevators, and working in or near elevator shafts.

Table 3.14
Average Estimated Annual Deaths Involving Elevators and Escalators, 1992-2009

	Elevator related	Escalator related	Total
Working on or near	15.5	0.5	16.0
Passenger while at work	5.2	0.2	5.4
Passenger not at work	7.0	3.0	10.0
Total	27.7	3.7	31.4

CPWR analysis of the Census of Fatal Occupational Injuries showed 263 elevator-related deaths while working in or near elevator shafts and elevators in the 17 years from 1992–2009—about 15 deaths per year (Table 3.12). During this same period, 8 escalator-related deaths occurred while working on escalators; most involved installing or repairing the escalator.

Fifty-seven percent of the deaths of workers working in or near elevator shafts were due to falls into the shaft. Incidents where workers were caught in/between moving parts of elevators caused 18% of deaths, and incidents where workers are struck by elevators or counterweights caused 17% of deaths. Deaths related to escalators are much less frequent; of those deaths, 75% involve falls.

Table 3.15
Deaths Involving Work on or Near Elevators, By Cause and Activity, 1992–2009

Cause	Installing & repairing	Working in elevator shaft/car	Working near elevators	Number	Percent
Falls	38	23	88	149	56.6%
Caught	32	8	8	48	18.3%
Struck by	24	10	10	44	16.7%
Collapse	8	**	**	10	3.8%
Other	8	**	**	12	4.6%
Total	**110**	**46**	**107**	**263**	**100%**

** Data does not meet BLS publication criteria

Installing & repairing: Almost three-quarters of these 110 deaths involved elevator constructors. The remainder included industrial machinery repairers, engineers, construction supervisors, electricians, janitors, and maintenance workers. At least 13 of the deaths involved workers who were unqualified—not trained in elevator repair—trying to fix jammed elevators.

Falls caused over one-third of the deaths of workers installing and repairing elevators; many of the fatal falls were of workers who were not classified by the Bureau of Labor Statistics as elevator installers or repairers.

Working in shaft/car: The 46 deaths in this category involved such activities as retrieving keys and other objects that had dropped into a shaft, cleaning inside an elevator shaft or elevator, fixing stuck elevators, and collapses of platforms over elevator shafts. Occupations included elevator constructors, janitors/cleaners, building managers and supervisors, and elevator inspectors.

Working near elevators: Almost all the 107 deaths involved construction workers, none of them elevator constructors. Forty-nine of these deaths (45 of them falls) occurred during work next to unguarded or improperly guarded elevator shafts.

Table 3.16
Deaths Involving Work on or Near Elevators, By Occupation, 1992–2009

Occupation	Deaths
Elevator installers & repairers	83
Other construction workers	86
Janitors/cleaners & supervisors	22
Construction supervisors/engineers	20
Others	52
Total	263

CPWR analysis of the Bureau of Labor Statistics showed 89 elevator-related passenger deaths in the 17 years from 1992–2009—about 5 deaths per year (Table 3.17). These included supervisors/managers, clerks/stock handlers, janitors/cleaners and their supervisors, plus a wide variety of other occupations. Three-fifths of these deaths involved falls, almost all the falls into elevator shafts, including 30 deaths when an elevator door opened and there was no elevator car due to the car leaving the floor in question and the hoistway interlock or door closer failed mechanically or electrically. The "caught in/between" and "struck by" deaths mostly involved people getting caught in the elevator door or between the elevator and door or shaft. The "other" category included 6 elevator collapses.

Table 3.17
Deaths Among Passengers Using Elevators While at Work, By Cause, 1992–2009

Cause	Deaths
Falls	52
Caught in/between	24
Other	13

From 1997 to 2010, the CPSC reported 91 non-work related deaths of elevator passengers, about seven deaths per year (Table 3.18). Falls caused over half the deaths, and about half the falls were to the same level (e.g. slips and trips), especially while exiting from the elevator, and the rest occurred from falls down elevator shafts.

During this same period, the CPSC reported 39 non-work related deaths of escalator passengers in 15 states and the District of Columbia – about three per year (Table 3.18). Seven of the 29 fall-related deaths occurred due to falling off the escalator while riding the escalator side rails. Nine "caught in/between" deaths resulted after clothing or articles became trapped at the bottom or top of an escalator or between a stair and escalator sidewall.

Table 3.18
Deaths Among Elevator or Escalator Passengers While Not at Work, By Cause, 1997–2010

Cause	Elevator Deaths	Escalator Deaths
Falls	51	29
Caught in-between	33	9
Other	7	1

The CPSC estimated that 75% of the escalator injuries resulted from falls, 20% from entrapment at the bottom or top of an escalator or between a moving stair and escalator sidewall, and 5% of the incidents were categorized as "other," including sudden stops of the escalator and reversal of direction. The "caught-in" incidents generally resulted in more serious injuries than did falls. Of concern is the fact that half of the approximately 1,000 sidewall-entrapment injuries involved children under age five. The children's injuries were mostly caused when a child's hands or footwear, including dangling shoelaces, became caught in an escalator comb plate at the top or bottom of an escalator, or in the space between moving stairs and an escalator sidewall. Two recent studies examined elevator and escalator related injuries among adults age 65 and older using data from the Consumer Product Safety Commission's National Electronic Injury Surveillance System (NEISS), which collects injury data on consumer products from selected hospitals nationwide. The 2008 study found an estimated 39,500 escalator-related injuries and no deaths to people over age 65 from 1991–2005, which is an average of 2,633 injuries per year. Almost all the injuries were caused by a slip, trip or fall. During this study period, the rate of escalator injuries doubled. The second study found an estimated 44,870 elevator-related injuries from 1990-2006, an average of 2,639 injuries per year. More than half of the injuries were caused by a slip, trip or fall. Three-quarters of the injuries in both studies involved women.

A third study, also using the NEISS data, examined elevator-related injuries among children from 1990 to 2004. They found an estimated 29,030 elevator-related injuries in children age 19 and younger, or an average of 1,935 injuries per year. The most frequent cause of injury was an elevator door closing on a body part.

The National Institute for Occupational Safety and Health (NIOSH) investigates work-related deaths through its Fatality Assessment and Control Evaluation (FACE) reports (http://www.cdc.gov/niosh/face/). These reports are produced through investigations conducted by NIOSH researchers at the federal level of government and by state health department personnel tasked with investigating and assessing work-related fatalities at the state level. FACE reports include 45 elevator-related deaths from 1982, the year the FACE program began, until 2010. These deaths are consistent with BLS guidelines for inclusion in the BLS Census of Fatal Occupational Injuries reports and are included in the CFOI narratives. NIOSH FACE reports included:

- 26 falls down elevator shafts (57%), with 8 during construction, 8 during maintenance/inspection and 10 during routine use
- 8 deaths (17%) involving being struck by an elevator car, caught in an elevator mechanism or struck by a counterweight
- 4 deaths (9%) from elevator collapses with a worker in or on the elevator
- 3 electrocutions (7%) during maintenance
- 4 deaths (9%) from other causes, including explosion, falling material and unknown circumstances

In addition to the elevator-related deaths, the California FACE program investigated the 2001 death of an elevator mechanic helper who was crushed in an escalator while performing maintenance (California Department of Health Services, 2001).

The following are examples of different types of elevator related fatalities:

- A 53-year-old male elevator construction foreman was killed and his helper, an elevator constructor, was injured, when the hydraulic elevator car they were working under fell on them. The two were adjusting the hydraulic cylinder when the car fell, trapping them in the elevator pit. Two wooden poles (4x4 by approximately twelve-feet long) used to keep the elevator from falling were placed leaning against the guide rails. The car was approximately fifteen inches above the poles, which they did not tie in place. The poles were knocked out of position when the car fell due to the sudden loss of hydraulic pressure and trapped the two workers under the car. The elevator apparently did not fall evenly to the bottom of the pit. This permitted the rescue team to enter the pit area and extract the injured. However, rescuers had to use air bags to help raise the car to remove the victim. The field investigator concluded that to prevent similar future occurrences, employers should:

- Train employees in the recognition of hazards and methods to control hazards
- Develop, set up and enforce comprehensive written instructions for adjusting hydraulic elevators

- The 46-year-old owner of a clothing manufacturing company was killed after falling 15 feet down a freight elevator shaft. The incident occurred in a large three-story warehouse where the victim was renting space for his clothing manufacturing business. At about 5 P.M., the owner was trying to move a customer order from his second-floor work shop to the loading dock on the first floor. Because the call buttons on the freight elevator were not functioning, the victim went to the first floor to raise the elevator to the second floor. Not realizing that the elevator was on the second floor, the victim opened the elevator door in the dark vestibule and stepped into the empty elevator shaft, falling 15 feet into the warehouse basement. Investigators concluded that, to prevent similar incidents in the future, these safety guidelines should be followed:
  - Building owners and employers should insure that elevators are maintained in proper working order
  - Building owners and employers should insure that entrances, exits, and work areas are properly illuminated
- A 42-year-old elevator service technician died after being crushed by an elevator counterweight while at work. The victim was an employee of an elevator repair company and was doing general maintenance contract work for a hotel. He was working alone at the time of the incident. The service dispatcher at his company had tried to reach him (via his pager) on several occasions earlier on the afternoon of the incident. When the dispatcher was unable to reach the victim, another service technician was sent to the hotel to find him. The co-worker met with the hotel's chief engineer and together they looked in the area where the victim had last been seen working. The victim was found in an elevator lying over counterweights and pinned between spreader beams on the second floor of the hotel. The victim may have been using the spreader beam between car #1 and #2. as a work station. The co-worker stated that the victim was obviously already deceased. The hotel engineer called 911 and police and paramedics arrived a short time later. The investigator concluded that, to prevent similar future occurrences, employers should:

    - Require rigid screens or walls between adjacent hoistways with side-mounted counterweights
    - Have signs posted between the elevator spreader beams stating that caution should be taken due to the position of the counterweights.
- A 34-year-old manufacturing supervisor died after falling approximately 35 feet into an elevator shaft. The victim had been showing his family members his place of employment. The incident occurred when the victim tried to prevent the elevator from going up a level. He attempted to detain the elevator by grabbing the elevator platform's edge and lost his grip. The victim had to be removed by firefighters from the shaft bottom. He was pronounced dead by a paramedic at the scene. The investigator concluded, that to prevent similar future occurrences employers should:
    - Have all elevators inspected and serviced on a regular basis by a licensed elevator technician.
    - Evaluate their current safety program and incorporate specific training procedures emphasizing the importance of recognizing and controlling hazards in the workplace. These procedures should include, but not be limited to, conducting hazard evaluations before initiating work at a job site and implementing appropriate controls.
    - Identify areas that may be hazardous to personnel, and restrict or prohibit the use of, or access to, these areas.

Endnotes

1. Florida Department of Business Professional Regulation

2. Uneasy Ride, Council of the City of New York, April 1999.

3. Elevator-Related Accidents and Fatality at NYCHA Public Housing. New York City Department of Investigation, March 2016

4. Deaths and Injuries Involving Elevators and Escalators, 1992-1998.2010. The Center to Protect Workers' Rights. July 2004., September 2013 (Updated from May, 2006)

Chapter 4

Reasons for and Causes of Accidents, Improving Safety and Limiting Liability

Synopsis

4.1 Introduction

The main purpose of this chapter is to describe the types of, causes of and general reasons for elevator and escalator accidents, and to provide methods for improving safety and limiting liability. It can be used as a reference to assist in determining why the accident happened and what could have been done or can be done to prevent it, as well as to assist in reconstructing the accident.

It should be noted that all the possible types of accidents involving elevators and escalators cannot be contained in a single treatise. For example, defects caused by improper manufacturing, shipping, or raw materials are possible but beyond the scope of this book. The reader is referred to one of the many books on this subject. The following discussion centers on the most prevalent or noteworthy reasons.

In most cases, accidents happen for one or more of the following reasons:

- Negligent or improper maintenance or repair
- Defective design in one or more of the system's components
- Misapplication of one or more of the system's components
- Improper installation or omission of one or more of the system's components
- Defective design in one or more of the system's components
- Improper operation, abuse or misuse
- Failure to provide sufficient warning of an impending hazard and/or operating instructions
- External factors, such as power failures, brownouts and acts of God

Many persons use elevators and escalators every day. They come from all walks of life, and vary considerably in their educational, social and economic backgrounds. Vertical transportation equipment must consistently deliver passengers and freight safely and efficiently throughout a building or complex.

Unlike most other complex electrical or mechanical equipment, modern elevators are operated by untrained personnel, by tenants and by visitors to buildings. These same people are exposed to moving parts as they ride on escalators, which would probably require guarding if it were machinery in a production facility.

Many parties are responsible for ensuring safe elevator and escalator operation. These include:

- The architects who designed the building
- The contractors who built the building
- The consultant who wrote the elevator or escalator specifications and assured compliance with those specifications
- The elevator or escalator designer and manufacturer
- The company that installed the elevator or escalator
- The code-enforcing authority (i.e., AHJ) that inspected and tested the equipment following installation and periodically thereafter
- The maintenance contractor or personnel whose job it is to keep the equipment "like new"
- The riding public and others who must use the equipment responsibly
- The building owner or manager

Although listed last in the preceding list, the building owner/manager is the first line of responsibility in ensuring the safe operation of the elevators and escalators under their control. This is recognized in most building codes, which make the building owner responsible for the maintenance of the equipment. They are the ones that usually choose the architect, the elevator or escalator installer, the manufacturer, the consultant, and the contractor. They are responsible for establishing a maintenance program to ensure safe and efficient operation, either through hiring an outside contractor or using a competent internal work force. This includes effective monitoring to ensure that the maintenance work is performed and ensure that the equipment is operating as intended. They are responsible for providing an acceptable and safe environment for the equipment and their users. Periodic inspections and tests conducted by the AHJ are coordinated through them. They must also promptly correct any deficiencies found. Good and accepted industry practice is to report accidents promptly to the responsible AHJ, whether or not they are legally required.

Unfortunately, many building owners/managers think that once they hire a maintenance contractor, their responsibility ends or that they have purchased an "insurance policy" against liability. This folly will be quickly exposed once an accident happens and litigation begins. Good and accepted industry practice requires that a building owner/manager effectively evaluate the maintenance being performed by their contractor. This not only provides an independent means to ensure that the equipment is being maintained in a safe condition, it also provides an economic benefit—making sure that they get what they pay for, and provides the opportunity to learn if the equipment could be made safer. Relying on the state-mandated inspections to determine this is inadequate, since violations can only be cited after the fact. There are many conditions (e.g., worn components) that are not yet code violations but can develop into a condition that causes an elevator malfunction before the next inspection and therefore cause injuries to passengers. If the building owner/manager has no expertise in elevator/escalator maintenance, then good and accepted industry practice would be to utilize an elevator/escalator consultant.

This is not to imply that the other parties have no responsibility for ensuring the safe operation of elevators and escalators. Indeed, these other parties usually will have a more direct role in the causes of any accident, but the fact remains that the building owner or manager has the most influence on the daily operation of elevators and escalators.

No vertical transportation equipment will be totally free of potential hazards. This is just the nature of the beast. No matter how well maintained, no matter how code compliant, no matter how good the training programs, no matter how comprehensive the warning signs—accidents will still occur. **However, the hazards are usually well-known and therefore accidents are preventable in most cases.** Therefore, it is the responsibility of all parties to identify and eliminate the hazards that are under their control, and to identify and notify the responsible party of those hazards outside of their control. Warnings can initially be oral, but they must be followed up and effectively conveyed in writing. If impending dangers exist, then the equipment must be taken out of service until the situation is corrected.

Advances in technology, additional safety features, improved service, reduced maintenance requirements, increased service life, and improved reliability are all excellent reasons to modernize outdated equipment. Usually an important dividend from the modernization of equipment is reduced liability. Many times the bulk of the existing equipment can be reconditioned and reused, and the remaining equipment can be modernized in stages.

Although many companies may perform good maintenance, any need for engineering design changes or extensive modifications can usually be done more efficiently by the original equipment manufacturer, who has access to the original design and application database. Examples of extensive modification would be alteration to the equipment requiring changes of speed or capacity, or adding an additional unit to a group operation. Also, some elevator and escalator companies specialize in modernization and can provide acceptable alternatives.

One of the most significant changes in the vertical transportation industry was the introduction of microprocessors in the 1980s. These microprocessors permitted programmable features on both the control and supervisory systems. Before this, changing equipment operation in response to changing usage patterns required costly hardware changes and extensive downtime. System performance information and error messages, so valuable to a mechanic troubleshooting equipment malfunctions, were previously virtually nonexistent. Also, the required maintenance had to be more intensive on older equipment.

There are many other measures that can be taken by all of the parties involved to prevent accidents. Some of these are discussed below.

The purpose of ASME A17.3 Safety Code for Elevators and Escalators *"is to establish minimum requirements that will provide a reasonable degree of safety for the general public"* and is intended *"to enhance the safety of the general public."* Therefore, even if not required by the AHJ, compliance with ASME A17.3 is not only prudent but also strongly advisable.

The addition of certain safety devices can always be accomplished, even if they were not required by code when the equipment was originally installed. Combplate stop switches (not to be confused with comb-step impact devices) on escalators reduce the severity of injuries for combplate entrapments. Installation of these devices is retroactively required on all escalators in New York City. Although these devices are not required by ASME A17.1, they have been provided as optional devices for many years and are easier to retrofit on existing equipment than comb step impact devices. Non-contact door reopening devices on elevators can prevent the doors from striking objects and people. Hoistway access switches and car top operating devices can assist the mechanics and inspectors gain safe access to the hoistway and control elevator operation when inside of the hoistway. Controlled stop brakes can reduce falls on escalators from sudden stops. Ascending overspeed protection, to prevent elevators from striking the hoistway overhead structure, and door monitoring, to prevent an elevator from leaving a floor with the doors open, due to the failure of the driving machine brake, motor, coupling, shaft, gearing or control system can be economically provided by aftermarket devices.

Although it is beyond the scope of this treatise to analyze design defects, there are certain bottom line precautions that would be prudent for any designer to take. One of these is the concept of "fail safe." In essence, this concept requires that if a device or component fails to operate then it must not result in a dangerous situation. This may require shutting down the elevator or escalator, or other precautionary action.

Proper lighting can enhance the safety both of users of vertical transportation equipment and maintenance mechanics. Included are machine rooms, elevator car tops and pits, inside elevator cars, escalator steps and landings. The ASME A17.1 code requires certain lighting intensities inside the car, in the pit, at the landing sills, and in the machine room for elevators and at landing plates and exposed steps for escalators. In addition for escalators the lighting must be uniform and not materially contrast with the surroundings. Local building codes may contain additional requirements.

Yellow striping on low overheads, ledges, rotating equipment, and at pinch points assists the technician in being aware of these dangers. Marking escalator steps with a yellow stripe along the sides of the step treads adjacent to the skirt panels and at the interface with the adjacent step's riser helps alert passengers to the potential entrapment areas and hopefully causes them to stand away from these areas. In at least one case, steps were marked with footprints to indicate the correct position to stand.

Yellow combs can be installed on escalators alerting passengers to the combplate-step interface. Skirt panels can be stiffened to limit deflection, lubricated to limit friction, and adjusted to minimize the running clearance between the steps and the skirt panels. Aftermarket devices can be installed to limit the running clearance between the steps and the skirt panels, or to prevent entrapments of children's calves in the running clearance between the steps and the skirt panels.

The use of "pre-opening the doors on approach" for elevators can be eliminated to reduce the probability of trip and fall accidents on elevators.

Unreliable or inaccurate leveling or landing systems can be replaced with accurate and reliable systems to reduce trip and fall accidents on elevators.

The list can go on and on. Yet even implementing just the ones mentioned could eliminate many elevator and escalator accidents and reduce the severity of many of those that do happen. The best source for accident prevention ideas is the elevator/escalator consultant. Many of these preventive actions can be easily and economically implemented for existing equipment. Others are simply common sense and prudent practice. Those requiring considerable expense and disruption can be phased in.

4.2 General Reasons for Accidents

A. Improper Maintenance

The importance of proper maintenance in preventing accidents and improving safety cannot be stressed enough. Probably the most important thing that can be done to prevent elevator/escalator accidents is to have an effective maintenance program in effect. Improper maintenance of a system reduces its reliability and subjects its owner to increased liability.

A very disturbing development in the elevator industry is the corporate management decision to focus on profits at the expense of providing proper maintenance. For example, increasing maintenance personnel workloads (i.e., number of units maintained) dramatically, decreasing maintenance frequency dramatically (but the bills still being sent at the same frequency), reducing the scope of maintenance tasks (e.g., limiting maintenance to riding an elevator and visual examinations), delaying necessary repairs, hiring management personnel for their business skills rather than their technical skills, etc. The significant negative effect on the accident rate will be predictable. Acronyms such as **TLOM** (**T**otal **L**ack **O**f **M**aintenance) and **GLOM** (**G**eneral **L**ack **O**f **M**aintenance) have sprung up to describe this phenomenon. Ironically, this continued after vastly expanded maintenance requirements were included in the 2000 Edition of the A17.1 *Safety Code for Elevators and Escalators*[1] in response to substandard maintenance.

Improper maintenance is very often the cause of elevator and escalator accidents. Even the best designed and installed equipment must be properly maintained for it to continue to operate safely. Therefore, the importance of proper maintenance cannot be stressed enough.

Improper maintenance covers a multitude of sins. It can include the lack of maintenance, inadequate scope or frequency of work, substandard methods of performing the work, inadequate monitoring of the work performed and the operation of the equipment, substandard training or skills of the mechanics performing the work, and so on. Each of these types of deficiencies has caused accidents.

By definition, maintenance is the work of keeping something in proper working order. In many cases this requires the replacement or repair of components in order to restore the system to its original operation. In general, maintenance consists of Cleaning, Lubrication, Examination, Adjustment, Repair or Replacement and Testing of various equipment, components and systems (remember CLEAR-T).

An effective maintenance program will be very similar whether internal employees or outside vendors are used. Such a comprehensive maintenance program is referred to as a maintenance control program (MCP). It describes in detail what maintenance tasks must be performed, when and how these tasks are performed, how they are documented and how the maintenance is evaluated.

It starts with establishing the frequency of maintenance and identifying the tasks that need to be performed. Then the work should be scheduled through using work orders, establishing a route or similar methods. Next, the work must be performed and documented. This must be done so that the mechanics are aware of what they must do for each elevator and escalator and when it is to be done.

Traditionally, the minimum frequency of maintenance tasks established was monthly, with other certain maintenance tasks performed quarterly, semiannually and annually. Then the race to the bottom began to cut costs at the expense of safety. For some maintenance companies the minimum frequency slipped to quarterly, then semiannually, then annually and now at least one company is using a minimum frequency of 18 months.

The importance of documenting maintenance and repairs cannot be stressed enough. This is the primary method for mechanics working on the equipment to know what problems are occurring with the equipment, what work needs to be done on the equipment, and what work has been performed on the equipment. This documentation can be in the form of a check chart, an electronic database, or other retrievable form. However, the records must be available to the mechanics before they start work on the equipment.

The lack of detailed maintenance records is at best an indication of lackadaisical maintenance, and at worst incompetent maintenance. Sometimes the lack of maintenance records is portrayed as proof that nothing was wrong with the equipment, and therefore the inference is that the accident did not occur. This self-serving position is not only unprofessional, it also has no basis. If records are not kept, then it is impossible to ensure that the required tasks were being performed at the correct frequency or were being performed at all. The failure to document normal maintenance may foreshadow a failure to document an accident. The best defense against claims of improper maintenance is comprehensive and well-kept maintenance records.

The 2000 Edition of the A17.1 *Safety Code for Elevators and Escalators*[1] introduced vastly expanded maintenance requirements from previous versions. Notable among the new provisions are identifying many more tasks that must be performed, requiring that wiring diagrams be available in the machine rooms and codifying requirements for maintenance records and procedures. Where these requirements do not yet have the force of law, they still represent good and accepted industry practice.

There have been numerous iterations of the maintenance requirements since then. One was requiring a formal Maintenance Control Program. This code-required Maintenance Control Program must be written and available to elevator personnel, although only certain documentation (On-Site Documentation and On-Site Maintenance Records) is required to be physically on-site. The instructions for locating or viewing the portion of the Maintenance Control Program not maintained on-site must be located in the controller or means necessary for testing. The MCP must include, but is not limited to, examinations, maintenance, and tests of equipment and the cleaning, lubricating, adjusting and repairing or replacing components. Maintenance records must be kept at a central location and be available to elevator personnel. They must include a description and dates of maintenance tasks performed, examinations, tests, adjustments, repairs, and replacements. They must also include a description, dates and the corrective actions for all callbacks (trouble calls) or information that is reported to elevator personnel by any means.

While the code-required Maintenance Control Program must include all the maintenance specified in the A17.1 code, it is not limited to them. A good example of comprehensive maintenance tasks that should be included in any maintenance control program are contained in the NEII Maintenance Guidelines.[2]

Finally, there needs to be some feedback mechanism. This can take many forms. Periodically using an independent third party to evaluate the condition of the equipment is an effective way to accomplish this. Monitoring callbacks and using diagnostic equipment to determine the operating condition of the equipment can be done together or independently.

The elevator industry refers to unexpected shutdowns or improper operation of the equipment as "callbacks," because the equipment owner usually has to call the maintenance company for the mechanic to come back to the building to resolve the problem.

How do we know if maintenance is being performed adequately? One way is to monitor callbacks. Having someone, such as a consultant, knowledgeable about elevators and escalators do this is recommended. **The importance of monitoring callbacks as a standard for measuring maintenance performance cannot be overemphasized. Therefore, it is essential that proper maintenance records be maintained.**

This can be monitored by retrieving each problem that has been registered into the elevator maintenance logbook. The elevator company usually records this information, either electronically in a database or in writing (e.g., logs kept in the machine room). This applies whether a resident mechanic is assigned to the building or the building is just one on a route that the mechanic covers. Cross-reference all documents to make sure the list is complete. Categorize the problems by cause, which can be derived from the descriptions entered by the elevator technician. Look at the list for problems associated with the unit, the associated dates, the various components involved, any reported causes, and any corrective measures taken.

Repeated problems frequently are caused by improper maintenance. The frequency of callbacks may be a sign of improper maintenance. In general, the average number of annual callbacks that many companies consider acceptable is two for escalators, three for hydraulic elevators and four for the more demanding traction-type elevators. More callbacks per year than those numbers are usually considered excessive and the reasons for the callbacks should be investigated.

Callbacks of the type that are beyond the control of the elevator maintenance company should be analyzed separately to determine any detrimental environmental conditions. These include passenger misuse, dropping of keys into the elevator pit requiring removal by the elevator technician, inadvertent activation of the emergency stop button, misuse, abuse, and vandalism. Other marginal problems should at least be put in a separate category. Included are signal lamp failures, excessive waiting times, and callbacks due to minor noises.

The importance of monitoring callbacks as a standard for measuring maintenance performance cannot be overemphasized. Therefore, it is essential that proper maintenance records be maintained.

Frequently, components start to fail intermittently. This can result in callbacks where the responding mechanic is unable to find any problem, which is commonly referred to as "running on arrival" or "ROA." Many times the responding mechanic is not the same individual who normally maintains the equipment or the one who responded to a previously reported similar problem. The availability of maintenance records is critical in these cases. Otherwise, mechanics are left to their own devices to try to guess what the problem is based solely on the current reported problem, without any current problem to observe or the benefit of the history of past problems with the equipment. Often the equipment is placed back in service (BIS) without any remedial action taken. This will in many cases result in an accident that could have been avoided if the proper maintenance records were available.

The building owner's or manager's responsibility is to ensure that the elevators and escalators are being maintained in a safe condition. This can be accomplished by ensuring that competent mechanics are maintaining the equipment and by having an effective and comprehensive maintenance program in place. The questions then become who will perform the maintenance, how often it will be performed, how it will be performed and how it will be monitored.

An effective maintenance program will be very similar, whether internal manpower or outside vendors are used. It starts with establishing the frequency of maintenance and identifying the tasks that need to be performed. Then there must be a way to schedule the work, which can be done through work orders, establishing a route, or similar methods. This must be documented in some manner so that the mechanics are aware of what they must do for each elevator or escalator and when it is to be done. This can be in the form of a check chart, an electronic database, or other retrievable form. Next, the work must be performed and documented. Finally, some feedback mechanism is needed. This can take many forms. Periodically using an independent third party to evaluate the condition of the equipment is an effective way to accomplish this. Monitoring callbacks and using diagnostic equipment to determine the operating condition of the equipment can be used in conjunction with this or independently.

Therefore, the building owner or manager must first decide if maintenance is to be performed by internal staff or if an outside contractor will be hired. Some building owners opt to use their own workers to perform maintenance. If internal staff is to be used, then a competent work force must be assembled and trained. This practice has its advantages and disadvantages. Using internal manpower usually provides a greater degree of control over costs and quality than using outside vendors. However, using outside vendors usually provides a greater level of technical knowledge and experience. If the industry is doing well, it will be difficult to retain competent workers who usually obtain higher wages working for an outside vendor. If the industry is doing poorly, competent mechanics may be attracted to the relative stability of a building owner. If internal manpower is chosen, then the building owner will have to assemble a cadre of competent workers and implement an effective training program.

The vast majority of building owners and managers will opt to hire an outside contractor. Therefore, more decisions need to be made. What type of maintenance contract will be used, which contractor will be selected, how often will maintenance be performed, and so on?

An elevator-escalator consultant can be of vital assistance to a building owner or manager in making these decisions. Many building owners are driven by the bottom line—how much it will cost. Choosing an elevator or escalator contractor based solely on initial costs is shortsighted and usually more costly in the long term. More commonly, the building owner or manager will sign a contract prepared by the maintenance contractor. Again, this is another shortsighted decision.

Maintenance contracts can be awarded to the firm that originally installed or upgraded (modernized) the equipment, or to a company that only performs maintenance. At this writing, several U.S. companies and many European companies are ISO 9000 certified. This or an equivalent certification requires a rigorous documentation of operating procedures by the company as well as periodic compliance inspections by the certifying organization. While this certification is certainly laudable and desirable from the equipment owner's perspective, it does not guarantee anything.

Most elevator and escalator maintenance contracts generally fall into one of the following four categories:

1. Oil and grease. As the name implies, this type of agreement only requires the contractor to lubricate the moving components of the system, examine the equipment's operation and make minor adjustments. All repairs or replacements will cost extra. The cost for this type of contract is minimal, which is its major allure to building owners. The contrac-

tor will attempt to make profits by performing repair and replacement work. It is apparent that there is not much incentive for the contractor to keep the equipment in good operating order, but quite the opposite. The contract will specify the frequency, typically monthly.

2. Oil, grease and parts. This is similar to the oil and grease type of contract, but it includes the repair and replacement of certain specified components.
3. Full-coverage preventive. This type of agreement requires the maintenance contractor to perform what is commonly referred to in the elevator industry as "preventive maintenance." The operative word is "preventive." It means simply that the maintenance functions are frequent and comprehensive enough to prevent most equipment failures.
4. Predictive. This type of maintenance is usually performed as an adjunct to other maintenance tasks and not as a stand-alone function. Generally, operating parameters of the equipment are measured using diagnostic equipment and recorded. In its most comprehensive form, a history of these measurements is kept and trends are identified. These trends are used to predict an impending failure well before it occurs, and proactive actions are taken. More commonly, each set of measurements is interpreted individually to detect any indication of impending failure. This type of maintenance is not common for elevators and escalators.

Of these four main types of elevator and escalator maintenance contracts, the oil and grease type and the oil, grease and parts type cover minimal maintenance. In fact, many companies charge less than would a repairman coming to your house to fix an appliance. The contractor attempts to make a profit by performing repair and replacement work. It is apparent that there is not much incentive for the contractor to keep the equipment in good operating order, but quite the opposite. The contractor usually shows up monthly just to get paid for this "maintenance."

On the other hand, preventive maintenance, perhaps in conjunction with predictive maintenance, offers the best opportunity to maximize safety and limit liability. Having a resident mechanic will obviously be more advantageous than having a mechanic periodically visit the building to perform maintenance. However, the cost for this is higher and therefore not chosen by most building owners unless they have a sufficient number of elevators or escalators to justify a resident mechanic or a premium is placed on service/safety.

Many contracts will typically exclude the following items: cabs, cab finishes and flooring; doors, door frames and sills; light fixtures and lamps; power switches and breakers, electrical feeds to the equipment that are on the "line" side of the main disconnect switch; hoistways; smoke detectors; external emergency power equipment; underground piping and cylinders on hydraulic elevators; and the renewal or refinishing of all exposed trim on an escalator. Therefore, the onus is on building owners or managers to assure the integrity of these components, or include them in the maintenance contract. **However, just because a component is excluded by the contract does not mean that the contractor can ignore problems with that component.** It simply means that an extra cost will be charged. Also, the contractor must warn the owner of any condition that may affect the safe operation of the equipment.

The maintenance contract should specify the frequency and scope of maintenance functions. Based on this, a maintenance schedule should then be developed. The maintenance schedule should indicate what is to be done and when it is to be done. Typically it will be in the form of a chart or list. When the tasks are completed and documented, it usually is referred to as a maintenance log. It can take many forms: for example it can be a written document that resides in the building or it can be an electronic database, which can then be stored in various locations.

The first obligation is to establish a frequency of maintenance that will ensure that the equipment remains operating as it did when originally installed. Generally this should be done at least on a monthly interval. One reason is practical. The maintenance contractor usually sends monthly invoices to the building owner or manager as required by the contract. Billing monthly is supposed to mean "showing up" monthly. However, recently some maintenance companies have reduced their maintenance frequencies to quarterly or even semiannually or annually, but still invoice monthly, with the predictable increase in frequency of malfunctions. Another reason is to shorten the time in which problems can develop. These monthly visits may be sufficient to catch any "lack of maintenance" problems. It depends on the usage of the equipment, its operating environment, its age and its design. Each elevator or escalator is unique. No two will require exactly the same degree of maintenance. Certain maintenance tasks may be performed based on usage (running hours for example). One industry rule of thumb provides for the following minimum hours of maintenance: one hour a month for a hydraulic elevator, two hours per month for a geared traction elevator, three hours per month for an escalator and four hours per month for a gearless traction elevator.

There are three main types of maintenance schedules:

1. *Time-based* maintenance. This involves a fixed amount of time between scheduled maintenance. For example, routine maintenance tasks are performed monthly, while certain periodic maintenance tasks are performed quarterly, semiannually, or annually.

2. *Use-based* maintenance. Maintenance is performed depending on the occurrence of some milestone event, such as the number of stops or running hours. Microprocessor-based equipment has features that facilitate the acquisition of this information, and in some cases the information can be remotely accessed.
3. *Use and time based* maintenance. This is a combination of use-based and time-based maintenance scheduling. For example, if the operating history of an elevator indicates that it may make 8,000 stops in a six-week period, then the routine maintenance tasks would be performed at six-week intervals regardless of the current usage. If the number of shutdowns or callbacks and customer satisfaction indicate that the maintenance is adequate, then the frequency will be continued. If not, the interval will be shortened. This method proves to be more effective on older equipment when the number of stops and running hours is available. If stop counters and running-time accumulators are installed, the routine maintenance can be performed at fixed intervals and the periodic maintenance can be performed based on usage. This approach is usually more productive when more frequent visits are required by contract.

Routine maintenance tasks are those performed every time maintenance is performed. Monthly is the most common frequency. Typical tasks for an electric elevator would include, but not be limited to, checking elevator ride quality, door operation, leveling, signal and communication operation, lubrication, cleaning, relay function, checking all rotating equipment, checking brake function, checking firefighters' service if provided, adjustment and replacement as required. Typical tasks for an escalator would include, but not be limited to, checking the steps, handrails, skirt panels, combs, brake function, key switches, emergency stop switches, lubrication, cleaning, adjustment and replacement as required.

Periodic maintenance tasks are performed less frequently than routine maintenance tasks. This may include brake adjustment, tests, vacuuming out a controller, and more thorough examinations of the various components.

The comprehensiveness of the maintenance tasks is the second critical variable for proper maintenance. Just doing something frequently, but not doing it correctly, does not accomplish much. Therefore, in conjunction with the maintenance schedule, procedures should be established governing how the maintenance tasks are to be performed. This is sometimes referred to as the maintenance guide. It may consist of a procedure, a manual, a book, or a database. Most equipment manufacturers supply maintenance instructions. Often included in these instructions is a list of the parts expected to need periodic replacement, (along with the part number and ordering instructions), lubrication requirements, adjustment procedures and a troubleshooting guide.

Good preventive maintenance is, therefore, simply performing comprehensive maintenance tasks at an appropriate frequency that reasonably assures against equipment breakdowns or failures. This type of maintenance has a strong incentive for the contractor to perform at its best, because costs can be incurred otherwise.

The importance of monitoring the operation of the equipment cannot be overemphasized as a tool for preventing accidents. Properly performed, it can determine the adequacy of the maintenance being performed and can detect incipient conditions that presage impending equipment failure. A building owner or manager that contracts out maintenance or issues work orders without having an effective feedback mechanism is asking for trouble. Maintenance must be properly managed for it to be effective. Too many building owners and managers blindly rely on their maintenance service contractors. All too often this turns out like having the fox watch the chicken coop. Having a consultant periodically perform maintenance evaluations is a wise investment for a building owner or manager.

Remote monitoring systems are readily available in today's market, and are considered to be one of the "state of the art" peripherals for today's vertical transportation. These systems can be adapted to most types of equipment. In addition to providing maintenance documentation and performance information, remote monitors can transmit live data on the current state of the elevator or escalator system, similar to the information on an automobile's dashboard but with much more detail. Recurring malfunctions, equipment status and alarms, as well as system performance information can be transmitted, as they occur, to the central watch station computer. Some monitoring systems have two-way communication to the elevator, helpful for consoling entrapped passengers and deterring equipment misuse.

A typical remote monitoring system will employ monitors in the security officer's room, at the desk of the lobby attendant and in the machine rooms for use by the technician. Valuable information is supplied to all parties and can be programmed to alert them when certain performance parameters are exceeded. This information documents how efficient the elevator system performs, as well as any faults that occur within the control system as described above. The information can be stored for long periods of time and the database can be accessed to document the exact time of the occurrence of a fault.

If an elevator has a telephone line, then it is possible with some equipment for this information to be transmitted directly to the elevator maintenance company. It is also possible for elevator companies to transmit software changes in this manner or take remote control of the elevator. While the potential benefits are substantial, so are the potential liabilities.

Computerized maintenance monitoring is commonly used today for documenting maintenance. The maintenance technician displays the scheduled task on a laptop computer, handheld terminal, or phone, then enters data as the task is completed. The entry records what maintenance tasks were completed, when and by whom. The program compares the date due versus the date completed, permitting a performance log. A microprocessor stores the information, perhaps for years when battery backups are provided, and when equipped with a modem can transmit the information periodically to a central station to be saved. These records should be available to the mechanics before they perform their maintenance and repair tasks, so that they have a complete history of the equipment.

Another effective method, although less high-tech, is monitoring equipment breakdowns manually and performing an analysis, which was discussed above.

For hydraulic elevators it is very important to document all additions of hydraulic fluid to the system. This permits an analysis to determine if a small underground leak exists in the system. Undetected underground leaks could result in an uncontrolled descent of the elevator (i.e., free fall) and seriously injure or kill anyone inside the elevator.

B. Failures to Warn

Failures to warn of any potentially dangerous conditions have resulted in causing or contributing accidents and in settlements in favor of plaintiffs. In general, if an owner, manufacturer, installer, maintainer, consultant or inspector of an elevator or escalator has reason to believe that average people using the equipment in a reasonably prudent manner might inadvertently injure themselves, then an appropriate warning or other safeguard is necessary.

The building owner or manager has ultimate control of the vertical transportation equipment, and therefore has the ultimate responsibility for this equipment. This is recognized by most codes. However, an elevator maintenance company, an elevator consultant or an elevator inspector has a duty to warn the building's management of potential dangers. The warning should first be conveyed orally to the appropriate representative of the building owner or manager and followed up with written correspondence (a certified mailing is recommended). The building owner or manager is then obligated to correct the condition, warn the users of the equipment, or both. These warnings must be commensurate with the hazard. Of course, since the maintenance contractor is in intimate contact with the equipment and the users of the equipment then it may be necessary for the contractor to provide warnings independent of those of the building owner or manager and to take other corrective action to protect herself from litigation.

Nevertheless, merely warning a building owner or manager of a potential hazard may not be sufficient. If an imminent hazard exists, then the maintenance company should take action. This may entail shutting down the equipment and refusing to place it back in service, locking it out of service, and notifying the building owner or manager and the AHJ. Of course, the maintenance service company cannot force the building owner to alter or repair its equipment, but the maintenance company must not turn a blind eye to an imminent hazard. **It would be prudent to discontinue servicing that equipment until corrective actions are taken.**

A maintenance company can become liable for hazardous conditions even if it was only tangentially involved with the equipment. For example, if the company only performs call-in repairs, but becomes aware of a hazardous condition (or should have become aware of it), then as an elevator/escalator expert it must take appropriate action to warn the building owner or AHJ, or both, about the hazardous condition. **It would be prudent to discontinue servicing that equipment until corrective actions are taken.** After an accident the building owner or manager may often try to blame the maintenance contractor and claim, "They should have warned me!"

Warnings to users of the equipment are also very important. These include posting "Out of Service" signs at each entrance of an elevator or escalator when appropriate, and erecting necessary barricades in accordance with industry standards. The Elevator Industry Field Employee Safety Handbook provides recommended barricading methods. It must be remembered that in many cases the passengers of elevators are in effect operating the equipment. Therefore, appropriate warnings are necessary. For example, freight elevators are many times operated by freight-handlers. If the building owner or manager has chosen not to provide an attendant, then sufficient warnings are necessary to warn the freight-handlers of known hazards, such as automatic closing of the doors or the fact that in most cases the doors close vertically both from the top and the bottom. The users of escalators are exposed to moving parts as they ride the equipment. Therefore, warnings of known hazards are necessary to alert the passengers to these hazards. For example, providing yellow markings of hazardous features is often an effective method of warning passengers.

Although mechanics are familiar with the equipment, this does not eliminate the need to provide sufficient warning of known hazards. For example, posting signs warning of limited working clearances, and marking rotating equipment or shear hazards in yellow are effective methods of avoiding certain accidents.

It must be recognized that warnings are the lowest level of action that can be taken. If a hazard can be eliminated then it should be eliminated, and warnings only provided for any residual hazards. Many times the warnings are ineffective or ignored. Therefore, supplemental action is often appropriate.

Effective signage is an easy and inexpensive method of reducing the probability of certain types of accidents. The codes, regulations and laws in effect for the equipment require certain signs. Additional signs can also be provided by the building owner or manager to reduce the probability of accidents and limiting their liability.

The following are some examples of the signage requirements contained in the ASME A17.1—2010 / CSA B44—10 Code:

- Capacity plate showing rated load inside the car
- DO NOT USE IN CASE OF FIRE pictograph above each landing call station (recommended, but may be required by the building code)
- Danger signs on emergency doors in blind hoistways and elevator pits
- Class of loading (general, motor vehicle, industrial truck, concentrated loads) for freight elevators
- Sign restricting the use of freight elevators for operators, freight and their handlers
- Danger signs on the hoistway doors for hand-operated elevators
- NO RIDERS sign inside dumbwaiters
- Operating instructions for firefighters' service operation
- Escalator and moving walk caution signs
- Markings for the emergency stop button on elevators and escalators
- Identification of equipment of different elevators located in the same machine room or hoistway

Also, certain signage is required by other applicable codes, and local regulations and laws. This usually entails raised lettering and numbering, Braille characters, or both.

Additional caution, warning, danger or traffic management signs should be placed in appropriate areas. While only certain signs are required by code, these additional signs are good practice and widely accepted in the elevator and escalator industry.

An example would be posting ELEVATOR OUT OF SERVICE signs or placing yellow caution tape across elevator entrances when an elevator is being serviced. Another example would be DANGER, ELEVATOR MACHINE ROOM signs on elevator machine room doors. Signs on switches and disconnects controlling equipment lighting and power circuits reading ALWAYS LEAVE ON EXCEPT WHEN SERVICING may help in preventing hydraulic elevators inadvertently drifting downward. It has also been required by ASME A17.1 for many years. Signs near escalators directing passengers to elevators, and prohibiting wheeled vehicles, can help in preventing wheeled objects such as baby carriages, strollers, and wheelchairs from being transported on escalators.

Since ASME A17.1-2013, the code has allowed signage on escalator and moving walk handrails. The handrails are a highly visible location for safety information, and handrail signage gives the passenger cues to handrail speed and direction.

Although only equipment of different elevators located in the same hoistway or machine room are required to be identified, it is prudent to establish a unique identification for each elevator in a building. Typically, each elevator will be numbered sequentially from left to right and clockwise. All major components of the elevator should be marked with that identifying number/letter. This includes control panels, disconnect switches, motor generators, driving machines, tanks, governors, car tops, pit equipment and car operating panel. Not only will this help prevent the wrong equipment from being worked on or the wrong switch being operated (preventing personnel injury or equipment damage), it also permits passengers to identify malfunctioning equipment or report an entrapment accurately. Marking each landing entrance with the equipment number can prevent misidentification of elevators by users, emergency personnel and elevator personnel.

Marking each hoistway landing entrance with its associated floor number will not only help passengers to determine whether they are on the right floor, it permits them to accurately identify problems on certain floors. Marking the hoistway side of the landing doors with each floor number can greatly assist mechanics working on the equipment and inspectors inspecting the equipment.

Other vertical transportation equipment (escalators and dumbwaiters) should also be similarly marked to avoid any confusion in identifying the equipment.

C. Defective Designs

Defective designs of vertical transportation equipment have similarities with other transportation, motor control and machinery designs. Simply put, a defectively designed component within the system is unreliable, unsafe, short-lived or incompatible with the system.

Most of the vertical transportation equipment manufacturers have test towers where a newly created elevator or escalator system is put through its paces. The purpose of this is to verify that the overall design performs as intended and to verify that the components of the system have no weaknesses susceptible to conditions such as heat, stress or friction. Monitors gauge the equipment and the results are recorded.

The tests are followed by design-review meetings. These meetings involve many company departments. Design engineers, manufacturing, marketing, application, procurement, shipping, installation, maintenance and spare part managers attend these meetings to assure that the new product fits into the company's product line, and that they can support the product. They evaluate the design to ensure that the system can be manufactured (especially for the parts that are made in-house), installed at the site, and maintained once installed. Also present at these meetings are the financial representatives of the company. Does the product meet the financial goals of the company? If not, then the product is redesigned, or the procurement managers are instructed to buy less costly components. In either case, the whole process is repeated again and again until the CEO allows the product to be released.

When released the product is again verified at the first field installation. More changes may be required.

If the product is released for sale before its reliability is assessed, problems may occur. For example, at several locations throughout the United States, an entire elevator controlling system had to be replaced with its predecessor because its solid-state electronic components were simply too sensitive to the environment and to static discharges to function properly. Because the company had a presence in many other markets, its reputation would have been highly diminished or destroyed had it not undertaken such a monumental replacement.

When defective parts are identified, a "product letter" is usually sent by certified mail to all of the owners of the equipment. In essence, this is similar to recall notices issued for other products, such as automobiles. In some cases, the defective part may take a long time to identify. Unfortunately, sometimes a product letter is released only after a series of accidents have occurred.

Defective designs can take many forms, many of which are not readily apparent. The most common weak link is maintenance. Even the best-designed equipment will fail if it is not properly maintained. The design of the equipment has a major effect on its maintenance. Maintenance personnel usually have a limited time to perform the required maintenance tasks. If the conditions are so severe (poor access, confined working space, components too heavy to be moved easily, etc.) that maintenance is difficult (and in some cases is impossible without major efforts), then chances are that it will not be done. The consequences are obvious.

D. Misapplication

Misapplication of equipment occurs when the item has been applied incorrectly. It is not defective as described above. It may work fine in less demanding situations, but it just does not work correctly when used in more demanding circumstances (at higher speeds, more frequent usage, greater loads, etc.) than it was designed to operate in. This is a very important distinction because it may appear on the surface that the manufacturer of the equipment is at fault, when in actuality the installer or user simply misapplied the equipment.

Since vertical transportation equipment is manufactured for a variety of applications, this occurrence is quite common because no two buildings are the same. The installing company generally takes the same course of action as described above for defective designs. A product letter is issued notifying the building owners of the problem along with the consequences of not taking remedial action. This at least reduces the installing company's liability, even if the owner does not take remedial action. Naturally, the installing company should keep a copy of the letter and produce it if an incident occurs.

E. Improper Installation

Improper installation of one or more of a system's components or the omission to install these components affects the operation of the elevator or escalator to varying degrees. Depending on the components, the elevator may not operate as designed. This type of error can occur during the original installation of the elevator, during the replacement of components, or during alterations to the equipment.

For example, if the electrical wiring of an elevator or escalator were installed incorrectly, the elevator or escalator would not function as intended despite the best design and maintenance. Unlike mechanical defects, which in most cases are readily observable, electrical defects might not be so evident. This is because mechanical defects usually prevent a mechanism from operating or otherwise become readily apparent, while an electrical defect in many cases allows the mechanism to work, but not properly. Once this situation develops, the problem may persist undetected for quite some time until an accident occurs. If this incorrect installation were to compromise a safety device, then the consequences are clear.

The failure to install components can have the same consequences. In addition, if the component is peripheral to the operation of the elevator or escalator then the omission may not be noticed until after an accident. For example, if a guard were to be removed during a repair but not be replaced, then the operation of the elevator would not be affected. The guard may even be discarded once it is no longer in place. The potential consequences are unmistakable.

In the elevator and escalator industry, maintenance workers will commonly not question the operation of the equipment if there have been no complaints. The common refrain is, "It always did that" or "It was like that when I got here." This tendency perpetuates problems created by improperly installed components. For example, in one instance a major elevator and escalator company designed, installed and maintained an escalator for over 20 years. A switch in the machine space (upper pit) was marked in a handwritten fashion "Do Not Use." None of the maintenance workers knew the switch's function. They were afraid to operate it and evidently could not find out its function from their own company. The switch activated a safety device that mechanically immobilized the escalator during maintenance. While this is not an example of an improperly installed device, it illustrates how the status quo is often perpetuated blindly.

F. Improper Use, Misuse, and Abuse

Improper use, misuse and abuse of elevator and escalator equipment can be attributable to almost anyone using them, including the operator, passengers, building engineers, maintenance workers and the elevator technician while performing repairs. All possibilities of abuse or misuse of the equipment must be considered during the reconstruction of any accident.

The operator of an elevator, while usually trained in its proper operation, can cause numerous types of injury to his passengers. During the span of an eight-hour shift, the operator may become complacent, considering the fact that he may make up to 800 trips. Passengers may get hit by the doors and some seriously injured, particularly on freight elevators having very heavy doors up to 20 feet wide that open and close vertically. Freight handlers can be struck by either the landing doors or the car's gate or door. To further compound the problem, the operator's vision can be obscured on a crowded or heavily loaded elevator. Some elevators do not have automatic leveling operations. If the operator does not position the cab substantially level with a landing floor, then trips and falls can occur. Both of these types of accidents may be attributable to operator error.

Most passenger elevators are equipped with a special operating feature, known as independent service. This allows the passenger, if provided with an access key, to commandeer the elevator and in effect become an operator. This can result in similar hazards as described above.

Passenger abuse or misuse can also be the cause of many types of accidents. Included are sudden stops due to emergency stop switch activation or pulling open the car's (inside) door while the elevator is in motion.

Abuse can be in the form of horseplay or fighting within or outside of the elevator, and the subsequent damage. One case in point took place in a college dormitory containing a long, narrow elevator corridor with a marble floor. As a form of recreation, the students would put soapy water on the floor and slide down the floor. The elevator was at the end of the hall. One student slid into the elevator hoistway door. The bottom door guides (gibs) were knocked off by the impact and the bottom of the door swung open into the hoistway. The student fell down the hoistway and was killed.

In two other cases, passengers tried to transport a baby grand piano and a mall-vending cart down an escalator. These large objects became caught in a narrow opening and were destroyed in one case and became stuck in the other.

Luckily no one was hurt in either case, but the potential was there for serious injuries, because of thoughtless actions.

In another case, the steps of an escalator were taken out so that the interior of the unit could be cleaned. Someone who regularly used that escalator found the unit out of service, but instead of taking an alternate route pushed aside the barricades and started to walk up the step axles! Again, luckily no injuries resulted, but the potential for serious injuries was clearly present.

Injuries attributable to sudden stops and entrapments can be caused by loss of power due to building personnel pulling the incorrect power disconnect switch. Building personnel can also cause injuries by dropping objects down the hoistway from the overhead machine room or into the space between the car sill and a landing sill. More often building personnel cause injuries when removing passengers from elevators that are stuck. Although emergency evacuation procedures are well documented and available to all, the training of building personnel is often inadequate. Even when the experienced elevator technician is involved during evacuations injuries can occur, sometimes because passengers may panic under the stress of the moment.

Elevator technicians have been known to cause accidents in a number of ways. This includes forgetting to restore controls to their correct settings after performing maintenance. Commonly, jumper wires are used to bypass normal electrical safety devices during maintenance and testing. If these jumpers are not removed upon the completion of the maintenance or inspections, serious accidents can and do occur if the equipment is placed back in service. Therefore, the use of jumpers should be strictly regulated. This can entail using jumpers with brightly colored insulation, using long lead wires so they are easily spotted, and numbering jumpers so that the mechanic can account for all of them. Mechanics have also caused accidents by inadvertently working on the wrong control panel, usually an adjacent one, assuming it was the control panel for the elevator that was supposed to be serviced because the control panels were not numbered. Not installing temporary barricades around an open hoistway or at the top and bottom of escalators can also result in accidents.

Although most mechanics have the technical ability to properly maintain escalators, many of them dislike working on escalators as opposed to elevators. This often limits the practical experience of many mechanics to work on escalators. In one instance, an escalator was found by the resident mechanic shutdown when he arrived in the building in the morning. Being an experienced escalator mechanic, he followed proper procedure after he started the escalator and waited for the escalator steps to make a full revolution even though he saw nothing out of the ordinary. Amazingly one of the steps was missing. Apparently, other "elevator" mechanics, assigned the job of cleaning the escalator's interior, had cleaned the escalator the day before but forgot to reinstall the step. If the resident mechanic had not followed the proper procedure or if someone else who was not as knowledgeable had started the escalator, a very serious accident could have occurred.

Failure to properly secure the equipment when working on it can lead to serious injuries. Proper lockout or tag-out procedures should be used whenever the equipment is worked on. This entails securing the equipment both electrically and mechanically from inadvertent movement and posting appropriate signs.

G. External Factors

External factors such as power failures, earthquakes, tornados, high winds resulting in sway of tall buildings, floods, fire, and building structural failures have been and will continue to be the cause of accidents.

Elevator and building codes help reduce the effects of these causes. When investigating accidents of these types, it is necessary to determine if the elevator was designed and installed to meet the required codes. For example, elevators installed in earthquake zones are required to meet the earthquake code requirements that apply in that jurisdiction. These codes help assure that the elevator and its associated counterweight remain in their guide rails and do not collide with each other. Earthquake zones exist in many areas of the U.S. besides the West Coast, including the East Coast and Midwest.

Elevator malfunctions are often related to power supply problems. Failures of power will usually cause all building equipment that relies on electricity to stop, including elevators and escalators. Brownouts can cause only one or two elevators in the building to be troublesome and are usually more difficult to attribute to any equipment malfunction. The same arguments can be made for water and fire or smoke damage. Settling or subsidence of the building can result in structural damage. Water damage is a common cause of damage to elevators and escalators. This can be from sources such as overflowing plumbing, sprinklers, floor cleaning machines and actual floods. In at least one instance someone became stuck in an elevator during flooding and drowned inside it. Tall buildings sway during high winds and therefore appropriate safeguards must be provided to ensure safe operation.

Poor lighting has contributed to many elevator and escalator accidents. Proper lighting can enhance the safety of both passengers and mechanics. Proper lighting should be provided in machine rooms, elevator car tops and pits, inside the elevator car, at escalator steps and at landings. The ASME A17.1 code requires certain lighting intensities inside the car, in the pit and in the machine room for elevators and at landing plates and exposed steps for escalators. In addition, the lighting for escalators must be uniform and not materially contrast with the surroundings. Local building codes may impose additional requirements.

4.3 Elevator Accidents and Their Causes

The general reasons for accidents that were outlined earlier (improper design, improper maintenance, improper operation, abuse or misuse, misapplication, improper installation, insufficient warnings and external factors) apply to elevators.

The most frequent elevator accidents are trips or falls and being hit by the doors. While significant injury can occur from these types of accidents, they are seldom in the realm of death and disfigurement. Probably the biggest potential danger to elevator passengers is falling down the hoistway (shaft). The potential for serious injury and death is probably greater for elevator mechanics than for passengers because mechanics often work in inherently hazardous locations that the general public never enters (e.g., pits, top of car, machine room).

The following sections will explain some of the various causes of elevator accidents.

A. Trips and Falls

Trips and falls occur quite often while entering or exiting the elevator due to the elevator floor being above or below the landing floor. This, along with door strikes, accounts for the vast majority of elevator injuries.

Improper leveling can result in serious injuries and even can result in death due to subsequent complications. The elderly do not recover fully from broken bones in most cases and in many of those cases death occurs in the months following the more severe accidents.

The cause of improper leveling can vary (e.g. improper maintenance, type of control, type of selector and landing devices). Improper leveling is most common on elevators with poor control technology (e.g. single speed AC elevators, which do not have leveling control but stop by sliding through the brake, similar to how an automobile stops and unlike most elevators where the brake normally is applied after the elevator has been stopped electrically, similar to an automobile parking brake) and those requiring intensive maintenance (e.g. elevators equipped with a mechanical selector or motor-generator control), both of which have been superseded by new technology, and elevators with "pre-opening upon approach" door operation.

Elevator accidents that involve tripping and falling while entering or exiting the elevator cab can occur as the elevator approaches the floor, or when the elevator stops above or below the corridor's floor level with the doors open.

Many traction elevators start to open their doors before reaching floor level. This is referred to as "pre-opening the doors on approach" and is done to improve performance times, often at the expense of safety. The sooner the doors start to open, the more quickly the passengers will enter and exit the elevator. If "pre-opening" is provided, the doors should be less than 24 inches open, that is, less than the width of a person when the elevator is within ½-inch from floor level. However, the devices that sense elevator positions or leveling speeds can fail, causing the elevator doors to open at a distance of several inches from floor level or significantly more on older elevators. When exiting, unsuspecting passengers seldom look down. They typically look straight out of the elevator, either to see if the floor is theirs, or if other persons are approaching to enter the elevator. When entering an elevator, the passenger would look forward to see if there is enough room in the elevator to board. Trips or falls can occur in both situations.

Tripping and falling can also occur when the elevator stops are adjusted so that the car sill is not substantially level with the landing sill when the doors are open. This is commonly known as "misleveling." The cause of a misleveling incident will vary depending on the equipment involved. Generally, the acceptable difference in level is plus or minus ½-inch per ADA Accessibility Guidelines. However, the ½-inch dimension is nominal. In addition, most types of elevators have controls that are capable of ¼ to ⅛ inch maximum tolerance for leveling accuracy. In addition, A17.1 requires that elevator must be substantially level with the corridor floor or at rest for the hoistway door to be fully open. Depending on the type of control that exists on the elevator, the dimension may be increased to ¾ of an inch. However, for single-speed AC-type controls it is possible for the degree of "misleveling" to be considerably more, depending on the load in the car, the speed of the car, the direction of travel and the temperature and humidity in the machine room. This is because the brake is used to stop the elevator at full speed in this type of control and the elevator slides through the brake to a stop analogous to how an automobile stops. In essence this type of control does not have leveling capability. In most other types of control the elevator is stopped electrically, and the brake is merely a holding brake, analogous to an automobile parking brake. Even if the car sill for electric elevators stops level with a landing sill, the ropes or the spring shackles at the rope ends stretch in response to the load changing inside the car and can cause the elevator to be off level. Therefore, re-leveling must be provided to maintain the car sill level with the landing sill, or trips and falls can occur.

Hydraulic elevators present another tripping hazard. The elevator is usually supported on a column of hydraulic fluid (oil). When the elevator is operating, the oil quickly becomes heated. If the elevator is idled, the oil cools and the elevator creeps downward as the oil contracts and has less volume. The elevator must be designed with a feature, known as "anti-creep leveling," to maintain the car sill substantially level with the landing sill. However, the A17.1 Code permits the car sill to be up to 1 inch below the landing sill with the doors open before this operation will re-level the car. Trips and falls can easily result if the design permits this much vertical distance between the car sill and landing sill.

An elevator stopping more than 18 inches above or below floor level will not normally open its doors automatically. The length of the door clutch or vane physically limits the distance above or below the landing that the landing doors can be opened automatically.

All newer car doors are provided with a means (commonly known as door restrictors) to prevent the car door from being manually opened from inside the car when it is outside the unlocking zone, while many older doors are not. If the doors are forced open by an entrapped passenger attempting to exit the elevator, serious accidents can occur.

Falls down the hoistway sometimes occur when passengers jump from an elevator that has stopped approximately 3–6 feet above the floor. They pull open the car door and open the lock on the hoistway door to pull it open. They jump down to the landing floor, lose their balance and fall backward under the elevator and down the elevator shaft. This can occur because the car's platform entrance is usually only guarded to a point less than 2 feet below the car sill, and at times the guard is not secure and can be pushed toward the hoistway when contacted by the falling victim.

It is therefore very important that entrapped passengers wait for an authorized person to release them, so that the extrication can be done safely. They can contact emergency personnel by using the alarm and communication system located in the elevator's cab. Of course those answering the calls for assistance from trapped passengers must convey proper warnings. Passengers should attempt to move the elevator only with the floor buttons and stay clear of the doors. They must never exit on their own through the top emergency exit because this is equally dangerous. The top emergency exit cover must not be able to be opened from inside the cab, in order to prevent passengers from getting into the hoistway and falling down the hoistway or contacting moving elevator components. Side emergency exits must be used only by trained emergency personnel and not be operable from inside the car without a key. When a side emergency exit is opened, by code the elevator must be provided with a switch to prevent the elevator from moving. Top emergency exits are in some cases also provided with a switch that prevents the elevator from moving. Side emergency exits have not been permitted for a number of years and certain alterations require existing ones to be permanently fixed in the closed positions due to injuries during extrication from stalled elevators.

Brochures instructing tenants of a building about the safe operation and riding practices for elevators are available from several safety authorities and elevator companies. Some are posted on state government or elevator company websites. Building managers and owners should periodically distribute these instructions to their tenants and train their employees in the proper procedures. The

ASME A17.4 Guide for Emergency Personnel provides safe procedures for the evacuation of passengers trapped in elevators.

Sometimes trapped passengers cannot summon help because alarm bells or communication devices (phones, intercoms) have malfunctioned. Also, many elevators only have an alarm bell, but do not have a means of communicating between the car and those responsible for rescuing trapped passengers. If the trapped passengers do not receive some prompt form of confirmation that help is on the way, then serious accidents can occur when they try to evacuate on their own.

Commonly, after the first few entrapments occur in a building, the trapped passengers tell other people about their experience. As the word spreads, the tenants fear that it will happen to them. When and if it does, then the person may panic and try to escape by pulling the doors open or climbing through the emergency exit unaided. This can result in falls causing serious injury or death, as described above. Therefore, the elevator technicians must quickly identify the reason for the entrapments and eliminate the cause.

Falls down elevator hoistways have occurred for other reasons. They can result from the circumventing of the interlock on the hoistway door either electrically or mechanically, unauthorized or untrained personnel using a hoistway door unlocking tool, malfunctioning mechanisms on multi-paneled hoistway doors that result in a panel becoming dislodged, the failure of a mechanical door closer to properly close the hoistway door, missing or deficient top or bottom door guiding devices, or the application of excessive force on the landing side of the hoistway door. To reduce these risks, frequent and thorough hoistway door maintenance is necessary. Door interlocks, hangers, retainers, sills, bottom guides (gibs), relating cables and closers must be in good condition. Door interlocks should not be circumvented unless absolutely necessary, and then only by an elevator technician when the elevator is out of normal service. Otherwise the technician may forget that the interlocks are "jumped out" (i.e., circumvented) and allow the car to run with the doors open. This can be disastrous! If a landing door is open or unlocked because of a defective component on that particular door, and the elevator is at another floor, a substantial barricade must immediately be placed in front of the opening and the elevator removed from service until repaired.

Newer elevators are required by A17.1 to be provided with a means to monitor the door's position to prevent operation of the elevator with faulty or by-passed landing door interlocks or car door contacts. This provision can prevent many of the serious injuries and deaths that result from falls down the hoistway. These devices also prevent serious injuries and fatalities due to the elevator running when someone is situated between the landing door and the car door when they are entering or exiting an elevator.

Many elevator doors are equipped with a means (unlocking device) for opening the hoistway door while the elevator is at another floor or landing. This allows properly trained personnel (elevator personnel, emergency workers, inspectors, etc.) to gain access to the hoistway for maintenance or inspection purposes or to help evacuate trapped passengers. Access in this manner is commonly permitted for no other purpose and requires a special tool. The tool is sometimes stored under a glass cover outside the main floor door of the elevator, when required by local regulations. Unauthorized persons may obtain the door-opening tool. It can be dangerous when used by untrained persons. Even experienced personnel have incurred injuries while entering the hoistway in this manner. Once the door is opened in this way, there are risks, including the chance for falls down the hoistway. If the AHJ requires that the tool be accessible then you're "damned" if you permit access in this manner and "damned" if you do not. While A17.1 requires that common tools cannot be used to open a locked hoistway door, some designs are more susceptible to being defeated by common tools. If the elevator is not taken out of service when using a hoistway door unlocking device, then serious injuries to fingers can occur if the elevator returns to that floor and opens the door resulting in fingers becoming crushed.

Some elevators are provided with a safer method of gaining access to the hoistway, namely by access switches. These are key-operated switches that permit movement of the car with the landing door (where the switch is located) open, but under the control of the person operating the switch. Unfortunately, if these devices fail, then access to the hoistway can become blocked if an unlocking device is not also provided. This can lead to the use of jumpers to bypass the door interlock, which is potentially dangerous.

Another common cause of falls down hoistways of elevators that only can be operated from inside the car and are provided with manually operated hoistway doors occurs when someone is able to open a landing door without the car being at that landing. Typically they park the car at a landing, leave the car and then someone else takes the car to another landing and when the first person returns they think the car is there but that the light inside the car has malfunctioned or been turned off. Unsuspectingly the person steps into the hoistway and either falls into the pit or onto the car. ASME A17.1 required "parking devices" for many years to help prevent opening a door when the elevator is at another floor, however these devices can be easily circumvented. ASME A17.1-2000 and later editions no longer permits parking devices on new elevators, but they are still required for certain alterations and by A17.3 for certain circumstances. Recently some codes (e.g. A17.3) have been revised to require that there be no means to turn the lights off inside a car when parking devices are provided in order to provide a visual cue that the lights were not intentionally turned off in the hopes that anyone attempting to enter the car will check to see if the elevator is there before stepping in.

B. Hit by Doors

Elevator accidents involving passengers being struck by the doors while entering or exiting the elevator's cab are very common. This, along with trips and falls, accounts for the vast majority of elevator injuries.

Most elevator passengers are aware that the doors close automatically. They assume that the door reopening devices are working properly. However, these devices are not usually effective in the path of the closing landing doors, but only effective in the path of the car doors, unbeknownst to the average passenger. Furthermore, these devices may be defective or turned off by the building engineer or other personnel with a key to the elevator control panel inside the cab. The device could also be shorted or intentionally circumvented, and the elevator will continue to operate without door protection. When this happens, tenants of the building are surprised when the door does not reopen as it always has in the past when they put their hands or briefcases on the door's edge or between the closing doors. The doors can then strike the passengers or squeeze them.

Accordingly, the ASME A17.1 Code limits the squeezing force of horizontally sliding doors to be a "safe" value of 30 lbs maximum, should the closing doors trap someone. This is measured with a force gauge. Horizontally sliding doors are typically provided on passenger elevators.

In addition, the Code requires the striking energy (known as the kinetic energy) of horizontally sliding doors to be limited. This kinetic energy is based on the combined weights of the closing car and hoistway doors and any associated hardware, the closing speed of the doors to the second power, and the rotating kinetic energy of the door operator.

The closing speed of the doors for the kinetic energy limitations is based on the travel of the doors in what is known as the code zone. This ignores the first and last inch or two of travel, depending on the type of doors involved, in order to factor out the acceleration and deceleration at the extreme limits of travel.

Traditionally, ASME A17.1 has placed limits on the kinetic energy based on an average closing speed in the code zone. Average kinetic energy is determined by timing the door travel in the code zone. Since the weight of the doors and the rotational energy of the door operator are not easily determined in the field, it is common to estimate the weight of the doors based on industry standards. The minimum permissible closing time will vary for the same size doors depending on if the doors are single speed opening, side opening, multiple speed opening or center opening. Heavier doors such as stainless steel, ornamental bronze doors or extra wide or tall doors require extra closing time (i.e., slower speed) because they are heavier than standard doors. All other things being equal, these heavier doors closing at the same speed as lighter doors will have a greater kinetic energy. Newer elevators will have a data plate on the door operator or the car crosshead that will indicate the minimum door closing time(s).

ASME A17.1-2000 introduced additional kinetic energy limits based on the actual speed at any point in the code zone. Instantaneous kinetic energy can be determined using a mechanical measuring device. However, this will yield the instantaneous kinetic energy at only one point in the code zone and it can only be measured in a limited location of door travel due to space constraints. The instantaneous kinetic energy will be greater than the average kinetic energy depending on the door operator and where the measurement is taken in the code zone.

Most elevator doors can be adjusted intentionally by the service technician, who is frequently unfamiliar with codes, to close with greater force and energy than permitted by code. Some have argued that this fact makes the door system having these characteristics "defective by design." These systems are especially vulnerable in buildings where wind, caused by the stack or chimney effect, stalls the doors and keeps them from opening or closing. Usually the maintenance mechanic will then increase the speed, in order to overcome the wind resistance. After the wind subsides, or when the elevator is at a landing with less inrush of wind, the door closing speeds and forces will exceed the safe values. Also, building owner's demands to try to decrease waiting times by decreasing door close times frequently result in excessive door closing speeds.

State-of-the-art systems now have what is referred to as "closed-loop feedback" circuitry that monitor the speeds and forces on the door, and will automatically make corrections to the system. The door closing forces and energies will almost always comply with code.

Horizontally sliding car doors must be provided with a reopening device if the kinetic energy is above a certain limit. The maximum kinetic energy of the doors is limited to a higher amount when a reopening device is operative. If the reopening device is rendered inoperative, then the kinetic energy must be reduced to the lower limit. This usually occurs if a feature known as "nudging" is provided. If the doors are prevented from closing, then after a predetermined time interval the door reopening device may be bypassed and the doors close at reduced speed in order to try and "nudge" any obstruction out of their path. While ADAAG (ADA Accessibility Guidelines) permits nudging to take effect after 20 seconds, this feature should not be enabled in hospitals or nursing home type buildings or accidents will predicably occur.

Vertically sliding doors have different requirements than horizontally closing doors. Freight elevators typically have vertically sliding doors. For many years, ASME A17.1 required sequence operation (i.e., the car door/gate closes most of the way before the hoistway doors begin to close), an audible warning prior to door closing, momentary pressure door opening buttons at each landing, and a reopening device; it also limited the average closing speeds for hoistway doors and car door or gate. The door reopening device was historically required contact to operate, but non-contact types have been available for many years. Recently these requirements were significantly revised. For example, the audible signal requirement was eliminated; when sequencing operation was revised; a non-contact reopening device was required, with exceptions, that could detect certain sized and shaped objects at various locations; a yellow and black diagonally striped hazard warning was required on the leading edge of the lower door panel; the closing speed of biparting doors was limited further when the panels were a certain distance apart; and several new requirements must be met if the reopening device was rendered ineffective.

There are three main types of door reopening devices, with a variety of designs available under each: mechanical, electronic and photoelectric.

Mechanical types (i.e., *safety edges*) require contact with an obstruction to operate. For horizontally closing doors, their sensing edge must lead the car door by a sufficient distance when it closes for it to operate effectively. Many times they were combined with 2 optical beams located 5 inches and 29 inches above the floor to meet ADA requirements. Historically, vertically sliding doors were provided with pressure-sensitive devices (e.g., pneumatic) on the leading edge of the upper car door or gate.

Photoelectric devices detect obstructions when the photoelectric beams across the door opening are blocked by the obstruction. These devices do not require contact with an object to operate, which increases safety. For many years these devices use infrared light, while older devices used less reliable visible light. These types of devices have been available for many years for vertically sliding doors and gates on freight elevators.

Newer designs provide an important safety enhancement. They typically use infrared beams to detect people as they approach to enter the car from the landing. These newer devices usually combine the proximity feature with the more common infrared feature that detects people in the path of the closing doors. This provides in effect a 3D detection zone instead of the normal 2D detection zone. However, the 3D protection typically can be turned off.

Electronic door reopening devices sense an object close to the doors. Some older types work on the principle of conductive obstructions (which include the human body) inducing a change in a sensing device when they come in proximity to the device. Historically, many of these devices were too sensitive.

Several important issues should be noted regarding door reopening devices. First, the ASME A17.1 code does not specify what specific type of reopening device is required, just when one is required. Therefore, it is left up to the designer or installer of the equipment to provide the most appropriate protection for passengers. It is obviously better for safety not to require contact with a person in the path of the closing doors for the device to work. Second, the reopening device is almost always provided on the car door. This means that it is possible, especially if a mechanical type reopening device is used, for the landing doors to strike someone trying to enter the car before the reopening device can detect the person. The use of devices with 3D capabilities in addition to the standard non-contact type greatly diminishes this possibility.

It should be noted that the code is silent on the reaction time when an object is detected and the door begins to reopen. The drift of the door can be several inches and hit the obstruction, especially if the kinetic energy is at or higher than its upper limits and on older mechanical safety edges.

A common type of crushing injury to hands and arms occurs with manually operated vertically bi-parting doors. The person closing the doors pulls down on the straps attached to the upper panel and does not get their hands/arms out of the way in time before they become caught between the two panels. This can occur because one or more straps are: missing; too short; configured into a loop; or not properly secured to the inside and outside of the door panel. Injuries can be severe, especially on older doors that have panels with overlapping metal edges when the doors are in the closed position instead of a non-crushing and non-shearing astragal (see photos of both the straps and the edges can be viewed in Chapter 2 of this book).

C. Abrupt Stops

Elevator accidents involving passengers injured when the elevator stops abruptly or moves abnormally are quite common. The stops can occur for numerous reasons described below. Abnormal or spurious movements include faster than normal accelerations or decelerations and abrupt reversals. Either can cause unsuspecting passengers to lose their balance and fall, or to be injured from forces imposed on them by the sudden stop or change of direction.

The likely magnitudes of forces imposed by common types of sudden stops are:

- Stop button or other electrical safety circuit, including main power trips while elevator is traveling at full speed—*less than one g force*
- Setting of the mechanical safety—*one or more g force*
- Car or counterweight strikes the buffer—*one or more g force*
- Car collides with the counterweight—*several g forces*
- Car hits top ceiling of the hoistway or collides with another obstacle—*several g forces*

- Hydraulic elevator supporting jack rapidly loses fluid and falls—*many g forces*
- Car free-falls down the hoistway because of sheared cables and without the setting of the mechanical safeties—*many g forces*

The values above are approximate and are given only to establish the relative severity of each type of stop. Elevators commonly have rated speeds of 50 to 2,200 feet per minute or approximately ½ to 25 miles per hour, although higher speed elevators have been installed in limited cases. While the speed can be important variable in the forces created by an elevator stop, the most important factor is the deceleration rate. As the old saying goes, "It is not the fall that kills you, but the sudden stop."

The load in the elevator car and the direction of travel will affect the severity of the stop. For example, the ASME A17.1 Code requires that a car buffer have a maximum average retardation of one g force. This is for the down direction with a full-rated load inside the car. If the load in the car is lighter than the rated load, which is the most likely scenario, then the resulting stop will be more abrupt.

A g force is equal to the force due to gravity. While this would appear to be safe to the average person, a more robust or an unsuspecting person can be injured. For example, the body of a 250-pound person who experiences a one-g force will be subject to a 250-pound force, and the body of a 120-pound person that experiences a one-g force will be subject to a 120-pound force. This may explain why heavy persons tend to suffer injuries from abrupt stops in elevators more easily than a light person.

It is also very important to note that these g-force estimates are based on the **average deceleration**. Historically, the A17.1 Code has sought to limit the average deceleration to a "safe" one-g force. More recently it has been recognized that the **peak deceleration and its duration** are equally important factors than the average deceleration. Peak deceleration values can easily surpass the average deceleration values by significant amounts. In contrasts, an elevator traveling at full speed may be adjusted to achieve approximately 1/8 g forces or 4 feet per second squared.

Abnormal movements, including fast acceleration and deceleration rates, are almost always caused by a problem with the regulation or control mechanism. Since elevators must compensate for the number of passengers in both directions of travel, the controlling mechanisms are complex. Most traction-type elevators are equipped with speed or current sensors that send information back to the speed-regulating circuitry. Faults in the circuitry can result in incorrect information being sent back to the controlling mechanism, causing the hoisting motor voltage to be unstable. This can cause the elevator to accelerate abruptly in either direction or even to change directions abruptly. The latter may be described by the passenger as a "yo-yo" effect. The effect typically would be less than 1 g force, but under certain conditions could cause g forces greater than one g. Again, while 1 g may appear to be safe to the "average" person, a less robust or an unsuspecting person can be injured.

Furthermore, the forces described above consider only those forces that exist in the vertical plane of travel and assume that the elevator will not twist. An elevator can twist or jerk from front to back or side to side while traveling through the hoistway creating horizontal forces on people or objects inside the elevator. Some reasons why this happens include improperly adjusted or damaged guide rollers or guide rails, unequal tension on traction cables, improperly adjusted cab steady plates and unbalanced cabs. Under certain conditions this can cause people or objects to be propelled horizontally inside the car and in extreme cases cause the car or counterweight to strike the fixed objects in the hoistway, or to collide, which would likely destroy the car.

Most of the above causes for spurious and unintended motion of the elevator are within the control of the elevator maintenance company and each cause must be addressed during routine preventive maintenance.

Hydraulic elevators having leaks or unaccounted oil losses are potentially dangerous. Unlike electric elevators that are required to have a speed governor and a car safety device to detect and stop an "overspeeding" elevator traveling downward mosy hydraulic elevators are not required to have these safety devices. A pipe or cylinder rupture can cause an elevator to descend rapidly and hit the bottom springs with great force. Injury or death is likely. Complete records of any additions of hydraulic oil must be kept. The reasons for any oil loss must be accounted for and assurances made that none is attributable to small leaks in the underground cylinder. Small leaks will eventually cause a blowout of the cylinder and an uncontrolled descent of the elevator. Unaccounted oil loss must be immediately investigated. Most hydraulic cylinders are inaccessible because they are located in the ground (similar to a well casing), thereby making direct physical examination impossible. The hydraulic cylinders typically corrode at their bottom.

Since ASME A17.1-1971 ,cylinders have been required to be provided with a safety bulkhead (aka double bottom), which limits the descending speed of a hydraulic elevator if the bottom of the cylinder leaks when it is buried underground without any effective means to prevent corrosion. However, many cylinders were installed without such protection and therefore are prime candidates for failure. Since ASME A17.1b-1989 cylinders buried underground have been required by A17.1 to have an effective means to prevent corrosion.

Some hydraulic elevators are provided with an overspeed valve, which stops a hydraulic elevator's descent if the speed in the down direction exceeds a limit (from a loss of pressure in the supply piping for example). However, this will not protect against overspeed from a leak in a hydraulic cylinder.

To recognize this problem, the A17.1 Code was revised to require as part of maintenance that car safeties be provided for all hydraulic elevators that do not have a safety bulkhead. This provision has met with opposition from building owners, where these provisions now apply. In response, some AHJs are exempting the hydraulic elevators under their jurisdiction from these provisions. As of 2011, the A17.1 Code has been revised to permit "plunger grippers" to be used in lieu of car safeties. A plunger gripper is a device that engages the plunger of a hydraulic elevator to stop its descent upon the detection of a loss of pressure.

D. Entrapments

Entrapments on elevators can result in some of the most tragic accidents that happen on elevators.

It occurs when a child or thin person is caught between the elevator hoistway (landing) door and the door or gate on the elevator cab. The most common cases involve elevators equipped with swing-type hoistway doors. In this case, each floor that is served by the elevator has a door that swings open when the entering passenger pulls or exiting passenger pushes on the manually operated door. This is similar to doors in homes or office buildings, except it is metal to meet the fire ratings. It is heavier and thicker than the sliding-type elevator door, and it is self-closing. The closing force of the door will vary depending on the device (e.g., spring) used to automatically close the door, the method used to check (i.e., slowdown) the closing of the door, and the weight of the door. The inside door on the elevator in these cases is usually a scissor-type collapsing gate.

As the person enters the elevator, she pulls open the outside (landing) door and then steps between the two doors while attempting to pull open the inside (car) gate. The outside door closes and locks before the elevator gate is opened, and the person is trapped in between the door and the gate. How this actually occurs will have to be determined in each specific case. Another person or child playing with the elevator could push the outside door, the person could lose her balance and fall against the gate, or the closing door may simply overwhelm the person.

Similar situations occur on private residence elevators, where the landing door is similar to a manually operated swing type home closet door with a passage type lock and the car door is a folding type similar to a folding closet door or a collapsible gate. A child is able to close the landing door with the car folding door or collapsible gate closed and becomes trapped.

Some elevators can have a space of 6–10 inches between the car gate and the landing door. This is especially the case for even recently installed private residence elevators due to improper installation and the significantly increased clearances caused by the V-shaped spaces (aka "valleys") of folding car doors formed by the folds of the door panels. In addition, the car gate or folding car door can deflect significantly when the person is forced into it by the closing door, which further increases the space between the door and the gate. The deflection could be as much as 2 inches depending on the design and condition of the car gate or folding door.

When the outside door closes and locks, the elevator can run in response to a call. When the elevator travels a few feet, the space for the person is reduced significantly. If the elevator stops at that point the person usually is squeezed and death can result from mechanical asphyxiation, or other serious injuries can result. If the elevator travels to the next floor then the person is either killed or critically injured, especially if travelling up.

This type of accident is horrible and tragic, and more saddening is the fact that the victim is usually a small child five to twelve years old and the accident results in brain damage or death. Just as saddening is the fact that space guards are available and inexpensive, and can prevent most of these accidents. They will in most instances prevent the swing door from closing and locking, thereby preventing the elevator from running if someone is caught between the car gate and the swing door. They are required when the space between the car door or gate and the landing door exceeds a maximum distance. See Chapter 2, Figures C.19–C.22.

Similar accidents occur on elevators equipped with sliding doors. When the space between the car door and the landing door is excessive, a sight guard is required by the ASME A17.1 code. Usually, when these accidents occur the sight guard, sometimes referred to as a non-vision wing, is missing. This commonly happens when the fastening screws are in open-ended slots rather than holes. Pinning the sight guard is highly recommended. This sight guard is similar to a space guard except that it is only installed along the open edge of the door, instead of filling in most of the space. This type of entrapment can also occur when the landing doors are disengaged from the inside car doors, trapping a slim person or child between the doors. The effect on the entrapped person is the same as described for space guards.

Unfortunately, the A17.1 code does not contain requirements for retrofitting existing elevators with space or sight guards under most circumstances. ASME A17.3 does contain such provisions for existing equipment. It should be noted that many versions of ASME A17.1 require that all the requirements of ASME A17.3 must be met whenever an alteration (which is defined in the Code) is made to an existing elevator or escalator regardless of the type of alteration. This is in addition to any specific requirements for each type of alteration. In fact, even if the AHJ did not adopt A17.3 as a stand-alone code, it would apply if the AHJ adopted the alteration requirements of ASME A17.1. Also, some jurisdictions have their own retroactive requirements for space and sight guards.

It is imperative that building owners install space and sight guards when they are required, and should provide them even if they are not specifically mandated if the distance between the car door or gate and the landing door exceeds the maximum limit established in the code. It is also imperative for the AHJ to enforce the applicable code requirements for space and sight guards. Elevator maintenance companies should alert the building owner or manager to the potential hazard, correct it, or report it to the AHJ as applicable. The hazard is well known and can easily be prevented in most cases.

E. Unauthorized Access

Unauthorized access to vertical transportation machinery rooms and hoistways can be hazardous and is the reason for many accidents.

The A17.1 Code requires that the machine room doors be self-closing and self-locking, and that only authorized personnel be permitted entry. These rooms must not be used for storage of other than elevator-related maintenance equipment and parts needed for vertical transportation. Not only does this prevent unauthorized personnel from entering these areas, it also reduces the potential for fires. In one case, a person sleeping in the machine room stopped an elevator by tripping the speed governor to keep down the noise.

Similarly, hoistways and pits should only be accessible to elevator personnel. These areas are inherently hazardous, more so than machine rooms. Storing large objects in the pit underneath the counterweight area can damage the frame, which in turn can dislodge the counterweight from its guide rails. A resulting collision between the car and the counterweight could destroy the elevator cab and injure or kill its occupants. This is not a doomsayer's fantasy; such collisions have occurred. Incredibly, in one case a mattress was found in a space underneath an escalator within a few inches of the moving steps and in other case a chair was found adjacent to the counterweight guide rails in the pit. The results could have been fatal in either case.

These areas can also contain dangerously high voltages and many moving parts. The ASME A17.1 Code requires that pipes, ducts, conduits, and equipment not related to the operation of the elevator not be installed in the elevator machine rooms or hoistways. This is to limit non-elevator personnel from entering these areas for maintenance or repairs, and also to limit the potential for these devices to impair the elevator's operation (water leaks, interferences, etc.). If cleaning personnel, painters and others are allowed to enter these areas then someone who recognizes the potential hazards should also be present. Locked doors and restricted use of those keys will help keep unauthorized personnel out.

In recognition of the need to restrict access to elevator machine rooms and hoistways, the A17.1-2001 code was revised to establish security levels for keys used to access and operate elevator equipment. Four levels of security were established: Group 1 is restricted to elevator personnel, Group 2 is restricted to authorized personnel, Group 3 is restricted to emergency personnel and Group 4 applies when the other levels do not.

F. Working Conditions

Working conditions significantly affect the level of safety of both elevator personnel and passengers. If elevator personnel can't safely maintain an elevator then passenger safety is jeopardized.

The *Elevator Industry Field Employees' Safety Handbook* is the foremost publication devoted to delineating the proper safety practices that should be used when working around elevators and escalators. While this document is intended for use by mechanics, it has many parts that are applicable to other elevator personnel (e.g., inspectors). The latest edition when this book was being written was the 2015 edition. In the past revisions were held until sufficient material was available to justify the cost of publishing a supplement. However, now revisions will be published electronically as soon as they are approved. Printed supplements will also be published periodically.

Elevator personnel are subject to the same general hazards as the general public (e.g. falls, being struck by objects hazards, shear hazards, crushing hazards, electrical hazards, being caught in between objects hazards). However, elevator personnel are typically faced with all of these hazards on a daily basis that are significantly more hazardous in nature. Therefore, this section addresses workplace accidents. See Section 3.2C for workplace accident statistics.

Elevator personnel are exposed to many of these hazards during the installation of elevators and escalators when many of the safeguards that protect the public are not yet installed or functional. Therefore, proper safeguards must be put in place to protect them (e.g. fall protection (guardrails, barricades and fall-arrest systems) and personal protection equipment (e.g. proper clothing, hard hats, hearing protection, safety glasses, safety boots and respiratory protection)).

Elevator personnel frequently work on top of elevators and therefore are subject to extreme fall hazards. The 2000 Edition of ASME A17.1 codified requirements for car top safety railings when the distance between the car top edge and the adjacent hoistway wall exceeds 12 inches. However, the vast majority of installed elevators do not have these railings. These handrails can easily and economically be installed in most cases. One potential obstacle is insufficient overhead clearances. However, this can be overcome with retractable safety railings and electric contacts to prevent operation with the railing deployed during normal operation.

When an electric elevator is moving in one direction, the counterweight is moving in the other direction. An elevator with only a 2,500 lb. capacity can have a counterweight that weighs 1.5 tons or more. The counterweight usually doesn't make sufficient noise to be heard when it is moving. Serious injuries or death will result if someone is struck by the counterweight. Also, side counterweights are required, instead of being installed at the rear of the hoistway, when front and rear openings are provided. This can cause elevator personnel to let their guard down when working on the side of the car top because they do not expect the counterweight to be there. This can be an issue even if the side counterweight is installed on an adjacent elevator in the same hoistway. Sometimes chains are hung from the bottom of the counterweight to create noise, but usually elevator passengers object to the noises and they are removed. Guarding is required in many cases in the pit to protect elevator personnel and when a counterweight is located between elevators.

While elevator control voltages are typically low (e.g. 24 VDC) and ancillary voltages will be in the 110/120 VAC range, main power voltages typically will be in the 220-480 volt range. These higher voltages are a serious shock hazard.

Failure to properly secure the equipment when working on it can lead to serious injuries. Proper lockout or tag-out procedures should be used whenever the equipment is worked on. This entails securing the equipment both electrically and mechanically from inadvertent movement and posting appropriate signage.

Yellow striping on low overheads, ledges and rotating equipment and at pinch points will warn the technician of these dangers. Warning signs on access doors for hoistways are required. Signs warning of high voltage (technically over 600 volts) are required, and signs warning of voltages higher than 110/120 volts would be prudent.

Hoistway access switches have been provided for many years to enable elevator personnel to safely gain access to the car top. However, many elevators are not provided with hoistway access switches and those that do have them frequently become disabled by building cleaning operations.

When used appropriately, hoistway access switches and hoistway unlocking devices assist the technician to safely enter the hoistway. Devices of this type should meet the requirements of ASME A17.1 (new equipment) and A17.3 (existing equipment). They obviate the necessity of having to "jump out" (circumvent) the door locks in order to gain access to the car top or pit areas for maintenance purposes. This of course eliminates the possibility of forgetting to remove any door lock jumpers before returning the elevator to service, because no jumpers are required to run the elevator during maintenance. The function of these devices is regulated by code. Access to the hoistway by unauthorized personnel or improper operation of these devices can result in serious injuries and deaths. In one fatal accident that was recorded, by a surveillance camera at the building, a mechanic was attempting to run the elevator down apparently trying to gain access to the car top using an inspection control switch inside an elevator car operating panel with the bottom half of his body lying down on the landing floor and the top half of his body sticking into the car. His body was crushed when he apparently lost control of the elevator.

For many years car top controls have been required so that elevator personnel can safely control the operation of the elevator when they are on the car top. Top-of-car operating devices are essential for proper inspections and maintenance inside the hoistway and therefore critical for both elevator personnel and passenger safety. While these devices are now required by the ASME A17.1 codes, many existing old elevators are not provided with this important safety feature. However, ASME A17.3 contains retroactive provisions for these devices. If these devices are not provided, then safe working conditions inside the hoistway on top of the car cannot be expected. The installation of car top controls typically can be installed economically.

Maintenance and workplace safety is enhanced with proper lighting in all working areas, whether required by code or not. These work areas include the machine rooms, car tops, and pits.

G. Dumbwaiters, Material Lifts, Vertical Reciprocating Conveyors and Material Hoists

Dumbwaiters share many characteristics with elevators, but are very limited in size and capacity, and are not permitted to carry riders. Therefore, they must also conform to the applicable requirements of ASME A17.1, but are exempt from a number of requirements that apply to elevators. Accidents related to dumbwaiters are not very common, but in many cases they result in serious injuries or deaths. These accidents share many of the same characteristics of some types of elevator accidents, but are somewhat unique to dumbwaiters.

If landing door interlocks are bypassed then someone can open the landing door, stick his head in the hoistway to look for the dumbwaiter and be hit by the moving dumbwaiter. Similar hazards exist for missing door vision panels.

Many dumbwaiters are winding-drum types. Many older dumbwaiters have no car doors or gates. A typical accident scenario would be for the objects inside the dumbwaiter to shift and cause a descending dumbwaiter to become stalled. If a slack rope or chain device is not provided or if it is defective, then the suspension rope or chain can continue to be wound off the winding drum. This creates slack in the suspension rope or chain. If someone frees the dumbwaiter without taking precautions against inadvertent movement due to gravity, then the dumbwaiter will descend uncontrolled. Serious injuries, including deaths, have occurred in this manner.

Material lifts in the U.S. have traditionally been essentially very large dumbwaiters and, therefore, were not permitted to carry any riders. When ASME A17 was "harmonized" with CSA B44 in 2000, these devices were designated as Type A material lifts; and Type B material lifts that were already included in CSA B44 were added to ASME A17.1. Type B material lifts are permitted to carry only one operator and have a number of restrictions, including access and usage limited to authorized personnel, limited speed and travel, restrictions on penetrating floors and limited to only continuous pressure type controls. Type B material lifts are not prevalent in the U.S. All material lifts are required to be inspected and tested by AHJs by ASME A17.1.

Accidents related to Type A material lifts will generally share many of the characteristics of elevators and dumbwaiters, while those of Type B material lifts will have more distinct characteristics. General causes of accidents will be similar.

There are devices known as vertical reciprocating conveyors (VRCs), which can be confused with material lifts. VRCs are covered by the less stringent, less prescriptive and less costly requirements of ASME B20.1 Safety Standard for Conveyors and Related Equipment.[27] VRCs are typically not inspected or tested by AHJs, and are located in industrial settings. They are supposed to be installed, maintained and operated by trained personnel, but often are not. VRCs are not permitted to carry riders, but sometimes are ridden. These factors can result in serious injuries, including fatalities. These devices are beyond the scope of this book. Accidents related to these devices will have distinct characteristics from those of elevators, but general causes will be similar.

It should be noted that there are devices known as material hoists, which can be confused with material lifts. Material hoists are covered by ANSI/ASSE A10.5 Safety Requirements for Material Hoists.[14] This standard applies to material hoists used to raise or lower materials during construction, alteration or demolition. It is not applicable to the temporary use of permanently installed personnel elevators as material hoists. These devices are beyond the scope of this book. Accidents related to these devices will have characteristics distinct from those of elevators, but general causes will be similar.

H. Private Residence Elevators

The main purpose of this section is to provide a brief history of private residence elevators and their intended installation, and further describe the types of and causes of private residence elevator accidents.

Private residence elevators have been manufactured and installed throughout the United States for many years. Further, early residential elevators were rather simple mechanisms comprised of electric or hydraulic driving machines; a basic elevator car enclosure; collapsible or accordion style car gate; constant pressure push button control; swing-style landing doors; and, limited safety devices. Although early residence elevators may appear similar to commercial elevators of that era, they are limited by size, speed, rise and load, and were only intended to be used by members of a single family under the control of the head of the family pursuant to ASME A17.1-1955.

Since their inception, private residence elevators have evolved technologically to include automatic push button operation, microprocessor technology (e.g., programmable logic computer), power-operated doors, soft start and variable speed motor control and battery backup operation. They have also become increasingly sophisticated and present fits and finishes worthy of architectural and master craftsmanship awards. Examples of such craftsmanship include matching architectural metal and hardwood finishes, and cut glass and leaded crystal elevator car enclosures. Private residence elevators have also become popular with architects, and custom home builders and owners, and seem to have an increasing appeal to baby boomers.

According to a January 2011 report, there are approximately 77.6 million baby boomers (people born between 1946 through 1964) in the U.S., who control a significant amount of wealth and spending power in the economy. Pursuant to same, 36 percent of Boomers (approximately 28 million people) will move or plan to move to a smaller house or adult community when their children move out. If the above is true, then private residence elevators may present a viable alternative to those boomers who wish to build a multi-story retirement dream home or those who wish to remain in their existing multi-story home for whatever reason.

Regardless of their design, appeal and functionality, special attention and consideration should be given to the installation, maintenance and service of a private residence elevator, as a majority of municipalities or authorities having jurisdiction (AHJs) exempt private residence elevators from routine inspection and testing following initial acceptance, or exempt them altogether from state and municipal elevator safety laws and ordinances. Therefore, it should come as no surprise that some accidents and incidents involving private residence elevators and personal injury or death have drawn national media attention.

In spite of the above limitations and exemptions, manufacturers continually review their elevator designs to assure conformity with applicable safety code requirements to mitigate potential hazards and risks. However, not all installations conform to national, state, or local building and elevator safety codes, and as such, a seemingly harmless two or three stop elevator may become a significant hazard to unsuspecting riders and service technicians. For example, although residence elevators are specifically designed for installation and use in single-family private residences, they have been installed in churches, assembly halls, and commercial and industrial locations without suitable modification for public use, and therefore would not meet the intent of the elevator safety code for such applications.

Disabling or removal of safety devices by owners/users of private residence elevators have resulted in accidents, including fatal ones. For example, gate switches, which prevent the car from moving with the car door or gate open, have been disabled, space guards have been removed, car gates have been removed (found under a bed after one accident). Further complicating things is that many owners of private residence elevators do not have them regularly maintained and only have them fixed when they malfunction.

Among the most tragic accidents are those that involve young children who get trapped between the landing doors and the collapsible car gate or folding car door due to excessive clearances between them, which result in brain damage or death although the hazards have been known in the elevator industry since at least 1931 and more current building codes limiting baluster clearances to 4 inches based on anthropometric data of children. In many cases the doors and gates are not provided or installed by the elevator manufacturer and hoistways are poorly constructed and do not comply with applicable code requirements.

Initially, since the first edition of the A17 safety code (1921) private residence elevators had to meet the same requirements as commercial type elevators. Then ASME A17.1.5-1953 created a standalone new section for ASME A17.1 that applied only to private residence elevators and it was incorporated into ASME A17.1-1955. This included limiting the distance between car door and the landing sill to 2 inches and limiting the clearance between the landing doors and the car gate or door to 4 inches. However, ASME A17.1-1981 increased the permitted clearances to 3 inches and 5 inches respectively. Subsequently, the introduction of folding car doors, created situations where the installed clearances significantly exceeded even these relaxed limits due to the spaces (aka "valleys") formed by the folds of the door panels. Recently, ASME A17.1 has reduced the permitted clearances to account for anthropometric data for children.

The number of children seriously injured or killed may never be fully known due to protective orders and destruction of documentation. One major manufacturer reported that 34 children were injured or killed from 1983 to 1993 in New Jersey and southern New York State alone and notified building owners and offered free space guards to address the hazard.

Accidents involving private residence elevators may include one or more of the following reasons:

- Defective design in one or more of the system's components
- Misapplication of one or more of the system's components
- Improper installation or omission of one or more of the system's components
- Improper maintenance or omission of maintenance
- Improper operation, abuse or misuse
- Ignorance
- Failure to comply with adopted safety codes
- Failure to provide sufficient warning of an impending hazard and/or operating instructions
- External factors outside the control of the manufacturer or intended application that may include acts of God
- Failure to monitor or supervise or suitably restrict use and operation

As previously mentioned in other sections, all the possible types of accidents cannot be contained in this single treatise. Nonetheless the following list of some accidents involving private residence elevators serves as a reminder that things are not always as they appear:

- On Christmas Eve in 2010 a three year old boy in Georgia became trapped between the swinging landing door and the folding car door due to excessive clearances. The elevator moved in response to a call from another landing and the boy's chest was crushed in the small space between the car sill and the bottom landing sill depriving him of oxygen before emergency responders could free him using the "jaws of life". He suffered permanent brain damage. This led to a safety notice being issued by the State of Georgia recommending all private residence elevators to be inspected to verify that they meet applicable code clearance requirements and installing space guards if found non-compliant.
- A private residence elevator was installed in a rental property in Myrtle Beach, SC despite the applicable code prohibiting this. A 10 year old boy was seriously injured during a family reunion at the property, which resulted in him becoming quadriplegic with catastrophic brain damage due to the lack of oxygen when his crest was crushed in the small space

between the car sill and landing sill. His upper body was found lying on the floor of the cab while his head was under the platform. Incredibly, the elevator manufacturer designed the elevator such that it could move even if the folding car door was open under certain conditions. During subsequent investigation, it was determined that the elevator would run continuously up and down the hoistway with the car door open when the emergency alarm was pressed and a car call button was pressed.

- A private residence elevator was installed in a church in New York despite the applicable code prohibiting this. Parishioners were using the elevator in 2009 when it descended uncontrolled into the pit. Subsequent investigation determined that the car safeties, which are required to prevent free fall, failed to function when the winding drum worm gear (similar to a spur gear) could no longer mechanically hold the elevator due to it being significantly worn out in its center in a "spooning effect" by the worm (screw gear) due to the lack of lubrication.
- In 2002 two girls, aged 6 and 7, of a groundskeeper at a multimillion dollar home were killed on a private residence elevator in New Jersey. The elevator was able to run with the car gate open and the girls were reportedly lying down in the car with their heads partially past the car sill and their heads became wedged as the car ascended. The gate switch, which prevents the elevator from running with the car or gate open, was reportedly found taped over.
- An elderly couple in Georgia dies from dehydration in their residential elevator after it malfunctions while they are home alone. A post-accident investigation revealed that the elevator had a history of malfunctions and did not include a telephone for emergency use. Pursuant to ASME A17.1, private residence elevators shall include a telephone connected to a central telephone exchange. The absence of a telephone was determined to have caused or contributed to this incident.
- An unattended young boy in Texas was almost strangled by a descending elevator. A post-accident investigation revealed that the elevator was installed in an existing and historic private residence, but no steps were taken by the installer or homeowner to reduce the space between the landing doors and elevator. Further, the distance between the hoistway face of the landing doors and elevator car gate exceeded 24 inches; and the car gate electric contact located on top of the elevator did not include a guard to ensure the contact was positively opened by the elevator car gate. Pursuant to the applicable ASME A17.1 the car gate electric contact shall be positively opened by a lever or other device attached to the car door or gate, and shall prevent the operation of the

elevator unless the door or gate is within 2 inches of the closed position; and the distance between the hoistway face of the landing door and elevator car gate shall not exceed 5 inches. The 24-inch space between the landing door and car gate permitted the young boy to stand on the landing threshold as the elevator descended with the car gate open and his sibling relatives inside. The boy subsequently attempted to enter the elevator and got his head and neck caught between the landing threshold sill and elevator door header. If it were not for the quick thinking and actions of the sibling relatives which raised and suspended the boy's body until help arrived, the boy would have most certainly suffered fatal injuries. Improper installation of the elevator and the absence of a guard on the car gate electric contact and landing door space guards were determined to have caused or contributed to this incident.

- A young girl in Pennsylvania is fatally injured when she is caught between an ascending elevator and landing entranceway. A post-accident investigation revealed that the distance between the hoistway face of the landing door and elevator car gate exceeded 7 inches. The excessive distance between the hoistway face of the landing door and car gate and the absence of landing door space guards was determined to have caused or contributed to this incident.
- A church facility maintenance person in Pennsylvania is seriously injured when the private residence elevator in which he is riding fails catastrophically and falls three floors into the elevator pit. A post-accident investigation revealed that the elevator service provider failed to examine, lubricate and test the elevator's safety system and suspension means during routine maintenance and service. Accordingly, the elevator's suspension means, which is comprised of wire ropes and sheaves (pulleys), failed catastrophically after a metal shaft that supported one of the suspension sheaves became severely worn and failed due to lack of field lubrication. This incident was exacerbated by the fact that the elevator's instantaneous mechanical safeties were defective. As such, the elevator fell into the elevator pit without the benefit of the safeties which are intended to stop and hold the elevator if the suspension means fails. Ironically, the elevator's suspension means had been previously repaired and replaced, but the safeties were not subsequently tested to ensure fail-safe operation pursuant to ASME A17.1. The failure and negligence of the service provider to provide sufficient warning of an impending hazard, and failure to provide routine examination, lubrication and testing the elevator's safety system and suspension means to ensure proper fail-safe operation, was determined to have caused or contributed to this incident.

- An unattended infant girl from Missouri is seriously injured when she falls two floors when the elevator she was riding malfunctions due to construction and service wiring defects. A post-accident investigation revealed that the girl was vacationing with her family and grandparents in a beach-front rental property in South Carolina that included a private residence elevator. The family, homeowner and leasing agent were unaware that the elevator equipment installer/service provider had improperly adjusted the car gate and its electric contact, and thereafter by-passed the electrical wiring in the hoistway door interlocks. As such, the elevator was defective and would operate with the car gate open. Given that the girl was too small to open the landing door, she apparently walked off the elevator platform at the second floor or stood on the landing sill as the elevator ascended with the car gate open, and then fell down the elevator shaft after the elevator passed. Although the infant girl was unattended at the time of the incident, the failure and negligence of the elevator installer/service provider to identify and correct defective equipment conditions, provide sufficient warning of an impending hazard, and comply with the manufacturer's specifications and adopted safety codes was determined to having caused or contributed to this incident.
- An unoccupied private residence elevator in Illinois malfunctions and then fails catastrophically when the anchor bolts which secure the elevator driving machine pullout of the concrete floor. A post-accident investigation revealed that the elevator installer failed to provide and install the correct concrete anchors and a machine isolation system for the elevator driving machine. As such, the elevator fell and stopped abruptly on its mechanical car safeties when the driving machine pulled up and out of the concrete floor and became wedged between the machine room wall and ceiling. The failure and negligence of the elevator installer to comply with the manufacturer's specifications and adopted safety codes was determined to have caused or contributed to this incident.
- An elevator service provider employee/technician in New York seriously injured while servicing an electric traction private residence elevator located in a veterinary clinic. A post-accident investigation revealed that the equipment owner failed to have the elevator inspected by the AHJ in accordance with local ordinances; that the subject suspension ropes had been previously replaced by another local elevator service provider who secured the suspension ropes to the elevator's counterweight by U-bolt clamps; and that suspension ropes, which support the elevator

car enclosure and counterweight assembly, separated from the counterweight assembly while the elevator was being examined by a local service mechanic during a service call. The mechanic was unaware that the suspension ropes had been secured to the elevator's counterweight assembly via U-bolt rope clamps (a practice which has been prohibited by ASME A17.1 since 1955) and that the elevator's instantaneous safeties would not stop and hold the elevator should its suspension means fail.

In this case, two $^{3}/_{8}$-inch diameter suspension ropes were secured to the elevator car by Babbitted sockets and then routed over and around numerous idler sheaves (pulleys), deflector sheaves, and a driving sheave before they were secured to the elevator's counterweight assembly by four U-bolt rope clamps. The U-bolt clamps were secured to a compensating hitch plate that was secured to the counterweight assembly by two eyebolts and two steel pins which passed through the eyebolts, and were held in place via cotter pins and flat washers. The U-bolt clamps also included rope thimbles which passed through and wrapped around the eyebolt to support the rope and prevent deformation. Further, the subject elevator driving machine was located adjacent to the elevator at the ground floor, and the elevator suspension ropes were routed over and around numerous idler and deflector sheaves (pulleys) before they were connected to the elevator car and counterweight. This configuration produced rotational and twisting forces on the eyebolts, ropes, and U-bolt clamps (fastenings) and ultimately caused one eyebolt and two U-bolt clamps to become loose and unbalance the tension of one suspension rope. Thereafter the remaining rope and its fastenings experienced additional loading and rotational forces (previously shared by the second rope), which caused the eyebolt assembly to experience unusual twisting. This action compromised one of the eyebolts and caused it to become separated from the counterweight assembly, as the eyebolt did not possess a cotter pin to prevent its anchor nut and safety nut from becoming loose and unthreaded. When this occurred, the weight of the elevator and counterweight were suspended by the remaining rope, steel pin and cotter pin which were subsequently pulled through the eyebolt causing the suspension ropes to become separated from the counterweight. Thereafter the suspension ropes, which were still attached to the elevator and routed around and over the deflector sheaves, idler sheaves and driving sheave, permitted the elevator to gradually descend into the elevator pit where the mechanic was working. Although the elevator did possess instantaneous car safeties, they failed to stop and hold the elevator when the counterweight suspension means failed. Ironically, this incident could have been easily prevented by the use of adjustable tapered Babbitted shackles or sockets or wedge clamp sockets, as these devices would have eliminated the use of four U-bolt rope clamps, two rope thimbles, two eyebolts, two steel rods, four flat washers, and four cotter pins. Further, as the tapered Babbitted shackles or sockets or wedge clamp sockets are independent of each other, the elevator would not experience a complete failure and separation of the suspension means should one socket or rope fail and separate. The failure and negligence of the equipment owner, elevator manufacturer and local service provider to comply with local ordinances, national safety codes, and adopted safety codes was attributed to have caused or contributed to this incident.

I. Platform (Wheelchair) Lifts and Staircase Chairlifts

1. Introduction

The main purpose of this section is to provide a brief history of platform (wheelchair) and stairway chairlifts, and their intended installation, and further describe the types of and causes of platform (wheelchair) and stairway chairlift accidents. This section and writing will revolve around commercial and residential vertical and incline platform (wheelchair) lifts.

2. Platform (wheelchair) lifts

Platform (wheelchair) and stairway chairlifts have been manufactured and installed throughout the United States for many years pursuant to various accessibility standards which include ICC/ANSI A17.1 Standard on Accessible and Usable Buildings and Facilities; the Rehabilitation Act, Section 504 (1973); and the Americans with Disabilities Act (1990). While the above standards were initially intended to eliminate discrimination against people with disabilities in programs or activities receiving Federal funding, it became apparent that platform (wheelchair) and stairway chairlifts provided a means to eliminate in many instances physical barriers preventing access to the physically disabled (see Section 1.4 for ADA issues).

Here again, platform (wheelchair) and stairway chairlifts are rather simple mechanisms comprised of unsophisticated but varied driving machines (e.g., screw, winding drum, hydraulic); a basic lift platform; swing-style car gate; sometimes a folding ramp; constant pressure push button control; swing-style landing gates; and limited safety devices. These lifts are also limited by size, speed, rise and load, and are only intended to be used by persons that are physically disabled pursuant to ASME A17.1 and subsequently ASME A18.1.

Since their inception, platform (wheelchair) and stairway chairlifts have evolved technologically to include soft start and variable speed motor control, attendant operation, microprocessor technology, low-impact power-operated landing gates, battery backup operation, and paneled (e.g., polycarbonate) enclosures. Given their functionality and intended use, their fits and finishes are becoming quite diversified and sophisticated to meet architectural needs and designs.

Accidents involving platform (wheelchair) and stairway chairlifts may be due to one or more of the following reasons:

- Defective design in one or more of the system's components
- Misapplication of one or more of the system's components
- Improper installation or omission of one or more of the system's components
- Improper maintenance or omission of maintenance
- Improper operation, abuse or misuse
- Ignorance
- Failure to comply with adopted safety codes
- Failure to provide sufficient warning of an impending hazard and/or operating instructions
- External factors outside the control of the manufacturer or intended application that may include acts of God
- Failure to monitor or supervise or suitably restrict use and operation

As previously mentioned in other sections, all the possible types of accidents cannot be contained in a single treatise. Nonetheless the following list of accidents involving platform (wheelchair) and stairway chairlifts serves as a reminder that things are not always as they appear:

- A physically disabled man in Missouri was injured when he fell from the upper landing of a vertical platform lift in his wheelchair. A post-accident investigation revealed that the lift was installed in a commercial office building in conformity with national and local building and safety codes including ASME A17.1; that the man's judgment was significantly impaired at the time of the incident; and, that the lift's manually operated upper landing gate interlock had been disabled which permitted the gate to be openable when the lift was absent from the landing. The failure and negligence of the building owner/manager to comply with the manufacturer's specifications and adopted safety codes including ASME A17.1 and ASME A18.1 was attributed to have caused or contributed to this incident.

- A severely disabled girl in Missouri injured when she fell from the upper landing of a vertical platform lift that had been installed in her parent's private residence. A post-accident investigation revealed that the wheelchair bound girl and her father/attendant fell while attempting to enter the lift through the upper landing doorway. The subject lift was installed by a local lift dealer/installer, and was not installed in conformity with national, state or local building and safety codes including ASME A17.1. Further, the upper landing door included an electric strike and passage lock that were not properly installed. Hence the landing door was openable when the lift was absent from the landing. The failure and negligence of the local lift dealer/installer to comply with the manufacturer's specifications and adopted safety codes was attributed to have caused or contributed to this incident.
- An elderly woman in Missouri sustains fatal injuries when the outdoor vertical platform lift in which she was a passenger fails catastrophically. A post-accident investigation revealed that the lift had been originally installed out-of-doors at a private residence for several years before it was subsequently re-purchased by the original lift dealer/installer, who then re-sold it to the decedent's family. The dealer claimed to have examined and tested the lift before it was sold and re-installed at the decedent's residence by a member of her family. However, examination of the sales agreement and discovery materials in this matter revealed that the lift was sold and installed without the benefit of the manufacturer's installation manual or technical information, or knowledge of any applicable safety codes. Thereafter, the decedent used the outdoor lift for approximately two years without any reported incidents until the primary lifting means failed. Examination of the acme screw lifting means revealed that the primary plastic lift nut had become stripped and the bronze safety nut had become dislodged from its safety catch. Subsequently, the lift platform and decedent fell approximately 4 feet before striking the concrete pad to which the lift was anchored. These facts are important as ASME A17.1 and A18.1 require the safety nut to limit the distance in which the lift may fall to $^1/_2$-inch in the event that the driving means or drive nut fails. The failure and negligence of the lift dealer/installer to thoroughly examine and test the lift to determine nonconformity with the manufacturer's specifications and adopted safety codes was determined to have caused or contributed to this incident. Further, the failure and negligence of the lift manufacturer to design a fail-safe

lift nut and safety nut, and provide sufficient warning of an impending hazard was attributed to have caused or contributed to decedent's fatal injuries.

3. Stairway chairlifts

Stairway chairlifts covered by ASME A18.1 (previously covered by ASME A17.1) are not recognized by ICC/ANSI A117.1 and the ADA Standards as components of accessible routes. They are usually installed in private residences. They generally consist of a chair with a folding seat and footrest, a seat belt and two arm rests that travel on a runway along a stairway.

They are provided with a few basic safety devices. One of the most serious hazard is the crushing hazard created when the footrest comes in close proximity to the steps. This is especially true for young children.

ASME A18.1 requires a footrest obstruction device to stop the upward motion if an object is detected between the footrest and the step risers and nosings. However, in many cases the unit will not be able to run in either direction if this device is actuated. This typically will trap a child with no easy way to remove the crushing force. A similar hazard can result if a child is laying on the step treads when the unit is running down.

ASME A18.1 requires that a stairway chairlift be controlled from stations at each landing and the chair by continuous pressure type controls. However, portable remote controls have become common contrary to this code requirement. These portable remote controls increase the hazards to children.

ASME A18 (and ASME A17.1 previously) required inspections and tests by the AHJ. However, as with private residence elevators, many AHJs exempt stairway chairlifts from periodic inspections and tests following initial acceptance inspections and tests or exempt them altogether from inspections and tests.

J. Elevators Used for Construction, Personnel Hoists and Employee Elevators

Elevators used for construction are governed by ASME A17.1. This classification applies to elevators temporarily used for construction or demolition to provide transportation for construction personnel, tools and materials only. In effect, it is a special application of a regular elevator. Inspections by the AHJ are required by ASME A17.1 on a more frequent basis than when the elevator is in normal use. Accidents related to these elevators will generally share many of the characteristics of elevators, but will have distinct characteristics. General causes of accidents will be similar.

Personnel hoists and employee elevators are covered by ANSI/ASSE A10.4 Safety Requirements for Personnel Hoists and Employee Elevators on Construction and Demolition Sites.[15] This standard applies to the design, construction, installation, operation, inspection, testing, maintenance, alteration and repair of hoists and elevators that are not an integral part of buildings, are installed inside or outside buildings or structures during construction, alteration, demolition operations and are used to raise and lower workers and other personnel connected with or related to the structure. They may also be used for transporting materials under specific circumstances defined in the standard. Accidents related to these devices will have distinct characteristics from those of elevators used for construction, but general causes will be similar. These devices are beyond the scope of this book.

4.4 Escalator Accident Causes

The general reasons for accidents that were outlined earlier (improper design, improper maintenance, improper operation, abuse or misuse, misapplication, improper installation, insufficient warning, and external factors) apply to escalators as well as elevators. The main differences will be in the specific causes, since the equipment is very different.

Moving walks are susceptible to some of the same types of accidents as escalators, because of their similar construction. However, since there usually is little or no difference in height between the ends of a moving walk, they are far less susceptible to injuries from falls. Also, the lack of relative motion of the standing surfaces greatly limits their susceptibility to certain injuries from entrapments that occur on escalators.

The following sections will explain the various causes for escalator accidents. In general, most escalator accidents are related to either trips and falls or entrapment of body parts. However, there are many different causes within these two broad categories. Although the vast majority of escalator accidents are related to trips and falls, the most serious escalator accidents are related to entrapment of body parts. Entrapments have resulted in amputations, degloving injuries, disfigurements, scalpings, and deaths. Tragically, the victims are usually young children.

For many years, A17.1 has required that certain safety devices require a manual reset before the escalator can restart. This occurred after a woman became entrapped inside an escalator when the step she was standing on collapsed and the safety devices kept resetting because the start switch was stuck in the starting position. Similarly the starting switch requirements were changed so that the escalator would not start unless the starting switches were in a neutral position.

A. Signage

For many years ASME A17.1 and A17.3 has required that caution signs be located at each landing. This caution sign is shown in Figure D.3 in Chapter 2. It contains the words CAUTION, PASSENGERS ONLY, HOLD HANDRAIL, ATTEND CHILDREN, and AVOID SIDES. In addition there are two pictographs contained on the sign. The first pictograph, which has been required for many years, corresponds to the written cautions. The second pictograph, added a number of years ago, is intended to denote that wheeled vehicles are prohibited. CAN/CSA B44 required this symbol in Canada for a number of years prior to it being adopted by A17.1.

No standard location has been established for the required signs, except that they must be located at the top and bottom of each escalator and must be readily visible to boarding passengers. Sometimes this can result in the signs not being easily read and comprehended. Commonly the sign consists of a decal applied either to the balustrades or the inner decking of the escalator, but it can be otherwise constructed and displayed.

There has been considerable debate whether this type of caution sign is adequate or effective. The sign was originally added to the A17 Code after a request from the Consumer Product Safety Commission (CPSC) many years ago. Some argue that a more appropriate sign would indicate "WARNING" instead of "CAUTION" and add the safety alert symbol (an equilateral triangle with an exclamation point inside it) among other changes to make the sign fully conform to newer safety signage standards (ANSI Z535.2[4] and ANSI Z535.4[5]) versus older signage (OSHA[3]). In general, there are three increasing levels of hazard situations that safety signs must convey: caution, warning and danger. In general, *caution* is used to denote a hazardous condition that if not avoided could result in minor or moderate injury, while *warning* is used to denote a hazardous condition that if not avoided could result in death or serious injury. *Danger* is used to denote a hazardous condition that will result in death or injury if not avoided.

The equipment owners may at their discretion install additional signs or warnings. These may include posting signs or voice messages. The code states the minimum requirements. Depending on the circumstances, other signs may be required simply as "good and accepted practice." For example, a readily seen sign can be placed near the escalator, directing the aged and less agile to the location of the elevator. However, later versions of the A17.1 Code restrict the location and content of additional signs in order to prevent them from distracting passengers.

Recently, the code began allowing signage on escalator and moving walk handrails. The handrails are a highly visible location for safety information, and handrail signage gives the passenger cues to handrail speed and direction. Studies have shown that passengers are far more likely to notice handrail signage than other signs. However, for many years escalator handrails have been available with markings e.g. (diamonds or dots) to provide a visible cue for handrail speed and direction, which likely would be less distracting than advertising. Typically handrails with these markings cost more than those without them, but advertising can generate revenue.

It must be recognized that for any warning or caution to be effective, it must be readily comprehended and obeyed. This places responsibilities on both those doing the warning/cautioning and those being warned/cautioned. Signs can prevent accidents and can be more effective when workers and passengers are made aware of the meaning of the signage. The awareness factor comes from training workers through programs such as NEIEP (National Elevator Industry Educational Program) and NEII (National Elevator Industry Inc.) safety programs. Public awareness is taught by programs such as the elevator industry programs reaching out mostly to second graders and senior citizens called the EESF (Elevator Escalator Safety Foundation).

B. Trips and Falls

Trips and falls result in the vast majority of escalator accidents. However, there are many different causes for these accidents.

1. Handrail-related

If an escalator's handrail is moving at a substantially slower speed than the steps or stops moving, then those who are holding the handrail must reposition their hands throughout the ride; otherwise their upper bodies will move backward in relation to their feet. This is especially dangerous on an ascending escalator, since a person will fall backwards down the incline. The elderly seem to be particularly at risk, because they have a tendency to hold on to the handrail even tighter as they sense they are falling. Ironically, these persons are complying with the HOLD HANDRAIL directions of the code-required caution sign.

ASME A17.1 presently requires a handrail-speed monitoring device that is required to shut down an escalator and apply the driving machine brake if the handrail is moving significantly (more than 15 percent) above or below the speed of the steps continuously within a 2–6 second range. It is noted that an escalator traveling at 90 fpm moves a person 1.5 feet (18 inches) in only 1 second. Therefore, it is possible for people to lose their balance before the device activates. Some earlier code versions required that the device work after only 2 seconds, which reportedly caused inadvertent shutdowns of the equipment. Other earlier code versions required only a stopped-handrail device, which was required to shut down an escalator only if the handrail stopped (for more than 15 seconds).

These devices are not required retroactively and most existing escalators do not have these devices. However, many years before the code required these devices, some manufacturers did provide devices that would sense if a handrail drive chain or the handrail were excessively slack or broken, which could cause the handrail to stop.

For a number of years ASME A17.1 has included requirements for the minimum force that the handrail drive system must overcome.

2. Transporting objects

The transportation of wheelchairs, baby strollers, freight and other bulky or heavy objects on escalators has resulted in trips and falls. If the object somehow becomes stationary between the entrance and exit points (wedged between the balustrades for example) then the other persons riding the escalator behind them are subsequently forced into them by the moving steps with predictable results.

As indicated above, the code-required caution sign states in part PASSENGERS ONLY. This cautionary note is intended to warn riders not to bring these types of objects on the escalator. However, one only has to go to any mall to see parents taking baby strollers on escalators, or an airport to see luggage carts transported on escalators. In two other cases, passengers tried to transport a baby grand piano and a mall-vending cart down an escalator. These large objects became caught in a narrow opening and were destroyed in one case and became stuck in the other. Luckily no one was hurt in either case, but the potential was there for serious injuries, because of thoughtless actions.

The code-required caution does not appear to be effective. Apparently, it is too vague, not understood, or ignored. Also, in most cases signs are not provided near escalators directing passenger to an elevator as an alternate means of vertical transportation, thereby contributing to the problem. The A17.1 Code currently also has a pictograph intended to covey that the transportation of wheeled vehicles on escalators is not permitted (see Photo D3 in Chapter 2). CAN/CSA B44 required this symbol in Canada for a number of years prior to it being adopted by A17.1.

3. Sudden stops

Sudden stops by an escalator are a common cause of falls by passengers on the escalator. The cause of the escalator's stopping can be a power supply failure, someone activating the emergency stop switches located at each landing, or one of the escalator's internal safety devices.

If a power failure is the cause, then there will be no warning to the passengers on the escalator that it is about to stop. If this is the cause of the escalator's stopping, it likely will be readily evident because it most likely will have affected other equipment in the building.

Emergency stop switches (buttons) are located either near the landing floor where the handrail enters and exits for many existing escalators or in a more accessible position (either on the balustrade or on a post) for most escalators that have been installed during the last 30 years. In the former case, the switch is located such that anyone using it would likely have to get on his knees. This location is usually a deterrent to inadvertent activation, but it also makes the switch very difficult to find and use in an emergency. In the latter case, the A17 Code requires that a cover be provided over the accessible switches as a protection against inadvertent activation. It also requires that an alarm sound when the cover is lifted, supposedly to alert passengers on the unit. But the alarm may not provide its intended warning since passengers on the escalator most likely will not know its significance (i.e., there is no requirement for any signage related to the alarm) or ambient noise levels may make the alarm difficult to hear. If the emergency stop switch was the cause of the escalator's stopping it will be more readily evident (i.e., alarm sounding or someone kneeling near the newel) than if an internal safety switch had been activated.

A number of electrical safety devices are present on escalators, many of which are required by code. These safety devices will shut off power to the escalator's driving machine and apply its brake. Since the activation of these devices is usually the result of an abnormal condition, which could result in an accident or major equipment damage, a delay in activation of the brake is not permitted by code. Most of these safety devices are located internally and not accessible to the general public. When any of these safety devices activate, usually no warning is given to passengers riding on the escalator. However, some of these devices are vulnerable to inadvertent activation as a result of improper maintenance or installation of the devices, or misuse or abuse by passengers.

Many existing escalators have no means of providing a controlled stop of the escalator. For many years the ASME A17.1 Code has required that the deceleration resulting from the activation of the driving machine brake be limited. However, proper adjustment of the brake is essential to achieve this maximum deceleration. In many cases retrofitting existing escalators with a controlled stop brake is not only feasible, but readily available and is certainly a good and accepted practice.

Controlled stop braking has been required with the adoption of the ASME A17.1-1983 code. The service brake is required to stop the escalator, running usually at a speed of 90 or 100 feet per minute, not instantly but with approximately five inch slide of the steps. However this code rule like most all of the code rules is the minimum standard for safety. Most manufacturers require a slide of 9 to 11 inches when the brake is actuated stopping the escalator. This will resulted in much smother stop and not likely to cause a passenger to fall.

All escalators are required by code to be equipped with a service brake (driving machine brake), generally an integral part of the drive unit located at the top of the escalator. On many escalators the drive unit connects to the step drive sprocket axle with a drive chain as the method to propel the steps. The drive chain is equipped with a switch that when activated due to excessive slack in the chain or broken chain will cause the service brake to set and the power be removed from the escalator. It will also set the emergency/safety brake on the escalator if so equipped. This will cause the stop to be more abrupt than if only the service brake trips. Generally only the slack drive chain switch or an overspeed condition will cause both brakes to set simultaneously. Any other safety switch generally will set the emergency brake seconds after the escalator stops and in those cases its primary purpose would then be to prevent the escalator from moving when people walk on a stationary escalator. Other escalators use belts to connect the driving machine motor and the gear reducer. A switch must be provided that will set the service brake if the belts break or there is excessive slack in the belts.

4. Disorientation

Falls may occur on escalators because of disorientation due to optical effects. In essence, when a repeating pattern exists, the human eye can be fooled into focusing such that depth perception is impaired (i.e., objects seem to be closer than they actually are, aka "the wallpaper effect").[6,7]

The surface of escalator step treads has a repeating alternation between cleats and slots. The slots are relatively deep compared to their width, which under certain lighting conditions creates a dark shadow in the slots. In addition, some manufacturers paint the bottom of the slots a dark color, thereby increasing the contrast between the cleat surfaces and the slot surfaces. The degree of disorientation can be remarkable under certain conditions.

5. Falls over the side

Another type of fall on escalators occurs when a passenger loses her balance and falls sideways over the top of the handrail many feet to the floor below. This typically occurs on escalators that do not have walls adjacent to them (e.g., in the common areas of malls). This usually results in serious injury or death. In many cases the passenger is intoxicated or otherwise impaired. However, it is possible for riders in full possession of their faculties to be forced over the side of the escalator through no fault of their own.

The handrail's height is usually at or below hip level, which makes people prone to losing their balance over the side of the escalator. Since 2002, the A17.1 code has required a handrail height of 35 to 39 inches. In comparison, OSHA requires that a guardrail be provided at 42-inch height where there is a hazard of falls.

The ASME A17.1 Code currently requires that floor openings adjacent to the entire length of the wellway be guarded in accordance with the local building code. Most building codes do not have provisions to prevent falls over the side of an escalator. However, some building owners and managers have provided guarding (see Chapter 2, Figure D.23) to correct this deficiency.[8]

6. Passenger misuse

Improper actions by passengers on escalators have resulted in injuries to themselves or other riders. These actions have included horseplay, facing backward, not holding the handrail, and walking in the opposite direction of the escalator's travel. If evidence exists that these actions occurred, then some, if not all, of the blame can be placed on the rider. However, it seems that the common refrain in defense of escalator accidents is to reflexively blame the victim without any substantive proof and as a catch-all excuse. Although injuries from falls can be the fault of someone riding the escalator improperly, the rider's conduct does not excuse entrapment injuries that result after such a fall.

7. Trips

Walking on stationary escalators is another cause of trips and falls. The steps at the entrance and exit ends are not of uniform height, since they have to articulate from the inclined to the flat position and vice versa. In addition, the height of step risers on the incline do not meet the requirement for stairs. This creates a known tripping hazard. For this reason, escalators are not permitted to be used as a required means of egress in most building codes anymore. More serious problems exist for persons walking on moving escalators. ASME A17.1 has for a number of years required that there be two flat steps at each landing entrance/exit.

8. Brake failures and reversals

Escalators used as stationary stairs can also be subject to crush loads, especially in arenas and stadiums. The cadence of people walking on the steps creates dynamic loadings in addition to the weight of the people. This can result in a condition in which the brake cannot hold the resulting load. The escalator will pull through the brake until it has dumped enough persons off at the bottom landing for the brake to stop the escalator and hold it again. This can result in a pileup of persons at the bottom landing. Once the escalator starts to move, very little force is needed to overcome any friction since an escalator with no passengers is a 100 percent counterbalanced mechanism.

The ASME A17.1 Code requires each escalator brake to have a capacity based on the width of the steps and the geometry of the escalator. A running capacity and a higher stationary capacity are required. Recently, ASME A17.1 increased the brake capacity (static) significantly to account for more realistic static loading. Other escalator codes (EN 115 for example) and standards (APTA Heavy-Duty Escalator Guidelines[9] for example), which these same manufacturers design some equipment to meet, require higher minimum brake capacities than A17.1. Typical causes for an escalator brake failing to hold the required loadings are: improper adjustment of the braking capacity and the braking capacity being degraded due to improper maintenance (e.g., the brake pads becoming glazed over from dragging).

Sudden reversal of ascending escalators can also occur, which can also result in a pileup of riders at the bottom landing. The ASME A17.1 Code requires that a reversal stop device detect the reversal of an ascending escalator and then shut off the escalator and set the driving machine brake. There are many different designs for this device, some more effective than others.

However, conditions can develop that will prevent this device from stopping the escalator at all. For example, if the main drive shaft connection to the main drive sprocket (commonly referred to as the "bull gear") fails, then the brake will in many cases be prevented from stopping the escalator.

9. Losing balance

Some persons are prone to falls on inclined surfaces, such as stairs, and falls on stationary stairs are common. It is not surprising, therefore, that falls on moving steps are prevalent, even when the steps and handrails are running at the same speed.

Most escalators travel at a speed of 90 feet per minute (fpm), although speeds of up to 125 fpm have been permitted. However, a number of escalators have been retrofitted to run slower than the normal 90 fpm, in order to help the less agile passengers keep their balance. Newer escalators travel at 100 fpm.

C. Entrapments

Entrapments of body parts in the moving parts of escalators result in serious injuries to both maintenance mechanics and passengers. It must be remembered that passengers on escalators are in close contact with many moving components of the escalator. There are many different causes for these accidents, but the components most likely to be involved are the handrail, the steps, the skirt panels and the combplate or combs.

1. Handrail-related

Escalator handrails are c-shaped. A small clearance exists between the handrail stand, which supports the handrail, and the edges of the handrail. ASME A17.1 has for a number of years limited this clearance, which increases as the handrail wears, but this requirement is not applicable for most existing escalators although the hazard is well known. Fingers, especially those of small children, can get into this space. This is not usually a problem until the handrail approaches a landing, when the clearance is drastically reduced. Serious injuries have resulted from this type of entrapment when a child's hand is forced into the opening of the balustrade. It is eye opening watching a security video of this type of entrapment. No signs are required to warn of this hazard. In fact, the code-required caution sign states HOLD HANDRAIL, but it is questionable whether signs would be effective.

The point where the handrails enter the escalator balustrade creates an opening in which young children's hands and arms are prone to be caught. Guards are required to be installed at these locations, but they become worn or dislodged over time. In addition, the handrails for most escalators are extended past the entrances and exits to discourage access to the handrail inlet areas. The ASME A17.1 Code now requires that a handrail entry device be provided to shut the escalator off and apply the driving machine brake if something gets caught in the space between the guard and the handrail. Many manufacturers provided this device long before it was required by code. However, many existing escalators do not have this safety device. The A17.1 code does not require signs to warn of this hazard, but it is questionable whether a warning sign would be effective, because the victims are usually unattended young children.

2. Broken or missing steps

Serious injuries or deaths can occur when step frames, components, rollers or axles are cracked or broken. This is another form of escalator entrapment, and perhaps the most serious. Riders fall inside the moving equipment when the step they are standing on fails to support them or they step into an opening created by a missing step. While these occurrences are not common, they have happened. The authors know of two cases that occurred a number of years apart, in which the same mechanic was maintaining two different types of escalators made by the same manufacturer (a coincidence perhaps?). Some designs are much more susceptible to this type of accident than others. Relatively simple design changes can help prevent someone standing on the step from falling into the escalator because of a failure of the step support components. Proper maintenance is essential in preventing these types of accidents.

The step structure can be weakened by improper maintenance, improper design, metal fatigue, manufacturing defects, or damage during improper usage of the escalator (such as from heavy objects being transported on the escalator). Periodic internal inspections of the steps are required by code to help insure the structural integrity of the steps. However visual inspections are not always conclusive in determining damage to the step frames and axles. While more sophisticated methods of determining the structural integrity of steps are available, they are rarely applied during periodic inspections. Usually they are performed only after a serious accident occurs.

The ASME A17.1 Code presently requires that a device be provided to detect whether a step is missing, which will shut off an escalator and apply the driving machine brake before the resulting opening emerges from the landings. Most existing escalators do not have this device. Also, it only detects a missing step, not one that will collapse if someone steps on it.

3. Between-step entrapments

The interface between the riser of a step and the tread of an adjacent step is an area that is prone to entrapment of body parts and shoes. Many older escalator steps have smooth risers. The ASME 17.1 Code limits the clearance ($^5/_{32}$-inch maximum) between the smooth step risers and the adjacent slotted step treads. This type of riser drastically increases the probability of entrapments between the steps. The ASME A17.1 Code has required cleated step risers for many years, and the cleats in the step risers must mesh with the slots in the adjacent step treads. This drastically reduces the probability of objects getting caught between the steps, provided that wear has not increased the gap such that the riser cleats no longer mesh with the step treads.

Excessive clearance between adjacent steps, either with cleated or smooth risers, is frequently caused by wear or damage to components, such as step-chain link bushings which causes the step chains to elongate. Another common cause is when step risers are dented. Recently, and unfortunately with increasing frequency, steps have been manufactured where the risers simply will not mesh with adjacent step treads. Objects such as children's fingers and shoes can then fit into these excessive clearances, especially on the incline portion of the escalator. It should be noted that these clearances are greater when the escalator is running than when it is at rest. This is because the step chains that propel the steps will be in tension when running, but relaxed when stationary. Where the steps articulate from the incline to the flat position, the relative motion of one step to another tends to draw any objects between them further inward. As the steps reach the landings, the clearances are reduced and any objects lodged between the steps will be subject to crushing and shearing at the combplate.

The ASME A17.1 Code requires that a step upthrust device be provided to shut down the escalator and apply the driving machine brake if a step fails to make the transition from the inclined to flat position at the lower landing correctly. Generally, a track is provided close to a microswitch. If the step fails to make the transition properly, for example, because an object is caught between the steps, then a part of the step assembly (e.g., a roller or tab) will be forced into the track, which in turn will activate the microswitch. Different manufacturers use different designs to achieve this, and some designs are more effective than others. Many manufacturers provide this device at both landings.

Proper maintenance is essential to prevent these excessive clearances from developing. The life expectancies of step chains depends on the operating conditions and lubrication. Proper lubrication delays wear and extends the life expectancies of these components considerably. However, a buildup of foreign matter can prevent the lubricants from reaching the wear-prone components, and rapid deterioration may occur. Therefore, keeping the step chains clean of foreign matter is essential. In most cases excessive elongation can only be corrected by replacing the step chains, which is relatively expensive. Replacement of the step chains is often included in the maintenance contract. However, if the contract is nearing expiration, many contractors will try to delay replacing the step chains until the contract expires and therefore will no longer be their responsibility.

The A17.1 code now requires that three edges of the step be marked with yellow lines, including the one between a step and the adjacent riser. This helps alert passengers to the potential entrapment area and, it is hoped, causes them to stand away from these areas. Some manufacturers have provided similar markings for many years, and in at least one case a building owner marked steps with footprints to indicate the correct position in which to stand.

4. Combplate entrapments

The stationary metal plates at each escalator landing under which the moving steps enter and exit is known as the combplate. Attached to the combplate are metal or plastic sections known as combs. These combs have multiple teeth (sometimes referred to as fingers), are detachable, and are adjustable vertically.

The purpose of the combs is to transfer objects from the moving steps to the stationary combplate. It is a very effective device if properly installed and maintained.

The comb teeth must be meshed with the slots in each step's tread surface so that the points of the comb teeth are always below the top of the step tread surfaces. The step tread slots are required by code to have a minimum depth. Most manufacturers require that the comb teeth be set at least halfway, 3/16 inches below the top of the step tread surface, but the exact amount varies among manufacturers.

If the escalator is not installed or maintained correctly, then objects, such as shoes, can become caught between the top of the step tread surface and the bottom of the combplate. Injuries related to combplate entrapments have included strangulations, amputations, and scalpings. This type of entrapment can occur from a number of causes, including the following:

- A comb section is set too high in relation to the steps, such that a clearance exists between the bottom of the comb teeth and the step tread surfaces. See chapter 2, photo D8B
- Worn or damaged step rollers or tracks and step chain rollers or tracks permit a clearance between one or more step treads and the bottom of the comb teeth.
- The comb teeth are designed to break if they come in contact with the steps. This prevents damage to the steps, which are relatively expensive in comparison to a comb section. The comb teeth therefore are prone to being broken by a number of other causes, such as impact loads or improper adjustment of the step guidance. Broken comb teeth create an opening or clearance between the bottom of the combplate and the step tread surfaces.
- Damaged step treads permit objects to get under the comb teeth. The comb section is broken in half horizontally due to an impact of a moving step. When this happens only the half that contains the screw exists.

The ASME A17.1 Code now requires that a comb-step impact device be provided at each landing of an escalator. This device is required to shut off the escalator and apply the driving machine brake if an excessive horizontal force in the direction of travel or a vertical upward force is applied to the combplate. The maximum horizontal forces permitted have been substantially increased from when this provision was first added to the code (112 pounds at each side of the combplate or 250 pounds in its center) to shortly afterwards (400 pounds at each end of the combplate and 800 pounds in the center). The vertical force (150 pounds) was not changed. One argument for the changes was that this device was primarily designed to protect the equipment from damage, which could cause a subsequent accident resulting in injuries, instead of preventing them directly. It was also argued that the device was prone to inadvertent activation at the lower horizontal force limits.

Most existing escalators are not provided with a step-comb impact device. However, many escalators were provided with what is known as a combplate stop switch. This device shuts off the escalator and sets the driving machine brake if an excessive vertical force is applied to the combplate. Unlike the step-comb impact device, which is significantly more costly to retrofit to existing escalators, the combplate stop switch can more readily and economically be retrofitted to existing escalators. In fact, New York City requires that a combplate stop switch be installed on every existing escalator and that the switch be set to activate at a low maximum vertical force limit (45 to 60 pounds depending on the width of the escalator).

The ASME A17.1 Code requires a step level device to sense a downward displacement of a step and subsequently shut off the escalator and apply the driving machine brake. Most existing escalators are not equipped with this device, but they can readily be retrofitted with one. It can help detect some of the conditions that would permit a clearance between the top of one or more step tread surfaces and the bottom of the comb teeth. All existing escalators in New Jersey have been required to be retrofitted with this safety device.

The ASME A17.1 Code also required for many years that two green fluorescent lights, known as step demarcation lights, be installed under the steps near each landing. These devices are intended to alert riders that the landing is approaching.

The AMSE A17.1 Code has for many years required that a visual contrast be created between the steps and the combs by using color, texture, or pattern. This is to alert the rider to the presence of the combs. The most effective distinction is through the use of yellow combs, which contrast with the aluminum-colored steps. Many other designs provide minimal if any noticeable contrast. These comb sections are relatively inexpensive to replace.

5. Side-of-step entrapments

Entrapment of body parts between the sides of the moving steps and the stationary skirt panels have led to serious injuries, such as amputations and degloving injuries. The causes of these types of entrapments have been known for a long time. Objects on the moving steps come into contact with the stationary skirt panels. These objects can include the shoes of riders, the calves of children sitting on a step, and so forth. Friction between the skirt panel and these objects causes the objects to slow down in relation to the steps. A running clearance exists between the stationary skirt panels and the moving steps. Objects get drawn into the running clearance, especially as the steps make the transition from the inclined position to the flat position. The skirt panels deflect to a varying degree, depending on their design, which increases the gap between the step and the skirt panel and allows the object to be drawn in further. The steps can shift creating larger gaps depending on the amount of lateral play permitted by certain worn components. There is a large hollow space on the sides of the steps. A curling action causes the object to enter the hollow space, thereby permitting the object to be further drawn in. Whether the entrapment occurs at the riser or the tread portion of the step will depend on the direction of travel (e.g. the riser is the trapping point for the down running escalator).

There are four main variables in this entrapment scenario. First is the running clearance between the steps and the skirt panels. Second is the coefficient of friction between the skirt panels and the object. Third is the amount that the escalator's components deflect or shift to permit the gap between the steps and the skirt panel to increase. The fourth is the hollow space on the sides of the steps.

For many years, the ASME A17.1 and A17.3 Codes limited the running clearance between the steps and the skirt panels to a maximum of $^3/_{16}$-inch on either side. Earlier versions of ASME A17.1 limited this clearance more restrictively ($^1/_4$-inch total for both sides with no more than $^3/_{16}$-inch on any one side). This more restrictive running clearance was subsequently increased substantially (to $^3/_8$-inch on any side) in the ASME A17.1 codes for a number of years (most of the 1970s). In response to increased entrapments on escalators with this increased clearance, the clearance was subsequently limited to a lower ($^3/_{16}$-inch maximum) maximum. Amazingly, these code requirements were still more lax than originally permitted ($^1/_4$-inch total for both sides with no more than $^3/_{16}$-inch on any one side). Most escalator manufacturers have specified their running clearances below (e.g., $^1/_8$-inch maximum) the permitted code dimension. It is also interesting to note that during the time period when these more permissive running clearances were permitted in the U.S. by A17.1, in Canada more restrictive running clearances (between 0.1875 and 0.197 inches on either side and not more than a total on both sides of between 0.25 and 0.236 inches) were required by CSA B44. Many manufacturers were installing the same equipment in both the U.S and Canada during this time, so existing equipment should be able to meet the more restrictive running clearances.

Skirt panels are usually adjustable toward or away from the steps, which is the main method of limiting the running clearance (gap). Worn components such as step chains axle bushings can allow the escalator steps to shift laterally, thus decreasing the gap on one side but increasing it on the other. If not properly maintained, the escalator can develop excessive clearances.

Aftermarket devices (step side plates) have been available, which not only limit this running clearance substantially (1/16-inch maximum) but also eliminate the hollow spaces on the sides of the steps. These devices are available for many new and existing escalators. There are no provisions in the ASME A17.1 Code to eliminate these hollow spaces.

For many years, the ASME A17.1 Code required that skirt panels be made of low friction materials or treated with friction-reducing materials such as silicone. Although the code specified "low friction," it did not define it, although some interpretations indicate that certain materials are not low-friction. Materials such as stainless steel, porcelain, or bronze are not considered low-friction materials. Most existing escalators are not provided with low-friction skirt panel materials.

When objects such as rubber footwear or human skin contact these non-low-friction surfaces, a high coefficient of friction can result. The coefficient of friction between any two objects depends on the materials the objects are made of and their surface conditions. The surface condition's effect on the coefficient of friction is substantial. The coefficient of friction is also sensitive to a number of variables such as environmental conditions (temperature, humidity, etc.), surface films (lubrication) and deposits (contamination). Significantly, under certain conditions, human skin can result in a higher coefficient of friction than rubber footwear.

Most escalator manufacturers now provide skirt panels with a Teflon® coating applied, although at least one manufacturer provides a skirt panel with the low-friction material imbedded in it. The applied coating is subject to damage and removal from contact with objects on the escalator (handcarts for example) or the escalator steps themselves (poor maintenance).

Skirt panels are usually lubricated by applying silicone. This application can be done easily, quickly, and in a way that prevents any silicone from being deposited on the steps, which would become a slip hazard. Incredibly, some escalator maintenance companies refuse to lubricate non-low-friction skirt panels. Typically, they insist on replacing the skirt panels with low-friction types, instead of lubricating them. While this replacement may reduce the potential for entrapments, continuing to run the escalator with non-low-friction skirt panels that are not lubricated certainly perpetuates a potentially hazardous condition. Treatment of non-low-friction skirt panels with a friction-reducing material is covered in the maintenance section of ASME A17.1.

The ASME A17.1 Code also requires that the skirt panel have a smooth surface adjacent to the steps. This is to reduce the coefficient of friction and eliminate snag points. Most skirt panels are constructed of a metal lamination adhered to plywood backing. Many times the metal lamination becomes damaged. This can result from contact with the steps due to poor maintenance and worn components, as well as contact with objects on the steps (handcarts for example). Sometimes, temporary repairs are made to damaged skirt panels that do not result in a smooth surface (with the use of pop rivets for example). While the resulting repaired skirt panel is probably safer than the damaged one, it still presents a safety hazard.

Entrapments on escalators occurring around the edges of the step can be reduced if passengers stand in the middle of the step. The A17.1 code now requires that three edges of the step be marked with yellow lines, including the ones adjacent to the skirt panels. This helps alert passengers to the potential entrapment area and it is hoped that it causes them to stand away from these areas. Some manufacturers have provided similar markings for many years, and in at least one case a building owner marked steps with footprints to indicate the correct position in which to stand. However, it is important to note that when young children hold an escalator handrail they usually are forced to stand very close to the handrail. This places their feet very close to the clearance between the skirt panels and the side of the steps. Ironically, by holding the handrail in order to reduce the potential of falling, young children expose themselves to a greater danger.

The code-required caution sign includes a pictograph that is intended to depict an adult holding the hand of a child (the other child's hand is not on the handrail), and does contain the cautionary words ATTEND CHILDREN and AVOID SIDES, but it also contains the cautionary words HOLD HANDRAIL. In many cases the code-required caution sign does not appear to be effective in conveying the potential hazard.

The ASME A17.1 Code requires safety devices, known as skirt obstruction devices (commonly called skirt switches) that stop an escalator if an object becomes caught between the steps and the skirt panel as the steps approach each landing. However, many existing escalators may not have these devices. There are two main types of skirt obstruction devices. The first type has a "trigger" plunger that protrudes through the skirt panels. If an object touches the trigger, a switch is opened that stops the escalator. The second type has the trigger mounted behind the skirt panels. This design relies on a deflection of the skirt panel to contact the trigger in order to open the switch to stop the escalator. Each type has its advantages and disadvantages. Some manufacturers provide devices that combine both attributes to overcome these shortcomings.

For many years the ASME A17.1 Code limited the deflection of skirt panels ($^{1}/_{16}$-inch under a force of 150 pounds). It should be noted that the Canadian equivalent to the A17.1 Code (CSA B44) added this same provision many years before it was required in A17.1. Most of the escalator manufacturers that were installing escalators after the Canadian code was revised also installed escalators in the U.S., but in some cases these escalators did not meet the more rigorous requirements specified in the Canadian code. Reinforcing skirt panels is relatively simple and inexpensive.

With the introduction of A17.1d-2000[10] (an addenda to A17.1-1996), a number of significant changes have been made to the requirements related to skirt panels. There is much confusion and misunderstanding regarding these changes even among those familiar with escalators. The following is provided to assist the reader in getting a very basic sense of these changes. It is important to note that these requirements are still very likely subject to revision.

First, it is easier to indicate what has not changed. The deflection and stiffness requirements remain the same, as does the maintenance requirement for lubricating non-low-friction skirt panels and the requirement for the skirt panels to be smooth.

One change was the permissive use of skirt deflector devices. Previously these devices, typically brushes mounted along the skirt panels, could not be installed without violating code requirements. These devices had been mainly used in the U.K. If young children sit on an escalator step, then their calves are subject to entrapment at the nose line of the steps. Skirt deflector devices can be very effective in preventing these calf entrapments. However, since these devices are only installed close to the step nose line, they are physically unable to prevent most other side-of-step entrapments (e.g., shoes entrapped at a step riser). Some argue that these devices provide a psychological warning to avoid the skirt panel area, while others argue that it is an attractive nuisance. These deflector devices are permitted, but not required on new escalators. In order to be installed on existing escalators, it would be considered an alteration and trigger any applicable requirements.

One main change was the introduction of a new parameter called the "loaded gap." This loaded gap consists of the running clearance between the steps and the skirt panels, together with the increase in the running clearance caused by the deflection of the skirt panels and the looseness (side-to-side motion) in the escalator's components under a relatively small force (25 pounds).

The other main change has been the introduction of a "performance index." This index, scaled from zero to one, is expressed as a mathematical formula with two main variables. These variables are the "loaded gap" and the coefficient of friction. The coefficient of friction is the sliding coefficient of friction of a polycarbonate test specimen on the skirt panels under that small force (25 pounds).

The code requirement for the running clearances (i.e., "unloaded gap") has been superseded by the loaded gap for new escalators, but retained for existing escalators. However, all escalators are required to meet certain performance index limits. In addition, the maintenance section provides for alternative running clearances, 4 mm (0.16 inches) on either side or 7 mm (0.28 inches) total for both sides for all existing escalators.

The introduction of this index and the other changes was controversial. The manufacturers fervently claim it is a dramatic improvement in safety and based on a sound scientific basis.[11,12] Others vehemently oppose the adoption of the index and the other changes for numerous reasons, including that the level of safety was being diminished. Who is correct still remains to be seen.

Interestingly, although a certain index limit (0.15) was established, which ostensibly would reduce the probability of entrapments, the code permits a significantly higher index value (0.25 or 0.40 for most existing units) if skirt deflector devices are provided. These deflector devices are permitted on new escalators, but are not required. Prudence dictates that the lowest reasonably achievable index value should be obtained for safety. This could entail reducing the running clearances, lubricating the skirt panels, stiffening the skirt panels, and so on.

It is noted that ASME A17.1-2013 eliminated the requirement to lubricate skirt panels that are not made of low friction materials, but it would be prudent to lubricate them as long as precautions are used when applying the lubrication to prevent deposits on the steps.

D. Working Conditions

Working conditions significantly affect the level of safety of both elevator personnel and passengers. If elevator personnel can't safely maintain an elevator then passenger safety is jeopardized.

The *Elevator Industry Field Employees' Safety Handbook* is the foremost publication devoted to delineating the proper safety practices that should be used when working around elevators and escalators. While this document is intended for use by mechanics, it has many parts that are applicable to other elevator personnel (e.g., inspectors). The latest edition when this book was being written was the 2015 edition. In the past revisions were held until sufficient material was available to justify the cost of publishing a supplement. However, now revisions will be published electronically as soon as they are approved. Printed supplements will also be published periodically.

Elevator personnel are subject to the same general hazards as the general public (e.g. falls, being struck by objects hazards, shear hazards, crushing hazards, electrical hazards, being caught in between objects hazards). However, elevator personnel are typically faced with all of these hazards on a daily basis that are significantly more hazardous in nature. Therefore, this section addresses workplace accidents. See Section 3.2C for workplace accident statistics.

Elevator personnel are exposed to many of these hazards during the installation of elevators and escalators when many of the safeguards that protect the public are not yet installed or functional. Therefore, proper safeguards must be put in place to protect them (e.g. barricades and personal protection equipment (e.g. proper clothing, hard hats, hearing protection, safety glasses, safety boots and respiratory protection)).

While escalator control voltages are typically low (e.g. 24 VDC) and ancillary voltages will be in the 110/120 VAC range, main power voltages typically will be in the 220-480 volt range. These higher voltages are a serious shock hazard.

Failure to properly secure the equipment when working on it can lead to serious injuries. Proper lockout or tag-out procedures should be used whenever the equipment is worked on. This entails securing the equipment both electrically and mechanically from inadvertent movement and posting appropriate signage.

Probably the most serious hazard is working inside the escalator step band and the escalator starting. This can be prevented by mechanically locking the step band. A number of these types of accidents have occurred when elevator personnel leave keys inserted into a starting switch and the weight of other keys on the same ring turns the switch and starts the escalator with disastrous results.

Endnotes

1. ASME A17.1-2000 *Safety Code for Elevators and Escalators*. American Society of Mechanical Engineers.

2. NEII-1-2000 *Building Transportation Standards and Guidelines*. Elevator World.

3. 29 CFR Part 1910.

4. ANSI Z535.2 *American National Standard: Environmental and Facility Signs*. National Electrical Manufacturers Association.

5. ANSI Z535.4 *American National Standard: Product Safety Signs and Labels*. National Electrical Manufacturers Association.

6. Cohn, Theodore E. 1984. "Escalators: The Visual Illusion". ITS (Institute of Transportation Studies/University of California). *Review*. August 1984, Vol. 7, No. 4.

7. Cohn, Theodore E. and Lasley, David J. 1990. "Wallpaper Illusion: Cause of Disorientation and Falls on Escalators." *Perception*. Vol. 19, pages 573-580.

8. Fruin, Dr. John. Open Side Guarding of Escalators. *Elevator World*. March 1993.

9. *Heavy-Duty Escalator Guidelines*. American Public Transit Association (APTA) Subcommittee on Elevators/Escalators.

10. ASME A17.1d-2000 *Safety Code for Elevators and Escalators*. American Society of Mechanical Engineers

11. Escalator Step/Skirt Performance Study. July 2, 1998. Arthur D. Little, Inc.

12. Escalator Step/Skirt Performance Standard. Final Report. September 16, 1999. Arthur D. Little, Inc.

13. ASME B20.1 Safety Standard for Conveyors and Related Equipment, American Society of Mechnical Engineers.

14. ANSI/ASSE A10.5 Safety Requirements for Material Hoists, American Society of Safety Engineers.

15. ANSI/ASSE A10.4 Personnel Hoists and Employee Elevators on Construction and Demolition Sites, American Society of Safety Engineers.

Chapter 5

Accident Prevention, Improving Safety, and Limiting Liability

5.1 Introduction

The main purpose of this chapter is to describe the methods for prevention of accidents, improving safety, and limiting liability. It can be used as a reference to assist in determining why the accident happened and what could have been done or can be done to prevent it, as well as to assist in reconstructing the accident.

No vertical transportation equipment will be totally free of potential hazards. This is just the nature of the beast. No matter how well maintained, no matter how code compliant, no matter how good the training programs, no matter how comprehensive the warning signs—accidents will still occur. However, the hazards are usually well-known and therefore accidents are preventable in most cases. Therefore, it is the responsibility of all parties to identify and eliminate the hazards that are under their control, and to identify and notify the responsible party of those hazards outside of their control. Warnings must effectively convey the hazards in writing. If impending dangers exist, the equipment must be taken out of service until the situation is corrected.

Unlike most other complex electrical or mechanical equipment, modern elevators and escalators are operated by untrained personnel, by tenants and visitors to buildings. These same people are exposed to moving parts as they ride on escalators, which would probably require guarding if it were machinery in a production facility. They come from all walks of life, and vary considerably in their educational, social, and economic backgrounds.

It should be noted that all the possible types of accidents involving elevators and escalators cannot be contained in a single treatise. For example, defects caused by improper manufacturing, shipping, or raw materials are possible but beyond the scope of this book. The reader is referred to one of the many books on this subject. The following discussion centers on the most prevalent or noteworthy causes of accidents for elevators and escalators.

In most cases, accidents happen for one or more of the following reasons:

- Negligent or improper maintenance or repair
- Defective design in one or more of the system's components
- Misapplication of one or more of the system's components
- Improper installation or omission of one or more of the system's components
- Improper operation, abuse or misuse
- Failure to provide sufficient warning of an impending hazard and/or operating instructions
- External factors, such as power failures, brownouts ,and acts of God

Many parties are responsible for ensuring safe elevator and escalator operation. These include:

- The architects who designed the building
- The contractors who built the building
- The consultant who wrote the elevator or escalator specifications and assured compliance with those specifications
- The elevator or escalator designer and manufacturer
- The company that installed the elevator or escalator
- The code-enforcing authority (i.e., AHJ) that inspected and tested the equipment following installation and periodically thereafter
- The maintenance contractor or personnel whose job it is to keep the equipment "like new"
- The riding public and others who must use the equipment responsibly
- The building owner or manager

Although listed last in the preceding list, the building owner/manager is the first line of responsibility in ensuring the safe operation of the elevators and escalators under their control. This is recognized in most building codes, which make the building owner responsible for the maintenance of the equipment. They are the ones that usually choose the architect, the elevator or escalator installer, the manufacturer, the consultant, and the contractor. They are responsible for establishing a maintenance program to ensure safe and efficient operation, either through hiring an outside contractor or using a competent internal work force. This includes effective monitoring to ensure that the maintenance work is performed and ensure that the equipment is operating as intended. They are responsible for providing an acceptable and safe environment for the equipment and their users. Periodic inspections and tests conducted by the AHJ are coordinated through them. They must also promptly correct any deficiencies found. Good and accepted industry practice is to report accidents promptly to the responsible AHJ, whether or not they are legally required.

Unfortunately, many building owners/managers think that once they hire a maintenance contractor, their responsibility ends or that they have purchased an "insurance policy" against liability. This folly will be quickly exposed once an accident happens and litigation begins. Good and accepted industry practice requires that a building owner/manager effectively evaluate the maintenance being performed by their contractor. This not only provides an independent means to ensure that the equipment is being maintained in a safe condition, it also provides an economic benefit—making sure that they get what they pay for, and provides the opportunity to learn if the equipment could be made safer. Relying on the state-mandated inspections to determine this is inadequate, since violations can only be cited after the fact. There are many conditions (e.g., worn components) that are not yet code violations but can develop into a condition that causes an elevator malfunction before the next inspection and therefore cause injuries to passengers. If the building owner/manager has no expertise in elevator/escalator maintenance, then good and accepted industry practice would be to utilize an elevator/escalator consultant.

Building owners are also responsible for designating what the code calls authorized personnel, who are to be instructed in the operation of the equipment. For example, the code requires escalators and moving walks to be started by authorized personnel, and has procedures to follow.

This is not to imply that the other parties have no responsibility for ensuring the safe operation of elevators and escalators. Indeed, these other parties usually will have a more direct role in the causes of any accident, but the fact remains that the building owner or manager has the most influence on the daily operation of elevators and escalators.

Advances in technology, additional safety features, improved service, reduced maintenance requirements, increased service life, and improved reliability are all excellent reasons to modernize outdated equipment. Usually an important dividend from the modernization of equipment is reduced liability. Many times the bulk of the existing equipment can be reconditioned and reused, and the remaining equipment can be modernized in stages.

One of the most significant change in the vertical transportation industry in the last 30 years was the introduction of microprocessors in the 1980s. These microprocessors permitted programmable features on both the control and supervisory systems. Before this, changing equipment operation required costly hardware changes and extensive downtime. System performance information and error messages, so valuable to a mechanic troubleshooting equipment malfunctions, were previously virtually nonexistent. Also, the required maintenance had to be more intensive on older equipment.

Although many companies may perform good maintenance, any need for engineering design changes or extensive modifications can usually be done more efficiently by the original equipment manufacturer, who has access to the original design and application database. Examples of extensive modification would be alteration to the equipment requiring changes of speed or capacity, or adding an additional unit to a group operation. Also, some elevator and escalator companies specialize in modernization and can provide acceptable alternatives.

There are many other measures that can be taken by all of the parties involved to prevent accidents. Some of these are discussed below.

The purpose of ASME A17.3 Safety Code for Elevators and Escalators "*is to establish minimum requirements that will provide a reasonable degree of safety for the general public* and is intended to *enhance the safety of the general public* Therefore, even if not required by the AHJ, compliance with ASME A17.3 is not only prudent but also strongly advisable.

The addition of certain safety devices can always be accomplished, even if they were not required by code when the equipment was originally installed. Combplate stop switches (not to be confused with comb-step impact devices) on escalators reduce the severity of injuries for combplate entrapments. Installation of these devices is retroactively required on all escalators in New York City. Although these devices are not required by ASME A17.1, they have been provided as optional devices for many years and are easier to retrofit on existing equipment than comb-step impact devices. Non-contact door reopening devices on elevators can prevent the doors from striking objects and people. Hoistway access switches and car top operating devices can assist the mechanics and inspectors gain safe access to the hoistway and control elevator operation when inside of the hoistway. Controlled stop brakes can reduce falls on escalators from sudden stops. Ascending overspeed protection, to prevent elevators from striking the hoistway overhead structure, and door monitoring, to prevent an elevator from leaving a floor with the doors open, due to the failure of the driving machine brake, motor, coupling, shaft, gearing, or control system can be economically provided by aftermarket devices.

Although it is beyond the scope of this treatise to analyze design defects, there are certain bottom line precautions that would be prudent for any designer to take. One of these is the concept of "fail safe." In essence, this concept requires that if a device or component fails to operate then it must not result in a dangerous situation. This may require shutting down the elevator or escalator, or other precautionary action.

Proper lighting can enhance the safety both of users of vertical transportation equipment and maintenance mechanics. Included are machine rooms, elevator car tops and pits, inside elevator cars, escalator steps, and landings. The ASME A17.1 code requires certain lighting intensities inside the car, in the pit, and in the machine room for elevators, and at landing plates and exposed steps for escalators. In addition for escalators the lighting must be uniform and not materially contrast with the surroundings. Local building codes may contain additional requirements.

Yellow striping on low overheads, ledges, rotating equipment, and at pinch points assists the technician in being aware of these dangers. Marking escalator steps with a yellow stripe along the sides of the step treads adjacent to the skirt panels and at the interface with the adjacent step's riser helps alert passengers to the potential entrapment areas and hopefully causes them to stand away from these areas. In at least one case, steps were marked with footprints to indicate the correct position to stand.

Yellow combs can be installed on escalators alerting passengers to the combplate-step interface. Skirt panels can be stiffened to limit deflection, lubricated to limit friction, and adjusted to minimize the running clearance between the steps and the skirt panels. Aftermarket devices can be installed to limit the running clearance between the steps and the skirt panels, or to prevent entrapments of children's calves in the running clearance between the steps and the skirt panels.

The use of "pre-opening the doors on approach" for elevators can be eliminated to reduce the probability of trip and fall accidents on elevators.

Unreliable or inaccurate leveling or landing systems can be replaced with accurate and reliable systems to reduce trip and fall accidents on elevators.

The list can go on and on. Yet even implementing just the ones mentioned could eliminate many elevator and escalator accidents and reduce the severity of many of those that do happen. The best source for accident prevention ideas is the elevator-escalator consultant. Many of these preventive actions can be easily and economically implemented for existing equipment. Others are simply common sense and prudent practice. Those requiring considerable expense and disruption can be phased in.

5.2 General Measures to Prevent Accidents, Improve Safety and Limit Liability

A. Proper Maintenance

Probably the most important thing that can be done to prevent elevator/escalator accidents is to have an effective maintenance program in effect. Improper maintenance of a system reduces its reliability and subjects its owner to increased liability. The importance of proper maintenance in preventing accidents and improving safety cannot be stressed enough.

Improper maintenance is very often the cause of elevator and escalator accidents. Even the best designed and installed equipment must be properly maintained for it to continue to operate safely. Improper maintenance covers a multitude of sins. It can include the lack of maintenance, inadequate scope or frequency of work, substandard methods of performing the work, inadequate monitoring of the work performed and the operation of the equipment, substandard training or skills of the mechanics performing the work, and so on. Each of these types of deficiencies has caused accidents.

A very disturbing development in the elevator industry is the corporate management decision to focus on profits at the expense of providing proper maintenance. For example, increasing maintenance personnel workloads (i.e., number of units maintained) dramatically, decreasing maintenance frequency dramatically (but the bills still being sent at the same frequency), reducing the scope of maintenance tasks (e.g., limiting maintenance to riding an elevator and visual examinations), delaying necessary repairs, hiring management personnel for their business skills rather than their technical skills, etc.

The effect on the accident rate will be predictable. Acronyms such as **TLOM** (**T**otal **L**ack **O**f **M**aintenance) and **GLOM** (**G**eneral **L**ack **O**f **M**aintenance) have sprung up to describe this phenomenon. Ironically, this continued after vastly expanded maintenance requirements were included in the 2000 Edition of the A17.1 *Safety Code for Elevators and Escalators*[1] in response to substandard maintenance.

By definition, maintenance is the work of keeping something in proper working order. In many cases this requires the replacement or repair of components in order to restore the system to its original operation. In general, maintenance consists of Cleaning, Lubrication, Examination, Adjustment, Repair or Replacement, and Testing of various equipment, components, and systems (remember CLEAR-T).

An effective maintenance program will be very similar whether internal employees or outside vendors are used. Such a comprehensive maintenance program is sometimes referred to as a maintenance control program (MCP) or maintenance plan (MP). It describes in detail what maintenance tasks must be performed, when and how these tasks are performed, how they are documented, and how the maintenance is evaluated.

It starts with establishing the frequency of maintenance and identifying the tasks that need to be performed. Then the work should be scheduled through using work orders, establishing a route, or similar methods. Next, the work must be performed and documented. This must be done so that the mechanics are aware of what they must do for each elevator and escalator and when it is to be done.

Traditionally, the minimum frequency of maintenance tasks established was monthly, with other certain maintenance tasks performed quarterly, semiannually and annually. Then the race to the bottom began to cut costs at the expense of safety. For some maintenance companies the minimum frequency slipped to quarterly, then semiannually, then annually and now at least one company is using a minimum frequency of 18 months.

The importance of documenting maintenance and repairs cannot be stressed enough. This is the primary method for mechanics working on the equipment to know what problems are occurring with the equipment, what work needs to be done on the equipment, and what work has been performed on the equipment. This documentation can be in the form of a check chart, an electronic database, or other retrievable form. However, the records must be available to the mechanics before they start work on the equipment.

The lack of detailed maintenance records is at best an indication of lackadaisical maintenance, and at worst incompetent maintenance. Sometimes the lack of maintenance records is portrayed as proof that nothing was wrong with the equipment, and therefore the inference is that the accident did not occur. This self-serving position is not only unprofessional, it also has no basis. If records are not kept, then it is impossible to ensure that the required tasks were being performed at the correct frequency or were being performed at all. The failure to document normal maintenance may foreshadow a failure to document an accident. The best defense against claims of improper maintenance is comprehensive and well-kept maintenance records.

The 2000 Edition of the A17.1 *Safety Code for Elevators and Escalators*[1] introduced vastly expanded maintenance requirements from previous versions. Among the new provisions are identifying many more tasks that must be performed, requiring that wiring diagrams be available in the machine rooms, and codifying requirements for maintenance records. Where these requirements do not yet have the force of law, they still represent good and accepted industry practice.

There have been numerous iterations of the maintenance requirements since then. One was requiring a formal Maintenance Control Program. This code-required Maintenance Control Program must be written and available to elevator personnel, although only certain documentation (On-Site Documentation and On-Site Maintenance Records) is required to be physically on-site. The instructions for locating or viewing the portion of the Maintenance Control Program not maintained on-site must be located in the controller or means necessary for testing.

The MCP must include, but is not limited to, examinations, maintenance, and tests of equipment and the cleaning, lubricating, adjusting, and repairing or replacing of components. Maintenance records must be kept at a central location and be available to elevator personnel. They must include a description and dates of maintenance tasks performed, examinations, tests, adjustments, repairs, and replacements. They must also include a description, dates, and the corrective actions for all callbacks (trouble calls) or information that is reported to elevator personnel by any means.

While the code-required Maintenance Control Program must include all the maintenance specified in the A17.1 code, it is not limited to them. A good example of comprehensive maintenance tasks that should be included in any maintenance control program are contained in the NEII Maintenance Guidelines.[2]

Finally, there needs to be some feedback mechanism. This can take many forms. Periodically using an independent third party to evaluate the condition of the equipment is an effective way to accomplish this. Monitoring callbacks and using diagnostic equipment to determine the operating condition of the equipment can be done together or independently.

The elevator industry refers to unexpected shutdowns or improper operation of the equipment as "callbacks," because the equipment owner usually has to call the maintenance company for the mechanic to come back to the building to resolve the problem.

One way to determine if adequate maintenance is being performed is to monitor callbacks. Having someone, such as a consultant, knowledgeable about elevators and escalators do this is recommended. **The importance of monitoring callbacks as a standard for measuring maintenance performance cannot be overemphasized. Therefore, it is essential that proper maintenance records be maintained.**

This can be monitored by retrieving each problem that has been registered into the elevator maintenance logbook. The elevator company usually records this information, either electronically in a database or in writing (e.g., logs kept in the machine room). This applies whether a resident mechanic is assigned to the building or the building is just one on a route that the mechanic covers. Cross-reference all documents to make sure the list is complete. Categorize the problems by cause, which can be derived from the descriptions entered by the elevator technician. Look at the list for problems associated with the unit, the associated dates, the various components involved, any reported causes, and any corrective measures taken.

Repeated problems frequently are caused by improper maintenance. The frequency of callbacks may be a sign of improper maintenance. In general, the average number of annual callbacks that many companies consider acceptable is two for escalators, three for hydraulic elevators, and four for the more demanding traction-type elevators. More callbacks per year than those numbers are usually considered excessive and the reasons for the callbacks should be investigated.

Callbacks of the type that are beyond the control of the elevator maintenance company should be analyzed separately to determine any detrimental environmental conditions. These include passenger misuse, dropping of keys into the elevator pit requiring removal by the elevator technician, inadvertent activation of the emergency stop button, misuse, abuse, and vandalism. Other marginal problems should at least be put in a separate category. Included are signal lamp failures, excessive waiting times, and callbacks due to minor noises.

Frequently, components start to fail intermittently. This can result in callbacks where the responding mechanic is unable to find any problem, which is commonly referred to as "running on arrival" or "ROA." Many times the responding mechanic is not the same individual who normally maintains the equipment or the one who responded to a previously reported similar problem. The availability of maintenance records is critical in these cases. Otherwise, mechanics are left to their own devices to try to guess what the problem is based solely on the current reported problem, without any current problem to observe or the benefit of the history of past problems with the equipment. Often the equipment is placed back in service (BIS) without any remedial action taken. This will in many cases result in an accident that could have been avoided if the proper maintenance records were available.

The building owner's or manager's responsibility is to ensure that the elevators and escalators are being maintained in a safe condition. This can be accomplished by ensuring that competent mechanics are maintaining the equipment and by having an effective and comprehensive maintenance program in place. The questions then become who will perform the maintenance, how often it will be performed, how it will be performed, and how it will be monitored.

An effective maintenance program will be very similar, whether internal manpower or outside vendors are used. It starts with establishing the frequency of maintenance and identifying the tasks that need to be performed. Then there must be a way to schedule the work, which can be done through work orders, establishing a route, or similar methods. This must be documented in some manner so that the mechanics are aware of what they must do for each elevator or escalator and when it is to be done. This can be in the form of a check chart, an electronic database, or other retrievable form. Next, the work must be performed and documented. Finally, some feedback mechanism is needed. This can take many forms. Periodically using an independent third party to evaluate the condition of the equipment is an effective way to accomplish this. Monitoring callbacks and using diagnostic equipment to determine the operating condition of the equipment can be used in conjunction with this or independently.

Therefore, the building owner or manager must first decide if maintenance is to be performed by internal staff or if an outside contractor will be hired. Some building owners opt to use their own workers to perform maintenance. If internal staff is to be used, then a competent work force must be assembled and trained. This practice has its advantages and disadvantages. Using internal manpower usually provides a greater degree of control over costs and quality than using outside vendors. However, using outside vendors usually provides a greater level of technical knowledge and experience. If the industry is doing well, it will be difficult to retain competent workers who usually obtain higher wages working for an outside vendor. If the industry is doing poorly, competent mechanics may be attracted to the relative stability of a building owner. If internal manpower is chosen, then the building owner will have to assemble a cadre of competent workers and implement an effective training program.

The vast majority of building owners and managers will opt to hire an outside contractor. Therefore, more decisions need to be made. What type of maintenance contract will be used, which contractor will be selected, how often will maintenance be performed, and so on?

An elevator-escalator consultant can be of vital assistance to a building owner or manager in making these decisions. Many building owners are driven by the bottom line—how much it will cost. Choosing an elevator or escalator contractor based solely on initial costs is shortsighted and usually more costly in the long term. More commonly, the building owner or manager will sign a contract prepared by the maintenance contractor. Again, this is another shortsighted decision.

Maintenance contracts can be awarded to the firm that originally installed or upgraded (modernized) the equipment, or to a company that only performs maintenance. At this writing, several U.S. companies and many European companies are ISO 9000 certified. This or an equivalent certification requires a rigorous documentation of operating procedures by the company as well as periodic compliance inspections by the certifying organization. While this certification is certainly laudable and desirable from the equipment owner's perspective, it does not guarantee anything.

Most elevator and escalator maintenance contracts generally fall into one of the following four categories:

1. Oil and grease. As the name implies, this type of agreement only requires the contractor to lubricate the moving components of the system, examine the equipment's operation, and make minor adjustments. All repairs or replacements will cost extra. The cost for this type of contract is minimal, which is its major allure to building owners. The contractor will attempt to make profits by performing repair and replacement work. It is apparent that there is not much incentive for the contractor to keep the equipment in good operating order, but quite the opposite. The contract will specify the frequency, typically monthly.
2. Oil, grease, and parts. This is similar to the oil and grease type of contract, but it includes the repair and replacement of certain specified components.
3. Full-coverage preventive. This type of agreement requires the maintenance contractor to perform what is commonly referred to in the elevator industry as "preventive maintenance." The operative word is "preventive." It means simply that the maintenance functions are frequent and comprehensive enough to prevent most equipment failures.
4. Predictive. This type of maintenance is usually performed as an adjunct to other maintenance tasks and not as a stand-alone function. Generally, operating parameters of the equipment are measured using diagnostic equipment and recorded. In its most comprehensive form, a history of these measurements is kept and trends are identified. These trends are used to predict an impending failure well before it occurs, and proactive actions are taken. More commonly, each set of measurements is interpreted individually to detect any indication of impending failure. This type of maintenance is not common for elevators and escalators.

Of these four main types of elevator and escalator maintenance contracts, the oil and grease type and the oil, grease, and parts type cover minimal maintenance. In fact, many companies charge less than would a repairman coming to your house to fix an appliance. The contractor attempts to make a profit by performing repair and replacement work. It is apparent that there is not much incentive for the contractor to keep the equipment in good operating order, but quite the opposite. The contractor usually shows up monthly just to get paid for this "maintenance."

On the other hand, preventive maintenance, perhaps in conjunction with predictive maintenance, offers the best opportunity to maximize safety and limit liability. Having a resident mechanic will obviously be more advantageous than having a mechanic periodically visit the building to perform maintenance. However, the cost for this is higher and therefore not chosen by most building owners unless they have a sufficient number of elevators or escalators to justify a resident mechanic or a premium is placed on service.

Many contracts will typically exclude the following items: cabs, cab finishes, and flooring; doors, door frames, and sills; light fixtures and lamps; power switches and breakers, electrical feeds to the equipment that are on the "line" side of the main disconnect switch; hoistways; smoke detectors; external emergency power equipment; underground piping and cylinders on hydraulic elevators; and the renewal or refinishing of all exposed trim on an escalator. Therefore, the onus is on building owners or managers to assure the integrity of these components, or include them in the maintenance contract. However, just because a component is excluded by the contract does not mean that the contractor can ignore problems with that component. It simply means that an extra cost will be charged. Also, the contractor must warn the owner of any condition that may affect the safe operation of the equipment.

The maintenance contract should specify the frequency and scope of maintenance functions. Based on this, a maintenance schedule should then be developed. The maintenance schedule should indicate what is to be done and when it is to be done. Typically it will be in the form of a chart or list. When the tasks are completed and documented, it usually is referred to as a maintenance log. It can take many forms: for example it can be a written document that resides in the building or it can be an electronic database, which can then be stored in various locations.

The first obligation is to establish a frequency of maintenance that will ensure that the equipment remains operating as it did when originally installed. Generally this is done at least on a monthly interval. One reason is practical. The maintenance contractor usually sends monthly invoices to the building owner or manager as required by the contract. Billing monthly means "showing up" monthly. Another reason is to shorten the time that problems can develop. These monthly visits may be sufficient to catch any "lack of maintenance" problems and they may not. It depends on the usage of the equipment, its operating environment, its age and its design. Each elevator is unique. No two will require exactly the same degree of maintenance. Certain maintenance tasks may be performed based on usage (running hours for example). One industry rule of thumb provides for the following minimum hours of maintenance: one hour a month for a hydraulic elevator, two hours per month for a geared traction elevator, three hours per month for an escalator and four hours per month for a gearless traction elevator.

There are three main types of maintenance schedules:

1. *Time-based* maintenance. This involves a fixed amount of time between scheduled maintenance. For example, routine maintenance tasks are performed monthly, while certain periodic maintenance tasks are performed quarterly, semiannually, or annually.
2. *Use-based* maintenance. Maintenance is performed depending on the occurrence of some milestone event, such as the number of stops or running hours. Microprocessor-based equipment has features that facilitate the acquisition of this information, and in some cases the information can be remotely accessed.
3. *Use and time based* maintenance. This is a combination of use-based and time-based maintenance scheduling. For example, if the operating history of an elevator indicates that it may make 8,000 stops in a six-week period, then the routine maintenance tasks would be performed at six-week intervals regardless of the current usage. If the number of shutdowns or callbacks and customer satisfaction indicate that the maintenance is adequate, then the frequency will be continued. If not, the interval will be shortened. This method proves to be more effective on older equipment for which the number of stops and running hours is available. If stop counters and running-time accumulators are installed, the routine maintenance can be performed at fixed intervals and the periodic maintenance can be performed based on usage. This approach is usually more productive when more frequent visits are required by contract.

Routine maintenance tasks are those performed every time maintenance is performed. Monthly is the most common frequency. Typical tasks for an electric elevator would include, but not be limited to, checking elevator ride quality, door operation, leveling, signal and communication operation, lubrication, cleaning, relay function, checking all rotating equipment, checking brake function, checking firefighters' service if provided, adjustment, and replacement as required. Typical tasks for an escalator would include, but not be limited to, checking the steps, handrails, skirt panels, combs, brake function, key switches, emergency stop switches, lubrication, cleaning, adjustment, and replacement as required.

Periodic maintenance tasks are performed less frequently than routine maintenance tasks. This may include brake adjustment, tests, vacuuming out a controller, and more thorough examinations of the various components.

The comprehensiveness of the maintenance tasks is the second critical variable for proper maintenance. Just doing something frequently, but not

doing it correctly, does not accomplish much. Therefore, in conjunction with the maintenance schedule, procedures should be established governing how the maintenance tasks are to be performed. This is sometimes referred to as the maintenance guide. It may consist of a procedure, a manual, a book, or a database. Most equipment manufacturers supply maintenance instructions. Often included in these instructions is a list of the parts expected to need periodic replacement (along with the part number and ordering instructions), lubrication requirements, adjustment procedures, and a troubleshooting guide.

Good preventive maintenance is, therefore, simply performing comprehensive maintenance tasks at an appropriate frequency that reasonably assures against equipment breakdowns or failures. This type of maintenance has a strong incentive for the contractor to perform at its best, because costs can be incurred otherwise.

The importance of monitoring the operation of the equipment cannot be overemphasized as a tool for preventing accidents. Properly performed, it can determine the adequacy of the maintenance being performed and can detect incipient conditions that presage impending equipment failure. A building owner or manager that contracts out maintenance or issues work orders without having an effective feedback mechanism is asking for trouble. Maintenance must be properly managed for it to be effective. Too many building owners and managers blindly rely on their maintenance service contractors. All too often this turns out like having the fox watch the chicken coop. Having a consultant periodically perform maintenance evaluations is a wise investment for a building owner or manager.

Remote monitoring systems are readily available in today's market, and are considered to be one of the "state of the art" peripherals for today's vertical transportation. These systems can be adapted to most types of equipment. In addition to providing maintenance documentation and performance information, remote monitors can transmit live data on the current state of the elevator or escalator system, similar to the information on an automobile's dashboard but with much more detail. Recurring malfunctions, equipment status, and alarms, as well as system performance information can be transmitted, as they occur, to the central watch station computer. Some monitoring systems have two-way communication to the elevator, helpful for consoling entrapped passengers and deterring equipment misuse.

A typical remote monitoring system will employ monitors in the security officer's room, at the desk of the lobby attendant, and in the machine rooms for use by the technician. Valuable information is supplied to all parties and can be programmed to alert them when certain performance parameters are exceeded. This information documents how efficiently the elevator system performs, as well as any faults that occur within the control system as described above. The information can be stored for long periods of time and the database can be accessed to document the exact time of the occurrence of a fault.

If an elevator has a telephone line, then it is possible with some equipment for this information to be transmitted directly to the elevator maintenance company. It is also possible for elevator companies to transmit software changes in this manner or take remote control of the elevator. While the potential benefits are substantial, so are the potential liabilities.

Computerized maintenance monitoring is commonly used today for documenting maintenance. The maintenance technician displays the scheduled task on a laptop computer or handheld terminal or phone, then enters data as the task is completed. The entry records what maintenance tasks were completed, when, and by whom. The program compares the date due versus the date completed, permitting a performance log. A microprocessor stores the information, perhaps for years when battery backups are provided, and when equipped with a modem can transmit the information periodically to a central station to be saved. These records should be available to the mechanics before they perform their maintenance and repair tasks, so that they have a complete history of the equipment.

Another effective method, although less high-tech, is monitoring equipment breakdowns manually and performing an analysis, which was discussed above.

For hydraulic elevators it is very important to document all additions of hydraulic fluid to the system. This permits an analysis to determine if a small underground leak exists in the system. Undetected underground leaks could result in an uncontrolled descent of the elevator (i.e., free fall) and seriously injure or kill anyone inside the elevator.

B. Proper Warnings

It must be recognized that warnings are the lowest level of action that can be taken. If a hazard can be eliminated, then it should be eliminated, and warnings only provided for any residual hazards. Many times the warnings are ineffective or ignored. Therefore, supplemental action is often appropriate.

Failures to warn of any potentially dangerous conditions have resulted in causing or contributing to accidents in settlements in favor of plaintiffs. In general, if an owner, manufacturer, installer, maintainer, consultant, or inspector of an elevator or escalator has reason to believe that average people using the equipment in a reasonably prudent manner might inadvertently injure themselves, then an appropriate warning or other safeguard is necessary.

The building owner or manager has ultimate control of the vertical transportation equipment, and therefore has the ultimate responsibility for this equipment. This is recognized by most codes.

However, an elevator maintenance company, an elevator consultant, or an elevator inspector has a duty to warn the building's management of potential dangers. The warning should first be conveyed orally to the appropriate representative of the building owner or manager and followed up with written correspondence (a certified mailing is recommended).

The building owner or manager is then obligated to correct the condition, warn the users of the equipment, or both. These warnings must be commensurate with the hazard. Of course, since the maintenance contractor is in intimate contact with the equipment and the users of the equipment then it may be necessary for the contractor to provide warnings independent of those of the building owner or manager and to take other corrective action to protect herself from litigation.

Nevertheless, merely warning a building owner or manager of a potential hazard may not be sufficient. If an imminent hazard exists, then the maintenance company should take action. This may entail shutting down the equipment and refusing to place it back in service, locking it out of service, and notifying the building owner or manager and the AHJ. Of course, the maintenance service company cannot force the building owner to alter or repair its equipment, but the maintenance company must not turn a blind eye to an imminent hazard. It would be prudent to discontinue servicing that equipment until corrective actions are taken.

A maintenance company can become liable for hazardous conditions even if it was only tangentially involved with the equipment. For example, if the company only performs call-in repairs, but becomes aware of a hazardous condition (or should have become aware of it), then as an elevator/escalator expert it must take appropriate action to warn the building owner or AHJ, or both, about the hazardous condition. After an accident the building owner or manager may often try to blame the maintenance contractor and claim, "They should have warned me!"

Warnings to users of the equipment are also very important. These include posting "Out of Service" signs at each entrance of an elevator or escalator when appropriate, and erecting necessary barricades barricades in accordance with industry standards. The Elevator Industry Field Employee Safety Handbook provides recommended barricading methods.. It must be remembered that in many cases the passengers of elevators are in effect operating the equipment. Therefore, appropriate warnings are necessary. For example, freight elevators are many times operated by freight-handlers. If the building owner or manager has chosen not to provide an attendant, then sufficient warnings are necessary to warn the freight-handlers of known hazards, such as automatic closing of the doors or the fact that in most cases the doors close vertically both from the top and the bottom. The users of escalators are exposed to moving parts as they ride the equipment. Therefore, warnings of known hazards are necessary to alert the passengers to these hazards. For example, providing yellow markings of hazardous features is often an effective method of warning passengers.

Although mechanics are familiar with the equipment, this does not eliminate the need to provide sufficient warning of known hazards. For example, posting signs warning of limited working clearances and marking rotating equipment or shear hazards in yellow are effective methods of avoiding certain accidents.

Effective signage is an easy and inexpensive method of reducing the probability of certain types of accidents. The codes, regulations, and laws in effect for the equipment require certain signs. Additional signs can also be provided by the building owner or manager to reduce the probability of accidents and limiting their liability.

The following are some examples of the signage requirements contained in the ASME A17.1—2010 / CSA B44—10 Code:

- Capacity plate showing rated load inside the car
- DO NOT USE IN CASE OF FIRE pictograph above each landing call station (recommended, but may be required by the building code)
- Danger signs on emergency doors in blind hoistways and elevator pits
- Class of loading (general, motor vehicle, industrial truck, concentrated loads) for freight elevators
- Sign restricting the use of freight elevators to operators, freight, and their handlers
- Danger signs on the hoistway doors for hand-operated elevators
- NO RIDERS sign inside dumbwaiters
- Operating instructions for firefighters' service operation
- Escalator and moving walk caution signs
- Markings for the emergency stop button on elevators and escalators
- Identification of equipment of different elevators located in the same machine room or hoistway

Also, certain signage is required by other applicable codes and local regulations and laws. This usually entails raised lettering and numbering, Braille characters, or both.

Additional caution, warning, danger, or traffic management signs should be placed in appropriate areas. While only certain signs are required by code, these additional signs are good practice and widely accepted in the elevator and escalator industry.

An example would be posting ELEVATOR OUT OF SERVICE signs

or placing yellow caution tape across elevator entrances when an elevator is being serviced. Another example would be DANGER, ELEVATOR MACHINE ROOM signs on elevator machine room doors. Signs on switches and disconnects controlling equipment lighting and power circuits reading ALWAYS LEAVE ON EXCEPT WHEN SERVICING may help in preventing inadvertent passenger entrapments, sudden stops or passenger panic on elevators or hydraulic elevators drifting downward. Signs near escalators directing passengers to elevators, and prohibiting wheeled vehicles, can help in preventing wheeled objects such as baby carriages, strollers, and wheelchairs from being transported on escalators.

Since ASME A17.1-2013, the code has allowed signage on escalator and moving walk handrails. The handrails are a highly visible location for safety information, and handrail signage gives the passenger cues to handrail speed and direction.

Although only equipment of different elevators located in the same hoistway or machine room are required to be identified, it is prudent to establish a unique identification for each elevator in a building. Typically, each elevator will be numbered sequentially from left to right and clockwise. All major components of the elevator should be marked with that identifying number/letter. This includes control panels, disconnect switches, motor generators, driving machines, tanks, governors, car tops, pit equipment, and car operating panel. Not only will this help prevent the wrong equipment from being worked on or the wrong switch being operated (preventing personnel injury or equipment damage), it also permits passengers to identify malfunctioning equipment or report an entrapment accurately. Marking each landing entrance with the equipment number can prevent misidentification of elevators by users, emergency personnel, and elevator personnel.

Marking each hoistway landing entrance with its associated floor number will not only help passengers to determine whether they are on the right floor, it permits them to accurately identify problems on certain floors. Marking the hoistway side of the landing doors with each floor number can greatly assist mechanics working on the equipment and inspectors inspecting the equipment.

Other vertical transportation equipment (escalators and dumbwaiters) should also be similarly marked to avoid any confusion in identifying the equipment.

C. Proper Design

Prevention of accidents due to defective designs of vertical transportation equipment has similarities with other transportation, motor control, and machinery designs. Simply put, a defectively designed component within the system is unreliable, unsafe, short-lived, or incompatible with the system.

Most of the vertical transportation equipment manufacturers have test towers where a newly created elevator or escalator system is put through its paces. The purpose of this is to verify that the overall design performs as intended and to verify that the components of the system have no weaknesses susceptible to conditions such as heat, stress, or friction. Monitors gauge the equipment and the results are recorded.

The tests are followed by design-review meetings. These meetings involve many company departments. Design engineers, manufacturing, marketing, application, procurement, shipping, installation, maintenance, and spare part managers attend these meetings to assure that the new product fits into the company's product line, and that they can support the product. They evaluate the design to ensure that the system can be manufactured (especially for the parts that are made in-house), installed at the site, and maintained once installed. Also present at these meetings are the financial representatives of the company. Does the product meet the financial goals of the company? If not, then the product is redesigned, or the procurement managers are instructed to buy less costly components. In either case, the whole process is repeated again and again until the CEO allows the product to be released.

When released, the product is again verified at the first field installation. More changes may be required. If the product is released for sale before its reliability is assessed, problems may occur. For example, at several locations throughout the United States, an entire elevator controlling system had to be replaced with its predecessor because its solid-state electronic components were simply too sensitive to the environment and to static discharges to function properly. Because the company had a presence in many other markets, its reputation would have been highly diminished or destroyed had it not undertaken such a monumental replacement.

When defective parts are identified, a "product letter" is usually sent by certified mail to all of the owners of the equipment. In essence, this is similar to recall notices issued for other products, such as automobiles. In some cases, the defective part may take a long time to identify. Unfortunately, sometimes a product letter is released only after a series of accidents have occurred. Also, sometimes known hazards are only communicated internally. While this results in correcting the problem for future products, it does not warn those who own, maintain, or use existing equipment.

Defective designs can take many forms, many of which are not readily apparent. The most common weak link is maintenance. Even the best-designed equipment will fail if it is not properly maintained. The design of the equipment has a major effect on its maintenance. Maintenance personnel usually have a limited time to perform the required maintenance tasks. If the conditions are so severe (poor access, confined working space, components too heavy to be moved easily, etc.) that maintenance is difficult (and in some cases is impossible without major efforts), then chances are that it will not be done. The consequences are obvious.

D. Proper Application

Misapplication of equipment occurs when the item has been applied incorrectly. This occurrence is quite common since vertical transportation equipment is manufactured for a variety of applications.

It is not defective as described above. It may work fine in less demanding situations, but it just does not work correctly when used in more demanding circumstances (at higher speeds, more frequent usage, greater loads, etc.) than it was designed to operate in. This is a very important distinction because it may appear on the surface that the manufacturer of the equipment is at fault, when in actuality the installer or user simply misapplied the equipment.

The installing or maintenance company generally takes the same course of action as described above for defective designs. A product letter is issued notifying the building owners of the problem along with the consequences of not taking remedial action. This at least reduces the installing company's liability, even if the owner does not take remedial action. Naturally, the installing or maintenance company should keep a copy of the letter and produce it if an incident occurs.

E. Proper Installation

Proper installation is important for an elevator or escalator to operate as designed. Improper installation of one or more of a system's components or the omission to install these components affects the operation of the elevator or escalator to varying degrees. This type of error can occur during the original installation of the elevator, during the replacement of components, or during alterations to the equipment.

For example, if the electrical wiring of an elevator or escalator were installed incorrectly, the elevator or escalator would not function as intended despite the best design and maintenance. Unlike mechanical defects, which in most cases are readily observable, electrical defects might not be so evident. This is because mechanical defects usually prevent a mechanism from operating or otherwise become readily apparent, while an electrical defect in many cases allows the mechanism to work, but not properly. Once this situation develops, the problem may persist undetected for quite some time until an accident occurs. If this incorrect installation were to compromise a safety device, then the consequences are clear.

The failure to install components can have the same consequences. In addition, if the component is peripheral to the operation of the elevator or escalator then the omission may not be noticed until after an accident. For example, if a guard were to be removed during a repair but not be replaced, then the operation of the elevator would not be affected. The guard may even be discarded once it is no longer in place. The potential consequences are unmistakable.

F. Other Measures

The purpose of ASME A17.3 Safety Code for Elevators and Escalators *"is to establish minimum requirements that will provide a reasonable degree of safety for the general public"* and is intended *to "enhance the safety of the general public."* Therefore, even if not required by the AHJ, compliance with ASME A17.3 is not only prudent but also strongly advisable.

Advances in technology, additional safety features, improved service, reduced maintenance requirements, increased service life, and improved reliability are all excellent reasons to modernize outdated equipment. Usually an important dividend from the modernization of equipment is reduced liability. Many times the bulk of the existing equipment can be reconditioned and reused, and the remaining equipment can be modernized in stages.

External factors such as power failures, earthquakes, tornados, high winds resulting in sway of tall buildings, floods, fire, and building structural failures have been and will continue to be the cause of accidents. Elevator and building codes help reduce the effects of these causes. When investigating accidents of these types, it is necessary to determine if the elevator was designed and installed to meet the required codes. For example, elevators installed in earthquake zones are required to meet the earthquake code requirements that apply in that jurisdiction. These codes help assure that the elevator and its associated counterweight remain in their guide rails and do not collide with each other. Earthquake zones exist in many areas of the U.S. besides the West Coast, including the East Coast and Midwest.

Elevator malfunctions are often related to power supply problems. Failures of power will usually cause all building equipment that relies on electricity to stop, including elevators and escalators. Brownouts can cause only one or two elevators in the building to be troublesome and are usually more difficult to attribute to any equipment malfunction. The same arguments can be made for water and fire or smoke damage. Settling or subsidence of the building can result in structural damage. Water damage is a common cause of damage to elevators and escalators. This can be from sources such as overflowing plumbing, sprinklers and floor cleaning machines. Tall buildings sway during high winds and therefore appropriate safeguards must be provided to ensure safe operation.

Poor lighting has contributed to many elevator and escalator accidents. Proper lighting can enhance the safety of both passengers and mechanics. Proper lighting should be provided in machine rooms, elevator car tops and pits, inside the elevator car, at escalator steps, and at landings. The ASME A17.1 code requires certain lighting intensities inside the car, in the pit, and in the machine room for elevators, and at landing plates and exposed steps for escalators. In addition, the lighting for escalators must be uniform and not materially contrast with the surroundings. Local building codes may impose additional requirements.

Although it is beyond the scope of this treatise to analyze design defects, there are certain bottom line precautions that would be prudent for any designer to take. One of these is the concept of "fail safe." In essence, this concept requires that if a device or component fails to operate then it must not result in a dangerous situation. This may require shutting down the elevator or escalator, or other precautionary action.

Proper lighting can enhance the safety both of users of vertical transportation equipment and maintenance mechanics. Included are machine rooms, elevator car tops and pits, inside elevator cars, escalator steps, and landings. The ASME A17.1 code requires certain lighting intensities inside the car, in the pit, and in the machine room for elevators, and at landing plates and exposed steps for escalators. In addition for escalators the lighting must be uniform and not materially contrast with the surroundings. Local building codes may contain additional requirements.

Yellow striping on low overheads, ledges, rotating equipment, and at pinch points assists the technician in being aware of these dangers. Marking escalator steps with a yellow stripe along the sides of the step treads adjacent to the skirt panels and at the interface with the adjacent step's riser helps alert passengers to the potential entrapment areas and hopefully causes them to stand away from these areas. In at least one case, steps were marked with footprints to indicate the correct position to stand.

Yellow combs can be installed on escalators alerting passengers to the combplate-step interface. Skirt panels can be stiffened to limit deflection, lubricated to limit friction, and adjusted to minimize the running clearance between the steps and the skirt panels. Aftermarket devices can be installed to limit the running clearance between the steps and the skirt panels, or to prevent entrapments of children's calves in the running clearance between the steps and the skirt panels.

The use of "pre-opening the doors on approach" for elevators can be eliminated to reduce the probability of trip and fall accidents on elevators.

Unreliable or inaccurate leveling or landing systems can be replaced with accurate and reliable systems to reduce trip and fall accidents on elevators.

Failure to properly secure the equipment when working on it can lead to serious injuries. Proper lockout or tag-out procedures should be used whenever the equipment is worked on. This entails securing the equipment both electrically and mechanically from inadvertent movement and posting appropriate signs.

The list can go on and on. Yet even implementing just the ones mentioned could eliminate many elevator and escalator accidents and reduce the severity of many of those that do happen. The best source for accident prevention ideas is the elevator-escalator consultant. Many of these preventive actions can be easily and economically implemented for existing equipment. Others are simply common sense and prudent practice. Those requiring considerable expense and disruption can be phased in.

G. Workplace Measures

Elevator personnel are subject to the same general hazards as the general public (e.g. falls, being struck by objects hazards, shear hazards, crushing hazards, electrical hazards, being caught in between objects hazards). However, elevator personnel are typically faced with all of these hazards on a daily basis that are significantly more hazardous in nature. Therefore, this section addresses workplace accidents. See Section 3.2(D) for workplace accident statistics.

Elevator personnel are exposed to many of these hazards during the installation of elevators and escalators when many of the safeguards that protect the public are not yet installed or functional. Therefore, proper safeguards must be put in place to protect them (e.g. fall protection, (i.e. guardrails, barricades, and fall-arrest systems) and personal protection equipment (e.g. proper clothing, hard hats, hearing protection, safety glasses, safety boots, and respiratory protection).

Elevator personnel frequently work on top of elevators and therefore are subject to extreme fall hazards. The 2000 Edition of ASME A17.1 codified requirements for car top safety railings when the distance between the car top edge and the adjacent hoistway wall exceeds 12 inches. However, the vast majority of installed elevators do not have these railings. These handrails can easily and economically be installed in most cases. One potential obstacle is insufficient overhead clearances. However, this can be overcome with retractable safety railings and electric contacts to prevent operation with the railing deployed during normal operation.

For many years car top controls have been required so that elevator personnel can safely control the operation of the elevator when they are on the car top for maintenance, repairs, and inspections. However, many existing old elevators are not provided with this important safety feature. The installation of car top controls typically can be installed economically.

Hoistway access switches have been provided for many years to enable elevator personnel to safely gain access to the car top. However, many elevators are not provided with hoistway access switches and those that do have them frequently become disabled by building cleaning operations.

When an electric elevator is moving in one direction, the counterweight is moving in the other direction. An elevator with only a 2,500 lb. capacity can have a counterweight that weighs 1.5 tons or more. The counterweight usually doesn't make sufficient noise to be heard when it is moving. Serious injuries or death will result if someone is struck by the counterweight. Also, side counterweights are required, instead of being installed at the rear of the hoistway, when front and rear openings are provided. This can cause elevator personnel to let their guard down when working on the side of the car top because they do not expect the counterweight to be there. This can be an issue even if the side counterweight is installed on an adjacent elevator in the same hoistway. Sometimes chains are hung from the bottom of the counterweight to create noise, but usually elevator passengers object to the noises and they are removed. Guarding is required in many cases in the pit to protect elevator personnel, but not the rest of the hoistway.

While elevator control voltages are typically low (e.g. 24 VDC) and ancillary voltages will be in the 110/120 VAC range, main power voltages typically will be in the 220–480 volt range. These higher voltages are a serious shock hazard.

The *Elevator Industry Field Employees' Safety Handbook* is the foremost publication devoted to delineating the proper safety practices that should be used when working around elevators and escalators. While this document is intended for use by mechanics, it has many parts that are applicable to other elevator personnel (e.g., inspectors). The latest edition when this book was being written was the 2015 edition. In the past revisions were held until sufficient material was available to justify the cost of publishing a supplement. However, now revisions will be published electronically as soon as they are approved. Printed supplements will also be published periodically.

Failure to properly secure the equipment when working on it can lead to serious injuries. Proper lockout or tag-out procedures should be used whenever the equipment is worked on. This entails securing the equipment both electrically and mechanically from inadvertent movement and posting appropriate signage.

5.3 Examples of Accident Prevention Measures

Example 1: Falls Down Hoistway Due to Dislodgement of Hoistway Doors

In one case the investigation and witness statements indicate that the injured was leaning against the elevator's 16th floor landing door, waiting for the adjacent passenger elevator to arrive. He was leaning against the door with his feet approximately 1 foot from the base of the door. Suddenly the door swung open from the bottom into the open hoistway. The top of the door remained on the track.

He fell down the shaft and on top of the elevator as it was traveling down at full speed. The elevator stopped below the 10th floor. He was wedged between the elevator and the hoistway wall and sustained injuries. The responding emergency crews removed him from the shaft. A representative of the elevator company who examined the subject landing doors saw the lower door guide (gib) bent with the bottom of the guide facing the hall at approximately a 45 degree angle.

Another case was in a college dormitory where the elevator faced a long hallway. The floor was marble coated. The students played a game that consisted of soaking the hallway with soapy water, then sliding down the hallway. The hallway door gibs, perhaps damaged by repeated blows, allowed a young man to dislodge the door and fall to his death.

In another case a young lady fell from the lobby floor into the pit and sustained permanent injuries. Repeated floor mopping caused the bottom of the door to rot out and the gib screws to become ineffective.

PREVENTION: Door gibs (see Chapter 2, Figure C.30) and hangers for horizontally sliding doors must be maintained in compliance with the applicable minimum code requirements and exceed them when appropriate.

- The ASME A17.1 code requires a lower door guide (gib) penetrate the sill track by a minimum ¼ inch. However, the gib should penetrate as much as possible without causing interferences when the doors move to provide maximum safety.
- The ASME A17.1 code requires one or more gib per hoistway door panel. However, good and accepted industry practice is to have at least two gibs. Having a single gib subjects it to misalignment and excessive wear and does not provide a backup.
- The hoistway door panels must be square, vertically plumb and must not be excessively warped in order to prevent the track channel from wearing. In some cases the gib screws are loosened either by the gib

binding in the track, or loosened by someone to reduce the door movement friction.

- The vertical leg of the gib bracket must be securely mounted to the door with all the required screws.
- It is **very important** that the gib bracket spans the entire depth (thickness) of the door. Otherwise if it is not deep enough it can bend and cause the gib to tilt reducing the penetration of the gib into the sill track and over time will chamfer the track. This chamfer will allow the gib to "jump the bottom track" more easily when a force is applied to the outside of the door panel.
- The door panel must also be able to support the screws and not strip the threads when tightened. Aging hoistway doors and hoistway doors in wet or corrosive environments can have the lower portions, where the lower guides (gibs) are fastened, become damaged and rusted to an extent where the gib screws are incapable of securing the gibs to the door. Columbia Elevator Products provides doors with stainless steel inserts in the bottoms and tops, when specified. See their website at www.ColumbiaElevator.com. It would be prudent to specify stainless inserts, especially in corrosive environments and near salt water and where tile or marble floors border the doors.
- **Frequent checking the condition of the gibs, sill tracks and tightening gib bracket screws are a must in any environment, and must be emphasized in the maintenance log.**
- The gib track must be square and not be worn such that the channel is down to ¼ inch or less. This is too prevalent on soft metal sills. Also the track must not be tilted or skewed, both of which prevents proper depth adjustments throughout the door travel.
- When replacing sills, use the newer T-groove type. The gib has a washer on the bottom that spans the width of the "T" to help prevent the door from leaving the track. This type of channel keeps the dirt and debris from lying adjacent to and damaging or gumming up the gib.
- The guiding member of gibs is usually a material like nylon that can melt in a fire or become damaged or dislodged. The gib is provided "fire tabs" that are made of metal and are bent into the sill to maintain the integrity of the bottom guides in case the nylon melts in a fire.
- Bottom and top safety retainers have been required in case the primary guiding means fails to prevent excessive displacement of the hoistway door panels under considerable forces A17.1b-1992 and later editions. These safety retainers must not be subject to wear or stress during normal operation or maintenance. **This is a significant safety enhance-**

ment to prevent falls down the hoistway due to landing doors being displaced. These safety retainers can be added to existing installations, but their ability to prevent displacement of hoistway door panels is limited by the strength of the existing door assembly. See Chapter 2, Figure C.30 for a photograph depicting a bottom safety retainer.

- The door closer must fully close an open door from any position, when the hoistway door is disengaged from the car door. Otherwise a door can be partially open when the car is at another floor. Door relating cables on center opening and multi-speed doors must be taught (no slack) to prevent the cable jumping the sheaves. Where broken arm type closers are used, they must be checked for tightness and securely mounted to the door and sill or wall.
- Door hangers and their tracks must be securely mounted to the door and the upper jamb or wall.
- The upthrust rollers must be properly adjusted and secure to prevent the door hanger rollers from jumping the upper track.
- The lip on the concave hanger roller must be deep enough so that a blow to the top of the door will not dislodge the roller from the track. The roller should not have cracks or worn bearings or bushings.
- Gibs must have at least ¼ inch engagement in the sill tracks, at least two gibs should be provided on each panel, and each gib must be properly secured.
- Sills with worn tracks must be replaced.
- *And finally and most importantly:* All of the above items must checked and rechecked by all personnel responsible for assuring elevator safety. This includes the inspector, the elevator consultant when making an audit or modernization survey, building management, and of course the maintenance technician and repair teams.

Example 2: Entrapments Between Swinging Hoistway Doors and Collapsible Cab Gates

TYPE OF EQUIPMENT: Swing type hoistway door (see Chapter 2, Figure C.19–C.22) with collapsible style car gate in a multifamily apartment building. The hoistway door is equipped with a space guard (See Chapter 2, Figure C.19–C.20) that does not meet the requirements in the ASME A17.3 *Safety Code for Existing Elevators and Escalators* (see Chapter 2, Figure C.21–C.22).

The child attempts to enter the elevator. The elevator "hoistway door to the collapsible gate" space (pocket) can be nine inches or more, with the higher value occurring when a force is applied to the gate (pushing it into the elevator).The child is blocked from full entry into the elevator by the closed elevator gate. The swing door closes, pushing the child into the gate and trapping them between the swing type outside door and collapsible type gate on the elevator. The elevator, in response to a call, is set in motion with the child trapped. When the running clearance on the elevator passes the narrowest point the child is crushed. These accidents, usually resulting in deaths or brain damage, continue to occur despite the fact that this space problem has been well known in the industry since at least the 1931 Edition of A17.1 and also published in ASME A17.3-1986. The cause of death or brain damage is generally attributed to mechanical asphyxiation.

PREVENTION: Most important in this example is that the space guard meets the requirements of ASME A17.3.

Gate gibs and hangers must be in compliance with code, of which requires a lower door guide (gib) on every 2nd vertical member and a hanger roller on every 4th member, and in good condition. This will help minimize the deflection of the gate.

The hoistway door must be square and must not be excessively warped. Also it must not have excessive clearance between the door hook and the interlock box. All of these conditions will increase the depth of the pocket where a child can be entrapped.

The running clearance (distance between hoistway sill and elevator cab sill) must not be excessive, i.e. exceeding the 1½ inch maximum permitted by code and if. If the running clearance can be adjusted to the ¾ inch permitted the entrapment pocket is further reduced.

Code enforcing authorities at times have been remiss in not citing the absence of a space guard and permitting the elevator to operate without the proper space guard for long periods of time (years). However they generally cite the violation immediately ***after*** the accident.

Example 3: Falls Due to Misleveling of an Elevator Above or Below a Landing

Trips and falls occur quite often while entering or exiting the elevator due to the elevator floor being above or below the landing floor. This, along with door strikes, accounts for the vast majority of elevator injuries.

Improper leveling can result in serious injuries and even can result in death due to subsequent complications. The elderly do not fully recover from broken bones in most of the cases and in many of those cases death occurs in the months following the more severe accidents.

The cause of improper leveling can vary (e.g. improper maintenance, type of control, type of selector and landing devices). Improper leveling is most common on elevators with poor control technology (e.g. single speed AC elevators) and those requiring intensive maintenance (e.g. elevators equipped with a mechanical selector or motor-generator control), both of which have been superseded by new technology, and "pre-opening upon approach" door operation.

Many years back, the elevator was not expected to be level with the floor. Passengers entered and exited with caution, always looking down as they stepped on and off the elevator. As the percentage of high performance elevators, with very accurate leveling capabilities continues to rise, more and more people expecting the elevator to be level with the floor and look straight ahead when they enter and exit an elevator.

Most electric elevators, except single speed AC controlled and two speed AC controlled elevators, stop electrically by slowing down the driving machine motor and the brake only sets after the elevator is stopped. In essence the brake is a parking brake. When properly maintained, the leveling accuracy should not exceed ½ inch, but for better types of control the accuracy can be 1/8 to ¼ inches or less. This creates false expectations for passengers when using single speed AC controlled and two speed AC controlled elevators.

Single Speed and Two Speed AC controlled systems, which can operate at relatively slow speeds of 100 or more feet per minute, do not have leveling capability. They receive a signal to stop and apply the driving machine brake at a predetermined distance away from a landing. The elevator then slides to a stop through the brake, similar to how an automobile brake functions. Therefore, the stopping accuracy is variable. It is dependent on conditions such as the amount of weight inside the car, the direction of travel, the adjustment of the brake, usage of the elevator, as well as temperature and humidity of the machine room.

Some excellent historical data can be found in past Elevator World articles (keyword: leveling), such as "Court Cases of Consequence" dated August, 1984 and "Leveling Accuracy-The Missing Standard" published in July, 1987 by John J McHale. He makes the point that we continue to let the courts establish the quantitative value for leveling accuracy, when it should be the responsibility of code writers.

The following is a summary of findings where an elderly lady tripped and fell while exiting the elevator and the time proven preventions:

The discovery documents indicate that a lady was injured when she exited an elevator that was not level with the landing floor. She had stepped out with her left foot and then fell as she attempted to pull her right foot from the elevator. She then crawled to her apartment, several feet down the corridor, and notified both her daughter and a building management employee that she had been injured in the fall.

The elevator maintenance contract obligated the maintenance company to supply trained employees, and further that those employees will use all reasonable care to keep the systems in proper adjustment and safe operating condition. It was a full coverage contract with 24 hour, 7 days a week callback service should repairs be needed.

Evidence indicated that either the brake was defective or was improperly adjusted on the date of her accident. The callback ticket submitted by the maintenance mechanic stated that the type of elevator (Single Speed AC) was prone to misleveling. While achieving this prevention is highly maintenance intensive, the maintenance contractor is never-the-less responsible by contract to provide an elevator operation that will consistently stop reasonably level at the floors within the capability of the control system. If they were unable to do so, and if the building management refused to upgrade the elevator equipped as recommended, then the contractor should have canceled the contract.

PREVENTION: Proper maintenance would have improved the stopping accuracy and lessened the probability of an injury.

Timely replacement of the control and landing system would have prevented the accident and injuries to the lady, by reducing the probability of a mislevel at the floor. To back up this claim a comparison was made of two elevators in the same complex: the subject elevator and an elevator that was equipped with a control feature (Variable Voltage Variable Frequency AC or VVVF AC) that varied the frequency and the voltage that is supplied to the motor. This control feature allows the elevator to land, level with the floor, even with variable loads. It accomplishes this by reducing the full speed (100 FPM) to 20% or less (less than 20 FPM) as the elevator reaches the floor level. This is as opposed to the elevator, without the features, approaching the floor level at 100 feet per minute while attempting to slide through the brake to try to stop level with the floor. The new landing system was also equipped with a newer floor-landing device.

The new features allowed the elevator to stop level when it was empty (no load) and also with an 850 pound load (70% capacity). The older elevator under the same tests stopped substaintially not level. Also, since the elevator had been experiencing a history of mislevels, building management was negligent in failing to warn the tenants and employees of the buildings that the floor position of the elevator could be off-level. Signage stating this fact should have been posted in the elevator as well as in the corridors adjacent to the elevator openings. In this day and age, it would be prudent to post signage on all elevators that "stop only with brake action."

Example 4: Hit by Doors

Elevator accidents involving passengers being struck by the doors while entering or exiting the elevator's cab are very common. This, along with trips and falls, accounts for the vast majority of elevator injuries.

Most elevator passengers are aware that the doors close automatically. They assume that the door reopening devices are working properly. However, these devices are not usually effective in the path of the closing landing doors, but only effective in the path of the car doors, unbeknownst to the average passenger. Furthermore, these devices may be defective or turned off by the building engineer or other personnel with a key to the elevator control panel inside the cab. The device could also be shorted or intentionally circumvented, and the elevator will continue to operate without door protection. When this happens, tenants of the building are surprised when the door does not reopen as it always has in the past when they put their hands or briefcases on the door's edge or between the closing doors.

Mechanical types (i.e., *safety edges*) require contact with an obstruction to operate. For horizontally closing doors, their sensing edge must lead the car door by a sufficient distance when it closes for it to operate effectively. Many times they were combined with 2 optical beams located 5 inches and 29 inches above the floor to meet ADA requirements. Historically, vertically sliding doors were provided with pressure-sensitive devices (e.g., pneumatic) on the leading edge of the upper car door or gate.

Photoelectric devices detect obstructions when the photoelectric beams across the door opening are blocked by the obstruction. These devices do not require contact with an object to operate, which increases safety. For many years these devices have used infrared light, while older devices used less reliable visible light. These types of devices have been available for a number of years for vertically sliding doors and gates on freight elevators.

Newer designs provide an important safety enhancement. They typically use infrared beams to detect people as they approach to enter the car from the landing. These newer devices usually combine the proximity feature with the more common infrared feature that detects people in the path of the closing doors. This provides in effect a 3D detection zone instead of the normal 2D detection zone. However, the 3D protection typically can be turned off.

Proximity door reopening devices sense an object close to the doors. Some older types work on the principle of conductive obstructions (which include the human body) inducing a change in a sensing device when they come in proximity to the device. Historically, many of these devices were too sensitive.

There are two main criteria relating to the closing forces of elevator doors: static force and kinetic energy.

The static force is the force necessary to keep the elevator door from closing once it is at rest. This force must not exceed 30 pounds. The force is a measure of the crushing force exerted by the doors. The kinetic energy is a measure of the dynamic impact that the doors can impart if they strike an object when closing.

The kinetic energy is based on the combined masses of the closing doors and any associated hardware, the average closing speed of the doors, and the rotating kinetic energy of the door operator.

The car doors must be provided with a re-opening device if the kinetic energy is above 2½ foot-pounds. The maximum kinetic energy of the doors is limited to seven foot-pounds when the re-opening device is operative. If the re-opening device is rendered inoperative, as is the case when the system is operating in the nudging mode, then the kinetic energy must be reduced to 2½ foot-pounds. For center-opening elevator doors, the re-opening device must operate such that an obstruction of either door panel when closing will cause the car and hoistway (landing) doors to stop and/or re-open. The re-opening device must protect the full height of the opening.

PREVENTION: To help prevent door strike accidents:

- modern 3D door automatic infrared door reopening devices should be installed,
- door closing speed and force must be maintained in code compliance and as low as possible to achieve acceptable operation,
- longer door open dwell times, lower door forces, slower door closing, and no nudging should be provided in buildings with large numbers of elderly or less ambulatory passengers (e.g. nursing homes, senior housing, hospitals),
- longer door open dwell times should be provided in main lobbies and in buildings where there are large numbers of transients (e.g. hotels, transportation centers).

Example 5: Escalator Entrapments

The most common escalator entrapments occur between two adjacent steps (i.e. the riser of one step and the tread of the adjacent step), the steps and the combplate, the moving steps and the stationary skirt panels (lower balustrade sides), or a combination of all of these. The injuries from these entrapments commonly involve young children and sometimes cause horrific injuries (e.g. amputations, degloving injuries, disfigurements).

PREVENTION: Preventions for entrapments are a derivative of good design, maintenance, inspection, and testing.

The main reasons for entrapments between step and the riser on the adjacent step is the gap between steps due to worn step chains and the condition of the step treads and any plastic demarcation inserts (if applicable). Assurance that there are no broken parts must be documented by both the person turning on the escalator as well as the service technician. On each visit the technician must also check the gaps between steps (a stiff business card can be used to verify that the step riser cleats mesh with the adjacent step treads or a "gap gauge" can be used to for old escalators with smooth risers).

The main reasons for entrapments between the sides of the step and the adjacent skirt panels are the gap between the sides of the step and the panels and the surface friction of the side panels with footwear. Good preventive maintenance will assure that the gaps stay at a minimum (usually 3/16 inches or less depending on the applicable code) and within the applicable code limits. Damaged/unsupported skirts or untreated skirts will facilitate entrapments. Frequent lubrication of skirt panels if they are not made from low friction materials is good and accepted industry practice.

The A17 code has required "Step/Skirt Performance Index" (SSPI) testing since 2001. This test is retroactive, and all escalators need to comply with the requirement. The test gathers the loaded gap (static gap between the step and the skirt panel, plus the deflection of the skirt panel, plus the step lateral stiffness (deadband) with 25 lbs applied between the step and the skirt), and the coefficient of friction between the skirt and the test device, then plugs them into a mathematical formula, and outputs the Step/Skirt Performance Index. The higher the "index," the higher the likelihood of entrapment between the step and the skirt. The index is required to be tested annually, with the goal being to maintain the escalator with the lowest possible index in an effort to minimize entrapments. Along with skirt brushes, if required, regular index testing and the maintenance that it necessitates should reduce entrapments.

However, there are a lot of misconceptions related to this test. One is that it has been erroneously claimed by some escalator maintenance companies that if skirt deflectors (brushes) are installed then the SSPI does not have to be performed. Another is that the 25 lb force is significantly less than the forces present during an entrapment. Another is that the test does not take into account what happens after the entrapment has already occurred. A wringing action occurs, which forces the entrapped body part into the hollow space on the side of the step. Also there may be sharp edges or protruding screws. This makes extrication of the body part difficult and can cause further damage to the body part.

Dynamic skirt panels (i.e. moving skirt panels) apparently have not been commercially viable. Skirt deflectors (e.g. brushes) have limitations, mainly because they are up to 9 inches above where most entrapments originate, except for preventing calf entrapments.

So what can be done to minimize the severity of injuries? This is one of the topics not addressed in most side of step entrapment studies.

Figure P.1 *Exposed screw*

First we must look at what happens to a foot or hand that becomes entrapped as the escalator travels down. The limb, after entrapment will be pushed by the skirt into the hollow opening in the side of the step, and underneath the top of the step. The limb will then be held by the sharp edges in the step casting (see P1 below). The entrapment will make it virtually impossible to remove the foot or hand without any damage such as amputation or de-gloving (stripping the skin from the bone).

Many escalator steps on the market today are dangerous because it "won't let go" if anything becomes entrapped between the skirt and the step. Body parts and objects are held by the inside of the step due to its hollow side opening (see P1) and the sharp edges, and in some cases protruding screws (P2). One of two things can then happen. Either the escalator continues to run with the entrapment and the object or body part is "sheared off" at the combs on the floor plates. Or the entrapped object causes the escalator to stop due to the action of the skirt switch. In this case the entrapped object is severely damaged due to the twist-

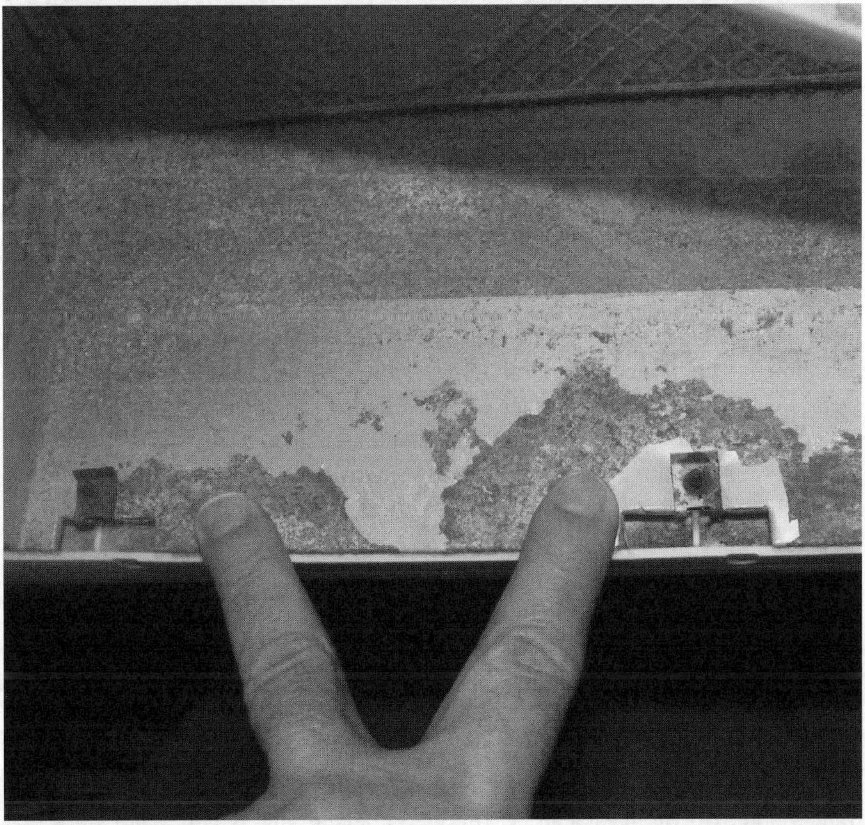

Figure P.2 *More exposed Screws*

Figure P.3 *Sharp edges on side void and exposed screws*

ing and pulling attempt to extricate the object. The code has addressed the skirt friction very well and ASME Escalator Committee should be commended for its inclusion into the Code of both friction reducing paint or periodic silicone applications and skirt index tests. But with these commendable inclusions, entrapments are occurring and the severity of the injuries needs to be addressed and minimized. Most studies do not address as to how to minimize the damage if an entrapment were to occur, but only how to minimize the likelihood of an entrapment. One must address the other side, the sides of the step facing the skirts for the achievement of a safely designed escalator step. However until a safer step is implemented the only avenue to safety is to reduce the likelihood of any step-to-skirt entrapment, e.g. smaller gaps and friction reduction.

Combplate entrapments can be prevented in most cases by replacing comb segments that contain broken teeth and adjusting the comb teeth tips to penetrate into the step treads a maximum distance that will not promote scraping as the step passes. Adjusting the penetration of the comb teeth into the step treads just so they mesh, as the code requires, is not enough. Combplate stop switches and comb-step impact devices will limit injuries from entrapments that do occur.

"CAUTION, PASENGERS ONLY, HOLD HANDRAIL, ATTEND CHILDREN, AVOIDS SIDES" are the caution signs required to be posted at the entrances and exits of all escalators. Yellow borders around the escalator steps that indicate the area on the step where your feet should **NOT** be placed are required on new escalators and are recommended for existing units. Yellow comb finger sections demarcate the ends of the moving steps and the beginning of the stationary combplate. These measures, at best, are only **reminders** to passengers of the imminent dangers that exist.

When falls occur for whatever reason, the incurred injuries are intensified by any sharpness in the escalator step treads. The knife-like edges are caused by either the steps not being burnished during manufacturing or by being honed when the escalator is in operation due to improper adjustment as the steps pass through the combs at the ends of the escalator. New steps must be burnished in the factory before being shipped. New steps must be checked by feeling the edges prior to installation into the escalator. The steps must pass through the combs without any interferences. Adjustments must be made to remedy any problems (e.g. adjustment of the combs vertically and adjustment of the step chains to assure that one side is not longer than the other side resulting in a skewed action as the steps pass through the combs).

Example 6: Escalator Trips and Falls

Many trips and falls while on the escalator can be prevented by the following actions:

- Escalators are not designed to be used as a stair case for several reasons (e.g. riser heights that are not uniform at entrances and exits, riser heights that do not meet standards for stationary stairs). Always barricade a stopped escalator. Barricades containing signage at the top and bottom will deter most passengers.
- Falls have frequently occurred when the speed of the handrails is slower that the step speed. Passengers fall when their feet get ahead of their upper body. Again this is a maintenance issue and handrails should be tested on each visit by the technician and by authorized personnel when an escalator is started or at least once per day.
- Many times on older escalators the fall is caused by an abrupt stop. This is most damaging when riding down due to the 120 degree fall pattern. The brake should be maintained to provide a stop that is not abrupt enough to cause falls but not too long that it could cause other injuries in an emergency situation. Current code requires a stopping rate of no greater than three feet per second squared, which equates to a stopping slide of approximately five inches when the running speed is 90 feet per minute. However, a 9 to 11 inch slide has become the industry standard to help reduce falls.

- While not required in ASME A17.1, guarding on the balustrade to prevent falls over the side of the handrail have been either required or installed on escalators in a number of countries.

Example 7: Escalator Runaways

Runaways happen when the heavily loaded escalator stops due to tripping of one of the 20 or more possible emergency safety switches and the brake does not hold the load. The speed of down running escalators increase dramatically uncontrolled until enough people are off the steps for the brake to hold the remaining load and up running escalators will stop and reverse direction with similar results. Often the brake does hold the load initially, but when people start using a stopped escalator as a stationary stair then the brake cannot hold the imposed loads.

In most cases the brake is found to be below specifications and lacks sufficient stopping torque capacity.

PREVENTION: Proper preventive maintenance.

Chapter 6

Pre-Suit Investigation

Synopsis

From the plaintiff's attorney's perspective investigation begins the moment the client walks through the attorney's door. Investigation continues from that moment through trial itself. Investigation is conducted both pre-suit and following suit. This chapter describes pre-suit investigation.

6.1 Meeting with the Plaintiff

The plaintiff's attorney has to be thorough and use great care when inquiring into the facts of the accident. Generally speaking, the plaintiff's recollection of the accident will be best at the early stages and will diminish as time passes, barring some unusual circumstances such as a head injury. Impressions will begin to be formed concerning the plaintiff's credibility, likeability, and ability to recall facts. The importance of a complete and thorough interview cannot be overemphasized, since often there are no other witnesses to the accident, and the plaintiff's recollection of how the accident occurred will be the only information available in determining what resources should be devoted to investigating the case. The initial client interview should seek to determine, at a minimum, the following:

- As precise a description of the accident as possible
- The plaintiff's familiarity with the elevator or escalator

- Condition of the escalator or accident from the plaintiff's perspective prior to the event
- Any previously existing conditions, disabilities or infirmities that other parties may try to later say contributed to or caused the event.
- Ruling out any distractions (i.e.> cell phone use) by the injured party
- Whether the injured party was under the influence of any prescription medication, drugs or alcohol that may later give rise to a claim that these were somehow factors in the event itself
- The identity of witnesses, including persons who used the equipment shortly before or after the accident, persons who may have actually observed the accident, or persons who were present only after the accident but may be able to provide information about what happened or physical facts useful in determining how the accident may have occurred
- The substance of conversations that took place at the time of the accident or immediately thereafter, including what the plaintiff may have said and statements by witnesses and employees of potential defendants
- Whether the plaintiff gave any statements to any parties before the initial interview, including statements to the compensation carrier or representatives of potential defendants
- Content and availability of the initial workers' compensation report of injury form or accident report and whether the plaintiff or someone else filled it out
- Damages, including injuries, medical treatment, loss of earnings, and potential future damages

6.2 Damages

Generally speaking, at the initial meeting with the client the plaintiff's attorney should be able to get a sense of the potential value of the case. Injuries should be evident or subject to description by the plaintiff. Similarly, economic losses, including medical bills and any lost time from work in the past, or likelihood of lost time from work in the future, can be estimated. If a case does not have sufficient damages then it is best to advise the plaintiff early and get out of the case at the beginning. Costs of suit, including depositions, investigation, fees for liability experts and fees for testimony of liability and damage experts add up quickly. As a result, early identification of a case that should not be undertaken is in the interest of all parties. The cost of litigating an elevator or escalator case involving only one liability expert, one physician as to damages, and half a dozen depositions will be at least $15,000.00. If the injuries are not significant or, if there is no loss of earnings or loss of future earning capacity, then the case simply may not warrant involvement. In some cases, the payments made by the workers' compensation carrier are such that even if there is a recovery the ultimate "net" benefit to the plaintiff is not significant. All of these factors must be considered even before contacting an expert liability witness. Litigation costs must be determined in each specific jurisdiction but there clearly are costs that make a threshold determination of value absolutely necessary. Do not take a case that is not economically feasible. An initial belief that a case is one of "perfect liability" so that even if the damages are not significant the defendant will be willing to "pay something" to settle the case is more times than not misguided. If the owner of the equipment is also the plaintiff's employer and immune from suit this information should be discovered as early as possible.

6.3 The Plaintiff's Account

Once the plaintiff has been interviewed the plaintiff's attorney should determine whether that account makes sense. Is it supported by other witnesses? Does it make sense from a common sense perspective? Do the statements that the plaintiff gave to the workers' compensation carrier or the plaintiff made in the initial report of injury to the compensation carrier coincide with what the plaintiff has told the attorney? Are the statements attributable to the plaintiff concerning how the accident occurred consistent with the emergency room records, hospital records, nurse's notes, and treating physician's notes? Sometimes the plaintiff's version of the facts is contradicted by the medical reports and records. While not fatal, such contradictions may later be used in efforts to impeach or undermine the credibility of the plaintiff by the defendants. If possible, and still available, efforts to obtain 911 tapes or logs of such calls may be useful to support contemporaneous reports surrounding the event itself by disinterested third parties.

6.4 Expert Liability Witness

Once a threshold determination has been made that the damages are sufficient to warrant proceeding, it is most important to select a competent expert liability witness. Without a competent liability expert the plaintiff's attorney will not be able to determine whether the case has merit. Spending a little money on a competent liability expert early in the case may save a lot of money later on. It is not unusual for a plaintiff's attorney to get involved in a case, take depositions, and then as he is approaching trial to go out and obtain an expert witness. Often a plaintiff's attorney will find that he has been pursuing the wrong theory, did not understand technical issues, and has no case. At this point he has squandered thousands of dollars and wasted his and the client's time. *The plaintiff's attorney must hire an expert liability witness immediately after determining that the dam-*

ages do warrant going forward. That expert witness will be able to assist the plaintiff's attorney in formulating theories, attending the site inspection, preparing the complaint and conducting discovery.

A competent elevator liability witness is *not* a witness who is a "jack of all trades." Do not hire an expert unless that expert has experience testifying. It makes no sense to hire an expert and then have to pay to coach that expert how to testify and how to present well in a courtroom. Desirable elevator and escalator experts generally are mechanical or electrical engineers. Attorneys should look for experts who have been involved in the elevator industry, either with inspections and tests, maintenance, installation, design, or a combination of these. A good elevator expert should have strong knowledge and experience working with elevator codes. Some experts may have highly specialized areas of knowledge, particularly those who have worked for a manufacturer. Whether it is better to choose a highly specialized expert or a more well-rounded expert (one involved in different phases of the industry, including inspections and tests, maintenance, and design) will depend upon the particular case. Selected experts should be willing and capable in testifying in support of their opinions and the underlying basis for the testimony. As discussed in Chapter 9, *Expert Opinion*, it is now more than ever essential that counsel retain a proper and competent expert whose opinion will be able to withstand challenges to its admissibility at trial.

6.5 Preservation of Evidence

Occasionally, the equipment involved in the plaintiff's accident will be subject to some type of security or surveillance cameras. This is most common in larger public areas such as hotel lobbies, casinos, governmental buildings, and airports. If so, in general there is a limited time during which the videotape or film will be available before it is simply recorded over. The plaintiff as well as the defendant facilities manager, property owner, or product manufacturer will be interested in this evidence. Plaintiff's counsel should ascertain as quickly as possible, through an informal site inspection or direct contact with potential defendants, whether videotapes may in fact be present at the scene of the accident and for how long they would normally be preserved before being recorded over. All jurisdictions are different but procedures are universally available for emergency applications to the court for preservation of evidence before filing the lawsuit.

It is also necessary to ensure that any equipment that is inspected be preserved in the condition that most closely resembles the condition existing at the time of the accident. If the evidence is destroyed or lost, depending upon the jurisdiction, there may be severe sanctions for the plaintiff if the evidence was under the plaintiff's control or the control of plaintiff's expert. Conversely, if the defendant removes critical evidence and does not make it available for inspection by plaintiff's expert, the plaintiff may be able to convince the court to limit defenses, or to instruct the jury that an adverse inference should be drawn based upon the defendant's failure to produce evidence within its control.

Some jurisdictions require that accidents that exceed a certain threshold be reported to the appropriate authorities, that an inspection be conducted by the proper authorities to determine the cause and/or to determine if the unit is safe to be placed back in service and prohibit the removal of damaged components unless approval has been granted.

Practitioners are encouraged to undertake preservation and inspection of evidence as part of the pre-suit process. This is arguably a critical component, when possible, of the pre-suit evaluation of any case. Some jurisdictions require, or mandate, that following an accident an inspection is undertaken. However, this does not mean one in fact takes place for a variety of reasons. This is true even where local ordinances, or state statutes, mandate an investigation or reporting to public authorities. Owners, their agents, and service companies are often allowed to police themselves when it comes to compliance as governmental authorities lack the resources to pro-actively monitor escalators and elevators absent a crisis or annual inspection.

Public safety requires vigilance by those knowledgeable of an accident on an escalator or elevator. Hazardous conditions, whether obvious or unexplained at the time, expose the public to the risk of serious injury. Timely notification to an owner may alert them to a problem, an actual incident requiring investigation, or the need for maintenance. Whether they, or their agents, act on information may be outcome determinative. Laws imposing duties to inspect, repair and maintain should be consulted to support the investigative effort.

With the advent of computers and software controlling access to landings or floors, seeking out the preservation of related data is warranted as soon as practical. Similarly, surveillance video may be helpful. While ultimately subject to interpretation by the Defense or a Plaintiff, data points provide information that could help evaluate symptoms of a problem or alternative explanations for an event. Experts may interpret data differently or identically; however, if it is not available, experts may not be in a position to assess fault or cast doubt on theories or defenses advanced by any litigant.

To this end, a property owner, their property manager, or other agents, including any contracted elevator service company, must consider saving information following notification of an event involving injury or death. Property Managers are often already versed in preparing an "Incident Report" with a view toward a potential legal claim. Service companies are often brought into legal cases, or subject to questions, where they are contractually obligated to maintain or service escalators or elevators. As a result, they may also be subject to requests for the preservation of evidence pre-suit or the production of any potential material evidence once litigation has been initiated.

With the undertaking of legal representation, practitioners should seek to identify, collect, and place a "litigation hold" on available documents, records, and electronically stored information relating to the operation of an escalator or elevator. Failing to preserve evidence can expose any party to cross-examination on what the evidence showed, or would have showed, if it was still available to an adverse party. Some jurisdictions allow for evidentiary burden shifting, or rebuttable presumptions against a party, where certain showings are made regarding previously available evidence that is lost, destroyed, or missing. Through early preservation requests or efforts to preserve evidence, a party may strengthen their legal theories and position and benefit the interests of their client.

As a general rule, the law encourages the repair of a condition in response to an event or accident. The repair itself may not be admissible, but the ability to recognize or address the condition before it required attention may be a fruitful area of inquiry. Documentation reflecting the need for remedial attention should be the subject of preservation requests to explore the underlying cause.

6.6 Cooperation with Workers' Compensation Carrier

The workers' compensation carrier for the plaintiff's employer will be paying medical bills and wage loss in connection with the accident regardless of fault. In most jurisdictions the plaintiff will be required to pay back to the compensation carrier a portion of the funds expended to pay her bills or lost wages. Depending upon the relationship between the employer and the compensation carrier, there may be a direct dollar-for-dollar credit or partial credit that will positively affect future workers' compensation rates. Accordingly, the employer and the workers' compensation carrier, if approached properly, will become the plaintiff's allies in connection with the lawsuit. If the injury is serious enough, the workers' compensation carrier will often investigate subrogation potential independently and may have photographs of the accident scene, statements of witnesses and access to repair or maintenance records. Photographs of the accident scene taken at the direction of the compensation carrier generally would be the ones closest in time to the accident unless, of course, there was an on-site facilities management company or prompt notification was made to those responsible for repair and maintenance of the elevator. Plaintiff's counsel should introduce herself to the compensation carrier as soon as possible in order to obtain cooperation and permission for a formal on-site inspection.

6.7 On-Site Inspection (OSI)

Plaintiff's counsel, the plaintiff and the plaintiff's expert must attend the OSI. Plaintiff's counsel must be present in order to learn the specific technical issues, how the particular piece of equipment works, what in all likelihood went wrong, as well as the likely defenses that will be raised during litigation and at trial.

It is necessary for the plaintiff to attend the site inspection to make certain that the proper elevator is identified and inspected. Sometimes the plaintiff describes the wrong elevator in the initial interview. Bringing the plaintiff to the on-site inspection should eliminate this problem. Having the plaintiff present may also promote more interaction with co-employees if it is a workplace injury. Additional information about prior incidents involving the product may be discovered. Observation of the plaintiff in the workplace environment will also assist in determining whether plaintiff was well-liked by co-employees and may provide the attorney with a sense of how co-employees will or will not cooperate with the lawsuit.

Plaintiff's counsel should address other significant concerns at the time of the initial inspection. These include how to present at trial photographic evidence of the specific equipment and the specific defect or condition that caused the accident. This may be the only site inspection permitted from which demonstrative evidence can be obtained. Plaintiff's counsel should also make certain throughout the process that the plaintiff's account makes sense given the physical location and specifics of the equipment involved.

To make the inspection productive, as much documentation as possible should be obtained and given to the expert in time for a thorough review before the inspection. However, if it is possible for the equipment to be altered in any way, then an immediate inspection is necessary. In this case, retention of all pertinent components should be arranged. An inspection will be most fruitful if little time has elapsed since the accident.

If a site inspection is allowed before suit is filed, extensive documentation may not be available at that time. Failing to have sufficient documentation available at the site inspection may necessitate additional site inspections, if permitted. If a site inspection is not permitted before the lawsuit is filed, or if an expert has not been retained before the suit is filed, then the on-site inspection should normally be deferred until document production has been completed. For a discussion of the types of documents that should be obtained after institution of suit and before an on-site inspection see Chapter 8.

During the inspection, while gaining technical insight into how the equipment works, plaintiff's counsel should also discuss with the expert all possible accident scenarios. Plaintiff's counsel must also investigate all possible accident scenarios that do *not* support the plaintiff's case so as to determine whether the case should be rejected or, if pursued, what types of defenses or obstacles to anticipate. Plaintiff's counsel can also determine at this point whether the right expert has been selected. While you hope that your initial selection of an expert witness is well-founded, sometimes it is not until you start asking questions and listening to your expert that you can truly judge the expert's worth. Does the expert appear knowledgeable? Does the expert explain technical issues simply and easily? Will the jury like the expert? If it appears that your expert is not all she should be, then it is better to learn this early and select another expert. The OSI provides this opportunity.

Is the OSI necessary? Yes, but maybe not if all of the components that could have caused the accident have been replaced. Some alternatives would be to reconstruct the accident on an exemplar product or another unit in the same building or complex that has not been altered. Many times useful information can be obtained during an OSI even if all the applicable components have been replaced and can counter criticism that an expert has not inspected the equipment or site. More importantly a request for production for documents that reveal the old components should be served, along with a spoliation order where applicable. Included in the request should be as many of the discovery items as practical that are listed in Sections 8.2 in Chapter 8. The reason being is that the expert must know the "make and model" of the equipment to know the applicable codes, accessories, etc. The reasons for *not* making an OSI should never include that the damages are not enough to absorb the cost. The reasons for making the OSI can include the demonstration/reconstruction of the accident with the plaintiff, the attorneys, the medical expert, the bio-mechanical expert as well as to gain access to the equipment's internal areas.

The OSI typically may include identification through photographing or videotaping of the: equipment characteristics; applicable electrical wiring diagrams; driving machine, controller and its peripheral equipment in the machine room or similar area; equipment on the top of the elevator, hoistway and/or pit, internal areas of an, escalator and other components that could have caused the accident. Equipment tests typically are also performed (see some typical tools shown in Chapter 2, Figures F.7 through F.12). See supplementary DVD that contains all photographs in Chapter 2 as well as a bonus video on a typical OSI.

6.8 Review of Maintenance Documents

Assuming the cooperation of the plaintiff's employer and that the employer owns the property, copies of invoices, logs and other similar maintenance documents should be available for review before filing suit. These documents provide, at a minimum, a history of repair and maintenance. Often, these documents will also include more detailed information about the specific nature of prior problems or complaints. Sometimes it is possible to discover a continuing problem with the equipment that necessitated service calls and that may support the plaintiff's theory of liability. These documents may also indicate that the owner was warned of problems by the service company yet ignored all warnings. Thus, comprehensive records may also provide an effective defense.

6.9 Applicable Codes and Standards

Safety codes for elevators and escalators are discussed in detail in Chapter 1. A good expert witness will be able to direct the plaintiff's attorney to those specific codes and sections of those codes that apply to the case. A review of the specific sections of the code applicable to the case must be made as part of the determination of whether or not the case has merit and should proceed. State laws and local ordinances may provide additional information and sources of codes in the name of public safety and welfare. These should also be identified and consulted as part of the investigative process.

6.10 Inspections and Tests

Code compliance tests typically are done by the code enforcing personnel working in conjunction with maintenance personnel, while inspections are typically performed by the code enforcement personnel alone. A detailed description of required inspection and testing of elevators and escalators is set forth in Chapter 1. Acceptance inspections are performed after installation and before placing the elevator or escalator in service. Periodic (routine) inspections and tests are generally conducted every six months whereas periodic tests are performed on an annual basis and to some extent every three to five years. Periodic inspections and tests may reveal trends with respect to a particular elevator or escalator. The results of inspections and tests are generally available from the applicable AHJ and should be obtained before filing suit. Some jurisdictions may require the public display or public availability of periodic inspections. These should be verified and cross-referenced with maintenance records.

6.11 Should a Lawsuit Be Filed?

If maintenance records have been provided, the plaintiff's version of the facts analyzed, an on-site inspection of the elevator performed, and appropriate guidance from an expert liability witness provided, it should be relatively easy to determine whether suit should be filed. *If the damages are sufficient to warrant the time and expense of the lawsuit, and liability and causation can be established, then the lawsuit should be filed.* Most cases are not so clear. If both the owner and the service company are potential defendants they may not be willing to provide documentation before filing suit. Without proper documentation, including service and maintenance records, the plaintiff's attorney can literally be in the dark about the history of the equipment. While an on-site inspection should reveal to a competent expert the significant parts and operation of the equipment, potential defendants may not permit an on-site inspection to plaintiff before suit is filed. On the other hand, some potential defendants may allow the plaintiff's expert to conduct an on-site inspection before suit, but may have the elevator or escalator adjusted or repaired before the plaintiff's attorney and his expert can inspect it, thus eliminating any pertinent deficiencies. Many times it is just not possible for an expert to be able to give the attorney an opinion on the merits of the case until after suit has been filed and discovery has been obtained. It may very well be that a lawsuit is the only way to obtain the documentation or on-site inspection needed to judge whether the case has merit.

Chapter 7

Legal Theories and the Standard of Care

Synopsis

Following injury on an elevator or escalator, the proper defendants must be identified. The typical defendants may include some or all of the following: the premises owner, the installer of the elevator or escalator, the service and maintenance contractor, the elevator or escalator manufacturer or component part manufacturer, the inspection and testing organization, and the facilities management company. The legal theories supporting causes of action against the defendants may involve negligence, warranty, or strict liability concepts.

7.1 Negligence

Causes of action based upon negligence theories require there to have been a duty or obligation recognized by law, a breach of that duty, and a causal connection between the breach of that duty and the resulting injury or damage. Generally speaking, all defendants identified in an elevator or escalator case can be and are sued based upon negligence theories. Some of the defendants may be sued on multiple theories, including negligence, warranty, and strict liability concepts as discussed in this chapter.

A. Premises Owner or Facilities Management Company

An owner or a facilities management company hired to maintain the premises is obligated to exercise reasonable care in maintaining the premises. The duty owed to an injured person is determined by whether the person is an invitee, licensee or trespasser. The vast majority of persons injured in elevator or escalator accidents are invitees. Restatement (Second) of Torts, §332, defines invitees and business visitors. Section 332 provides as follows:

> **332. Invitee Defined**
> (1) An invitee is either a public invitee or a business visitor.
> (2) A public invitee is a person who is invited to enter or remain on land as a member of the public for a purpose for which the land is held open to the public.
> (3) A business visitor is a person who is invited to enter or remain on land for a purpose directly or indirectly connected with business dealings with the possessor of the land.

Causes of action against premises owners or facilities management companies are based upon negligence principles. For example, a successful lawsuit was brought against a facilities management company claiming negligence for its failure to properly control the operations of its elevators and control the number of persons accessing the elevators.[1] Strict liability claims against the owner of the premises where the elevator or escalator in question is located are not likely to be successful because the defendant premises owner is generally not within the chain of manufacture, distribution, or sale of the elevator or escalator.[2] Elevator and escalator owners and facilities management companies have been held liable to business invitees based upon Restatement (Second) of Torts, §343. Section 343 provides as follows:

> **343. Dangerous Conditions Known to or Discoverable by Possessor**
> A possessor of land is subject to liability for physical harm caused to his invitees by a condition on the land if, but only if, he (a) knows or by the exercise of reasonable care would discover the condition, and should realize that it involves an unreasonable risk of harm to such invitees, and (b) should expect that they will not discover or realize the danger, or will fail to protect themselves against it, and (c) fails to exercise reasonable care to protect them against the danger.

The importance of §343 is that an affirmative duty to inspect and discover dangerous conditions on the land, including the conditions of elevators and escalators, is imposed on the premises owner or facilities management company. Failure to know of the existence of a dangerous condition is not an excuse if through the exercise of reasonable diligence that dangerous condition could have been discovered.

B. Installer

Although less common, installers are also often defendants in elevator and escalator cases. Depending upon the jurisdiction the installation of an elevator or escalator may be considered the sale or supply of a product subjecting the installer to liability under strict liability concepts discussed in subsection C. Most often, however, the theories against installers are based upon negligence concepts. Many jurisdictions have statutes of repose that require lawsuits to be brought within a specific time triggered by the date of installation or construction.[3]

C. Manufacturer

Suits against manufacturers are based upon negligence and strict liability, as well as warranty. For most jurisdictions the Restatement (Second) of Torts, §402(a), defines the responsibility and liability for the sale or supply of a defective product. Section 402(a) provides as follows:

> **402(a) Special Liability of Seller of Product for Physical Harm to User or Consumer**
> (1) One who sells any product in a defective condition unreasonably dangerous to the user or consumer or to his property is subject to liability for physical harm thereby caused to the ultimate user or consumer, or to his property, if (a) the seller is engaged in the business of selling such a product, and (b) it is expected to and does reach the user or consumer without substantial change in the condition in which it is sold.
> (2) The rule stated in Subsection (1) applies although (a) the seller has exercised all possible care in the preparation and sale of his product, and (b) the user or consumer has not bought the product from or entered into any contractual relation with the seller.

Thus, by virtue of a defendant's being engaged in the business of selling a product, a higher burden is placed upon the defendant for the safety of that product. This is made explicit by §402(a) in that it clearly states that liability will attach even though the seller has exercised all possible care in the preparation and sale of the product. The focus is on the condition of the product and whether or not it is safe or "defective" as opposed to whether or not the defendant manufacturer has exercised reasonable care with respect to the manufacture of the product. Elevator and escalator manufacturers, as well as manufacturers of component parts, such as sensor devices, controllers, leveling devices, and door reopening devices are sued under strict liability theories.

Defective products can be classified as having manufacturing defects or design defects. A manufacturing defect can simply be a failure in the manufacturing process or a breakdown in the particular product. A design defect is a defect that is inherent in the product by virtue of its design and has nothing to do with the manufacturing process or a breakdown or failure of the specific product itself. In design defect cases, many jurisdictions require the court to make a threshold determination as to whether the product is "unreasonably dangerous."[4] In making the determination as to whether or not the product is unreasonably dangerous the factors include, inter alia, the gravity of the danger posed by the challenged design, the mechanical feasibility of a safer design, the usefulness and desirability of the product or its utility to the user and to the public, the availability of a substitute product which would meet the same need and not be as unsafe, and the manufacturer's ability to eliminate the unsafe character of the product without impairing its usefulness or making it too expensive to maintain its utility.

Actions against manufacturers based on breach of warranty generally are based on either the Uniform Commercial Code's implied warranty of merchantability or warranty of fitness for a particular purpose.[5] In an action for breach of warranty, however, depending upon the law in the jurisdiction where the action is brought, the absence of privity between the plaintiff and manufacturer of the elevator or escalator may preclude recovery for personal injuries.[6]

D. Service and Maintenance Contractor

Premises owners or facilities management companies generally hire an independent contractor to provide some type of maintenance for their elevators and escalators. As discussed in this book, a number of different types of agreements can be entered into with maintenance personnel. The manufacturer of the elevator or escalator may provide its own service or maintenance agreements, or a contract can be entered into with an independent service and maintenance company as well as a preventative maintenance consultant. The service and maintenance contractor is almost always sued in elevator and escalator accident cases. When a contract has been entered into with a preventative maintenance consultant, the consultant can also be sued when an accident occurs.[7] The theories and causes of action against service and maintenance contractors are based upon negligence concepts.

By virtue of the fact that there are different types of maintenance contracts offered, an issue that often arises is whether a more comprehensive plan had been offered to the premises owner or the facilities management company. In these cases, it is commonly argued that a more extensive plan was offered but the owner was "too cheap" and did not accept the plan and that the service contractor was limited in the scope of its work. The types of service and maintenance contracts offered range from a minimum "oil and grease" to a more comprehensive preventive (full) maintenance arrangement. Often that defense argument reflects exactly what happens: to save money, elevator and escalator owners opt for a cheaper, less extensive contract.

E. Inspection and Testing Organization

In many jurisdictions governmental agencies inspect and test elevators and escalators. In some jurisdictions complete immunity or limited liability is extended to the agencies even for improper testing and inspections. Some jurisdictions require that "gross negligence" be proved in order to recover against a governmental agency. Therefore, when inspections and tests are conducted by non-governmental agencies or maintenance contractors, it is easier to establish liability. For example, when an insurer undertakes an inspection of the elevator or escalator in the course of a general inspection of the premises, some jurisdictions permit actions to be brought against the insurer for negligent inspection.[8] Frequency of inspections and the details of inspections vary from jurisdiction to jurisdiction.[9] See Chapters 1 and 4 for a detailed explanation of these testing and inspection requirements for both elevators and escalators.

7.2 Special Rules Applicable to Elevator or Escalator Operation

In some jurisdictions elevator and escalator owners, the premises owners, and the facilities management company are considered common carriers. Common carriers are generally defined as those who hold themselves out to the public as engaged in the business of transportation of persons or property from place to place for compensation. In some jurisdictions, common carriers are held to owe their passengers "the highest degree of care possible under the circumstances."[10] This is an advantage for the plaintiff's attorney and should be exploited through arguments contrasting the duty imposed of "normal and ordinary care" to that of "the highest degree of care possible under the circumstances."

7.3 Special Considerations of Proof

A. *Res Ipsa Loquitur*

Often a person is injured on an elevator or escalator and a great deal of time elapses before counsel is obtained and a site inspection is performed. It is also not uncommon for conditions to change, or, for whatever reason, the accident scenario cannot be duplicated. This makes it difficult, if not impossible, for the plaintiff's attorney to prove the case. Recognizing these practical difficulties, some jurisdictions have enacted special rules that reduce the burden of proof necessary for the plaintiff to establish her prima facie case. In many jurisdictions, some form of Restatement (Second) of Torts, §328(d), which sets forth the doctrine of *res ipsa loquitur,* has been adopted. This doctrine assists the plaintiff in making out a *prima facie* case of negligence by allowing an inference of negligence to flow from evidence on the theory that in the course of ordinary events the injury complained of would not have occurred in the absence of negligence. Section 328(d) provides as follows:

> **328(d) Res Ipsa Loquitur**
> (1) It may be inferred that harm suffered by the plaintiff is caused by negligence of the defendant when (a) the event is of a kind which ordinarily does not occur in the absence of negligence; (b) other responsible causes, including the conduct of the plaintiff and third persons, are sufficiently eliminated by the evidence; and (c) the indicated negligence is within the scope of the defendant's duty to the plaintiff.
> (2) It is the function of the court to determine whether the inference may reasonably be drawn by the jury, or whether it must necessarily be drawn.
> (3) It is the function of the jury to determine whether the inference is to be drawn in any case where different conclusions may reasonably be reached.

Res ipsa loquitur has been held to apply to premises owners, as well as to the service and maintenance companies, although, in some jurisdictions courts will not apply the doctrine of *res ipsa loquitur* to any potentially responsible parties in cases involving elevator accidents.[11]

Thus, when a malfunction is alleged, such as the sudden stopping of an escalator, or the sudden descent or ascent of an elevator at high rates of speed, even without direct proof of the cause of the accident, the plaintiff may be able to present his case to the jury if other potentially responsible causes, including the conduct of the plaintiff and third persons, are sufficiently eliminated by the evidence and the event is of a kind that ordinarily does not occur in the absence of negligence.[12] There are many cases in which it has been held that the plaintiff failed to establish the necessary prerequisites to invoke the doctrine of *res ipsa loquitur.*[13] By establishing the elements necessary for the application of *res ipsa loquitur*, the plaintiff essentially demonstrates that more probably than not, the defendant was negligent and that the negligent conduct caused the accident and resulting harm, despite the absence of direct evidence. For *res ipsa loquitur* to apply, the plaintiff must be in the class of persons within the scope of the defendant's duty.

One of the issues that arises concerning the use of *res ipsa loquitur* is what happens when some evidence of negligence is introduced but the exact cause of the accident is unknown to either side. It is generally agreed that a jury instruction is not available based upon *res ipsa loquitur* when clear evidence of negligence has been presented.[14]

B. Negligence *Per Se*

The duty owed by elevator and escalator maintenance contractors may be based upon statutes or administrative rules and regulations governing the operation and maintenance of elevators and escalators. See the extensive discussion of codes and regulations in Chapter 1, *infra*. A number of state and local authorities have adopted ASMEA 17.1 "Safety Code for Elevators and Escalators," as establishing the requirements for operation and maintenance of elevators and escalators. The defendant's violation of a statute enacted to protect against the type of harm sustained by the plaintiff can establish the duty and breach of duty elements required for a cause of action based upon negligence. Violation of a statute under these circumstances can constitute negligence *per se*. For example, under Pennsylvania law, Title 35, Chapter 15, of the Pennsylvania Code provides requirements pertinent to elevators and escalators. The violation of one of these provisions may be used to establish negligence *per se* and ease the plaintiff's burden of proof or establish both duty and breach of duty in a particular case. It has been held that the failure to have a locking device as required by statute is negligence *per se*.[15] Additionally, for a statute requiring elevators to receive four inspections a year, it was held that the statute established the minimum standard of duty. Compliance with the statute with respect to those inspections would prevent the finding of negligence *per se* but would not prevent the finding of negligence under the circumstances of a particular case.[16] While some jurisdictions do apply negligence *per se* based upon the existence of a specific regulation governing the standard of care of the defendant, other jurisdictions have held that those regulations only impose a standard of reasonable care.[17] In those jurisdictions, violation of statutes may serve as evidence of negligence and warrant a special jury instruction. Utilizing such statutes to force conduct that fell below the standard of reasonable care should be researched accordingly.

7.4 Additional Considerations Relative to the Standard of Care

Application of legal concepts to a particular factual scenario is never easy. In addition, discussion of the case and the legal theories involved in a framework of negligence or strict liability can often produce seemingly contradictory positions and produce more questions than answers. For instance, a violation of the applicable code could result in establishment of elements of a plaintiff's case based upon concepts of negligence *per se*. However, when the plaintiff argues that the defendant should have enacted safety measures beyond code requirements, most jurisdictions will allow the plaintiff to proceed to trial under the theory that the code itself only provides a minimum with respect to the standard of care or safety. One of the biggest complaints that manufacturers have is that the legal concepts concerning what is or what is not a "defective product" vary from jurisdiction to jurisdiction. Thus, the same product may result in an injury in one jurisdiction for which there is liability and for which in another jurisdiction there is no liability. Until there is a national codification of standards or tort law, differing results based upon the jurisdiction will continue.

Investigation of an accident may disclose that existing technology on a product had been replaced with a newer technology that would have prevented the accident. For example, older elevators typically were installed with a contact-type door reopening device. By design, these devices require actual contact with an object in the closing path before the closing door stops and reopens. For many years improved non-contact-type reopening devices have been available at a reasonable cost. By definition, these devices do not require any contact with an object in its closing path before the closing doors stop and reopen. Is it the responsibility of the owner of the elevator to keep abreast of new technology changes and implement same? Is it the responsibility of the service and maintenance company to advise the building owner that there is new and improved equipment that should be incorporated in the elevator? Most plaintiffs' attorneys would answer these questions in the affirmative.

What happens when the service company does in fact advise the owner that there are newer products which would make the elevator safer, or advises that there are general conditions that are unsafe and must be remedied but the building owner for economic reasons does not agree? This situation is one reason why it is vital that all parties, particularly the service company, keep written documentation. Should a building owner or elevator owner periodically have their vertical transportation equipment evaluated by an independent third party to determine whether any safety changes are necessary? These are just a few of the potential questions and issues that arise and must be determined on a case-by-case basis.

Endnotes

1. *Burch v. SMG*, 191 So. 3d 652 (La.App. 4 Cir. 2016). The plaintiff in *Burch* filed suit after she sustained injuries on an elevator at a football game in the Louisiana Superdome due to overcrowding of the elevator. The facilities management company was found to be negligent because the company had a duty to properly control the operations of its elevators and the number of people accessing the elevators after events because of known overcrowding and the company did not put an attendant or any plan in place to monitor or control the crowds using the elevators.

2. *Serna v. New York State Urban Development Corp.*, 586 NYS 2d 413, 185 A.D. 2d 569 (1992).

3. For example, in the Commonwealth of Pennsylvania there is a twelve-year statute of repose for construction projects. See 42 Pa. C.S.A.§5536. This provision requires that civil actions against those performing design, planning, supervision, observation of construction or construction of improvements to real property must be commenced within twelve years after completion of construction or the improvements.

4. *See, e.g., Azzarello v. Black Bros. Co., Inc.*, 480 Pa. 547, 558, 391 A.2d 1020, 1026 (1978).

5. UCC§2-314 provides as follows with respect to implied warranty of merchantability:

   > (1) Unless excluded or modified ...,
   > a warranty that the goods shall be merchantable is implied in a contract for their sale if the seller is a merchant with respect to goods of that kind

   UCC§2-315 provides the following with respect to implied warranty of fitness for a particular purpose:

   > Where the seller at the time of contracting has reason to know any particular purpose for which the goods are required and that the buyer is relying on the seller's skill or judgment to select or furnish suitable goods, there is unless excluded or modified under the next section an implied warranty that the goods shall be fit for such purpose.

6. UCC§2-318 provides various alternatives for adoption by states with respect to the necessary relationship to the purchases in order to be able to pursue a claim for personal injuries.

7. *See Trotman v. Mass. Bay Transp. Auth.*, 32 Mass. L. Rep. 112 (Mass. Super. Ct. 2014) (Plaintiff's lawsuit against a preventative maintenance consultant for the property owner was allowed to proceed because there was an issue of fact regarding whether he was negligent in failing to address the hazard on the escalator causing plaintiff's death, given that he was on notice of other deaths that occurred in a similar manner and because of his contractual obligation to be responsible for preventive maintenance oversight.)

8. *Fosgate v. American Mutual Liability Insurance Company*, 161 Ga. App. 376, 288 SE 2d 647 (1982). This case was decided in part upon §324A of the Restatement (Second) of Torts, which provides for liability of those who, although gratuitously, undertake to render services for others which are recognized as necessary to protect others and harm results from reliance on those services which were performed negligently.

9. For example, in the Commonwealth of Pennsylvania passenger elevators and escalators must be inspected four times each year. There are varying requirements for the frequency of inspection with respect to freight elevators, hoists, and temporary construction elevators. See 35 P.S.§1347.

10. Under Pennsylvania law it is well established that ordinary negligence concepts are superseded with respect to common carriers. The degree of care has been referred to as the "highest practical degree of care." *See, Petrie v. Kaufmann & Baer Company*, 291 Pa. 211, 213-214, 139 A. 878, 879 (1927) and *McGowan v. Devonshire Hall Apartments*, 278 Pa. Super. 229, 240, 420 A.2d 514, 519-20 (1980).

11. *See Villalba v New York El. & Elec. Corp.*, 2014 NY Slip Op 31155(U) (N.Y. Sup. Ct. Apr. 29, 2014) (Plaintiffs were entitled to invoke the doctrine of *res ipsa loquitur* based on the plaintiffs' testimony that the elevator began to descend and ascend at high rates of speed.).

12. *See Spencer v. Otis Elevator Co.*, 2016 U.S. Dist. LEXIS 132279 * (S.D. Ga. Sept. 27, 2016).

13. *See Backus v New Yorker Hotel Mgt. Co.*, 2016 NY Slip Op 31697(U) (N.Y. Sup. Ct. Sept. 8, 2016) (plaintiff's *res ipsa loquitur* claim was precluded becausee it could reasonably be determined that her conduct contributed to her injuries): *Pace v. Mainstay Suites Hotel*, 2008 U.S. Dist. LEXIS 91426 (E.D.

Pa. Nov. 5, 2008) (plaintiff failed to establish that the incident where the elevator door closed on his arm was of the type which ordinarily would not occur in the absence of negligence and failed to rule out other responsible causes); *Espinoza Ugaz v. American Airlines, Inc.*, 576 F. Supp. 2nd 1354, 1369 (S.D. Fla. 2008) (plaintiff's conduct was found to be a factor in the happening of the accident and thus *res ipsa loquitur* was not applicable).

14. *See, e.g., Williams v. Otis Elevator Company*, 409 Pa. Super. 486, 492, 598 A.2d 302, 305 (1991) and *McGowan v. Devonshire Hall Apartments, supra.*

15. *McGowan, supra.*

16. *McGowan, supra.*

17. *Phillips v. Fujitec Am., Inc.*, 2010 D.C. App. LEXIS 506, 1-2 (D.C. September 2, 2010), *Carcana v. New York City Housing Authority*, 2010 NY Slip Op 50460U, 4 (N.Y. Sup. Ct. 2010) (it is only the violation of a state statute that imposes a specific duty constituting negligence *per se* and where a statute refers to only a general duty to keep the premises in a safe condition, the prerequisites for negligence per se are not established.)

Chapter 8

Pleadings

Synopsis

This chapter contains sample complaints and affirmative defenses commonly raised in elevator cases.

8.1 Complaints

A. Excerpts from Sample Complaint in a Porch-Lift-Collapse Case

. . .

5. Prior to the date of accident, Defendant, [manufacturer], had designed, manufactured, fabricated, advertised, distributed, sold and supplied a certain vertical platform lift, and/or a "porch lift."

6. The aforesaid lift was then sold, distributed, and/or provided to Defendant, [distributor], and ultimately was installed at Plaintiff's residence by Defendant, [installer/repairer].

7. Prior to the date of the accident, Defendant, [manufacturer, distributor, installer/repairer], had designed, manufactured, sold, fabricated, promoted, advertised, and/or distributed said lift, including its component parts, for sale and distribution within ____________.

8. Subsequent to the date of installation and prior to the date of the accident, there were a number of incidents wherein said platform lift malfunctioned, did not operate, and had otherwise required repair and service.

9. Upon information and belief, prior to date of accident, Defendant, [installer/repairer], its agents, servants and/or employees, performed service and repairs to said product and/or its component parts subsequent to its installation.

10. On the date of accident, Plaintiff was seated in a wheelchair on the platform of said lift when suddenly, without warning, the lift platform collapsed, causing Plaintiff to fall with the lift platform and to sustain serious, permanent, and painful injuries.

11. The aforesaid accident and resulting injuries and damages sustained by Plaintiff were caused as a direct and proximate result of the negligence, carelessness, breach of warranty, strict liability and other liability-producing conduct of the Defendants, their agents, servants, workmen, and/or employees, and was due in no fashion whatsoever to any act or omission on the part of Plaintiff.

12. The product described herein was defective, unreasonably dangerous, not fit for the ordinary and particular purpose for which it was designed and sold, nor was it of fair and merchantable quality.

. . .

COUNT I
PLAINTIFF v. DEFENDANT, [MANUFACTURER]

19. Plaintiff incorporates by reference herein the allegations set forth in paragraphs 1 through ___ as though same were set forth at length.

20. The aforesaid accident and the resulting injuries and damages sustained by Plaintiff were caused as a direct and proximate result of the liability-producing conduct of the Defendant, [manufacturer], which consisted of the following:

a. failing to properly and adequately design, manufacture, test, inspect, maintain, adjust and repair said product prior to and after its sale and distribution to determine that the platform would not fall in a sudden and unanticipated fashion, causing injury to its user;

b. failing to properly and adequately manufacture said product, and its component parts, specifically those parts integral to the movement and stability of the lift platform;

c. failing to properly and adequately design, manufacture, test, inspect, maintain, adjust and repair the components of the lift platform assembly, including the worm, lift plate, fall or locking nut, plastic or synthetic nut, and sling;

d. failing to properly and adequately design, manufacture, test, inspect, maintain, adjust and repair said components of the lift platform assembly to determine that same would remain secure, structurally sound, and would prevent sudden and unanticipated falling of the lift platform during periods of normal and intended use;

e. failing to properly design and manufacture said product and its component parts, so as to contain features which would prevent "free falling" of the lift platform, including a structurally sound and operating fall or locking nut and a sufficiently tight fit of the nut to the worm in order to properly support the lift platform;

f. failing to properly and adequately lubricate said components of the lift platform assembly in order to prevent premature wear of said components, resulting in a "free fall" of the platform;

g. incorporating into said product materials that were substandard, defective, and likely to deteriorate during periods of normal and intended use resulting in "free fall";

h. failing to conform with all industry standards and practices pertinent to the design, manufacture, and sale of similar products, with respect to preventing lift platform "free fall";

i. liability for design, manufacture and sale of a product incorporating component parts that were defective in construction and fabrication;

j. failing to properly and adequately inspect said components prior to sale and/or distribution to determine that said components would not fail resulting in "free fall" of the lift platform during normal and anticipated use;

k. failing to properly design and manufacture said product with the result that it contained elements rendering it unsafe for its use and/or lacked all elements necessary to ensure its safe use, i.e., to prevent "free fall" of the lift platform during normal and intended use;

l. designing and manufacturing said product so as to make it unlikely that users, repair personnel and others would receive warning or be alerted to the fact that there was an impending failure of the fall nut and worm connection thereby likely to cause a "free fall" of the lift platform;

m. designing and manufacturing said product so that it was unreasonably difficult to install, and/or repair, with the result that during normal and intended use there would be "free fall" of the lift platform;

n. failing to provide all necessary and appropriate instructions concerning installation of said lift to prevent deterioration of components and subsequent "free fall";

o. failing to provide all necessary instructions pertinent to maintenance, repair, service and lubrication of said product to prevent lift platform "free fall";

p. liability for malfunction of a product in that the lift platform assembly failed resulting in "free fall" during normal and intended consumer use.

. . .

COUNT II
PLAINTIFF V. DEFENDANT, [MANUFACTURER]

22. Plaintiff incorporates by reference herein the allegations set forth in paragraphs 1 through ___ as though same were set forth at length.

23. Defendant, [manufacturer], at all times material hereto, was engaged in the business of designing, manufacturing, fabricating, assembling, promoting, selling, supplying, delivering, and distributing certain products and consumer goods, including the aforesaid porch lift and component parts.

24. The aforesaid product was in a defective and dangerous condition and lacked all elements necessary to ensure its safe use at the time it left the hands of each Defendant, including a lift platform which malfunctioned resulting in "free fall," component parts in the lift platform assembly which wore prematurely, were composed of materials which were not sufficiently structurally sound to prevent "free fall," which contained a locking nut which failed to hold the lift platform resulting in "free fall," as well as failure to warn of these limitations and defects of said product resulting in the accident herein.

25. The defective and dangerous condition of said product, including the design, manufacturing and warning defects, as well as product malfunction, as set forth herein were proximate causes of the accident described herein and the injuries sustained by Plaintiff while said product was being used for its ordinarily intended purpose.

26. Upon information and belief, prior to the aforementioned accident, there had been no substantial or material change in the condition of the product as pertains to the lift platform assembly and the integrity of same, from the time when it was designed, manufactured, sold and/or distributed by each Defendant herein.

. . .

COUNT III
PLAINTIFF V. DEFENDANT, [MANUFACTURER]

. . .

29. The sale and distribution of the product involved herein constituted a sale of goods so that in connection with said sale certain warranties were created by law. Additionally, by virtue of instructional, sales and other material accompanying the sale, distribution and advertisement of said product express and implied warranties as to the safety, fitness, and longevity of said product were made and/or created.

30. Warranties of fitness for a particular purpose, i.e., as a porch lift, as well as fitness for the ordinary purpose for which said product was intended were created by virtue of the sale of said product, as well as the other written material accompanying the sale and distribution, as well as advertisement of said product.

31. The express and implied warranties which were created by law, or which arose as a result of sales, instructional or advertising materials were breached in that the product was not fit for its intended purpose, was not safe, malfunctioned and did not have sufficient structural integrity to promote longevity and usefulness of said lift for its intended and normal life expectancy.

. . .

COUNT VII
PLAINTIFF V. DEFENDANT, [REPAIRER/INSTALLER]

. . .

50. The negligence, carelessness, recklessness, and other wrongful and liability-producing conduct of the Defendant, [repairer/installer], its agents, servants, workmen, and/or employees, which was the proximate cause of the accident herein, consisted of the following:

a. failing to employ persons capable and competent in installing, repairing, and servicing the porch lift described herein;

b. failing to properly and adequately train employees, agents, workmen and/or servants with respect to installation, inspection, repair and maintenance of the product herein;

c. failing to provide adequate instructional materials, manuals, and similar documents to employees, agents, workmen, and/or servants pertinent to the installation, inspection, service, repair, and/or maintenance of the porch lift involved herein;

d. failing to adequately and properly install, service, repair, and/or maintain the porch lift involved herein;

e. failing to properly and adequately lubricate all necessary moving parts of the lift involved herein, specifically the lift platform assembly, at the time of the installation as well as on subsequent service calls prior to the date of the accident herein;

f. failing to adequately and properly inspect said product, including the lift platform assembly, to determine that the parts contained therein were of sufficient structural integrity to adequately support the lift platform assembly and its user during normal and intended use;

g. failing to provide and/or install parts necessary to provide adequate structural integrity to the lift platform assembly in order to prevent "free fall";

h. failing to adequately and properly discuss with the manufacturer and distributor proper methods of installation, inspection, repair, and/or maintenance to prevent premature wear and tear of parts resulting in "free fall" of the lift platform assembly;

. . .

WHEREFORE, Plaintiff demands judgment in her favor and against each Defendant herein in an amount in excess of $____________, to be determined at the time of trial.

B. Excerpts from Sample Complaint Involving Gate Striking Plaintiff on Freight Elevator

. . .

3. Upon information and belief and subject to discovery, it is averred that Defendant, [facilities manager], was at all times material hereto, the manager, operator, owner and/or tenant in possession of [the premises] and owed a duty to its business invitees to repair, inspect and maintain the premises including the elevator described herein in a safe and defect-free condition.

. . .

5. Upon information and belief, and subject to discovery, it is averred that the Defendant, [owner], was at all times material hereto, the owner of the premises where the accident occurred, and owed a duty to its business invitees to repair, inspect and maintain the premises including the elevator described herein in a safe, defect-free condition.

. . .

7. Upon information and belief, and subject to discovery, it is averred that Defendant, [maintenance and repair company], was, pursuant to an agreement and/or contract between Defendants, at all times material hereto, charged with the duty of maintenance, examination and repair of the elevator in which Plaintiff was injured.

8. Upon information and belief and subject to discovery, it is averred that Defendant, [maintenance and repair company], was also the manufacturer of the elevator at the aforementioned premises.

9. At all times relevant hereto, the building's elevators were designed, manufactured, distributed, sold, installed and maintained by Defendant, [maintenance and repair company].

10. On the date of the accident, Plaintiff was a business invitee upon the premises in the course and scope of employment for his employer, ________, and was using a freight elevator to move furniture when a metal gate from the elevator struck him on the head causing him to sustain serious personal injury.

. . .

COUNT I
PLAINTIFF v. DEFENDANT, [FACILITIES MANAGER] [OWNER]

. . .

19. At all times material hereto, it was the duty of Defendant, [facilities manager] [owner] to inspect, repair and maintain the aforesaid premises, including the freight elevators thereon in a reasonably safe condition for those lawfully upon the premises.

20. The negligence of the Defendant, [facilities manager] [owner], by and through its agents, servants, and/or employees, consisted of, but is not limited to:

(a) Failing to maintain the premises in a safe condition;
(b) Failing to keep the premises in proper repair;

(c) Allowing the defective condition as heretofore described to exist on said premises;

(d) Failing to take reasonable and adequate measures to prevent such an occurrence;

(e) Failing to adequately and periodically inspect and test said elevator in order to ascertain whether it was working properly and safely;

(f) Failing to warn the Plaintiff and others lawfully upon the premises of the dangerous and hazardous condition then and there existing;

(g) Failing to incorporate all devices necessary to warn of impending elevator gate closing;

(h) Failing to incorporate all devices necessary to eliminate the possibility of gate closing and injuring the user;

(i) Failing to incorporate all electrical systems including interlocking devices necessary to prevent unintended gate closing;

(j) Failing to post any and/or adequate warnings that the elevator in which Plaintiff was injured was being repaired;

(k) Failing to exercise that degree of care required for the safety of the Plaintiff, a business invitee, under the circumstances;

(l) Failing to inspect and effectuate repairs as necessary based upon prior malfunctions and/or repair history;

(m) Failing to discharge obligations existing under contract between Defendants;

(n) Failing to hire competent elevator repair personnel;

(o) Failing to accept responsibility for a dangerous artificial condition existing upon its premises;

(p) Failing to incorporate elevators with safeguards and interlock devices;

(q) Otherwise being negligent at law.

. . .

COUNT II
PLAINTIFF v. DEFENDANT, [MAINTENANCE COMPANY]

. . .

27. At all times material hereto, it was the duty of Defendant, [maintenance company], to inspect, supervise, repair and maintain the aforesaid premises, including elevators thereon in a reasonably safe condition for those lawfully upon the premises.

28. The negligence of the Defendant, [maintenance company], by and through its agents, servants, and/or employees consisted of but is not limited to:

(a) Failing to properly maintain the elevator/product;

(b) Failing to properly and adequately maintain the safety devices with regard to operation of gate and/or doors of said product;

(c) Failing to adequately and periodically inspect and test said elevator in order to ascertain whether it was working properly and safely;

(d) Failing to adequately and periodically inspect and test said elevator in order to determine whether or not its gates and doors were operating properly and safely;

(e) Failing to incorporate all devices with regard to the operation of gate and/or doors necessary to warn of impending elevator gate closing;

(f) Failing to incorporate all devices necessary to eliminate the possibility of gate closing and injury to the user;

(g) Failing to incorporate all electrical systems including interlocking devices necessary to prevent unintended gate closing;

(h) Failing to post any and/or adequate warnings that the elevator in which Plaintiff was injured was being repaired;

(i) Failing to inspect and effectuate repairs as necessary based upon prior malfunctions and/or repair history;

(j) Failing to hire competent elevator repair personnel;

(k) Failing to incorporate elevators with safeguards and interlock devices with regard to the operation of gates and/or doors;

(l) Failing to properly test the elevator and its associated components with regard to the operation of gates and/or doors;

(m) Failing to properly inspect the elevator and its associated components with regard to the operation of gates and/or doors;

(n) Failing to recommend or require repair or replacement of the original existing metal safety gate and/or door mechanism with another similar product with a safer design;

(o) Failing to timely recommend essential inspection, maintenance and testing procedures to minimize or alleviate the risk of an uncontrolled and/or unexpected dropping of the metal gate;

(p) Violation of applicable statutes and regulations of the City of Philadelphia and Commonwealth of Pennsylvania relating to elevator safety with regard to the operation of gate and/or doors;

(q) Violation of applicable construction/industry standards pertinent to the operation of said product with regard to the operation of gate and/or doors;

(r) Failing to have in force, a necessary and proper inspection and repair schedule for said elevator.

. . .

COUNT IV
PLAINTIFF v. DEFENDANT, [MANUFACTURER]

. . .

32. At the time of the aforesaid design, sale, manufacture, supply, maintenance and/or distribution of the elevator involved in Plaintiff's accident, said product was unsafe, defective in design, unreasonably dangerous, and otherwise lacked all elements necessary to ensure its safe use, including those elements set forth in the body of this Complaint, i.e. pertinent to door mechanism and/or safety gate closing, the physical equipment necessary to effectuate same, rendering Defendants strictly liable to Plaintiffs under Restatement (Second) of Torts §402A.

33. The defects in said product included the failure to provide proper and necessary warnings and the failure to provide all elements necessary to ensure the products safe use with regard to the operation of gate and/or doors, which were the proximate cause of the incident and injuries sustained by Plaintiff.

WHEREFORE, Plaintiffs demand judgment in their favor and against each Defendant herein in an amount in excess of $___________, to be determined at the time of trial.

C. Excerpts from Sample Complaint by Plaintiff Who Entered Through Open Elevator Doors and Fell Down Shaft

. . .

2. The Defendant, [elevator repair company], is a business corporation organized and existing under the laws of the Commonwealth of Pennsylvania, authorized to do business in the Commonwealth of Pennsylvania, and transacting business in Philadelphia at the above address.

3. At all times material and relevant hereto, the Defendant acted or failed to act through its agents, servants, workmen and/or employees in the course and scope of such relationship.

4. At all times material hereto [owner], owned, operated, managed and/or controlled a warehouse known as _______ Warehouse, located at ___________, Philadelphia, PA.

5. On or about date of accident, and for sometime prior thereto Defendant, [elevator repair company], was the elevator service company who serviced the __________ Warehouse elevators.

6. On or about __________, one of the elevators at the owner's premises, referred to as the Combined Passenger Freight (hereinafter "CPF"), was sealed by the Commonwealth of Pennsylvania, Department of Labor, because of an unsafe condition.

7. On or about ________, Defendant, [elevator repair company], became aware that the aforesaid elevator was sealed by the Commonwealth, and continued to service the unsealed elevator and/or the CPF elevator.

8. Subsequent to ___________, and for a period of time up to the date of the accident, Defendant placed the sealed elevator back into service, violating the laws and regulations of the Commonwealth of Pennsylvania, by placing the aforesaid elevator back into service.

9. The CPF elevator was unsafe for use and created an unreasonable risk of serious injury to anyone using said elevator.

10. Defendant, [elevator repair company], knew or, in the exercise of reasonable care, should have known that the CPF elevator was being used by [owner] in violation of the seal order by the Department of Labor and Industry.

11. On or about the date of the accident, the decedent unknowingly entered the empty elevator shaft, plunging to the bottom of the shaft, resulting in injuries which led to his death on ________.

12. The injury and subsequent death of the decedent was due to the negligence, carelessness and reckless disregard of the Defendants, and was due in no manner whatsoever to the actions of the Plaintiff.

COUNT I
PLAINTIFF V. DEFENDANT, [ELEVATOR REPAIR COMPANY]

. . .

14. The negligence, carelessness, and recklessness of Defendant, [elevator repair company], consisted of any and all of the following:

(a) failure to properly service and/or repair the subject elevator;

(b) failure to inspect the subject elevator;

(c) placing the subject elevator into service in violation of the Commonwealth seal on the elevator;

(d) failure to warn Defendant, [owner], of the dangers of running the elevator which had been sealed by the Commonwealth;

(e) failure to cordon off or place adequate warning signs by the sealed elevator;

(f) failure to properly service the "emergency key" feature of the elevator;

(g) failure to advise the Commonwealth of [owner's] use of the sealed elevator; and

(h) any and all acts which may become apparent during the discovery process.

. . .

WHEREFORE, Plaintiffs demand judgment in their favor and against each Defendant herein in an amount in excess of $___________, to be determined at the time of trial.

8.2 Affirmative Defenses

The following are typical affirmative defenses raised in elevator or escalator cases by defendants.

1. Plaintiff's Complaint fails to state a cause of action upon which relief may be granted.

2. The alleged injuries of Plaintiff are the result of her own negligence which exceeded any negligence of the answering Defendant, all such alleged negligence by answering Defendant being expressly denied and therefore, pursuant to the applicable Comparative Negligence Act, Plaintiff's claims are barred.

3. Plaintiff's claims are further barred or mitigated by the theory of contributory negligence and/or voluntary assumption of the risk.

4. Plaintiff, having knowledge of, understanding and appreciating the consequences of the alleged unsafe condition, nonetheless voluntarily chose to encounter same, thereby voluntarily assuming the risk of her injuries relieving answering Defendant from liability.

5. Plaintiff's injuries and damages as alleged were not proximately caused in any manner whatsoever by answering Defendant.

6. The alleged injuries to the Plaintiff were caused or contributed to, in whole or in part, by the negligence or want of due care by persons, parties, and/or organizations other than answering Defendant and over whom said Defendant had no control or right of control.

7. If answering Defendant was negligent in any respect as alleged, such negligence was passive and the injuries sustained by the Plaintiff were the result of an intervening negligent act of a third person or persons which was a superseding cause of her injuries, thereby relieving answering Defendant from liability.

8. Answering Defendant owed no duty to Plaintiff.

9. At the time of the alleged accident the product was no longer in the condition when it left the control of answering Defendant.

10. At the time of the accident the product had been substantially changed and/or altered from its original condition thereby relieving answering Defendant from liability.

11. The conduct of the Plaintiff and others which contributed to the accident was not foreseeable and/or constituted foreseeable misuse thereby relieving Defendant from liability.

12. At the time of the accident the product was being used in a fashion which was not foreseeable, was unsafe, and therefore such as to relieve answering Defendant from liability.

13. The product, as originally designed and manufactured, contained safety features which would have prevented the accident had they not been disabled by Plaintiff or third parties over whom Defendant had no control or right of control.

14. The product involved in Plaintiff's accident was designed and manufactured according to Plaintiff's employer's specifications and accordingly, answering Defendant cannot be liable for an allegedly defective condition of same.

15. The Plaintiff, and others, failed to heed all warnings and instructions which would have prevented the accident thereby relieving answering Defendant from liability.

16. The product was not properly maintained by Plaintiff's employer and third parties over whom Defendant had no control or right of control thereby relieving answering Defendant from liability.

17. The product involved in Plaintiff's accident conformed with all applicable safety standards, codes, and regulations at the time of its design and manufacture.

18. Plaintiff's claims may be barred in whole or in part by alteration and/or substantial change of the product after delivery.

19. Plaintiff's claims may be barred by the applicable Statute of Limitations and/or the applicable Statute of Repose.

20. Plaintiff's causes of action against answering Defendant may be pre-empted by any applicable state, federal and/or local rule, regulation, law or code.

21. Plaintiff's claims and causes of action against answering Defendant may be barred by the Doctrine of Spoliation of Evidence.

22. The product was not defective, nor was it unreasonably dangerous for its intended use.

Chapter 9

Discovery

Synopsis

This chapter provides sample interrogatories, requests for production of documents, and corporate designee notices. A good expert witness can provide help in drafting discovery to elicit the information necessary to prove a case, as well as to review materials provided in response to discovery.

9.1 Interrogatories

These interrogatories are comprehensive but also may be specific with respect to particular issues. Not all of these interrogatories will apply in every case. It is recommended that the attorney consult with his expert so that the pertinent information can be obtained.

A. Equipment-Specific Examples

1. Elevator basic

- Provide all the identification numbers of the incident elevator (e.g., building ID, maintenance company ID, inspection authority ID).

- Indicate in detail the type of the incident elevator (e.g., traction, hydraulic, roped hydraulic).
- Indicate in detail the type of service of the incident elevator (e.g., passenger, freight, service).
- Indicate in detail the type of operation (e.g., automatic, designated attendant) of the incident elevator.
- Indicate in detail the type of control (e.g., motor generator, SCR, solid state, relay logic) of the incident elevator.
- Indicate in detail the manufacturer, type and model of the elevator controller.
- Indicate the capacity of the incident elevator.
- Indicate the rated speed of the incident elevator.
- Indicate the rise of the incident elevator.
- Indicate the number of landings and openings of the incident elevator.
- Indicate in detail the manufacturer of the elevator and any model type.
- Indicate the installer of the elevator.
- Indicate the date of installation and any alterations of the elevator and indicate the applicable code(s). Set forth all bases for that answer.
- Provide details of all alterations to the elevator, when they were done and by whom.
- Indicate in detail the type of driving machine (geared traction, gearless traction).
- For hydraulic elevators indicate the type of jack (e.g., single stage telescopic, in-ground).
- Describe in detail the type, material and construction of floor covering inside the elevator cab.
- Describe in detail the lighting in the cab of the elevator, including the type and description of each fixture, wattage for each fixture, and number of fixtures.
- What is the height and width of the elevator cab entrance(s) when the doors are fully open?
- Indicate in detail the type and operation of car door(s) or gate(s) (e.g., single speed side opening, manual).
- Indicate in detail the type and operation of hoistway (landing) doors (e.g., single speed center opening, automatic).
- What is the estimated number of people who use this elevator each day? Set forth all bases for that answer.
- Provide a complete copy of any and all indemnity or contribution agreements between the owner of the elevator, owner of the real property where the real property is situated and any third party, as well as any and all policies of insurance for any of these entities or potential parties.

- What is the estimated number of hours this elevator carries passengers each day? Set forth all bases for that answer.

2. Elevator door strike/crush

- Indicate in detail the type and operation of car door(s) or gate(s) (e.g., single speed side opening, manual).
- Indicate in detail the type and operation of hoistway (landing) doors (e.g., single speed center opening, automatic).
- Indicate the height and width of the elevator cab entrance(s) when the doors are fully open.
- Indicate in detail the manufacturer, type and model of all automatic door operating devices (e.g., door operator, door reopening or protective devices, door control buttons).
- Indicate when the door operating device was installed and the date of any alteration. Set forth all bases for that answer.
- Indicate the number of landings and openings of the incident elevator.
- Indicate in detail the materials and construction of the car door or gate and the landing doors (e.g., hollow metal doors, ornamental coverings, bronze cladding, stainless steel).
- Indicate who determined the door opening, open dwell and closing times and the door closing force for the elevator involved in plaintiff's accident. Set forth all bases for that answer.
- Indicate in detail the performance criteria used for the door opening, open dwell and closing times and the door closing force for the elevator. Set forth all bases for that answer.
- Indicate in detail when the door opening, open dwell and closing times and the door closing force for the elevator were last checked and adjusted prior to the incident and by whom. Set forth all bases for that answer.
- What is the estimated number of times the doors of this elevator open and close each day? Set forth all bases for that answer.
- Describe in detail the leading edges of the doors, including the materials, type, composition, width and thickness.
- Is the door open (dwell) time controlled by the flow of passenger traffic across the elevator entrance? If yes, describe in detail how the flow of passenger traffic controls the doors.
- Were the doors of the incident elevator designed or equipped so as not to close on the body of a passenger, and if so, describe the mechanism or control that prevents or limits such closing?

- On the date of plaintiff's accident was there any device or mechanism in place to prevent the doors of the elevator from ever closing on the body of a passenger? Describe fully the mechanism and/or component parts and their normal operation.
- Relative to your answer to the preceding interrogatory, indicate whether said mechanism or device was operating properly on the date of plaintiff's accident. Set forth all bases for that answer.
- Indicate the date the equipment was last inspected and adjusted prior to plaintiff's accident. Set forth all bases for that answer.
- Indicate in detail the manufacturer, model and type (e.g., door open button, mechanical safety edge, dual beam photo-eyes, 2-D infrared photoelectric light curtain, electronic inductive) of all door reopening devices present on the elevator at the time of the incident. Provide details.
- Indicate in detail when these devices were last inspected and adjusted prior to the incident. Set forth all bases for that answer.
- On the date of plaintiff's accident, were there any circumstances under which the doors of the elevator could fully close on the body of a passenger? If so, describe in detail said circumstances and the force that would be exerted by the doors on the passenger and the speed of the closing doors.
- Indicate in detail if the controls permit the door reopening device(s) to be rendered ineffective after a predetermined time (i.e., nudging). Provide details. If yes, what is the normal setting of the predetermined time before nudging begins? When was it last checked and adjusted prior to the incident? Set forth all bases for that answer. If yes, then what is the performance criteria for the nudging door closing speed? When was it last checked and adjusted prior to the incident? Set forth all bases for that answer.
- Indicate in detail if there are there any other controls or devices that limit the door closing force and/or speed. Provide details.
- Indicate in detail whether the manufacturer of the elevator and/or equipment designed to control the opening and closing of elevator doors recommends regular periodic inspections of the doors and if so, please set forth the time schedule for periodic inspections and the detail of the inspection to be performed.
- How many times have the doors or related mechanisms (e.g., door operator, door reopening devices) of the elevator in which plaintiff was injured been repaired since their installation? Set forth all bases for that answer.
- Relative to each repair made to such doors or related mechanisms (e.g., door operator, door reopening devices) in the past five years indicate in

detail the date of all said repairs, the name, address and employer of the person making the repairs and a description of the repairs. Set forth all bases for that answer.

- Please set forth the last date prior to plaintiff's accident when the doors or related mechanisms (e.g., door operator, door reopening devices) were repaired. Set forth all bases for that answer.
- Identify and provide information regarding any prior claims of injury involving the subject elevator

3. Elevator improper leveling

- Indicate in detail the type and operation of car door(s) or gate(s) (e.g., single speed side opening, manual).
- Indicate in detail the type and operation of hoistway (landing) doors (e.g., single speed center opening, automatic)
- Indicate the height and width of the elevator cab entrance(s) when the doors are fully open.
- Indicate the length of the car door vane or clutch and the corresponding landing door vanes.
- Describe in detail the type of door opening device (e.g., door operator) on the elevator involved in plaintiff's accident.
- Indicate in detail the manufacturer and model of all automatic door operating device(s).
- Indicate when the door operating device was installed and the date of any alteration. Set forth all bases for that answer.
- Indicate in detail who last inspected and adjusted the door operating device prior to the incident and when this was done. Set forth all bases for that answer.
- Indicate in detail when the doors on the elevator involved in plaintiff's accident were supposed to begin to open (i.e., pre-opening before the elevator reaches floor level and how far from the floor, or after reaching floor level).
- Indicate in detail who last inspected and adjusted the elevator prior to the incident to determine door opening calibration relative to distance from floor level and when this was done. Set forth all bases for that answer.
- Describe in detail the devices and controls in place for the elevator involved in plaintiff's accident that controlled the leveling, re-leveling and/or stopping accuracy.

- Indicate when the devices and controls in place for the elevator involved in plaintiff's accident that controlled the leveling, re-leveling and/or stopping accuracy were installed and the date of any alteration. Set forth all bases for that answer.
- Indicate in detail who last inspected and adjusted the devices and controls in place for the elevator involved in plaintiff's accident that controlled the leveling, re-leveling and/or stopping accuracy and when this was done. Set forth all bases for that answer.
- Describe in detail the devices and controls in place for the elevator involved in plaintiff's accident that sensed or determined elevator position.
- Indicate when the devices and controls in place for the elevator involved in plaintiff's accident that sensed or determined elevator position were installed and the date of any alteration. Set forth all bases for that answer.
- Indicate in detail who last inspected and adjusted devices and controls in place for the elevator involved in plaintiff's accident that sensed or determined elevator position and when this was done. Set forth all bases for that answer.
- Describe in detail the type of devices and controls in place for the elevator involved in plaintiff's accident that determined leveling speed, leveling accuracy, speed feedback and speed control.
- Indicate when the devices and controls in place for the elevator involved in plaintiff's accident that sensed or determined leveling speed, leveling accuracy, speed feedback and speed control were installed and the date of any alteration. Set forth all bases for that answer.
- Indicate in detail who last inspected and adjusted devices and controls in place for the elevator involved in plaintiff's accident that sensed or determined leveling speed, leveling accuracy, speed feedback and speed control and when this was done. Set forth all bases for that answer.
- On the date of plaintiff's accident, at what distance from floor level would the doors begin to open? Set forth all bases for that answer.
- Indicate whether the elevator involved in plaintiff's accident had any device which would prevent door opening based upon elevator stopping at a predetermined distance from floor level. Describe in detail said device and its calibration at the time of plaintiff's accident. Set forth all bases for that answer.
- Indicate whether in the five-year period prior to plaintiff's accident there were any complaints relative to improper leveling of the elevator.
- Indicate whether during the five-year period of time prior to the accident there had been any service or repair on the elevator to correct or

adjust elevator car leveling relative to outside floor level. If so, indicate each and every date. Set forth all bases for that answer.

- If a hydraulic elevator, indicate whether the elevator involved in plaintiff's accident contained an "anti-creep leveling" device. If so, describe in detail its operation.
- At the time of plaintiff's accident, what was the permissible tolerance above and below the floor landings that the elevator car could be located for the elevator would be permitted to remain in service?
- Indicate in detail when the elevator involved in plaintiff's accident was last inspected prior to the incident to determine whether or not the elevator car was stopping at floor level or some distance away. Set forth all bases for that answer.
- Describe in detail any and all documents generated in the course of inspection, repair, or maintenance which describes leveling or improper leveling conditions.
- Describe in detail each and every document, manual, service bulletin, or similar document which describes the procedures for inspection, repair, maintenance, and calibration of elevator components to prevent improper leveling.

4. Escalator basic

- Provide all the identification numbers of the incident escalator (e.g., building ID, maintenance company ID, inspection authority ID).
- Indicate the type of the incident escalator (e.g., conventional end drive, modular)
- Indicate the rise of the incident escalator.
- Indicate the width of the steps of the incident escalator.
- Indicate the rated speed of the incident escalator.
- Indicate the type of control (e.g., solid state, relay logic).
- Indicate the capacity of the incident escalator.
- Indicate the manufacturer and model of the escalator.
- Indicate the installer of the escalator.
- Indicate the location of the driving machine (e.g., upper pit, under the exposed steps).
- Describe in detail the manufacturer and type of brake(s) (e.g., driving machine, service, drum, disc, mechanically applied, hydraulically applied).
- Describe in detail the operating environment (e.g., outdoors, heavy usage, crush loads).

- Indicate the date of installation and any alterations of the escalator and indicate the applicable code(s).
- Provide details of all alterations to the escalator, when they were done and by whom.
- What is the estimated number of people who use this escalator each day?
- What is the estimated number of hours this escalator carries passengers each day?

5. Escalator combplate entrapments

- Indicate the manufacturer of the combplates, combs and steps of the escalator involved in plaintiff's accident.
- Indicate whether the combplate was fixed or could move horizontally and/or vertically.
- Indicate when the combplates, combs and steps were installed and the date of any alteration. Set forth all bases for that answer.
- Indicate in detail who last inspected and adjusted the combplates, steps, step rollers and tracks, and combs prior to the incident; and when it was done. Set forth all bases for that answer.
- Indicate in detail the manufacturer's requirements (e.g., height, width, condition) for the step tread slots of the escalator involved in plaintiff's accident. Set forth all bases for that answer.
- Indicate in detail the maintenance company's requirements (e.g., height, width, condition) for the step tread slots of the escalator involved in plaintiff's accident. Set forth all bases for that answer.
- Indicate in detail the specific tools and the procedures which were used to check the condition of the step tread slots.
- Indicate in detail who last inspected the step tread slots prior to the incident, and when it was done. Set forth all bases for that answer.
- Indicate in detail the actual recording of the condition of the step tread slots for the three-year period prior to plaintiff's accident.
- Indicate in detail the manufacturer's requirement for the depth of comb teeth setting into the step tread slots of the escalator involved in plaintiff's accident.
- Indicate in detail the maintenance company's requirement for the depth of comb teeth setting into the step tread slots of the escalator involved in plaintiff's accident.
- Indicate in detail the actual measurements for the depth of comb teeth

setting into the step treads at each landing of the escalator for the three-year period of time prior to plaintiff's accident.

- Indicate the specific tools and the procedures which were used to measure the depth of comb teeth setting into the step tread slots.
- Indicate in detail who last inspected and adjusted the combplate and the comb teeth prior to the incident, and when it was done. Set forth all bases for that answer.
- Do you contend that the comb teeth depth setting into the step tread slots on the date of plaintiff's accident was in conformity with the manufacturer's and maintenance company's recommendations. If so, set forth the recommendations, the actual depth measured and all bases for that answer.
- Describe in detail any damage noted to the steps, combplate or comb teeth after plaintiff's accident. Set forth all bases for that answer.
- Identify in detail each and every document that reports or reflects any damage to the step rollers, step chain rollers, or step chain tracks of the escalator involved in plaintiff's accident for the three-year period of time prior to the accident.
- Identify in detail each and every document that reports or reflects any damage to the steps, combplate or comb teeth of the escalator involved in plaintiff's accident from the date of plaintiff's accident and for one month subsequent.
- How soon after plaintiff's accident was the comb teeth depth measured, by whom, and what, if any, measurements were documented?
- How often during the three-year period of time prior to the accident was the depth of the comb teeth setting into the step tread slots inspected, measured and adjusted?
- Identify in detail each and every document generated by you, or any other entity, which reflects the measurement of the depth of comb teeth below the top of the step tread surface, or adjustments to comb teeth depth for the three-year period of time prior to the accident.
- Indicate in detail whether, after plaintiff's accident, any damage was noted to step rollers, step chain rollers, or step chain tracks, and if so, fully describe said damage.
- Identify in detail each and every document that reports or reflects any damage to the step rollers, step chain rollers, or step chain tracks of the escalator involved in plaintiff's accident for the three-year period of time prior to the accident.
- Identify in detail each and every document that reports or reflects any damage to the step rollers, step chain rollers, or step chain tracks of the

escalator involved in plaintiff's accident from the date of plaintiff's accident and for one month subsequent.

- Indicate whether the escalator involved in plaintiff's accident was equipped with comb-step impact devices, and if so, indicate the maximum horizontal and vertical forces permitted at each side of the combplate and at its center to actuate the devices.
- Indicate when the comb-step impact devices were installed and the date of any alteration. Set forth all bases for that answer.
- Indicate the manufacturer of the comb-step impact devices.
- Indicate whether the escalator involved in plaintiff's accident was equipped with combplate stop switches, and if so, describe the maximum vertical force necessary to activate same.
- Indicate when the combplate stop switches were installed and the date of any alteration. Set forth all bases for that answer.
- Indicate whether the escalator involved in plaintiff's accident was equipped with step level devices.
- Indicate when the step level devices were installed and the date of any alteration. Set forth all bases for that answer.
- Indicate in detail the manufacturer and type of the step level devices.
- How far from each landing is each step level device located?
- What is the minimum and maximum stopping distance for the escalator.
- Indicate in detail each and every occasion during the three-year period of time prior to plaintiff's accident when the comb step impact devices were maintained and tested, and the results.
- Indicate in detail each and every occasion during the three-year period of time prior to plaintiff's accident when the comb stop switches were maintained and tested, and the results.
- Indicate in detail each and every occasion during the three-year period of time prior to plaintiff's accident when the step level device was maintained and tested, and the results thereof.

6. Escalator sudden stops

- Do you admit that the escalator came to an abrupt stop?
- What condition or conditions do you contend caused the escalator involved in plaintiff's accident to come to a sudden stop? Set forth all bases for that answer.

- Do you contend that any equipment or parts of the escalator involved in plaintiff's accident failed causing the escalator to stop, and if so, identify all parts or equipment. Set forth all bases for that answer.
- Do you contend that an emergency stop switch was activated at the time of plaintiff's accident? Please identify the individual you contend activated the emergency stop switch at the time of plaintiff's accident. Set forth all bases for that answer.
- Please identify the location of each and every emergency stop switch for the escalator involved in plaintiff's accident.
- Please identify each and every safety device incorporated into the escalator's control system involved in plaintiff's accident which is designed to interrupt power to the escalator's drive machine or to apply its brake.
- Did any safety device activate on the date of plaintiff's accident with the result that the escalator came to a stop? If so, identify which safety device was activated. Set forth all bases for that answer
- Describe in detail the manufacturer and type of brake(s) (e.g., driving machine, service, drum, disc, mechanically applied, hydraulically applied).
- What is the minimum and maximum stopping distance and deceleration for the escalator? Set forth all bases for that answer.
- Describe in detail the procedure how the minimum and maximum stopping distance and deceleration of the escalator is adjusted and tested. Set forth all bases for that answer.
- Indicate in detail who last inspected and adjusted the brake prior to the incident and when it was done. Indicate in detail any recordings of the findings and measurements. Set forth all bases for that answer.
- Indicate in detail who last tested the minimum and maximum brake torque prior to the incident and when it was done. Set forth all bases for that answer. Indicate in detail all recordings of the brake torque.
- Indicate in detail each and every repair or replacement of the brake for 3 years prior to the incident and one month subsequent to the date of the incident. Set forth all bases for that answer.
- Indicate whether or not the elevator was equipped with any instrumentation that measured or collected data or information measuring the speed, deceleration or acceleration of the subject elevator prior to the date of the events at issue.
- Indicate whether the elevator was equipped with any camera equipment that recorded the interior of the elevator, or any information relating to the events at issue.

7. Side-of-step entrapments

- Please state whether the skirt panels of the escalator involved in plaintiff's accident were made of any low friction material, and if so, identify completely.
- Please state whether the skirt panels in the escalator involved in plaintiff's accident were lubricated at any time during the three years prior to the accident, and if so, identify each occasion, and state whether any documents reflect said work.
- Please state whether the skirt panels involved on the escalator involved in plaintiff's accident were replaced or repaired any time within the three years prior to the accident, and if so, identify the date of each said repair or replacement.
- Please set forth the running clearance between steps and skirt panels as recommended by the manufacturer for the escalator involved in plaintiff's accident.
- Please identify each and every occasion when the running clearance between steps and skirt panels of the escalator involved in plaintiff's accident was measured during the three-year period of time prior to the accident, and for each occasion, set forth the actual measurement.
- Do you contend that on the date of plaintiff's accident the running clearance between steps and skirt panels was within limits set by the manufacturer?
- Do you contend that on the date of plaintiff's accident the running clearance between steps and skirt panels was consistent with any code or code provisions, and if so, identify the specific code(s) and section(s).
- Did plaintiff become entrapped in the running clearance between the steps and skirt panels of the escalator involved in plaintiff's accident?
- How soon after plaintiff's accident did you, or any representative on your behalf, inspect the escalator involved in plaintiff's accident?
- When was the first time after plaintiff's accident that the running clearance between steps and skirt panels was measured, what measurement was obtained and who was the person who obtained said measurements?
- Please set forth each and every occasion within the three years prior to the date of plaintiff's accident when the running clearance between the steps and skirt panels was adjusted or changed.
- Please set forth for the escalator involved in plaintiff's accident the procedures necessary to adjust running clearance between steps and skirt panels.

- Please identify each and every warning or cautionary sign present on the date of plaintiff's accident.

8. Handicapped lift or porch lift collapse

- Please state whether or not a parts list exists for the lift platform assembly, including the worm or drive screw, lift plate and fall or locking nut for the porch lift involved herein.
- Please state whether or not any technical drawings, specifications or blueprints exist for the lift platform assembly, including the worm or drive screw, lift plate and fall or locking nut of the porch lift involved herein.
- Please state whether any service bulletins, repair manuals or maintenance procedures or policies exist for the porch lift involved herein, and if so, identify each completely.
- Is the model porch lift involved in the accident in suit still being manufactured and sold, and if not, identify by model number the replacement product, if any?
- Are there any service bulletins, repair manuals, maintenance manuals or similar documents which set forth the following: (a) the frequency with which the porch lift involved in the accident herein should be inspected; (b) the frequency with which the porch lift involved in the accident herein should be lubricated?
- Please identify the specific materials used in the design and manufacture of the fall or locking nut of the lift platform assembly in the porch lift involved in this lawsuit.
- Have you received notice of any accidents, suits or claims in which it was alleged that the lift platform assembly fell unexpectedly in any porch lift that you design, manufacture, sell, install, repair or maintain and if so, set forth the date, name and address of persons involved, court caption including jurisdiction, term and number of any lawsuit filed?
- Other than the porch lift involved in this lawsuit, do you manufacture or distribute any other porch lifts, and if so, please set forth the model numbers and descriptions of same?

B. General Examples

1. Identification of defendants

- As to each defendant, please state the corporate name, state of incorporation and principal place of business.
- Please state the name, present business address, job title, and employer of the individual answering these interrogatories.

2. Notice of plaintiff's accident

- Please state how defendant first became aware of plaintiff's accident.
- By what method did defendant receive said notice.
- Please state whether the first notice of plaintiff's accident was received in writing, and if so, describe the nature of said document.
- Please identify any and all incident reports relating to the plaintiff's event. To the extent that work product protection is claimed over these materials please identify them with sufficient particularity to allow the court to consider the applicability of this claim. This should include any applicable privilege log.

3. Witnesses

- Please state the name, address, and employer of all known eyewitnesses to the accident.
- Please identify whether or not any of defendant's employees were eyewitnesses to the accident.
- Please identify each and every person, providing names, addresses and employer, of all witnesses who have any knowledge whatsoever concerning the facts leading up to the accident in question.
- Relative to your answer to the preceding interrogatory, please state the knowledge or information of each witness identified.
- Please identify each and every person who has been interviewed by defendant or by defendant's representatives and set forth the date of the interview, the identity of the persons present, whether the interview was recorded, and if so, the manner of recording.
- Please identify whether or not any statements, written or recorded, have been taken or are available for any of the persons identified in answer to these interrogatories.

- Please set forth the name, address, and employer of each and every person for whom a statement, recorded or written, has been taken.
- Please identify each and every statement in the possession of the defendant, oral, typed, written, taped, transcribed, or memorialized in any fashion, pertinent to the facts alleged in plaintiff's complaint.

4. Investigation and examination

- Please state whether defendant examined or inspected the product identified in the definitions to this set of Interrogatories (elevator and/or escalator) and if so, please set forth for each examination or inspection the date, time, name, address, and employer of the person conducting said investigation or examination.
- Please identify by name, address, and employer, all investigators, representatives, or employees of defendant who have inspected the accident location and/or product.
- For each investigation or examination, please identify the name, address, employer, of the investigator and set forth the results or conclusions of the investigation.
- For all investigations or examinations identified, please set forth whether the results of the examination or investigation are set forth in any written document, and if so, identify completely.
- Was any report of this accident made to any municipal or state authority, and if so, please identify the name and address of the person who made the report, the date the report was made, the names and addresses of each person who furnished the information included in the report, and a summary of the conclusions thereof.

5. Evidence

- Please state whether there are any photographs which depict the product (elevator or escalator) involved in plaintiff's accident, and if so, set forth the date, identity of the person taking the photographs, and the subject matter of said photographs.
- Please identify whether there are any videotapes of the product (elevator or escalator) in existence involved in plaintiff's accident, and if so, set forth the date, identity of the person taking the videotape, and the subject matter of said videotape.

- Was the product involved in plaintiff's Complaint (elevator or escalator) and adjacent area subject to routine videotaping or surveillance at the time of plaintiff's accident, and if so, please state whether any videotapes exist for the time of plaintiff's accident.

6. Prior complaints, notice, and accidents

- Please state whether the defendant, for the period of time five years prior to the accident and to the present, has ever received any complaint from any person or entity regarding the product in question, and if so, please set forth the date, name and address of person making the complaint, the subject matter of the complaint, and whether the substance of the complaint was memorialized or documented.
- Please identify the method by which defendant records and memorializes complaints made pertinent to products (elevator or escalator) it installs, services, and/or owns.
- Please identify each and every accident involving the product in question which occurred five years prior and to the present, providing the name and address of the injured person.
- For each and every accident identified, please state whether or not any claim or lawsuit was brought against defendant or any other entity for personal injuries and if so, please provide the name and address of the plaintiff's attorney, court term and number of any lawsuit, and the outcome of the lawsuit.
- Please identify each and every claim or lawsuit brought against defendant for the period of time five years prior to the accident and to the present alleging negligence with respect to the installation, repair, maintenance, or service of products similar to that involved in plaintiff's accident.

7. Contact with the plaintiff

- Please state whether any representative of defendant interviewed the plaintiff at any time, and if so, please set forth the date, name and address of person conducting the interview, and whether the interview was recorded or whether there is any written document memorializing the substance of the interview.
- If it is claimed that plaintiff made any admission relating to the accident or plaintiff's injuries and damages, please state the name, address and

employer of the person or persons to whom said admissions were made, and the date thereof.

- Please set forth in detail the substance of any and all conversations, statements, or remarks made by plaintiff to any person concerning the accident in suit.
- Please state whether any personal injury or accident report form was completed by you, or any other entity pertinent to the accident in suit and if so, then identify completely.

8. Ownership, control and service

- Please identify the owner of the product involved in plaintiff's accident.
- Please identify by name, address, and date the entity or person responsible for installing the product on the premises where the accident occurred.
- Please identify by name and address the entity responsible for the service, repair, inspection or maintenance of the product involved in plaintiff's accident on the date of plaintiff's accident.
- Please identify each and every entity responsible for the maintenance, service, inspection or repair of the product involved in plaintiff's accident for the five-year period of time prior to the accident.
- Please identify each and every entity responsible for hiring or arranging for the hiring of entities responsible for service, repair, inspection or maintenance of the product involved in plaintiff's accident on the date of plaintiff's accident.
- Were any persons or entities not referred to in your answers to the preceding interrogatories in possession or control of the premises where the product was located on the date of plaintiff's accident, and if so, state the name and address of all said persons or entities.

9. Manufacture

- Please identify the manufacturer of the product involved in plaintiff's accident [or component parts].
- Please state the date of manufacture of the product involved in plaintiff's accident [or component parts].
- Please identify all documents furnished by the manufacturer of the product involved in plaintiff's accident.

- Please identify all instructions for installation provided by the manufacturer of the product.
- Please identify all written materials, instructions, operators' instructions or similar information provided by the manufacturer relative to maintenance and use of the product involved in plaintiff's accident.

10. Installation and alteration

- On what date was the product involved in plaintiff's accident first installed at defendant's premises.
- Please identify by name, address and employer all persons responsible for purchasing or ordering said product.
- Please identify by name and address each person, firm, or business who installed or assisted in the installation of the product involved in plaintiff's accident.
- Indicate the applicable standards and codes, including applicable edition, that the elevator was required to conform to when it was installed.
- Indicate specific details of all alterations of the equipment, the date(s) they were made and by whom. Indicate the applicable standards codes, including applicable edition, that the elevator was required to conform to when it was altered.

11. Maintenance and repair contracts

- Please state whether there was any type of maintenance contract or any other type of contract in existence at the time of the plaintiff's accident for the repair, service, or maintenance of the product and if so, identify by name and address all parties to the contract.
- Please identify by name and address the person or entity which you contend had the contractual obligation to service, maintain, or repair the product on the date of plaintiff's accident.
- At any time during the five-year period of time prior to the accident, did defendant, or any representative on behalf of defendant, enter into any contract with any entity to perform service, maintenance, or repair on said product, and if so, identify by name and address said entity?
- Please describe the type of contract which existed at the time of the accident for the repair, service, and/or maintenance of the product involved in plaintiff's accident.

- Please identify by name and address each and every entity responsible for the repair, service, or maintenance of the product involved in plaintiff's accident for the five-year period of time prior to plaintiff's accident until 30 days after the accident.
- Please identify the nature of the documents generated by each and every service, repair, or maintenance visit involving the product identified in plaintiff's accident.
- Please identify precisely the nature of any service, repair, or maintenance performed on the product involved in plaintiff's accident for the period of time thirty days prior to and including the date of the accident.
- Please list each and every date for the five-year period of time prior to the accident that any representative of defendant inspected, repaired, serviced, or performed any type of maintenance work whatsoever to the elevator involved in plaintiff's accident.
- Relative to your answer to the preceding interrogatory, please state whether written records exist for each and every visit identified, and if not, please set forth each and every date for which records are not available.

12. Elevator and escalator inspections and tests

- Please state whether regular and periodic inspections or tests of the elevator or escalator are required by state or local government, and if so, please identify the department that requires such inspections and tests, the frequency with which such inspections and tests are required, the type and extent of the inspection and test required and the results of the last inspection prior to plaintiff's accident.
- With respect to all required periodic inspections of the elevator or escalator in the five years prior to plaintiff's accident, please set forth each and every recommendation or violation from the inspector as to necessary repairs or modifications.
- Please identify the date of each and every inspection of the product involved in plaintiff's accident for the five-year period of time prior to the accident through the present time and set forth the name, address and employer of the inspector.
- Please identify each written document which sets forth the results of every inspection of the product involved in plaintiff's accident for the five-year period of time prior to the accident through the present.

13. Insurance

- Please identify each and every policy of insurance providing coverage for defendant for the accident in suit.
- For each insurance policy identified, set forth the limits of coverage and state whether there are any deductibles, or co-pays, and the amount of same.
- Please state whether any non-waiver or reservation of rights letters have been issued with respect to claims arising from plaintiff's accident, and if so, please state the basis for same.
- Please identify the named insured, or any additional named insured, on any and all potentially available policies of insurance
- Please identify any and all available med-pay or medical payment benefits available under any potential policy of insurance

14. Expert witnesses

- Identify by name, address, occupation, and title each person whom you expect to call as an expert witness at trial and state with respect to each:
  - (a) His or her field of expertise, including any areas in which he or she believes to have special qualifications;
  - (b) Educational background;
  - (c) Any special training in the field of elevator or escalator accident investigation or reconstruction;
  - (d) Any special training in the field of elevator or escalator design, installation, repair, service or maintenance;
  - (e) General professional background, i.e., job title, duties, employer(s) and the term of each position;
  - (f) Papers and/or books published or reported;
  - (g) Lectures on subjects involving elevators or escalators; and
  - (h) Membership in professional societies and/or organizations.
- For each expert witness identified, please set forth the following:
  - (a) The frequency with which he or she has testified in matters involving elevators or escalators;
  - (b) The frequency with which he or she has testified on behalf of defendant; and
  - (c) The caption and court term and number of all cases in which he or she has been involved, inspected products, offered expert opinions,

provided depositions, or testified at trial and the percentage of total income received from testifying.

- For each person you expect to call as an expert witness, set forth the following:
  (a) The subject matter to which the expert is expected to testify;
  (b) The substance of the facts and opinions to which the expert is expected to testify;
  (c) A factual summary of the grounds for each such opinion; and
  (d) Whether the facts and opinions set forth are contained in any written report, memorandum or other transcript.
- For each expert you expect to testify at the time of trial, state the following:
  (a) Is the opinion of the expert based in whole or in part on any code, regulation, governmental or otherwise, and if so identify said code or regulation and specifically set forth the section relied upon;
  (b) If the opinion of any expert witness is based in whole or in part upon any scientific or engineering textbook or other publication, identify said test or publication completely; and
  (c) Identify by author, title, publication date and publisher each and every document in the nature of a "learned treatise" upon which the expert may rely at the time of trial.
- For each expert identified, please list each and every document provided to that expert in order for him or her to render an opinion in this case.

15. Product testing and reenactments

- Please state whether any tests of the product involved in suit was made by you or your representatives, and if so, state the date, location, and all parties present at the time of the test.
- For each test of the product involved in this lawsuit, please describe fully the observations made in the course of each test, and whether any written documents record or memorialize the test results.
- For all testing performed on the product in suit, state whether any photographs, videotapes, measurements or readings of any type or nature whatsoever were made, and if so, state the nature of each.

16. Surveillance of the plaintiff

- State whether any surveillance was conducted of plaintiff by defendant, or any other entities, and if so, please set forth the date of all said surveillance, the name and address of the investigator performing same, and whether or not photographs or videotapes were produced as a result.
- Please state whether any written document exists which sets forth the nature and scope of the surveillance performed and identify the custodian of same.
- Please set forth whether defendant is in possession of any photographs, videotapes, films, or other visual representations of plaintiff's activities, and if so, please set forth for each and every photograph or visual representation the date same was made.
- Please set forth the name, address, and employer of the photographer or videographer if different from the person conducting the surveillance.
- Please set forth the name, address, and employer of each and every person who may be called upon to testify at trial concerning the surveillance, or observations of plaintiff's activities.

17. Custodian of records

- Please identify by name, address, and employer the person or persons presently in custody of documents pertinent to installation, inspection, service, repair, and/or maintenance of the product involved in plaintiff's accident.

18. The plaintiff's conduct

- If you contend that the plaintiff was contributorily or comparatively negligent, please set forth all facts to support said contention.
- Please identify by name, address, and employer each and every person who will provide facts to support defendant's claim that plaintiff was comparatively or contributorily negligent.
- Please set forth your contention as to how the accident involving plaintiff occurred.

9.2 Request for Production of Documents

After a lawsuit is filed and before the post-suit inspection, it is to the plaintiff's attorney's advantage to obtain as much information as she can to make the site inspection more productive. Expert witnesses often complain that the discovery information received from the attorney does not contain all the documents that are necessary to reconstruct the accident or form an opinion as to liability issues. Therefore, for purposes of the site inspection, evaluation of the case, and preparation for trial, comprehensive records must be obtained.

A. Examples of Key Documents

- The wiring diagrams (control schematics) for the incident elevator/escalator
- All maintenance and repair documents (e.g., callback records, work tickets, time tickets, logs) for the incident elevator/escalator for two years prior to the incident date and six months after it
- The maintenance contract/specifications in effect on the incident date
- All incident reports
- All witness statements
- The complete inspection file for the incident elevator/escalator, including all accident investigations
- Detailed description (including dates) and documentation of all modifications to the elevator/escalator since it was installed
- All proposals for modifications and repairs to the incident elevator/escalator
- All insurance reports related to the incident
- All video recordings of the incident
- All consultant reports related to the incident elevator/escalator
- All installation, adjustment, maintenance, repair and owner's manuals for the incident elevator/escalator
- Detailed description of all known substantially similar incidents (alleged or otherwise) for the incident elevator/escalator
- The written Maintenance Control Program (MCP) for the incident elevator/escalator as defined by ASME A17.1

It is important to request these documents from all defendants. Different defendants may have different but related documents (e.g., maintenance log books, building engineering log books, security log books, electronic documents, work tickets, invoices, call back records, trouble call records) that need to be cross referenced for a more complete analysis. The timeframe indicated above is important for analysis of intermittent type malfunctions, notice and the probable cause(s) of the incident. In general, the more complete the documentation obtained, the more complete the analysis.

B. General Examples

1. Statements

- Any and all statements of plaintiff.
- Any and all statements of any witnesses to the accident.
- Any and all statements of witnesses to the condition of the product involved in the accident before and after the time of the accident.

2. Accident and injury reports

- All personal injury or accident report forms completed for the accident in suit.

3. Litigation materials

- Any and all documents identified in defendant's answers to plaintiff's Interrogatories.
- All reports of experts that defendant intends to call as expert witnesses at the time of trial.
- Any and all documents defendant intends to introduce as exhibits at trial.
- Any and all documents provided to experts who defendant intends to call at the time of trial.
- Any and all investigation materials, including statements, photographs and any other documentary evidence.

4. Evidence

- Copies of any and all photographs or videotapes depicting the product involved in plaintiff's suit.
- Copies of any and all routine or periodic surveillance or videotapes that depict the accident location involved in suit.

- Copies of any and all documents reflecting or evidencing surveillance conducted on the plaintiff.
- Copies of any and all surveillance videotapes.
- Copies of any and all investigative reports pertinent to surveillance.

5. Identification of product

- Copies of any and all documents evidencing the sale and distribution of the product involved in suit.
- Copies of any and all documents evidencing the installation of the product in suit.
- Copies of any and all documents identifying the manufacturer of the product in suit.
- Copies of any and all sales brochures, operator's manuals, installation manuals, or similar documents pertinent to the product in suit.
- Copies of any and all documents including sales slip, receipt, invoice, charge account statement, billing, cancelled check, purchase order, lease or agreement or other writing which was issued or recorded because of the sale, purchase or lease of the product [or component part] which was involved in plaintiff's accident.
- Copies of any and all documents, written, printed, or graphic representations, including catalogs, statements, circulars, manuals, brochures, advertisements, or other writings which were made by or on behalf of any defendant and which mention or describe or otherwise refer to the virtues, capacities, qualities, characteristics, or capabilities of the product involved in suit.

6. Documents pertinent to product

- All blueprints, diagrams, schematics, plans, technical drawings pertaining to the product in suit [or component parts].
- Operator's and/or owner's manual, instruction manual, safety manual, or other similar document pertaining to the product in suit.
- Parts list or catalog for the product in suit.
- Copies of any service bulletins or service updates pertinent to the product in suit [specific component part].
- Copies of all engineering change notices or engineering change orders for the product in suit [or component part].

7. Inspections and examinations

- Copies of all evaluations and/or examination records for the product in suit from the date of installation through the present.
- Copies of any and all documents purporting to set forth the results of inspections of the product in suit from the date of installation through the present.
- Copies of any and all documents indicating inspection or testing on a periodic basis for the product in suit from the date of installation through the present.

8. Maintenance and repair

- Copies of any and all maintenance contracts, service contracts, or similar types of contracts pertinent to the product from the date of installation through the present.
- Copy of the maintenance log in force for the product involved in plaintiff's accident from the date of installation through the present.
- All field test and data reports related to the product in suit from the date maintenance and/or repair first began on the product to the present time.
- A summary of all contract data for all maintenance and repair service records that relate to the product in suit from the date that maintenance or repair commenced on the product to the present time.
- All technical articles available for use in maintaining and/or repairing the elevator involved in plaintiff's accident from the date that maintenance and/or repair on the elevator commenced to the present time.
- All field bulletin indices and/or field education articles available for use in maintaining or repairing the type of elevator involved in plaintiff's accident from the date that maintenance or repair commenced on the product to the present time.
- All service letter indices and/or service letters available for use in maintaining or repairing the elevator involved in plaintiff's accident from the date that maintenance and/or repair commenced on the product to the present time.
- Copies of all your manual and computer callback, maintenance and repair, site history reports, and any other type of documents for the product involved in suit from the date maintenance and/or repair first began until the present time.

- All trouble work tickets and/or all callback reports by field personnel that relate to the product involved in plaintiff's accident from the date maintenance and/or repair first began on the elevator to the present time.
- All maintenance record cards and files for the product involved in plaintiff's accident from the date maintenance and/or repair first began on the product to the present time.
- All sales information data and owners' information pertinent to the product available for use in maintaining and repairing the product from the date maintenance or repair first began until the present time.
- Copies of all maintenance manuals available for use in maintaining and repairing the elevator from the date maintenance or repair first began to the present time.
- Copies of all construction, service and adjustment manuals available for use in installing, adjusting, maintaining or repairing the product from the date maintenance or repair first began on the product until the present time.
- All training manuals available for use in maintaining and repairing the elevator from the date maintenance or repair first began to the present time.
- All installation manuals available for use in maintaining and repairing the elevator from the date maintenance or repair first began to the present time.
- All assembly and detail drawings for the product's component parts available for use in maintaining and repairing the elevator from the date maintenance or repair first began on the elevator to the present time.
- All assembly and detail drawings of vendor supplied components incorporated into the product available for use in maintaining and repairing the elevator from the date maintenance or repair first began to the present time.
- All service supervisors' manuals available for use in maintaining and repairing the elevator from the date maintenance or repair first began to the present time.
- All combination weekly time reports or their equivalent by employees that relate to all work performed on the product from the date maintenance or repair first began to the present time.
- A copy of all preventive maintenance guidebooks or their equivalent available to field service personnel that perform work on the product from the date maintenance or repair first began to the present time.

- All preventive maintenance schedules and/or check charts for the product from the date you first began to perform maintenance or repair to the present time.
- All of your maintenance evaluation reports for the product from the date you first began to perform maintenance or repair to the present time.
- All correspondence, memos, notes, inspection reports, and documents of any kind, however recorded, transmitted and received from any entity, that relate to the product that was available for use or relied on any time during the period of time from the date maintenance or repair first began to the present time.
- All documents generated, referred to, used and relied upon that relate to the electric speed control system and its components that are a part of the product involved in suit from the date maintenance or repair first began to the present time.
- All documents generated, referred to, used and relied upon that relate to the automatic leveling device that is a part of the product involved in suit from the date maintenance or repair first began to the present time.
- Copies of any and all documents setting forth standard operating procedures, rules, guidelines, and/or similar documents provided to field service personnel that performed work on the elevator involved in suit from the date maintenance or repair first began to the present time.
- Copies of any and all documents provided to employees for the purposes of maintenance and repair that relate to design, adjustment, maintenance and/or repair of products of the type at issue with respect to user and passenger safety from the date maintenance or repair first began to the present time.
- Copies of any and all documents including, but not limited to reports on maintenance, dynamics, testing, certification, repair, trouble calls, adjustments in performance that were required by the maintenance contract for the product involved in suit from the date maintenance or repair first began to the present time.
- Copies of any and all documents including sales slips, receipts, invoices, charge account statements, billing, cancelled checks, purchase orders, or other writings which were issued or recorded because of repairs, service, modifications or maintenance performed on the product involved in plaintiff's accident from the date maintenance or service first began through the present time.
- All diagnostic instrumentation data recorded relating to the product from the date of the maintenance contract to the present time.

- All examiner certificates of examination and service route sheets that have a reference to the product from the date maintenance and/or repair first began to the present time.
- Copies of all records of field service personnel performing repair, inspection, service or maintenance on the product.

9. Expert reports

- Copies of any and all reports of expert witnesses who will testify at trial.
- Copies of any and all articles, treatises, or publications that the expert(s) will rely upon at the time of trial.
- Copies of any and all codes, regulations, or standards that the expert(s) will rely upon at the time of trial.

10. Investigation and examination

- Copies of any and all reports reflecting post-accident investigation or examination of the product in suit.
- Copies of any and all photographs or videotapes reflecting post-accident investigation or examination of product in suit.

11. Prior complaints, notice and accidents

- Copies of any and all reports, notes, records, memoranda, or other documents referencing complaints from any person or entity regarding the product in question.
- A copy of defendant's complaints/notice/accident log.
- Copies of any and all documents reflecting injury or accidents involving the product in suit or similar products for the period of time five years prior to the accident to the present time.
- Copies of any and all documents reflecting complaints for the product involved in suit made five years prior to the accident to the present time.
- Copies of all complaints, summons, or similar documents filed to recover for personal injury for accidents involving the product in suit and similar products for the period of time five years prior to the accident to the present time.

12. Miscellaneous from building owner

- A copy of the complete set of elementary wiring diagrams (schematics) for the product involved in suit including the bank of the elevator's supervisory system.
- Copies of any and all inspection reports performed by the applicable code authorities for the period of time five years prior to the accident to the present time.
- A copy of video of elevator or escalator activity on the date of the accident including one half hour before until one half hour after the accident.
- Copies of any proposals for modernization or upgrades of the product from product manufacturers, designers, and repair personnel from the time of installation to the present time.
- Copies of all independent consultant's reports that relate to the product in question, passenger safety, design and/or maintenance from the date of installation to the present time.
- All governmental and consultant safety inspection and test reports including, but not limited to acceptance, semi-annual, annual and five-year inspections that relate to the product involved in suit.
- Copies of any and all proposals for maintenance or service provided by manufacturer and/or installer whether or not entered into.
- A list of any and all agents, employees, independent contractors or vendors that have been granted or authorized to enter into, or work within, the elevator machine room for any reason during the past three (3) years.

9.3 Depositions of Corporate Designees

Local and federal rules permit noticing the deposition of the corporate defendant and then requiring that defendant to designate one or more persons who will testify about specific areas of inquiry. The testimony of persons designated by a named defendant in response to a properly drafted Notice of Corporate Designee is binding against the defendant. Accordingly, most jurisdictions permit the reading into evidence at the time of trial of the questions and answers of the corporate designee. This can assist in proving required elements of the case, laying a groundwork for the plaintiff's expert's opinion, or cross-examining the defendant's expert. Reading into evidence the answers of the corporate designee can also be used if counsel believes it would be advantageous not to have to elicit this information at trial live from the opposing party's representative. Normally corporate depositions of the manufacturer, the service and repair company, the building owner, or the facilities manager are taken. Counsel should also consider whether the corporate deposition of the defendant should be videotaped. If useful or damaging information is obtained from the corporate designee it is much more effective to present it at trial through a videotaped deposition as opposed to reading a question and answer or even having an enlargement of the desired question and answer from the transcript. The following are sample questions.

Notice of Corporate Designee

PLEASE TAKE NOTICE that on **Tuesday, November 20, 2001 at 10:00 A.M.**, Plaintiff shall take the deposition of the Corporate Designee of (defendant), at the law offices of _________________, upon oral examination pursuant to ______, before a notary public or other officer similarly authorized by law to administer oaths.

Inquiry will be made concerning all paragraphs set forth below pertaining to document production. This deposition is *not* limited to document production and will involve questioning concerning the topics set forth below.

Pursuant to Pa. R.C.P. 4007.1(d) and 4009, the person(s) designated by the defendant, (defendant), to testify on its behalf shall bring with him or her, for the purposes of inspection and/or copying, the complete records and/or files of (defendant), relative to the following:

General information

- Specifications prepared by the purchaser (building owner and/or other or their agent) regarding elevator involved in plaintiff's accident.
- The identity of the company which installed the elevator, doors and gates, involved in this accident as set forth and identified in plaintiffs' Complaint.
- Identification of the model freight elevator, doors and gates involved in this lawsuit.
- Agreements or contractual arrangements entered into between defendants and non-defendants relating to elevator identified in complaint.
- Repair or maintenance contracts pertinent to the elevator, doors and gates involved in this case.
- Installation, operation and maintenance manual with regard to the elevator and/or doors/gate of elevator involved in plaintiff's accident.

- Repair or maintenance brochures or instructions pertinent to the model elevator doors and gates involved in this lawsuit.
- Recommendations for service, operation and maintenance of the product by any entity including but not limited to defendants at the time of installation and any time thereafter.
- Maintenance and/or log books related to elevator involved in plaintiff's accident.
- Maintenance and repair of the elevator, doors and gates involved in this accident.
- Service calls to repair or maintain or inspect any elevator, doors and gates located at ___________.
- Documents reflecting periodic testing and inspection and/or maintenance from any governmental agencies or entities.
- Complaints from any source regarding the operation or use of the elevator involved in plaintiff's accident.
- Notice of lawsuits wherein it was alleged that elevator, doors and gates involved in this lawsuit had caused damage and/or injury by virtue of striking an object and/or individual.
- Wiring diagrams and/or schematics and manuals for the elevator including but not limited to the elevator and/or doors/gate.
- Information pertinent to the sensor beam and/or reversing edge of the elevator involved in plaintiff's accident.
- Any alterations to the gate, doors, door operating systems or re-opening devices.
- Operation of the elevator, including the doors, under all conditions.

Door strike

- Description of the operation of the doors of the elevator involved in plaintiff's accident.
- Identification and description regarding the leading edges of the doors of the elevator involved in plaintiff's accident.
- Description of the mechanism in place which controlled door opening and closing on the date of plaintiff's accident.
- Door opening times for the elevator involved in plaintiff's accident.
- Equipment, devices or mechanisms in place on the date of plaintiff's accident to prevent doors from striking or closing on passengers.

- All service or maintenance calls reflecting repairs or service to the doors, or mechanism controlling the opening or closing of the doors of the elevator involved in plaintiff's accident.
- Identification of the manufacturer of the equipment designed to control the opening or closing of the elevator doors involved in plaintiff's accident.

Misleveling

- Description of the equipment in place on the elevator involved in plaintiff's accident that sensed or determined elevator position relative to floor level.
- Description of the equipment or devices in place in the elevator involved in plaintiff's accident that determined leveling speed.
- All service or maintenance performed on the elevator involved in plaintiff's accident to determine door opening calibration relative to distance from floor level.
- Description of each and every service or maintenance call to correct or adjust elevator car level relative to outside floor level.
- Description of all equipment in place on the date of plaintiff's accident to prevent door opening based on pre-determined distance from floor level.

9.4 Depositions and Maintenance Documents

This section describes the background of personnel commonly employed in the elevator industry. It also describes basic maintenance documents. Examples of typical questions to be asked at depositions are also supplied. The specific series of questions to be asked will be based upon the particular facts of a given accident. It is strongly suggested that consultation with an elevator and escalator expert be done before conducting any depositions. Expert witnesses frequently complain that attorneys do not follow through on a promising line of questioning, fail to obtain key information, fail to understand and properly use important maintenance documents, and do not gather the information necessary to make the deposition productive.

A. Understanding Job Duties and Responsibilities of Personnel

1. Field technicians, adjusters, repair and service, or installers

Generally, field technicians typically will be involved in one or more of the following elevator or escalator field disciplines: installing new equipment; modernizing existing equipment; or servicing existing equipment, which can include cleaning, lubricating, examining, adjusting, and replacing parts or components. Therefore, their expertise in certain areas may vary considerably. The following discussion is geared toward outside contractors, since most building owners do not use internal technicians.

These technicians are either union or non-union, depending on their employers. Journeymen, known as mechanics, begin as apprentices, known as helpers. Certain mechanics will be elevated to an adjuster status, in recognition of their expertise, and will be responsible for handling problems other mechanics cannot solve or for making final adjustments to newly installed equipment.

The union technicians, with few exceptions, are members of the International Union of Elevator Constructors (IUEC). Typically they serve two to five years as helpers before being promoted to mechanic. During this apprenticeship their salaries typically are lower than a mechanic's salary (usually approximately 50 percent for the first six months and 70 percent thereafter).

During almost all of the apprenticeship the helpers report to and work under the direction of a mechanic. The union helpers are required to attend "night courses" that are divided into modules. The modules are developed by the National Elevator Industry Educational Program (NEIEP) for the U.S. and the Canadian Elevator Industry Educational Program (CEIEP) in Canada. The local offices of the IUEC administer the courses. The modules ostensibly teach them to perform the work disciplines listed earlier in this section. When the helper completes the modules, he is eligible to take the mechanic's examination. If the helper passes the examination he is eligible to be promoted to mechanic. The employer would then promote the former helper to a mechanic's position provided the employer has a need for such a person. If not, then the mechanic may seek employment with another contractor as a mechanic, or remain as a helper with the present company. The IUEC sometimes orchestrates the move. This is one of the benefits of being in a union. Union workers pay quarterly dues and negotiate their salaries and benefits collectively. Of course, technicians' training, salaries and advancement may be varied by contractual provisions.

The non-union technicians generally obtain their electrical or mechanical background from technical or trade schools, or from working in other, similar trades. Their progression from helper to mechanic is much less defined as compared to union workers. This progression is sometimes based solely on the volume of work. Their skills as mechanics would be well honed if they were given enough time to develop, but may be deficient if promoted to mechanic too soon. Also, helpers may often work alone without direction from a more experienced person, unlike their union counterparts. This can help develop them, but helpers "biting off more than they can chew" could make serious mistakes, and be a liability. The salary and sometimes the benefits for non-union workers are comparable to union workers in the area. This is especially true for the better-performing mechanics and helpers, because the contractor wants to retain the employees.

An increasing number of mechanics are Certified Elevator Technicians (CET®), but many others are not. This type of certification consists of a self-paced program structured to meet federal apprenticeship requirements of 144 hours of related instructions in 12 courses (typically via the Internet) and 2,000 hours on-the-job training annually for four years. It is administered by the National Association of Elevator Contractors (NAEC). It requires passing a certification exam. Many experienced mechanics have had requirements grandfathered and take a modified exam. Related are Associate Elevator Technician (AET™), CET-Modernization and Construction (CET-MC), CET-Maintenance and Repair (CET-MR), CET-Escalator (CET-E)and CET supervisor/administrator (CET-S).

Also related for accessibility type equipment is the Certified Accessibility and Private Residence Lift Technician (CAT®), which has the same training and experience requirements, but only for two years. Related are the CAT-Vertical Platform Lift (CAT-VPL), CAT-Inclined Platform Lift (CAT-IPL), CAT-Inclined Stairway Chairlifts (CAT-ISC), CAT Private Residence Elevator (CAT-PRE) and CAT supervisor/administrator (CAT-S).

In general, the line of questioning in a deposition or trial should establish the technician's professional development, workload, experience related to the specific equipment, the documentation of the maintenance tasks she performs and the particulars related to any accident.

2. The field manager or the superintendent

Field managers and superintendents typically direct the activity of the mechanic and usually have the same background. In addition they are responsible for showing profits. They do this by allotting enough units of equipment (elevators or escalators) to the mechanic to service so that the route can generate a substantial profit margin. Therefore, the line of questioning for the field manager or superintendent should be targeted to establish whether the mechanic had enough time to perform proper preventive maintenance for the equipment. One obvious basis for a claim of negligent maintenance would be the lack of time to maintain the equipment because the mechanic was assigned too many units. The elevator expert can usually determine a "maintainable" workload for the average mechanic. It would be too presumptuous to describe such a workload here.

3. Code enforcing authorities

The code enforcing authority, known as the Authority Having Jurisdiction (AHJ), is the entity that typically certifies elevators and escalators for safe operation. Inspectors may be employed by the AHJ, or a private inspection agency contracted by the AHJ or by an independent third party such as an insurance company. The certification of the equipment is first done at the completion of the initial elevator or escalator installation, and then periodically thereafter (typically every six months). The actions include performing inspections and tests, or witnessing elevator contractors making tests. When the inspections and tests are completed, a certificate of compliance is issued to the building owner or manager where the elevator or escalator is located. If safety violations exist on the equipment, the elevator is either given a temporary compliance certificate or, for more serious violations, is locked out of service. This certificate covers a fixed period, and must be posted either in the elevator or elsewhere on site (e.g., the building manager's office). It should be noted that some AHJs may have no inspection program and may not even have adopted an elevator code.

Frequently inspectors obtain certification by taking a Qualification of Elevator Inspectors (QEI) course and the associated exam. Inspector's supervisors are similarly certified. However, an AHJ may have its own qualification program. The QEI program is based on the ASME A17.1 Code and the ASME A17.2 Inspector's Manual. QEI-certified inspectors and supervisors should be thoroughly familiar with the material contained within these documents. Therefore, when examining this type of witness, obtain copies of these documents and focus the questioning to determine the inspector's competence in testing and inspecting the equipment pertinent to the case. Even if the inspector or supervisor is not QEI certified, the inspection and test procedures given in these documents can be used as a baseline for the standard of care in the elevator industry.

At present only three organizations administer QEI certification programs. These organizations usually provide continuing elevator and escalator education for their members. It should be determined what continuing education, if any, the inspector or supervisor has been taking, especially in the areas most involved in the case at hand.

Many AHJs assign too many units to an inspector for them to adequately inspect or test. This can lead to units not being inspected at the required frequency or in a substandard manner.

The line of questioning in a deposition or trial should establish the inspector's professional development, workload, experience related to the specific equipment, the documentation of the tasks performed and inspections and tests of the pertinent components.

4. Design engineers and managers

Elevator design engineers are generally limited in scope when compared to elevator field engineers. Many have been previously employed in other industries. Usually they specialize in one area of development, and therefore usually have a deep knowledge about a particular area. Since an elevator or escalator is an electromechanical device, the design engineers are usually either mechanical or electrical engineers. Their specialized areas are many times limited to component parts of the system. For example, on the electrical side, their specialization may include the control panel, the motors, the landing device, or the call buttons. On the mechanical side, the specialization may include the governor, the safeties, the guide rails, the cables or the system's structural integrity. Therefore, their knowledge may be limited.

When requesting a deposition of a witness for a design defect case, the elevator expert can help you to identify the person mostly responsible for that design.

B. Understanding Maintenance Documents for Use at Depositions

Answers to discovery requests will produce certain basic maintenance documents. These documents should include the maintenance contract, maintenance records, including logs and guides, electrical wiring diagrams, callback and repair records, and time tickets. Depositions of key elevator personnel should not be taken until these documents are obtained.

Maintenance personnel (mechanics and technicians) can be responsible for servicing 30 to 150 plus elevators or escalators, usually referred to as their route. Obviously, the more units that the technician must maintain in a given time frame the less time is available for maintenance of each unit.

Many of the records listed below are generated from observations and reporting by these technicians. Considering that each elevator and escalator has many components requiring maintenance actions, the technicians should document hundreds of actions each month. Their maintenance, callback and repair actions must be documented to assure that proper maintenance has been performed. Also if they expect to receive payment for the service, time tickets must be completed and submitted. A maintenance company database should include all of this information. This database, along with the maintenance log (sometimes only kept at the job site), will reveal the standard of maintenance provided by the maintenance company. Comprehensive records will help address allegations of improper or negligent maintenance.

Many times the back sides of the maintenance and repair records contain useful information that is not produced for review. For example, "codes" may be provided to decipher information contained on the front side.

1. Contract

Almost all elevator companies contracted to perform maintenance in a building or complex will enter into an agreement that explains the type of maintenance, equipment items covered and excluded, the actions that will be performed, and the (monthly) price for the services. If a component or task is not covered by the contract, the contractor cannot ignore it. He must always warn the building owner of any conditions that may affect safe operation of the equipment. Any work outside of the provisions of the contract will simply incur extra costs. A copy of the contract should be obtained so that all the items in the contract can be reviewed, particularly the dates of the contract and the scope of work. A maintenance control plan also may be included in the contract and this document should also be obtained.

2. Maintenance records

The maintenance records typically consist of a log and a guide. The maintenance logs contain the maintenance actions that have been performed and when the actions were performed. The maintenance guide explains how the actions are to be performed. The log tells *what* and *when*, the guide tells *how*.

Logs come in many shapes, sizes and formats. Many of the larger firms and some smaller companies are turning to computerized logs, using a handheld terminal similar to those used by express delivery personnel. The forms also vary by equipment type.

Some exemplar logs are shown and discussed below. It should be noted that these exemplar logs are for illustrative purposes only, and actual logs can and do vary significantly. Many required maintenance tasks are not shown in these logs.

Figure 9.1 shows an exemplar maintenance log for a traction elevator.

The log shown in Figure 9.1 is designed for documenting the maintenance tasks for (up to) eight elevators for a period of time, typically one year. However, it is also designed to implement "use-based" maintenance (similar to a chart for changing the oil in your automobile every 5,000 miles). It has two essential parts, the top part for documenting routine maintenance tasks, the lower part for periodic tasks. The latter involves maintenance in three areas, the elevator machine room, the car top and the hoistway pit. Almost all of the maintenance tasks are performed in these three areas.

Figure 9.2 shows an exemplar maintenance log for up to eight hydraulic elevators.

Some of the tasks are performed monthly, quarterly, semi-annually or annually. The "open boxes" control this frequency. For example, "Lubrication" has four open boxes under "Periodic" for each unit, which indicates it must be done

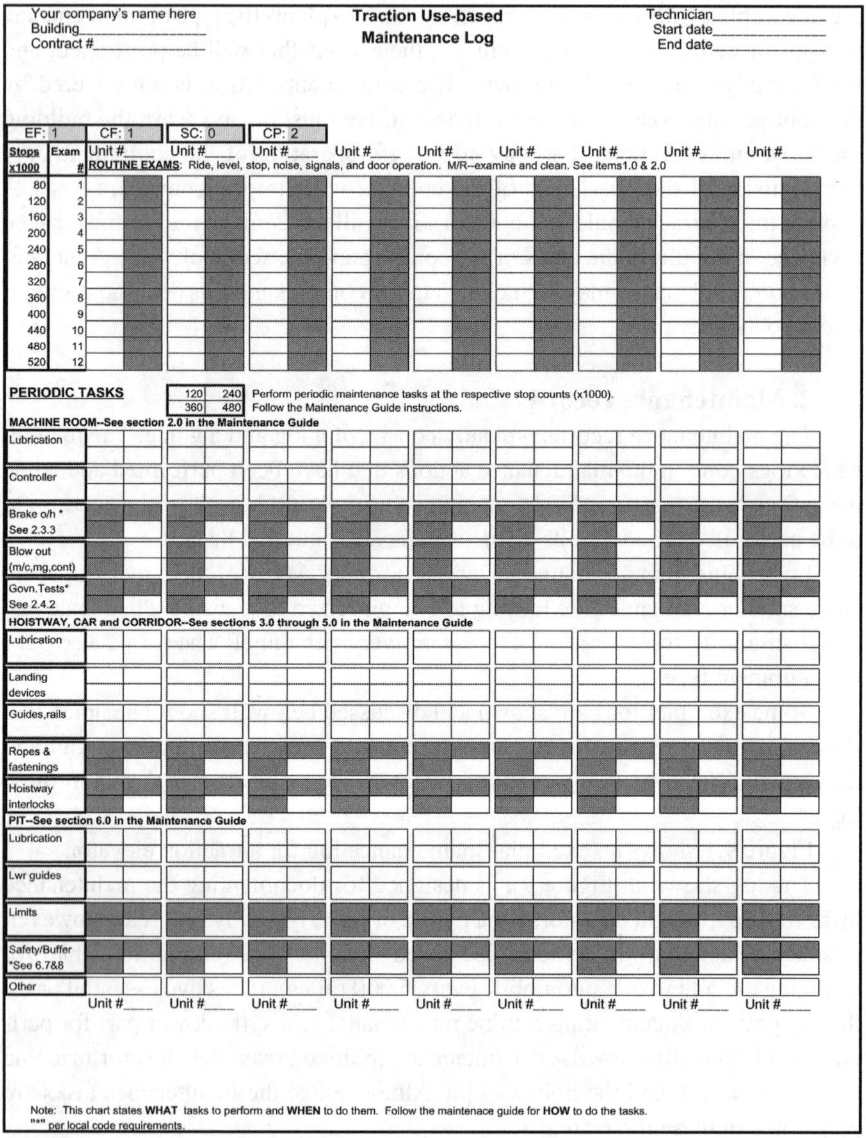

Your company's name here
Building_______________
Contract #_____________

Traction Use-based Maintenance Log

Technician_____________
Start date_____________
End date_____________

EF: 1 | CF: 1 | SC: 0 | CP: 2

Stops x1000	Exam #	Unit #___	Unit #___	Unit #___	Unit #___	Unit #___	Unit #___	Unit #___	Unit #___	Unit #___
80	1									
120	2									
160	3									
200	4									
240	5									
280	6									
320	7									
360	8									
400	9									
440	10									
480	11									
520	12									

ROUTINE EXAMS: Ride, level, stop, noise, signals, and door operation. M/R--examine and clean. See items1.0 & 2.0

PERIODIC TASKS 120 240 360 480 Perform periodic maintenance tasks at the respective stop counts (x1000). Follow the Maintenance Guide instructions.

MACHINE ROOM--See section 2.0 in the Maintenance Guide

Lubrication
Controller
Brake o/h * See 2.3.3
Blow out (m/c,mg,cont)
Govn.Tests* See 2.4.2

HOISTWAY, CAR and CORRIDOR--See sections 3.0 through 5.0 in the Maintenance Guide

Lubrication
Landing devices
Guides,rails
Ropes & fastenings
Hoistway interlocks

PIT--See section 6.0 in the Maintenance Guide

Lubrication
Lwr guides
Limits
Safety/Buffer *See 6.7&8
Other

Unit #___ Unit #___ Unit #___ Unit #___ Unit #___ Unit #___ Unit #___ Unit #___ Unit #___

Note: This chart states **WHAT** tasks to perform and **WHEN** to do them. Follow the maintenace guide for **HOW** to do the tasks.
"*" per local code requirements.

Figure 9.1 *Sample maintenance log for a traction elevator*

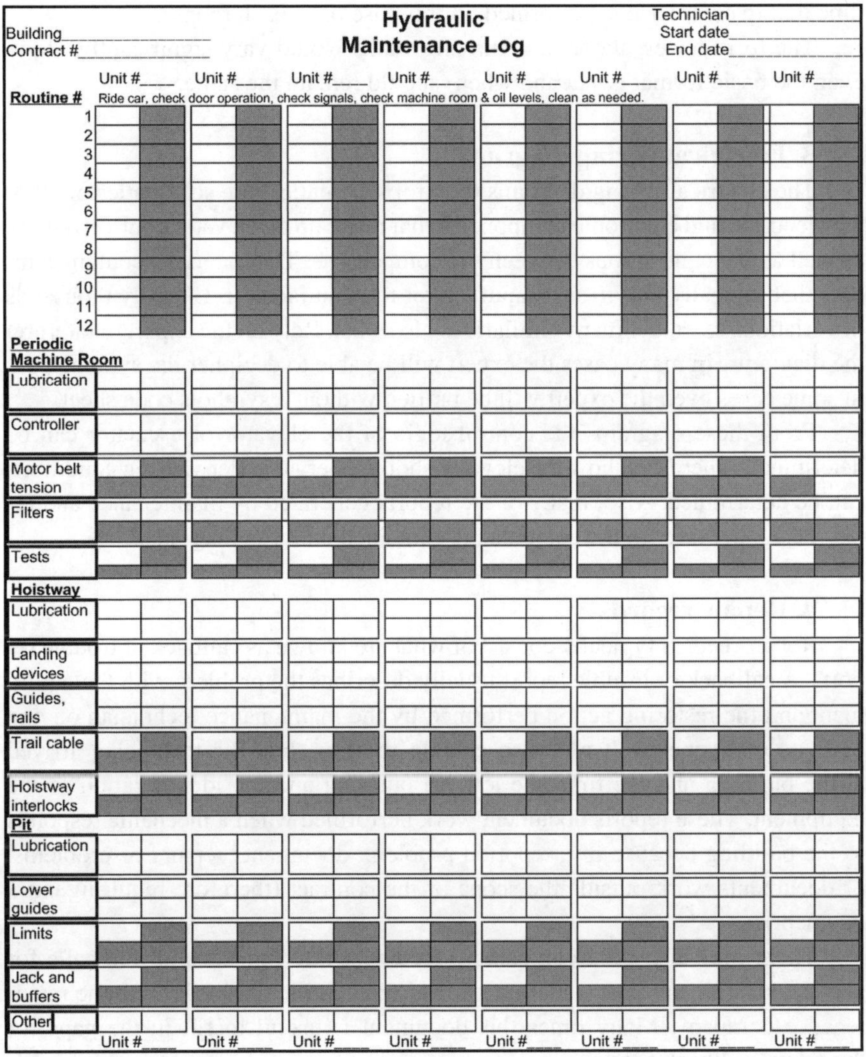

Figure 9.2 *Sample maintenance log for a hydraulic elevator*

quarterly (four times annually), while "Tests" has only one open box, which indicates that it must be done once annually. All of the routine items are done each time that maintenance is performed, in this case once each month.

The form for escalators and moving walks would vary significantly. However, the basic format (what and when) should remain the same.

3. Electrical wiring diagrams

The electrical wiring diagrams (control schematics) are schematics of all of the electrical and electronic components that make up an elevator control system, as well as the connections between the components. The diagrams contain symbols that typically vary from manufacturer to manufacturer. Literally thousands of variations exist, but many similarities also exist. Rely on the expert to interpret the diagrams. In many cases the expert will be able to decipher the symbols, but in some cases even the expert will be baffled without a symbols code sheet.

From these diagrams the control logic of the elevator or escalator can be determined. Therefore, how the elevator should operate under varying conditions can be determined. Also, many of the reports generated by maintenance and repair personnel refer to the components contained on these diagrams.

4. Repair records

Repair records typically consist of what are known as callback or trouble reports. A callback or trouble report usually describes the problem with the equipment and the restoring action performed by the maintenance technician on one or more components. It will also contain the time that the technician arrived at the building and the time she left the building and the identification of the equipment. These reports document work performed when a mechanic responds to the building because of a reported problem, documents repairs or problems, or documents work outside the scope of the contract (therefore requiring extra payment).

There may also be a companion document that indicates all the calls for service, such as equipment malfunctions, from a particular location to the maintenance company. Many times this document is useful to fill in the gaps for "missing" callback reports.

5. Time tickets

The maintenance technician will submit a weekly time ticket that documents building visits and the number of hours spent at each location. Many are coded with other information, much of which is only known to the maintenance company. Time tickets usually do not document the tasks performed at each building. Therefore, the expert will typically use this information only to establish the frequency of maintenance personnel being at a particular building location.

9.5 Sample Questions for Depositions

The following are some sample deposition questions. These questions are specific to certain circumstances and conditions. Therefore, they are not universally applicable. The key is to ascertain critical information pertinent to the specific case at hand.

A. Examination of a Field Technician or Mechanic—Exiting or Entering Passenger Fell because a Hydraulic Elevator was Misleveled

1. Have you received any *formal* training in the maintenance and repair of hydraulic elevators? What other qualifications do you have that would assist you in maintaining this type of elevator? Are you a Certified Elevator Technician? When did you obtain that certification?
2. Describe the incident elevator (i.e., manufacturer, model, age, capacity, speed, passenger/freight use, control, operation, driving machine).
3. Are you a union mechanic? Which union? Did your NEIEP Elevator Union training include maintaining this type of elevator?
4. How long have you been maintaining this type of elevator?
5. Describe *in detail* the maintenance that you performed on this elevator. How long did this take and how frequently was it performed?
6. Is the incident elevator under contract for maintenance with your company? What type of maintenance is performed on this elevator (e.g., cleaning, lubricating, adjustments, repairs, replacements, and testing)? How often is this maintenance performed? How many other elevators/escalators are covered by this contract? Does any one else perform maintenance or repairs on this elevator?
7. How many of this type of elevator do you have on your route? How many total units do you have on your route? Do you also answer callbacks during the workday?
8. Do you feel that you have sufficient time in your normal workweek to adequately maintain the units considering the volume of units that you service?
9. Does this type of elevator contain a fluid reservoir or tank? Does the fluid leave the tank as the elevator ascends upward? Does the fluid return to the tank as the elevator goes down?
10. How would the elevator react if the fluid in the tank were at a low level? Would it fail to level into the top floor?
11. How often do you typically check the fluid to assure against this happening?

12. Has this system had any leaks in the past years that would cause the fluid in the tank to be at a low level? What observations relative to fluid level were made of the jack, piping, valves, pump and the tank?
13. Based on your recollection (or documents) identify each occasion on which the elevator was leaking fluid prior to the accident.
14. For each of these occasions, what was determined to be the reason for the fluid leaking?
15. What repairs were made in response to these circumstances?
16. Do you typically account for fluid losses in the system? How? Has there been any unexplained fluid loss in this system? Could there be any underground leaks that would account for any fluid losses? Do you record the amount of fluid that you add to the tank and the date that the fluid was added? Is this information now available? From whom?
17. What equipment in the system was present which could cause the elevator to stop before reaching floor level?
18. Describe the operation of the landing (leveling) device on this elevator?
19. Describe the operation of the landing switches. Describe how they are adjusted.
20. Describe the operation of the limit switches. Describe how they are adjusted.
21. Describe the operation of the relays in the controller. Describe how they are adjusted.
22. Describe how improper adjustment of landing switches or limits can affect the leveling of the elevator.
23. Describe how the operation of the relays can affect the leveling of the elevator.
24. What other devices in the system could cause the elevator to stop before reaching the floor? Would the landing switches or limits, or both if defective or misadjusted, cause the elevator to stop short of the floor?
25. How often do you (or your company) check each of these devices?
26. Have there been any problems with these devices? Describe each one.
27. Have there been any alterations to these devices? Why were these changed and when?
28. What, if any, adjustments, repairs, replacement or alteration of parts was necessary with respect to these devices during the period one year prior to the accident to the present?
29. Where are records kept which document maintenance, service, repair, or fluid leaks?

30. Does your company use any computerized method to document callbacks/repairs/maintenance? Describe how that system works. Describe the type of documents or reports that can be printed from that system.
31. Describe the procedure through which a callback request after normal hours is generated, received, and documented.
32. Describe how callbacks after normal hours differ, if at all, from callbacks received during normal working hours.
33. Describe the procedures for communication and notification of your office relative to arrival, and departure from the site to which you were dispatched.
34. During the course of a service call, are you required to describe the conditions that you found by any method (phone, radio, etc.)? What documentation do you keep relative to callbacks? What documentation is kept by your company? Who is the person who has custody of documents pertinent to service, maintenance, callbacks, or communications from you and/or the customer?
35. Please describe the differences between traction type elevators and hydraulic elevators pertinent to floor leveling.
36. What experience do you or your company have with respect to the frequency with which hydraulic elevators "mislevel"?
37. Who is the person or persons (e.g., the building manager) that you communicate with pertinent to this elevator on site?
38. What conversations or discussions have you had with any persons on site pertinent to misleveling?
39. Have you received any complaints or questions from persons on site relative to misleveling?
40. Which code(s) do you use to maintain this elevator? Which versions of these codes do you use?
41. What tools are you issued by your employer? Are you personally responsible to supply any of your own tools? If so, which ones. Are there any tools that you are not allowed to use because of your position within the union or organization?

B. Examination of an AHJ Inspector—Plaintiff Fell Down an Open Hoistway

1. What training have you received for the inspection of elevators? Have you received any formal training for the inspection of elevators? Were you a QEI (Qualification of Elevator Inspectors) certified inspector on

the date of the accident? When did you become certified? Do you have any other qualifications or training to assist in inspecting this type of elevator? Did your elevator inspection training include training for this specific type of elevator?

2. What type of elevator was involved in the accident, (i.e., manufacturer, model, age, capacity, speed, passenger/freight use, control, operation, driving machine)? How long have you been inspecting this type of elevator?
3. How many times have you inspected this elevator? What documentation is necessary for each time you inspect this elevator? For what period of time have you inspected this elevator? Has anyone else performed any inspections on this elevator during that period of time?
4. What specific problems were identified during these inspections? How were those problems documented? Is it customary for you to discuss the results of your inspection orally on the date of your inspection? Did you ever do so with respect to this particular elevator? With whom?
5. What tools do you use when performing inspections?
6. What year was this elevator installed? Which code(s) do you use or refer to in performing your inspections? During the period of time that you inspected this elevator were different codes or different code sections in effect, or were different codes modified or updated? How does the date of installation or alteration of a major component in the elevator system govern the applicable code to be used when determining safety? What safety codes did you use to inspect this elevator? Which versions and applicable dates?
7. Describe in detail the procedures you use to inspect an elevator similar to the elevator involved in the accident? What documents, manuals, or other similar written materials do you refer to when inspecting an elevator similar to the one involved in the accident?
8. What year was this elevator installed? To your knowledge, has the elevator been modernized or altered in any fashion since its original installation?
9. Please describe your inspection route. How many total units are you assigned to inspect or test on a daily, weekly, or monthly basis? What written documents exist outlining the units that you are responsible for inspecting? What written documents are available outlining the units that you are responsible for inspecting during a six-month period of time prior to the accident? In addition to inspecting do you have other duties assigned to you during the workday? What duties? How do you determine whether or not you have sufficient time in your work week

to adequately inspect the units considering the volume of the units assigned to you for inspection? How many elevators of a similar type to the one involved in the accident do you have on your route? What specific documents or forms do you use when performing inspections similar to the one involved in this accident? Are you required to complete those forms or documents on site or do you complete them later after leaving the site?

10. Please describe the operation of the doors. Describe the number of panels and their operation. Are the doors manual or power operated? Are the landing or hoistway doors equipped with electrical/mechanical interlocks? If not, what type of locking mechanism is present? Are there any documents which reflect the type of locks for the landing or hoistway doors? Where on the document is it indicated?
11. What effect on the elevator's operation would there be if the outside doors were open? Would the elevator operate with the outside doors in the open position? Why? Why not? On each of your inspections do you check to determine whether or not the car will run if the doors are in the open position? Describe how you do that. Can you accomplish this test alone or do you need the assistance of any other person? Do you record on any documents the results of such a test?
12. What type of brakes are incorporated into this elevator? If drum brakes, please describe the purpose of the brake. What equipment was in place at the time of the accident to keep the elevator at a floor level even when the car is loaded to capacity? Had you performed a brake test on this elevator prior to the accident? When? Describe the results. When was the last load test of the brake prior to the accident? What conditions would result in the elevator car drifting? What specific conditions do you look for to determine proper operation of the brake? Did you observe any conditions which would affect the ability of the elevator car to remain at floor level when fully loaded? When empty?
13. What conditions would permit the elevator car to leave the floor with the doors in the open position? How do the relays in the controller affect operation of the elevator with the doors in the open position? How can the car move with the doors in the open position? What condition would the door locks have to be in to permit the elevator to operate with the doors open? Had you ever made any observations or determinations pertinent to the specific condition of the door locks or relays with respect to this elevator? Where on the forms are you required to complete these observations or note these findings noted?

14. Please describe each and every safety check that you made on the dates of your inspection of this elevator. Were you provided with any documents or reports from any other elevator inspectors reflecting problems with respect to these particular devices before the date of the accident? Did you request copies of the results of inspections performed prior to the accident and prior to your beginning to inspect this elevator?
15. Prior to the accident had there been any upgrades to door locks? What upgrades? Were you able to determine why these were changed? How were these upgrades documented?
16. Can the door-latching device be released to permit the door to open in order to gain access to the pit? Can one gain access to the elevator shaft on other floors? Can the elevator doors be opened even when the elevator is at another floor? How? What would happen if the door unlatching device was pulled when the elevator was running? Is the means to release the door unlatching device accessible so that untrained persons can activate it? How? Is a key required to access the means to release the unlatching device? On your inspections do you check to determine if the doors can be opened without the key? How do you perform that test? Do you use a screwdriver or bar to assist in opening the doors?
17. Do you inspect or determine the intensity or operation of the cab lights? Are there any codes that govern intensity of the cab lights? Do you check to determine the intensity at the corridor doorsill? Are there any codes which govern the light intensity at the corridor doorsill? How do you determine whether or not the lighting levels meet the applicable code? What equipment do you use? Who provides that equipment? What specific brand model light meter is employed?

C. Examination of a Field Technician or Mechanic—Passenger Fell because of a Sudden Stop of Elevator Due to Setting of the Car Safeties after Control System was Altered Resulting in Removal of a Safety Switch

1. Have you received any *formal* training in the maintenance and repair of hydraulic elevators? What other qualifications do you have that would assist you in maintaining this type of elevator?
2. Describe the incident elevator (i.e., manufacturer, model, age, capacity, speed, passenger/freight use, control, operation, driving machine).
3. What year was the elevator installed?
4. Are you a union mechanic? Which union? Did your NEIEP Elevator Union training include maintaining this type of elevator?

5. How long have you been maintaining this type of elevator?
6. Describe in detail the typical maintenance you performed on this elevator? What tools were required? How long did it typically take? Were you able to do the maintenance yourself? How long would it take if you did it yourself? How long would it take if you had a helper?
7. Does this type of elevator contain a traction-type driving machine that raises and lowers the car? Describe its operation. How is the movement of the machine controlled? How is the movement controlled when the elevator is going down? Going up?
8. How would the elevator react if the speed in the down direction of travel exceeded a safe speed level? How do you determine a safe speed level? How does the governor operate? What conditions cause the elevator governor to trip? Are there any conditions other than overspeed which can cause the governor to trip? What effect does a heavy buildup of grease on the governor have on elevator operation?
9. How often do you check the operation of the governor when maintaining this elevator? What documents do you utilize in maintaining or serving this elevator? What documents are you required to complete when maintaining or servicing this elevator?
10. Describe the operation of the governor, including the electrical switches. How do speed-reducing switches operate? If the elevator experienced an overspeed in the down direction and the governor contained a speed-reducing switch, if the elevator is properly maintained, what should happen? If the elevator experienced an overspeed in the down direction and the governor did not contain a speed-reducing switch, if the elevator is properly maintained, what should happen?
11. Does the elevator have car safeties? What are car safeties and how do they operate? When the governor trips do the car safeties set? On service calls do you check to determine the operation of the car safeties and governor? How do you perform that test?
12. When the car safeties set will the elevator stop more rapidly than normal? How rapidly? Will it be noticeable to occupants of the elevator cab?
13. Describe all devices on the elevator to prevent or detect overspeed conditions while the elevator is traveling downward. Describe their operation. Describe when they were last tested or inspected prior to the accident. Are these devices checked during normal service or maintenance calls? How often? Have there ever been any reported problems with these devices on this elevator?
14. Was the speed-reducing switch removed from the governor on the date of the incident? When was the switch removed? Does this photograph

show the governor? Does this photograph also show that the governor is missing the speed-reducing switch? When the new control system was installed, why wasn't the switch maintained? What equipment was in place after the new control system was installed to prevent the car safeties from setting? Describe its operation.

15. What instances of the governor tripping and the safeties setting were there with the old control system? Did that system have any components in the hoistway that, if they failed to activate, would result in an overspeed condition and the car safeties setting?
16. Did you or your company experience problems with any of these devices during the year of the accident? How often?
17. Did the owner of the premises or any users of the elevator make any complaints concerning sudden stopping of the elevator? Who? When? How often? Were these documented?
18. Is there a landing device on this elevator? Have there been any upgrades to landing devices or switches on any other elevators in the building? When were these changed? Why?
19. How does your company document callbacks, repairs and maintenance or service? What policies are there which regulate the documentation necessary? What are you required to document? What are you not required to document?
20. What conditions needed attention during the three months prior to the accident? Do these documents reflect any of those conditions? What work was performed? What indicates that the work was performed completely? Were there any instances where the owner of the building refused any recommendations for work? Does your company have a policy for documenting circumstances when work is recommended but refused by the owner?
21. Why did the governor trip on the date of the accident? How do you know? Was that problem ever corrected? How was it corrected? When? What equipment was installed?

D. Examination of a Field Technician or Mechanic—Passenger Fell because of Stopping of an Escalator Handrail and Steps

1. Have you received any *formal* training in the maintenance and repair of an escalator? What other qualifications do you have that would assist you in maintaining this type of escalator? Did your NEIEP Elevator Union training include maintaining this type of escalator?

2. What type of escalator was involved in the accident, (i.e., manufacturer, model, age, rise, width, speed)? How long have you been maintaining this type of escalator? How many of this type of elevator have you maintained?
3. How many escalators are under (*maintenance company*) contract at (*building address*)? Is the incident elevator under contract with (*maintenance company*)? Does anyone else perform maintenance on the escalator? Who does any necessary repair work on this escalator? How often?
4. How many units do you have on your maintenance route? Do you also answer callbacks during the workday? How many escalators do you have on your route?
5. Do you feel that you have sufficient time in your normal workweek to adequately maintain the units considering the volume of units that you service?
6. Does this type of escalator contain numerous safety switches or sensors?
7. Does the escalator stop if one of the switches is actuated?
8. Where are the switches located? Describe the operation of each switch.
9. Which safety switches are exposed? Which safety switches are within the escalator? How often do you check each of these switches? How do you check the switches? When were all of these switches checked for the period one year prior to the accident? What records were made regarding the operation and adjustment of these switches?
10. Describe all of the problems with any of these switches prior to the accident.
11. What adjustments or checks were made to any of these switches in the days prior to the accident? Weeks prior to the accident? Days following the accident? What, if anything, was recorded pertinent to the operation or adjustment of the switches on each of these occasions? What adjustments or checks were made to any of these switches in the days prior to the accident? What adjustments or checks were made to any of these switches in the days following the accident?
12. What devices are present which could cause the escalator to stop suddenly? Are there relays in the controller? How often are these checked?
13. Describe in detail the typical maintenance you performed on this escalator. What tools did you use? What codes or documents did you reference? What forms were you required to complete? How long did this typically take? How frequently did you perform maintenance on this escalator?

14. Do you know what caused the escalator to stop on the date of the accident? What conditions did you observe which may have caused the escalator to stop? Which conditions were observed by others and reported to you? When you first examined the escalator after the accident was the stop within limits required by all applicable codes? Describe these limits of the applicable codes.
15. Describe the service and maintenance history of this escalator during the three years prior to the accident.
16. Are there brakes on the escalator? How many? Which brake activated to cause the escalator to stop at the time of the accident?
17. When you first observed the escalator after the accident, had it been serviced or repaired by any other person? What work had been done? How do you know?
18. When servicing or maintaining the escalator, is it necessary to check the operation of the brakes? How do you do that? Is there a method for determining the stopping force of the brake?
19. What codes do you refer to when servicing or maintaining this escalator? What code provisions are applicable to brakes? What code provisions address brake tension or torque setting? When was the brake torque last checked prior to the accident? What was determined? Who checked it? Was the torque setting within the design limits? What was the setting? How were the limits determined? Were there limits stamped on the plate of the driving machine? Elsewhere? What are the maximum and minimum brake torque settings? How do you know that these are the correct limits? What section of the code is applicable? Do you have the ability to reference the code when servicing or maintaining escalators?
20. Where are records kept documenting maintenance, repair, service of the escalator? Where are records kept that document any problems with the escalator?
21. Has the escalator been altered in any fashion since it was installed? How?
22. Describe the policies and procedures your company utilizes to document callbacks, maintenance and repairs. Is there a specific policy for after hours callbacks? How do you communicate with your office during callbacks? Are logs kept relative to callbacks?
23. Do you reply back to your office after you leave the building to which you were dispatched? Would you give a description of what you found (by phone, radio, etc.) as to the type of problem or cause for the callback? Is this logged into a record? Would this record be available upon request? Who would one contact to obtain it?

Chapter 10

Expert Opinion

Synopsis

10.1 Introduction

Until recently expert engineering evidence in premises liability or product liability cases was more or less taken for granted. An attorney would hire an expert who had an appropriate degree, may have published an article or two, and had investigated a number of similar cases. At trial the attorney would present the expert by going through his curriculum vitae and turning the questioning over to the opposing attorney for cross-examination on "qualifications." Under the liberal Federal Rules of Evidence and state rules based on the federal rules there was seldom a dispute about whether the expert would be permitted to testify and give an expert opinion. The manner in which the expert arrived at his opinion was addressed in cross-examination but not in a preliminary inquiry into whether that witness should be permitted to testify at all. Many courts believed that the rules were so liberal that as long as an expert had a "reasonable pretension of expertise" the opinion should be admitted and it would then be up to the jury to decide how much weight, if any, to give the opinion.

As a result of recent significant court decisions, that is simply no longer the case. In every case in which expert opinion is required, more and more time is spent on trying to prevent the opposing expert from testifying at all by the use of pretrial motions, elaborate hearings, and testimony going far beyond what had been contemplated or done in practice until more recently. As a result of several significant court decisions, the trial judge has truly become a "gatekeeper" and trial judges are taking very, very seriously their obligation to make certain that the expert's opinion is not only relevant but reliable as well.

10.2 Federal Rules of Evidence

A. Federal Rule of Evidence 104

Federal Rule of Evidence 104 provides as follows:

> (a) Questions of Admissibility Generally. Preliminary questions concerning the qualification of a person to be a witness, the existence of a privilege, or the admissibility of evidence shall be determined by the court, subject to the provisions of subdivision (b). In making its determination it is not bound by the rules of evidence except those with respect to privileges.

B. Federal Rule of Evidence 702

Federal Rule of Evidence 702 provides as follows:

> If scientific, technical, or other specialized knowledge will assist the trier of fact to understand the evidence or to determine a fact in issue, a witness qualified as an expert by knowledge, skill, experience, training, or education, may testify thereto in the form of an opinion or otherwise, if (1) the testimony is based upon sufficient facts or data, (2) the testimony is the product of reliable principles and methods, and (3) the witness has applied the principles and methods reliably to the facts of the case.

10.3 Significant Court Cases

A. *Daubert v. Merrell Dow Pharmaceuticals, Inc.*[1]

In *Daubert* it was alleged that ingestion of the drug Bendectin by a pregnant woman caused birth defects in her children. The defendant, Merrell Dow, moved for summary judgment and presented expert testimony through an affidavit from a physician and epidemiologist contending that a review of all the literature on Bendectin and birth defects did not provide any sound evidence that the use of Bendectin created a risk of birth defects. The plaintiff was unable to controvert that summary of the literature; however, the plaintiff sought to establish medical causation through the testimony of chemists and statisticians who were able to find a link between Bendectin and birth defects as a result of animal studies. The plaintiff's expert's opinion had not been published, nor had it been subjected to peer review. It was therefore not considered to be "generally accepted" in the scientific community. General acceptance in the scientific community had been considered the benchmark for admissibility of novel opinion evidence since the landmark ruling in *Frye v. United States*.[2] *Frye* had involved the admissibility of the "systolic blood pressure deception test" to determine whether a defendant in a criminal proceeding was answering questions truthfully based upon variations in blood pressure. Since this was a new or novel expert opinion it was held that a general acceptance of the methodology in the applicable scientific community was necessary for admissibility.

In *Daubert*, the Supreme Court stressed that in order to be admissible the expert's opinion had to be both reliable and relevant. To be reliable an expert opinion must present "scientific knowledge" that necessarily "implies a grounding in the methods and procedures of science" and requires "more than a subjective belief or unsupported speculation."[3] Therefore, it was necessary for the Court to first determine "whether the reasoning or methodology underlying the testimony is scientifically valid and whether that reasoning or methodology properly can be applied to the facts in issue."[4] Having addressed the "reliability" issue, the Court then turned its attention to the "relevancy" issue. Since expert testimony must be helpful to the jury by helping them to understand evidence or determine a specific fact in issue, the Court stated that it must be determined that the expert evidence "fits" the facts of the case and that the "helpfulness standard requires a valid scientific connection to the pertinent inquiry as a precondition to admissibility."[5]

Replacing *Frye*'s single test for admissibility of a new or novel expert opinion, the Supreme Court identified four factors to be used in determining whether an opinion was scientifically valid:

- Whether a scientific theory or technique has been tested
- Whether the theory or technique has been subject to peer review and publication
- The known or potential rate of error for the theory or technique
- The general acceptance of the theory or technique within the relevant scientific community[6]

The Supreme Court also indicated that while general acceptance of the methodology employed by the expert within the applicable scientific community was no longer entirely dispositive, it remained a factor to be considered. Thus, most commentators believe that *Daubert* established a slightly less stringent test for admission of expert testimony than had been the case under *Frye*.

Federal Rules of Evidence 104 and 702 clearly established that before *Daubert* the trial judge had the power to determine admissibility. *Daubert's* significance lies in the fact that it clearly established that the trial court had not only the power but the obligation to act as a gatekeeper.

Following *Daubert*, it was unclear whether the factors set forth by the Supreme Court were to be used by the trial judge in her gatekeeping obligation in "nonscientific" cases, that is, whether the guidelines extended to cases involving experts giving opinions in areas of "technical, or other specialized knowledge."

B. *Kumho Tire Co. v. Carmichael*[7]

In *Kumho Tire Co. v. Carmichael,* the Supreme Court agreed to decide if the trial judge's gatekeeping obligations did in fact extend to technical evidence. In *Kumho*, suit was brought after a tire blew out on a minivan allegedly resulting in an accident in which one passenger died and others were seriously injured. The tire had been manufactured in 1988 and installed on a purchased vehicle, used by the plaintiffs in 1993. The plaintiffs claimed that the tire was defective and relied upon the testimony of an expert in tire-failure analysis who concluded on the basis of a visual inspection of the tire that the blowout was caused by a defect in the tire's manufacture or design. The trial judge agreed with the defendant that the *Daubert* gatekeeping obligation did apply even though the case did not involve a "scientific" expert opinion. The trial court reviewed the expert's basis for his opinion, including the visual inspection in light of the *Daubert* factors and concluded that none of the *Daubert* factors was satisfied. The testimony was excluded and the defendant's motion for summary judgment granted because the plaintiffs could not meet their burden without expert opinion.

On appeal to the Eleventh Circuit Court of Appeals, the trial judge's decision was reversed when the court held that *Daubert* only applied in the scientific context.[8] The court distinguished opinions relying upon the application of scientific theories which would be subject to the *Daubert* analysis and those opinions that were more based on the expert's "skill- or experience-based observations."[9]

On appeal, the Supreme Court unanimously rejected the Eleventh Circuit Court of Appeals' decision distinguishing between experts relying on the application of scientific principles from those opinions which were based upon "skill- or experience-based observations," holding that the trial judge had properly excluded the expert's opinion.

In *Kumho*, the Supreme Court adopted a flexible approach that focused on the particular circumstances of the specific case. The Supreme Court also clearly indicated that the expert would be required to observe the same standard of "intellectual rigor" in the courtroom as would be employed when addressing similar matters outside the courtroom.[10] The defendants had argued that *Daubert's* four-factor reliability test had to be applied in all cases. This position was specifically rejected and the Court stated that the *Daubert* factors "may or may not be pertinent" and the analysis would depend upon "the nature of the issue, the expert's particular expertise, and the subject of his testimony."[11] The fact that engineering testimony could rest upon both scientific foundations, as well as personal knowledge or experience, was clearly recognized.

The Court went to great lengths to analyze the record and determine whether the plaintiff's expert had properly accounted for how and why he had reached the challenged opinion. The Court noted that the tire was both old and repaired and some of its treads had been worn bald. The plaintiff's expert also conceded that the tire should have been replaced before the accident.

Perhaps most significant was the fact that the expert was not able to say with any certainty how far the tire had traveled. The expert was unable to say whether the tire had traveled less than 10,000 or more than 50,000 miles. The Court thought it particularly significant that if the expert, by a visual and tactile inspection, could not state with any certainty the life or travel time of the tire, how could the expert through the same visual and tactile inspection determine whether there had been a defect in manufacture or design? Similarly, it was demonstrated that the expert had concluded that the tire was defective after having looked at photographs of it but before visually or tactilely inspecting the tire itself. There was also no evidence in the record indicating that other experts, papers, or articles supported the expert's theory or method of analysis. Last, there was no evidence to support the proposition that had the expert still been employed in the tire industry, he would have used a similar analysis to report to his employer that a tire was in fact defective.

10.4 Engineering Testimony after *Kumho*

A. Selection of an Appropriate Expert Witness

Attorneys who have had some experience handling cases involving the use of experts are certainly aware of the expert who professes to have a great deal of experience and knowledge about many areas. Experts, especially in mechanical engineering, have been known to testify about products as varied as drain cleaners, lawn mowers, fork lifts, nip points in the poultry industry, scaffolding, piping, automotive design and crashworthiness, and elevator and escalator cases.

These "jack-of-all-trades" experts may have been adequate in the past, but in the authors' opinion are no longer so.

It is clear that *Daubert* and its progeny evolved because of attempts by plaintiffs to create novel causal links between chemical or drug exposures and birth defects and other injuries. However, it is apparent from *Kumho* and a multitude of other federal court decisions that the principles announced in *Daubert* and *Kumho* will apply to a wide variety of cases involving the use of expert opinion, including elevator and escalator accident cases.

Although it had always been advisable to employ an expert who had considerable experience in the specific industry, it would seem almost foolish not to do so under the present post-*Kumho* circumstances. Do not hire an expert who suggests that although he has no elevator or escalator experience, mechanical engineering principles are uniform and easily transferable from one industry to another. Selecting this type of an expert will leave a case vulnerable to having an essential expert opinion stricken before the trial even starts.

How can an expert employ the same "intellectual rigor" in expressing an opinion in the courtroom as he would have in the industry, if that expert has no experience in the particular industry? What problems will be created by obtaining from a network or group of experts one who can testify about years of performing forensic investigations but has limited or no experience in performing investigations in the industry? Will a "forensic expert" ever be in a position to address a judge's questions about whether the opinion being offered in the courtroom would be the same as for an employer in the industry if the expert had never been employed in that industry or had only gained his experience concerning elevators or escalators as a result of testifying in connection with lawsuits? Will an expert who has no connection with the industry, or a limited connection, be able to test his hypothesis about the cause of an accident, such as misleveling and door strikes?

From the attorney's perspective, selection of an appropriate expert who will be able to survive a *Kumho* challenge at the beginning of the case is essential. The best elevator and escalator experts will be those who have been in the industry and have had experience with installation, maintenance, inspections and code compliance.[12] Having practical experience and common sense is much more important than just having a good understanding of the engineering principles and theory. Being able to explain the engineering and technical concepts in a straightforward and understandable fashion to a lay jury is also critical. It is essential for the expert to appear professional, unbiased and disinterested in the outcome of the case. There are numerous national, state, and local elevator and escalator codes and it is essential that an expert have a familiarity and working understanding of the intricacies of these codes as they may apply to the particular piece of equipment. In limited scenarios, the use of an expert may not be necessary in an escalator or elevator case in jurisdictions recognizing the doctrine of *res ipsa loquitur*, but this is an exception and not the rule.[13]

B. Application of *Kumho* Factors to Elevator and Escalator Cases

Once an appropriate expert witness with the requisite qualifications has been obtained, then that witness must render an opinion that is both reliable and relevant. With the emphasis upon testing, studies and data, it should not be forgotten that opinions can still be based upon a particular expert's experience so long as the methodology employed to reach the opinion is sound. The expert must be able to support her opinion, particularly as to how and why the opinion was reached. Reviewing courts that have addressed the question of whether a trial court abused its discretion in either admitting or excluding an elevator or escalator expert's testimony not only looked at the expert's qualifications but also examined whether the expert's conclusory statements had sufficient supporting facts to substantiate the expert's claims.[14]

As an example, consider a door strike case. If the plaintiff's theory is based on the failure to have appropriate safety equipment, that is, an electric sensor or photoelectric beam, then the expert should perform a detailed and thorough analysis of the inadequacy of the existing equipment, and the availability of the proposed equipment, and how it would have prevented the accident.

C. Exclusion of Expert Testimony after *Kumho*[15]

1. Testing of the expert's hypothesis

In a case in which an elevator helper was injured while trying to remove "gunk" from elevator cables, the defendants challenged portions of the plaintiff's expert's report for failing to comply with the requirements of *Daubert* and Federal Rule of Evidence 702. Plaintiff's expert had 31 years of elevator industry field experience working as a mechanic, project engineer, and consultant. He had also worked with various elevator code enforcement agencies and published several articles on elevator technology. Plaintiff's expert opined that the cables' condition which resulted in the formation of the gunk was caused by a manufacturing defect and by depletion of the factory-applied cable lubricant. He specifically excluded as a cause any field or maintenance errors. The defendants conceded that the expert was qualified to opine about the worn condition of the cables but challenged his qualifications to opine about the causes of the gunk formation, as well as whether or not the cables were defectively manufactured. The expert admitted that he was not familiar with the particular type of gunk observed and also that he did not have any background in cable design or manufacture. Therefore, the defendants argued that it was improper for this expert to state with the requisite degree of certainty that a product was manufactured defectively if that expert did not have any experience or prior education in manufacturing or design processes. The court disagreed, determining that the expert reached his conclusion based upon his years of experience in the maintenance field and was able to conclusively rule out the condition of the cables as being caused by any maintenance error, thereby leaving the only likely explanation an error in manufacture. The defendants also complained that the expert's methodology did not satisfy the *Daubert* standard. Since the cables had not been preserved the expert was only able to rely upon photographs and witness descriptions of the materials. The defendants argued that the lack of ability to examine first hand the cables, the limited photographs and other "second hand" evidence did not satisfy the *Daubert* standard of reliability. The court noted that more flexibility is given when determining the reliability of experience-based methodology as opposed to other opinions which might lend themselves more easily toward laboratory testing. Thus, elimination of alternatives as a method of reaching one's opinion, as well as employing a methodology based upon experience, were held to satisfy the admissibility standards.[16]

In several cases the expert's opinion or report was criticized for lacking any reference to testing of the hypothesis that resulted in the expert's opinion. In a truck crashworthiness case an expert had opined that the front bumper and cab floor had been defectively designed. The plaintiff's expert's opinion was excluded because it was based only on his training and years of experience as an engineer and his subjective belief as opposed to being based on the methods and procedures of science. The expert had opined that the piercing of the cab floor by a guardrail rendered the truck not crashworthy because of defective design. However, the expert had calculated neither the forces inflicted on the truck nor the strength of the guardrail, and he had not tested his hypothesis with any testing or scientific data.[17]

Similarly, in a case in which the plaintiff's expert sought to give his opinion about whether a defect in a toaster oven had caused a fire, the trial judge determined that the expert's opinion appeared to have consisted of a testable hypothesis but that it was never tested. The expert had hypothesized that the fire had been caused by spontaneous welding of contacts in the toaster oven, which in turn caused overheating and combustion. Although a scanning electron microscope was used to produce evidence of fusion and melting, the expert did nothing further other than to offer his personal experience and belief that the product was defective. The expert hypothesized that had there been a thermal cut-off device, overheating and the resultant fire would not have occurred. The expert did not sketch the kind of device he recommended, did not produce an example of that device, and did no empirical research into how the device could have been incorporated into the toaster oven. In ruling that the plaintiff's expert was not qualified to give his expert opinion, the trial judge was critical of the fact that the hypothesis had never been tested even though it could easily have been tested using an exemplar product.[18]

2. Speculation or valid opinion?

In a case involving an injury to a worker who took a sidewalk lift to get from his basement office to a parking lot and was injured when the lift which had risen to sidewalk level suddenly fell back to the basement, the court held that the testimony of an elevator maintenance mechanic who had almost 50 years of experience in the industry lacked a reasoned basis or support from generally accepted scientific theories in the field and therefore should have been excluded at trial. The expert testified that based upon the snapped cable the lift's platform must have encountered an obstruction as it rose, causing the cable failure, and that the condition of the equipment had no bearing on that failure. The expert admitted that he had not examined the cable in detail but merely noted that it had broken. He reviewed no experts' depositions or other evidence, could not provide any guidance as to what could have obstructed the lift and, other than the broken cable, could point to no evidence indicating that there was in fact an obstruction. Finally, he offered no explanation or support for his opinion that only an obstruction, as opposed to wear or lack of lubrication, could have caused the cable to break. The court found that this expert's testimony provided absolutely no reasoned analysis for any of his conclusions. An expert's experience alone was insufficient to make the unsupported and unscientific opinion admissible.[19]

In a case in which the plaintiff alleged that he was injured while entering an elevator and the doors closed on him, the plaintiff's expert opined that the closing force was in excess of what was permissible and attributed it to poor maintenance. Plaintiff attempted to submit the case under the *res ipsa loquitur doctrine*. Under applicable New Jersey law, the doctrine of *res ipsa loquitur* was inapplicable where the injured party failed to offer evidence tending to exclude other possible causes of the injury. While the plaintiff need not eliminate the possibility of other causes, affirmative evidence must be presented that tends to exclude other possible causes of the injury. The court found that the expert had failed to provide an explanation in lay terms of the possible ways in which the accident could have occurred that would more likely than not point to defendant's negligence as a substantial contributing cause. The appellate court agreed with the trial court in tossing out the expert's testimony.[20] The appellate court stated that it was convinced that the expert testimony could not reasonably guide a jury in determining if the incident occurred, more likely than not, as a result of the defendant's negligence. In fact, a substantial portion of the expert's report concerned the possibility that the elevator doors were defectively designed. However, the plaintiff's claim against the defendant did not rest on the thesis of defective design, but rather the thesis of negligent maintenance. The expert claimed that the elevator doors were defectively designed because the placement of the electric eyes would not cause the doors to retract if the person entering the elevator bent down and straddled the entrance way. The Appellate Court pointedly noted, "We need not comment on the permutations of bodily contortions envisioned [by the expert] that could produce such a result. Suffice it to say that [the trial court] was clearly befuddled by some [of the expert's] statements, and for good reason."[21] The court was therefore not at all reluctant to point out the factual inconsistencies and lack of logic in the expert's opinion, but also the legal inconsistency in arguing inadequate maintenance as the cause of the accident when presenting evidence of defective design in a case based upon *res ipsa loquitur*. This case certainly underscores the need for selection of an appropriate expert and careful preparation of expert testimony. Since the expert testimony did not provide an explanation in lay terms of the possible ways in which the accident could have occurred that would be more likely than not suggestive of defendant's negligence, that opinion was not properly supported.

In an escalator case a plaintiff claimed injury when the handrail on an escalator stopped but the steps continued to move, throwing the plaintiff backwards. The plaintiff's expert testified that the cause of the accident was a failure to do preventive maintenance and that had there been proper maintenance the handrail would not have stopped. The expert could not specifically point to any mechanical problems which caused the handrail failure, nor was he able to describe what work would have been required to correct the alleged mechanical problem. His expert opinion was based upon his experience, the repair record of the escalator, and the testimony of the people who worked on the escalator, as well as a surveillance videotape of the accident itself which was equivocal as to whether or not the handrail had stopped moving. The expert attempted to infer, without providing any factual foundation, that there had been improper maintenance because the repair company had worked on the escalator several times in the months preceding the incident. The expert conceded that he could only speculate as to what had actually occurred and could only offer in the most general terms that defendants must have been at fault simply because the event had happened. The appellate court agreed with the trial court that there was not a proper factual and scientific basis for the expert's opinion and as such it was worthless. The appellate court characterized the expert's opinion as merely a bare conclusion unsupported by factual evidence or a "net opinion." It was incumbent upon the expert to give the why and wherefore of his expert opinion, not just a mere conclusion as a substitute for a reasoned explanation for an alleged causal connection between the act complained of and the injury or damage resulting therefrom.[22]

In a products liability motor vehicle accident case, the plaintiff's car was struck from the rear and propelled into the rear of a trailer, killing the occupants. The product liability action against the trailer manufacturer alleged that the rear bumper guard was defective because it lacked a vertical attachment between the edges that allegedly would have offered more protection against underride. The trial judge found flaws in all of the plaintiff's expert reports and concluded that the plaintiff's experts did not pass muster and their testimony would be excluded. The trial judge noted that no measurements, calculations or analysis had been done to establish that the intrusion would have been less had the underride guard been modified as plaintiff suggested. The expert did not test a vertical attachment design. Similarly, the auto safety design consultant's opinion was rejected as being based solely on personal evaluation and ignoring decades of federal agency studies of the balance between strength and energy absorption for rear trailer guards. Since the biomechanical engineer's opinion that the accident would have been survivable had the underride guard been modified was based solely on the opinions of the accident reconstructionist and auto safety design consultant, then that opinion was also not validly supported. The trial judge concluded that the methodology of all three experts was lacking since they looked only at the accident as it occurred and proposed a new design without presenting hard data on how the new design would have changed the outcome of the accident. The trial judge referred to one of the expert's opinions as "untutored intuition."[23]

In a case in which the plaintiff alleged that an elevator malfunctioned causing it to shake and fall and injuring her, the defendant filed a motion in limine to exclude plaintiff's liability expert from testifying contending that the expert's opinion was unreliable, speculative and misleading. Plaintiff's expert had, according to the court, used himself "as a sort of human guinea pig," attempting to recreate multiple movements and reactions to movements of the human body in an attempt to explain the mechanism of plaintiff's injury. Plaintiff's expert had been a physician and then later became an accident reconstructionist. The court cited other opinions in which the expert's testimony was excluded or limited approvingly and granted defendant's motion in limine.[24]

The expert must be prepared to give the court enough information to convince the court that the expert is knowledgeable, is applying the same standards to the forensic inquiry as experts in the industry would, and that the method is reliable. Would an expert be permitted to opine that a particular elevator was defective and was lacking certain safety equipment, if that expert did not actually inspect the elevator? If an expert contends that an accident was caused as a result of misleveling and on each inspection after the accident the elevator is seen to level perfectly, should that expert's opinion be excluded? Should not an expert be allowed to opine that misleveling was the cause of the accident, despite being unable to reproduce that condition, so long as the expert can demonstrate that the particular equipment in place at the time of the accident, if not maintained properly, could result in misleveling, and eyewitnesses in fact do testify to a misleveling condition?

In some cases testing may be appropriate and in other cases it may not. Although it is clear that mere speculation or "untutored intuition" will not be enough to permit an expert to testify, testing and re-enactments are neither required nor feasible in every case. An expert must convince the court that his opinion is based upon methods and procedures that are generally accepted within the given industry.

Endnotes

1. 509 U.S. 579 (1993).

2. 239 F. 1013 (D.C. Cir. 1923).

3. *Daubert*, 509 U.S. at 590.

4. *Daubert* at 593.

5. *Daubert* at 591.

6. *Daubert* at 593-594.

7. 526 U.S. 137 (1999).

8. *Carmichael v. Samyang Tire, Inc.*, 131 F.3d 1433, 1435 (11th Cir. 1996), rev'd sub. nom. *Kumho Tire Co. v. Carmichael*, 526 U.S. 137 (1999).

9. 131 F.3d at 1435.

10. *Kumho* at 1176.

11. 119 S. Ct. 1167.

12. In *Otis Elevator Company v. Tuerr*, 616 A.2d 1254 (D.C. 1992), the defendant elevator company's motion in limine to strike the plaintiff's liability

expert's testimony for failing to possess the requisite experience to qualify as an expert in the area of elevator maintenance was denied. The defendant had taken the position that although plaintiff's expert had been an engineer and designer for elevator companies, had been in charge of engineering and had numerous engineers working under him, and had been involved in redesigning certain equipment, he had never engaged in actual repairs. The court found that although the expert had not engaged in the actual business of repairing elevators he had directed others to do so and had actually monitored maintenance contracts. However, in *Murphy v. Montgomery Elevator Company*, 957 S.W. 2d 297 (Ky. 1997), the court of appeals upheld the trial judge's ruling permitting a mechanical engineer who had never designed, manufactured, serviced or maintained escalators to offer an opinion concerning the adequacy of warning signs on an escalator in an entrapment case despite the defendant's motion to exclude the testimony. See also, *Knight v. Otis Elevator Company*, 596 F.2d 84 (3d Cir. 1979), in which a consulting chemist and engineer who specialized in materials, engineering and safety was permitted to express an opinion about whether an unguarded elevator button constituted a design defect despite the fact he had no background in the design and manufacture of elevators. Whether these experts would be permitted to testify in a courtroom today, with the more stringent requirements that have been followed by the courts, is an open question.

13. In *Lazarus v. Port Auth. of N.Y. & N.J.*, 2014 N.J. Super. Unpub. LEXIS 2970 (App.Div. Dec. 29, 2014), the Court concluded that the Plaintiff could survive summary judgment without an expert in a case involving an injury sustained by the Plaintiff after the she stepped on an elevator that suddenly and without warning rose several inches causing the Plaintiff to fall forward and fracture her knee. The court reached this conclusion after finding that the Plaintiff could rely on the *res ipsa loquitur* doctrine because "[c]ommon knowledge suggests that elevators do not usually operate in the manner reported by plaintiff and that such an accident does not normally occur absent negligence." The elevator malfunction that occurred was of such a nature that "plaintiff can rely on the common knowledge and experience of the fact-finder to deduce what happened without an expert's opinion." Unlike in *Lazarus* and in line with the majority rule, the Court in *Camacho v. Schindler Elevator Corp.*, 2014 U.S. Dist. LEXIS 172664 (W.D. Tex. Dec. 12, 2014) held that the plaintiff needed to designate an expert witness to support her allegations of negligent maintenance of the escalator that she was injured on. The Plaintiff's shoe got caught in the gap between the escalator and the escalator wall, causing injury to her foot. The court found that "[b]ecause the maintenance and operation of an escalator system involves technical and specialized knowledge, [the plaintiff] cannot demonstrate a breach in the standard of care in operating or maintaining an escalator without a qualified expert."

14. *Furlan v. Schindler Elevator Corp.*, 516 Fed. Appx. 201 (3d Cir. Pa. 2013) (Expert's opinion that the finger guard on an escalator was worn down causing injury to a child's hand was excluded as "mere speculation" because the expert's opinion was based solely on an amateur photographer's pictures and the fact that the child got his hand past the guard. The expert did not compare the picture of the finger guard to that of a finger guard In new condition and he conducted no tests into the adequacy of the maintenance performed on the finger guard.): *Crawford v. Millar Elevator Service Company,* 2000 W.L. 573177 (Ohio App. 8th Dist., May 11, 2000, McMonagle, P.J., holding that the trial court was not required to consider the testimony from a technical elevator consultant who had no supporting facts to buttress his conclusion that a maintenance problem was the cause of plaintiff's injuries); *May v. The Dover Elevator Company*, 845 F. Supp. 377, 381 (E.D. Va. 1994) (Expert's opinion, which was admittedly not based on any visual evidence by witnesses at the scene, was found to be "wholly speculative, based entirely on conjecture, and contrary to the undisputed evidence" and thus excluded.). Similarly, in *Davis v. Schindler Elevator Corp.,* 98 Ohio App. 3d 18, 647 NE 2d 827 (8th Dist. Cuyahoga Cty. 1994), plaintiff's expert opinion that a valve failure which resulted in an elevator running into the pit was the result of poor maintenance was rejected because of an insufficient factual basis to support the opinion.

15. There has been some confusion concerning just when an expert's proposed testimony and opinion should be challenged. There has also been some confusion concerning the formality and extent of the "hearing" necessary to decide the relevancy and reliability of a proposed expert's opinion. In order to address those issues some jurisdictions have recently promulgated specific rules. For example, in the Commonwealth of Pennsylvania, Rule of Civil Procedure 207.1 provides as follows:

    Rule 207.1. Motion to Exclude Expert Testimony Which Relies Upon Novel Scientific Evidence.

    (a) If a party moves the court to exclude expert testimony which relies upon novel scientific evidence on the basis that it is inadmissible under Pa. R.E. 702 or 703,

    (1) the motion shall contain:

    (i) the name and credentials of the expert witness whose testimony is sought to be excluded,

    (ii) a summary of the expected testimony of the expert witness, specifying with particularity that portion of the testimony of the witness which the moving party seeks to exclude,

    (iii) the basis, set forth with specificity, for excluding the evidence,

(iv) the evidence upon which the moving party relies, and

(v) copies of all relevant curriculum vitae and expert reports;

(2) any other party need not respond to the motion unless ordered by the court;

(3) the court shall initially review the motion to determine if, in the interest of justice, the matter should be addressed prior to trial. The court, without further proceedings, may determine that any issue of admissibility of expert testimony be deferred until trial; and

(4) the court shall require that a response be filed if it determines that the matter should be addressed prior to trial.

16. *Sikora v. AFD Industries, Inc., et al.*, 221 F. Supp. 2d 920 (N.D. Ill. 2002).

17. *Oddi v. Ford Motor Company,* 234 F.3d 136 (3d Cir. 2000).

18. *Booth v. Black and Decker,* 2001 W.L. 366631 (E.D. Pa. April 12, 2001)(Reed, J.).

19. *Lombardo v. Reliance Elevator Company, et al.,* 315 Ill. App. 3d 111, 733 N.E. 2d 874 (2000).

20. *Gore v. Otis Elevator Company*, 335 N.J. Super. 296, 768 A.2d 292 (2000).

21. Id. 335 N.J. at 296, 768 A.2d at 303.

22. For an explanation of how New Jersey Courts handle the "net opinion" rule, see *Jimenez v. GNOC CORP., et al.*, 286 N.J. Super. 533, 670 A.2d 24 (1996).

23. *Rapp v. Singh et al.*, 00-2741 (E.D. Pa. May 1, 2001)(Dalzell, J.).

24. *Lascola v. Schindler Elevator Corporation, et al.*, 2010 U.S. Dist. LEXIS 23155, 10-12 (E.D. Ala. March 11, 2010

Chapter 11

The U.K. Experience

Synopsis

11.1 Types Of Action—Accident Cases

Accidents fall into two legal categories in the U.K. namely those that attract criminal action and those that attract civil action.

Criminal action is when the accident is deemed by the authorities to have been as a result of some input from the defendant, be that negligence or some other failure to meet its legal duties. In criminal cases the matter is brought to the court by the enforcement authority. In general terms this is either the local authority environmental health department or the Health & Safety Executive. Most commercial office environments come under the jurisdiction of the local authority unless the building is in fact owned by the local authority. In these cases the burden of proof is on the prosecution to prove "beyond reasonable doubt" that the defendant has breached a statutory law such as The Health & Safety at Work Act, Provision of Use of Work Equipment Regulations (PUWER), Lifting Operations & Lifting Equipment Regulations (LOLER). A list of statutory instrument follows. These cases sit in front of a jury who decides the outcome.

Civil action is when an individual or individuals take action against another individual, individuals or a company. This type of law is based on precedence where previous cases are cited and the claimant's legal team argue the case. Similar to criminal cases the burden of proof is still on the claimant, however the test is "in the balance of probabilities" rather than beyond reasonable doubt. These cases sit in front of a judge who decides the outcome based on the balance of the arguments placed before her.

11.2 Types Of Action—Disputes

When disputes arise over matters such as quality of workmanship, contractual differences of opinion, etc., these fall into the civil area of law and generally one of contract law.

There are four requirements of contract law that have to be satisfied for a contract to be deemed in place:

- An offer
- An acceptance
- The intent to form a legal relationship
- Consideration

When a contract is deemed valid the disputes generally fall into two categories which are further tested by the legal system:

- Is it fit for purpose?
- Is it of merchantable quality?

An example of "fit for purpose" would be if the specification called for an eight person passenger lift and the contractor supplied a four person passenger lift. The purchaser had made it clear that an eight person lift was required and what was supplied was not what was asked for. The counter argument is if the purchaser said "install a lift for me" with no reference to size, speed, etc. The contractor could then legitimately claim that it supplied what was asked for. It is similar to a taxi driver going into a garage and saying "I want to buy a car suitable for my job as a taxi driver" versus "I want to buy a car." Obviously a two-door, two-seater car would not be suitable for his job as a taxi, but in the latter case the garage would not know that—albeit it might be a very nice shade of pink!

An example of "merchantable quality" would be with reference to the quality of the equipment supplied. It is reasonable to expect the equipment to be safe and reliable, although longevity may be an argument based on the specification. If it transpires that the contractor has supplied a lift with no safety gear (an extreme case I know but bear me out) and it comes to light, then the equipment may be deemed unsafe and therefore not of merchantable quality. Similarly if the lift keeps breaking down because the door motor repeatedly burns out then this might be deemed unreasonable and a remedy might be to install a better door gear.

11.3 Compliance

In the U.K. there are statutory instruments (law), European & British Standards (recommended but not law) and Codes of Practice & Guidance notes.

As an example in the U.K. we have the Road Traffic Act. It is law. It says what maximum speed you are allowed to do in your car on different types of road, when you should put your lights on, how you should behave at traffic lights and so on. It is law and therefore a statutory instrument approved by our Government. But the Road Traffic Act has probably only been read by the police and lawyers, and it is all in legalese. When you take your driving test in the U.K. you are given a copy of the Highway Code. It is an easy to read book with many pictures and it is understandable to the majority of people. In simple terms if you comply with the Highway Code you are likely to be in compliance with the Road Traffic Act. Regarding lifts, if you comply with the EN81 code (a standard) you are most likely to be in compliance with The Lift Regulations (law).

11.4 Accident Types

The type of accidents seen with lifts and escalators in the U.K. are generally the same as those seen in the U.S. and therefore there is no need in this section to repeat the words of my U.S. colleagues; however I would say that with lifts there are a number of general types of accidents involving passengers including:

- Collision with closing doors
- Out of level trips/falls
- Midflight stops

It is also true to say that the U.K. experience is that a serious accident involving a passenger (i.e., where a fatality occurs) is extremely rare. Most accidents involving a fatality involve the technician that is working on the lift rather than the general passenger. There are, of course, occasional exceptions to the rule.

11.5 Statutory Instruments

The Supply of Machinery (Safety) Regulations 1992
Statutory Instruments 1992 No. 3073, as amended by the
Supply of Machinery (Safety) (Amendment) Regulations
Statutory Instruments 1994 No. 2063 and Supply of
Machinery (Safety) (Amendment) Regulations Statutory
Instruments 2005 No. 831 The Supply of Machinery (Safety) Regulations 2008
Statutory Instruments 2008 No.1587.

The Lifts Regulations 1997 Statutory Instruments 1997
No. 831.

The Construction (Design and Management) Regulations 2007 Statutory Instruments 2007 No. 320

The Provision and Use of Work Equipment Regulations 1998, Statutory Instruments 1998 No. 2306

The Lifting Operations and Lifting Equipment Regulations 1998 Statutory Instruments 1998 No. 2307

The Management of Health and Safety at Work Regulations 1992

Provision & Use of Work Equipment Regulations 1998

11.6 British and European Standards Applicable to Lifts and Escalators

BS EN 81: *Safety rules for the construction and installation of lifts and service lifts.*

BS EN 81 1: 1998: *Safety rules for the construction and installation of lifts and service lifts. Electric lifts*

BS EN 81-1: 1998 + A1 + A2: Consolidated 2006: *Safety rules for the construction and installation of lifts and service lifts. Electric lifts*

BS EN 81-1: 1998 + A3: 2009: Consolidated BS EN 81-1: 1998 + A1: 2005 + A2: 2004 + A3: 2009+ corrigendum September 1999: *Safety rules for the construction and installation of lifts and service lifts. Electric lifts*

BS EN 81-2: 1998: *Safety rules for the construction and installation of lifts and service lifts. Hydraulic lifts*

BS EN 81-2 + A1 + A2: Consolidated 2006: *Safety rules for the construction and installation of lifts and service lifts. Hydraulic lifts*

BS EN 81-2: 1998 + A3: 2009: Consolidated BS EN 81-2: 1998 + A1: 2005 + A2: 2004 + A3: 2009+ corrigendum September 1999: *Safety rules for the construction and installation of lifts and service lifts. Hydraulic lifts*

BS EN 81-3: 2000 + A1: 2008: *Safety rules for the construction and installation of lifts and service lifts.* Electric and hydraulic service lifts

prEN 81-5: *Safety rules for the construction and installation of lifts and service lifts. Screw lifts*

prEN 81-6: *Safety rules for the construction and installation of lifts and service lifts. Guided chain lifts*

prEN 81-7: 2002: *Safety rules for the construction and installation of lifts and service lifts. Rack and pinion lifts*

prEN 81-7: 2009: *Safety rules for the construction and installation of lifts and service lifts. Rack and pinion lifts* (under review)

PD CEN/TR81-10: 2004: *Safety rules for the construction and installation of lifts. Basics. System of the EN 81 series of standards*

PD CEN/TR81-10: 2008: *Safety rules for the construction and installation of lifts. Basics and interpretations. System of the EN 81 series of standards*

DD CEN/TS81-11: 2009: *Safety rules for the construction and installation of lifts. Basics and interpretations. Interpretations related to EN 81 family of standards*

BS EN 81-21: 2009: *Safety rules for the construction and installation of lifts. Lifts for the transport of persons and goods. New passenger and goods passenger lifts in existing building*

prEN 81-22: 10/30216944 DC: *Safety rules for the construction and installation of lifts. Lifts for transport of persons and goods. Part 22. Electric lifts with inclined path*

BS EN 81-28: 2003: *Safety rules for the construction and installation of lifts. Remote alarms on passenger and goods passenger lifts*

DD CEN/TS 81-29: 2004: *Safety rules for the construction and installation of lifts. Safety rules for the construction and installation of lifts. Lifts for the transport of persons and goods. Interpretations related to EN 81-20 up to EN 81-28 (includes EN 81-1:1998 and EN 81-2:1998)*

BS EN 81-31: *Safety rules for the construction and installation of lifts. Lifts for the transport of goods only. Accessible goods only lifts*

BS EN 81-40: 2008: *Safety rules for the construction and installation of lifts. Special lifts for the transport of persons and goods. Stairlifts and inclined lifting platforms intended for persons with impaired mobility* (formerly EN 81-32)

prEN 81-41: 2008: *Safety rules for the construction and installation of lifts. Vertical lifting platforms* (formerly EN 81-33)

BS EN 81-43: 2009: *Safety rules for the construction and installation of lifts. Special lifts for the transport of* persons and goods. Lifts for cranes

BS EN 81-58: 2003: *Safety rules for the construction and installation of lifts. Examination and tests. Landing doors fire resistance test* (formerly EN 81-8)

BS EN 81-70: 2003: *Safety rules for the construction and installation of lifts. Particular applications for passenger and goods passenger lifts. Accessibility to lifts for persons including persons with disability*

BS EN 81-71: 2005: *Safety rules for the construction and installation of lifts. Particular applications to passenger lifts and goods passenger lifts. Vandal resistant lifts*

BS EN 81-72: 2003: *Rules for lifts which remain in use in case of fire (Firefighters lifts)*

BS EN 81-73: 2005: *Safety rules for the construction and installation of lifts. Particular applications for passenger and goods passenger lifts. Behaviour of lifts in the event of fire*

BS EN 81-73 Amd 1: 2009: 09/30201228 DC: *Safety rules for the construction and installation of lifts. Particular applications for passenger and goods passenger lifts. Part 73. Behaviour of lifts in the event of fire*

prCEN/TR 81-76: 2006: *Evacuation of disabled persons using lifts*

BS EN 81-80: 2003: *Safety rules for the construction and installation of lifts. Existing lifts. Rules for the improvement of safety of existing passenger and goods passenger lifts*

DD CEN/TS 81-82: 2008: *Safety rules for the construction and installation of lifts. Existing lifts. Improvement of the accessibility of existing lifts for persons including persons with disability*

DD CEN/TS 81-83: 2009: *Safety rules for the construction and installation of lifts. Existing lifts. Rules for the improvement of the resistance against vandalism*

BS EN 115: 1995: *Safety rules for the construction and installation of escalators and passenger conveyors*

BS EN 115 + prA1: 1998: *Safety rules for the construction and installation of escalators and passenger conveyors*; *Amendment A1*

BS EN 115 + A1 + A2: 2006: Consolidated 2006: *Safety rules for the construction and installation of escalators and passenger conveyors*; *Amendment A1*

BS EN 115-1: 2008: *Safety of escalators and moving walks. Construction and installation*

BS EN 115-1: 2008 + A1: 2010: *Safety of escalators and moving walks. Construction and installation*

prBS EN 115-2: 2009: 09/30192761 DC: *Safety of escalators and moving walks. Part 2. Rules for the improvement of safety of existing escalators and moving walks*

PD CEN/TR 115-3: 2009: *Safety of escalators and moving walks. Correlation between EN 115:1995 and its amendments* and EN 115-1:2008

BS EN 292-1: 1991: *Safety of machinery. Basic concepts, general principles for design. Basic terminology, methodology*

BS EN 292-2: 1991: *Safety of machinery. Basic concepts, general principles for design. Technical principles and specifications*

BS EN 627: 1996: *Specification for data logging and monitoring of lifts, escalators and passengers conveyors*

BS EN 1050: 1997: *Safety of machinery. Principles for risk assessment* prBS EN 1570: 2008: 08/30180969 DC: *Safety requirements for lifting tables*

BS EN ISO 10535: 1998: *Hoists for the transfer of disabled persons. Requirements and test methods*

BS EN 12015: 1998: *Electromagnetic compatibility Product family standard for lifts, escalators and passenger conveyors. Emission*

BS EN 12015: 2004: *Electromagnetic compatibility Product family standard for lifts, escalators and passenger conveyors. Emission*

BS EN 12016: 1998: *Electromagnetic compatibility. Product family standard for lifts, escalators and passenger conveyors. Immunity*

BS EN 12016: 2004: *Electromagnetic compatibility. Product* family standard for lifts, escalators and passenger conveyors. Immunity

BS EN 12016: 2004 + A1: 2008: *Electromagnetic compatibility. Product family standard for lifts, escalators and moving walks. Immunity*

BS EN ISO 12100-1: 2003: *Safety of machinery. Basic concepts, general principles for design*

BS EN 12158: 2000: *Builders hoists for goods*:

BS EN 12158-1: 2000: *Builders hoists for goods. Hoists with accessible platforms*

BS EN 12158-2: 2000: *Builders hoists for goods. Inclined hoists with non-accessible load carrying devices*

BS EN 12183: 1999: *Manually propelled wheelchairs. Requirements and test methods*

BS EN 12184: 1999: *Electrically powered wheelchairs, scooters and their chargers. Requirements and test methods*

EN 12385-5: 2002: *Steel wire ropes. Safety stranded ropes for lifts*

BS EN 13015: 2001: *Maintenance for lifts and escalators. Rules for maintenance instructions*

BS EN 13015: 2001 + A1: 2008: *Maintenance for lifts and escalators. Rules for maintenance instructions*

BS EN 50214: 1998: *Flexible cables for lifts*

BS EN 61508: *Functional safety of electrical/electronic/programmable electronic safety-related systems*:

BS EN 61508-1: 2002 (IEC 61508-1: 1998 + Corrigendum 1999): *Functional safety of electrical/electronic/programmable electronic safety-related systems. General requirements*

BS EN 61508-1: 2010 (IEC 61508-1: 2010): *Functional safety of electrical/electronic/programmable electronic safety-related systems. General requirements*

BS EN 61508-2: 2002 (IEC 61508-2: 2000): *Functional safety of electrical/electronic/programmable electronic safety-related systems. Requirements for electrical/electronic/programmable electronic safety related systems*

BS EN 61508-2: 2010 (IEC 61508-2: 2010): *Functional safety of electrical/electronic/programmable electronic safety-related systems. Requirements for electrical/electronic/programmable electronic safety related systems*

BS EN 61508-3: 2002 (IEC 61508-3: 1998 + Corrigendum 1999): *Functional safety of electrical/electronic/programmable electronic safety-related systems. Software requirements*

BS EN 61508-3: 2010 (IEC 61508-2: 2010): *Functional safety of electrical/electronic/ programmable electronic safety-related systems. Software requirements*

BS EN 61508-4: 2002 (IEC 61508-4: 1998 + Corrigendum 1999): *Functional safety of electrical/electronic/programmable electronic safety-related systems. Definitions and abbreviations*

BS EN 61508-4: 2010 (IEC 61508-4: 2010): *Functional safety of electrical/electronic/programmable electronic safety related systems. Definitions and abbreviations*

BS EN 61508-5: 2002 (IEC 61508-5: 1998 + Corrigendum 1999): *Functional safety of electrical/electronic/ programmable electronic safety-related systems. Examples of methods for the determination of safety integrity levels*

BS EN 61508-5: 2010 (IEC 61508-5: 2010): *Functional safety of electrical/electronic/programmable electronic safety related systems. Examples of methods for the determination of safety integrity levels*

BS EN 61508-7: 2002 (IEC 61508-7: 2000): *Functional safety of electrical/electronic/programmable electronic safety-related systems. Overview of techniques and measures*

BS EN 61508-7: 2010 (IEC 61508-7: 2010): *Functional safety of electrical/electronic/programmable electronic safety related systems. Overview of techniques and measures*

BS EN 62305: *Protection against lightning*:

BS EN 62305-3: 2006: *Protection against lightning. Physical damage to structures*

BS EN 62305-4: 2006: *Protection against lightning. Electrical and electronic systems within structures*

11.7 Standards Applicable to the U.K. Only and Not Throughout Europe

BS 5588-8: 1999: *Fire precautions in the design, construction and use of buildings. Code of practice for means of escape for disabled people*

BS 5588-8: 1999: Amd 2004: *Code of practice for means of escape for disabled people*

BS 5776: 1996: *Specification for powered stairlifts*

BS 5900: 1999: *Specification for powered domestic lifts with partially enclosed cars and no lift well enclosures*

BS 5965: 1980: *Specification for manually driven balanced personal home lifts*

BS 6440: 1999: *Power lifting platforms for use by disabled persons. Code of practice* (under review)

BS7255: 2001: *Safe working on lifts*

BS7801: 2011: *Safe working on escalators & moving walks*

BS 8300: 2001: *Design of buildings and their approaches to meet the needs of disabled people. Code of practice*

BS 8300: 2009 + A1: 2010: *Design of buildings and their approaches to meet the needs of disabled people. Code of practice*

BS 9999: 2008: *Code of practice for fire safety in the design, management and use of buildings*

11.8 Interpretations to Standards

Safety standards are very necessary, but the documents that describe them often require detailed study to obtain a full understanding. Sometimes the meaning is still unclear and hence the use of requests for interpretations. It is very important that designers, manufacturers, installers, maintainers, owners, inspectors and consultants keep up-to-date with such interpretations. BSI publishes EN 81-11: *Safety rules for the construction and installation of lifts. Basics and interpretations. Interpretations related to the EN 81 family of standards* as DD CEN/TS 81-11: 2009. This replaces DD CEN/TS 81-29: 20.

Appendix A

Sample Expert Report

The following sample report has been prepared using absolutely no factual basis.[1] It does not even deal with elevators or escalators. Its purpose is not to teach someone how to write a report. It is intended to show how a typical report might be structured and presented. The methodology is the key point.

In this example the finding of a product defect is not intended to exclude other types of causes of an accident.

Any resemblance to fictitious characters or real persons is purely coincidental.

Enjoy!

1. This report is reproduced here courtesy of Jim Korczak, Summit Professional Resources, LLC, Hackettstown, New Jersey, www.summitresources.com.

Report

Wile E. Coyote v. ACME Industries, Inc.

Ref. 99-1234-P

Prepared for:

Anna Tate, Esq.
Quorum, Secundum & Winem, PC
444 Main Street
Downtown, NJ 08000

Prepared by:
Justin Tyme, P.E.

September 31, 1999

Synopsis

On August 10, 1968, Mr. Wile E. Coyote was pursuing his prey, Velocitous Maximus (Roadrunner) along a deserted stretch of road near Prescott, Arizona. To better facilitate capture of his fleet-footed foe, Mr. Coyote purchased a pair of "Jet Powered" roller skates from ACME Industries, Inc. (ACME). This device malfunctioned and caused Mr. Coyote to suffer temporary death.

Scope

The following addresses the suitability for use and design characteristics of the product as sold by ACME. This report does not address the actions of Mr. Roadrunner or his contribution to this unfortunate event.

Inspection

The actual skates used by Mr. Coyote were destroyed in the incident. However, an exemplar pair was obtained for purposes of measurement and testing. The inspection took place on January 5, 1969 at a classified military facility located in New Mexico. Present were Ms. Joy Phull, counsel for ACME, Mr. Grant Kenyon, counsel to Mr. Roadrunner, Anna Tate, counsel to Mr. Coyote and ACME expert Hy Erdgun, FOS. Photographs were taken and First Aid was administered to the injured.

Discussion

Mr. Coyote, a member of the species Appetitum Gigundim, pursues prey for sustenance. His preferred prey, Roadrunner, is a quarry capable of speeds worthy of Pole Position at the Daytona 500. Roadrunner speeds well in excess of 200 miles per hour have been verified using Arizona State Police Radar (Ref. 3). Mr. Coyote's maximum self-propelled velocity is about 40 miles per hour, making procurement of Roadrunner quite difficult. Use of guile, trickery and deviousness is often required. When these methods fail, direct pursuit of the quarry is used. Unfortunately, this seldom results in Mr. Coyote's capture of Roadrunner.

According to Mr. Coyote's testimony (Ref. 2), he sought a means by which he could increase the likelihood of catching Roadrunner. ACME supplies a diverse and dubious array of items to assist predators in their normal and expected activities. Mr. Coyote ordered a pair of ACME "Jet Powered" roller skates, Item number JPRS2114 (Ref. 4) from the ACME Winter Catalog #35 (Ref. 5).

Upon receipt of the product (photo 01-4), Mr. Coyote immediately removed them from the packaging and took them out to the road to await an opportunity to operate them (Ref. 2). After Roadrunner passed at a high rate of speed, Mr. Coyote put the skates on his hind feet, donned his crash helmet and lit the fuses. He immediately began to accelerate at a furious rate along the roadway. Mr. Coyote described a period of initial instability (Ref. 2, pg. 45, ln. 13), then indicated that he, in fact, began to gain on Roadrunner.

Unfortunately, as Mr. Coyote continued to accelerate, he began to lose directional control. Mr. Coyote is not a pilot and had no knowledge of the potential for flight with the ACME Jet Powered Roller Skates. Mr. Coyote became airborne, thereby losing directional control once the roller skate wheels were no longer in contact with the roadway. Although Mr. Coyote attempted to cut power to the propulsion system by means of the supplied "OFF" switch, the Jet Powered skates remained on. He continued on a linear flight path until he struck a sedimentary rock outcropping, thereby causing sudden, temporary death (Ref. 7). Arizona Highway Patrol estimated his speed at impact at greater than 300 miles per hour (Ref. 6).

This writer's examination of the exemplar skates and product packaging revealed a number of anomalous conditions. Of significance, this product is actually powered by a solid fueled rocket and is not, in fact, "Jet" powered. This is significant in that a solid fuel rocket has no output control and cannot be turned off once ignited (Ref. 9). The limited instructions do not indicate that fact, but do indicate that Roadrunner capture rates can be increased by 45% through use of the product (photo 01-7). No data is provided to substantiate that claim. The warnings do not comply with applicable standards (Ref. 8), which require the following with respect to warnings (Sect. 5 (a) (4)):

> *"Packaging for roller skate propulsion systems shall clearly indicate the means of propulsion and the method of controlling same."*

Mr. Coyote was denied the knowledge that would have allowed him to properly evaluate the hazardous nature of the ACME product.

Section 6 (b) (2) of the standard (Ref. 8) requires the following to appear on all packaging for the incident product:

> *"Sudden, temporary death may result from use of this product."*

No such admonition was found on the exemplar packaging.

An additional defective condition was found, in that the design of the exemplar skates did not include any means by which the operator could quickly release the foot bindings. Therefore, once Mr. Coyote had initiated their operation, he had no means of escape from their significant power. A quick release binding could have been incorporated at little additional expense, thereby allowing him to abort his flight before striking the rock. This violated good design practice, as this type of design feature is found on similar devices worn on the feet such as jet powered skis and ice skates. ACME even offered for sale a rocket powered skateboard with such quick release bindings in the same catalog from which Mr. Coyote made his purchase of the incident skates (Ref. 5, pg. 211).

Conclusions

Mr. Coyote purchased a pair of rocket powered roller skates from ACME Industries, Inc. in order to pursue and catch his prey. These skates were labeled and sold as "Jet Powered Roller Skates". The skates were defective, in that misleading, misrepresentative and incorrect labeling accompanied the product, preventing Mr. Coyote from evaluating their full hazard potential. The skates were also defectively designed in that they did not incorporate a quick release binding similar to those found on other products sold by ACME during the same period this product was sold to Mr. Coyote. An additional and significant defect existed, in that the "off" switch provided did not, in fact, disconnect power from the skate propulsion system. Mr. Coyote suffered sudden temporary death as a result of using this hazardous and defective product.

Opinion

It is the writer's opinion, to a reasonable degree of technical certainty, that the "Jet Powered Roller Skates" as sold by ACME Industries, Inc., were defective. The defective skates were a proximate and real cause of Mr. Coyote's sudden temporary death. Therefore, ACME Industries, Inc. bears responsibility for this incident.

Respectfully submitted:

Justin Tyme, P.E.
N.J. License # 12-3456

References

1. Deposition of Roadrunner, taken May 24, 1969.
2. Deposition of Wile. E. Coyote, taken May 23, 1969.
3. Speeding ticket for Roadrunner, dated June 2, 1967.
4. Receipt for purchase of ACME "Jet Powered Roller Skates"—item # JPRS2114, dated August 8, 1968.
5. ACME catalog #35, Winter 1967–1968.
6. Arizona State Police Incident Report #68-4456, dated August 10, 1968.
7. Certificate of Temporary Death, Prescott Arizona Coroner's Office, dated August 10, 1968, time of death 3:45 PM. Expires August 10, 1968, 11:59 PM.
8. Animated Manufacturers Standards Institute (AMSI) standard F208.4—"Jet and Rocket powered foot mounted propulsion systems," 1965.
9. *Solid Fuel Rocketry*, Robert Goddard, Michigan Press, 1940.

Photographs

01-2 Overall view of exemplar "Jet Powered Roller Skates"
01-4 Closer view of exemplar "Jet Powered Roller Skates" (Note fuse at arrow.)
01-7 View of exemplar package warnings and instructions

Glossary of Terms Used in the U.S., Canada, and the U.K.

IMPORTANT NOTE—See Section 2.1, *Terminology*, before using this glossary.

A17.1: See *ASME A17.1.*

A17.2: See *ASME A17.2.*

A17.2.1: See *ASME A17.2.1.*

A17.2.2: See *ASME A17.2.2.*

A17.2.3: See *ASME A17.2.3.*

A17.4: See *ASME A17.4.*

A17.5: See *ASME A17.5.*

A18: See *ASME A18.*

A117.1: See *ICC/ANSI A117.1.*

abstract: A summary sheet that indicates all the major features of the equipment.

AC: Abbreviation, see *alternating current.*

AC control: Type of motion control that uses an AC motor to operate the driving machine; among the types are single-speed, two-speed, variable-voltage, variable-voltage/variable-frequency, AC with DC injection.

AC control, single-speed: Type of AC control that has a single speed.

AC control, two-speed: Type of AC control that has two speeds.

AC control, with DC injection: Type of AC control that produces a retarding torque by injecting a DC current into the motor stator winding or a separate eddy current brake.

AC control, variable-voltage (VVAC): Type of AC control that varies the magnitude and direction of torque by controlling the voltage (magnitude and phase sequence) to the motor.

AC control, variable-voltage/variable-frequency (VVVF): Type of AC control that varies the magnitude and frequency of the voltage applied to the motor.

acceleration: The rate of change of a velocity with respect to time.

acceptance form: A document signed by the owner or their agent which indicates that they accept the equipment as is.

acceptance test: See *test, acceptance.*

acceptance inspection: See *inspection, acceptance.*

access door: Used for access to equipment located in various locations not accessible otherwise (hoistways, pits, machine rooms, etc.).

access switch, hoistway: Keyed switch located at a landing that permits operation of the car with the hoistway doors and car gate or door to open.

accidents: Unintentional or unexpected incidents which may cause injury or damage.

accumulator: A device that stores hydraulic fluid under pressure so that it can be available for immediate use.

active oil: Amount of oil available in a hydraulic elevator storage tank that can be circulated into a system.

actuator: Any device that puts a mechanism into motion (e.g., motor, hydraulic piston, etc.), or activates another device (e.g., a plunger).

ADA: Abbreviation, see *Americans with Disabilities Act.*

ADA Accessibility Guidelines: Published guidelines for meeting ADA requirements.

ADAAG: Abbreviation, see *ADA Accessibility Guidelines.*

addendum: Change or addition to a previously written specification or proposal.

adjunct: An applied section of architectural metal fastened to the edge of an escalator or passenger conveyor decking for the purpose of increasing the effective width.

adjustable chain tension device, escalator: A carriage that maintains proper tension on a step chain, usually through the use of springs or weights.

adjustable flow control: A valve that can be adjusted in order to restrict the flow of hydraulic fluid.

adjuster: Mechanic who adjusts newly installed or modernized equipment in order to ensure proper operation and code compliance, and who typically troubleshoots problems that other mechanics cannot solve.

adsil: An application applied to escalators and passenger conveyors to reduce the likelihood of static electricity.

advance door opening: See *pre-opening.*

AFR: Abbreviation, see *aramid fiber rope.*

AHJ: Abbreviation, see *authority having jurisdiction.*

air bleed: Device used to release air trapped in a hydraulic fluid system.

air breather: Device that permits the entry and exit of air into an oil storage tank as the oil discharges and returns.

air cord: Another term for *aircraft cable.*

aircraft cable: Small diameter wire rope used for a number of mechanisms, such as door relating cables.

air gap: (1) Space between mating contacts when open; (2) distance between an armature and a pole in a magnetic device.

air entrapment: Pockets of air trapped in hydraulic fluid.

alteration: A change to the equipment which cannot be classified as maintenance, repair, or replacement.

alternate landing: Landing that an elevator returns to when the smoke detector at the designated landing is activated and the firefighters' service key switch is not activated.

alternating current: Electrical current that continuously alternates in the form of a repeating sine wave between positive and negative values; abbreviated as AC; this is the standard available electricity.

American National Standards Institute: Organization that establishes national voluntary industry standards in the U.S. by adopting standards published by others under their auspices; abbreviated as ANSI.

Americans with Disabilities Act: A civil rights law applicable in the U.S. for removing barriers for people with disabilities; abbreviated as ADA.

American Society of Mechanical Engineers: Engineering society that publishes numerous codes and standards; this includes the A17 standards, under the general auspices of ANSI; abbreviated as ASME.

ammeter: Tool used to measure electrical current.

amp: Abbreviation, see *amperes.*

amperes: Unit of electrical current.

angle of contact: The part of a sheave contacted by a rope.

angle of inclination: The maximum angle at which escalator steps move with respect to the horizontal.

annunciator, car: Visual signal device in the car that indicates which hall call buttons have been activated.

anode: (1) a terminal or electrode with a positive charge; (2) electrode toward which electrons flow.

ANSI: Abbreviation, see *American National Standards Institute.*

ANSI A10.4: Standard used in the U.S. for personnel hoists.

ANSI A10.5: Standard used in the U.S. for material hoists.

ANSI A92: Standards used in the U.S. for mobile scaffolds, towers, and platforms.

ANSI A120.1: Standard used in the U.S. for powered platforms and equipment used for exterior building maintenance.

anti-creep: Re-leveling feature of a hydraulic elevator that allows the car to move upward even with the doors open if it is located within a certain distance of the landing.

anti-slide devices: Raised objects (e.g., knobs) on a high deck of an escalator to act as a deterrent to objects sliding down the deck; also known as baggage stops.

anti-reversal device: See *reversal stop device.*

anti-static coating: An application to escalators and passenger conveyors intended to reduce the likelihood of static electricity.

approved: Accepted by the authority having jurisdiction.

apron: See *platform guard.*

aramid fiber ropes: See *ropes, aramid fiber.*

arc: Flame formed when electrical current passes through a gap between two conductors.

arc quencher: Device that eliminates an arc when contacts are opened.

armature: (1) Rotating element of a DC motor or generator; (2) moving part of an electro-mechanical device, such as a relay, bell or contactor.

ASME: Abbreviation, see *American Society of Mechanical Engineers.*

ASME A17.1: *Safety Code for Elevators and Escalators*, most widely recognized code used in the U.S. for the minimum requirements for the design, construction, operation, inspection, testing, maintenance, alteration and repair of elevators, escalators, moving walks, dumbwaiters, and material lifts with automatic transfer devices; previously covered stairway chairlifts and wheelchair lifts.

ASME A17.2: *Guide for Inspection of Elevators, Escalators and Moving Walks,* a guide for elevator and escalator inspections in the U.S. Formerly titled *Inspector Manual for Elevators and Escalators.*

ASME A17.2.1: *Inspectors' Manual for Electric Elevators*, recommended guide for electric elevator inspections in the U.S. in accordance with A17.1.

ASME A17.2.2: *Inspectors' Manual for Hydraulic Elevators*, recommended guide for hydraulic elevator inspections in the U.S. in accordance with A17.1.

ASME A17.2.3: *Inspectors' Manual for Escalators and Moving Walks,* recommended guide for escalator and moving walk inspections in the U.S. in accordance with A17.1.

ASME A17.3: *Safety Code for Existing Elevators and Escalators,* a standard used in the U.S. for the minimum requirements for existing elevators and escalators.

ASME A17.4: *Guide for the Emergency Personnel*, a guide that explains the proper procedures to be used for the safe removal of passengers from stalled elevators in the U.S. Formerly titled *Guide for Emergency Evacuation of Passenger Elevators.*

ASME A17.5: *Elevator and Escalator Electrical Equipment,* establishes the requirements for labeling and listing electrical equipment used for starting, stopping, regulating, controlling, or protecting the equipment in the scope of the A17.1 standard in the U.S. (joint standard-CAN/CSA B44.1).

ASME A18: Standard used in the U.S. for stairway chairlifts and wheelchair lifts.

ASME A90.1: Standard used in the U.S. for manlifts.

ASME B20.1: Standard used in the U.S. for conveyors, including vertical reciprocating types.

ASME B30: Standard used in the U.S. for cranes, derricks, and hoists.

ASME B56: ASME standards for industrial type trucks.

astragal: Resilient, non-crushing and non-shearing molding used on the leading edges of car and hoistway doors.

asymmetric relay: See *reverse phase relay.*

attendant, designated: Person who is authorized to operate the elevator from inside the car; also known as an operator.

attendant service: Operation of an elevator by a designated attendant.

automatic operation: See *operation, automatic.*

authority having jurisdiction (AHJ): The organization responsible for enforcing the applicable code requirements.

authorized personnel: See *personnel, authorized.*

automatic transfer device: Mechanism that automatically transfers the load on or off a dumbwaiter or material lift.

auxiliary drive chain: See *chain, auxiliary drive.*

auxiliary isolating switch: See *disconnecting means, auxiliary.*

auxiliary lighting: See *lighting, standby.*

auxiliary rope fastening device: Device that will automatically support the car or counterweight if the rope fastening fails.

auxiliary supply: An alternate power supply.

axial: Located on, along or in the direction of an axis.

axis: Real or imaginary straight line that an object rotates around or is symmetrically arranged about.

axle, step chain: See *step chain axle.*

B44: See *CAN/CSA B44.*

B44.1: See *CAN/CSA B44.1.*

babbitt: Alloy used in bearings, sliding guides shoe liners and for tapered rope sockets.

backlash: Rocking action in the drive sheave or gear caused by excessive clearance between the worm gear and the worm teeth.

baggage stop: Common term for anti-slide devices.

balance weights: Weights added to the car underside or frame to evenly distribute the pressure on the guide shoes.

balustrade, escalator or moving walk: Assembly that supports the handrail.

balustrade deck: See *deck, escalator and moving walk.*

balustrade lights: Light fixtures installed in balustrades.

balustrade panel: Panels that enclose the interior and exterior of the balustrade.

bank: (1) A group of elevators or escalators adjacent to each other that serve the same floors; (2) a common grouping of devices (e.g., resistors).

bar lock: A type of lock used with manual hoistway doors.

basement machine: Driving machine located not directly over the hoistway, usually in the basement.

bearing: A device that supports a rotating element; among the types are anti-friction, ball, needle, roller, sleeve, taper rolling, and thrust.

bearing plate: Steel plate that is used to distribute loading (e.g., supporting an escalator truss).

bedplate: Support framework (foundation) upon which a driving machine is installed.

belt-driven machine: Indirect elevator with belts connecting the motor and driving sheave.

bevel: Angle other than a right (90-degree) angle, or a sloping surface

bias: Voltage applied to establish certain operating conditions.

bi-directional: Capable of operation in two directions.

bi-parting door: See *door, bi-parting.*

BIS: Abbreviation commonly used to denote that the equipment has been placed back in service

blade: Planed guide rail surface that the car guides ride over.

blind hoistway: Portion of the hoistway in which there are no landings served by the elevator.

block and fall: See *block and tackle.*

block and tackle: Pulley arrangement used to gain mechanical advantage when lifting; also known as a block and fall or rope fall.

blowout coil: Permanent magnet or electromagnet around a contact arranged so that its magnetic field extinguishes the arc formed when the contacts open.

BOCA: Abbreviation, see *Building Officials and Code Administrators.*

bolster: Bottom horizontal member of a hydraulic elevator car sling to which the platen attaches.

bonding: Method of establishing electrical continuity between different components.

brake: Electromechanical device that applies a force to stop and hold an escalator or moving walk; or hold and in some cases retard the motion of an elevator, dumbwaiter, and material lift; it is electrically released and can be applied by mechanical, hydraulic, magnetic or gravity means depending on the equipment and the applicable code.

brake arm: Lever that supports and transmits motion to the brake shoes.

brake armature: Component that moves the brake levers and linkages, in order to release the brake when it is moved by the brake coil.

brake, auxiliary: See *brake, emergency.*

brake coil: Solenoid that when energized moves the brake shoes away from the brake drum.

brake cooling circuit: See *cooling circuit, brake.*

brake, driving machine: Brake that is part of the driving machine.

brake disc: Disc connected to the drive shaft to which the brake pads apply for a disc-type brake.

brake, disc: Brake in which pads apply to a disk mounted on a rotating shaft.

brake drum: Smooth cylindrical surface connected to the drive shaft to which the brake shoes apply for a drum type brake.

brake, drum: Brake in which linings apply to a drum connected to a shaft.

brake, emergency: Mechanical mechanism used to stop and hold an elevator or escalator in lieu of the driving machine brake; can be applied to the guide rails, ropes (see *rope brake*), sheaves, sprockets, drive shaft (see *brake, main drive shaft*), and so on.

brake lift detector: Switch used to determine that the brake has fully released (lifted).

brake lining: Replaceable high friction material attached to the brake shoes that contacts the brake drum.

brake magnet: See *brake coil.*

brake, main drive shaft: An emergency brake that acts on the main drive shaft that applies a force to stop and hold an escalator or moving walk.

brake motor: Motor sometimes used to release the brake.

brake, operational: See *brake, driving machine.*

brake pad: Replaceable high friction material that contacts the brake disc.

brake release device: Mechanism, usually a lever, used to manually release the brake.

brake, rope: A type of emergency brake that applies on elevator ropes.

brake, service: A secondary brake to the driving machine brake which can be used when servicing the driving machine brake.

brake shoe: Moving part of the brake to which the lining is attached.

brake solenoid: See *brake coil.*

brake spring: Spring that is usually used to apply the brake.

branch circuit: Individual circuit of a main wiring diagram.

break: To open or disconnect (e.g., a contact opens when it breaks).

bridge rectifier: Full wave rectifier that uses four diodes.

British Standard: A system of rules or regulations (i.e., national standards) published in the U.K; abbreviated as BS.

broken arm closer: A type of door closer used with manually opened, self-closing hoistway doors.

broken drive chain switch: Electrical protective device that also applies a main shaft brake if a drive chain breaks between the main drive shaft and an escalator or moving walk driving machine. It also can activate from slack chain or jerks in the chain.

broken handrail switch: Electrical protective device that activates if the handrail breaks, or if the handrail is excessively slack.

broken rope/tape/chain switch: Electrical protective device activated when a rope, tape or chain connecting a normal terminal stopping device to a car breaks.

broken step chain device: Electrical protective device required to activate if an escalator step chain breaks, and can also activate for excessive slack in the chain or jerks in the chain. Commonly known as a carriage switch.

broken treadway device: Electrical protective device activated when the connection between pallets or the belt breaks on a moving walk.

brush: Device, usually made of carbon or graphite, used to complete an electrical circuit between a commutator and a non-rotating component.

brush assembly: Assembly made up of brushes and their holders, springs and flexible connections.

brush, skirt: See *skirt deflector*.

brush holder: Device that holds a brush in contact with the commutator.

brush, newel entry: See *handrail entry guard.*

BS: Abbreviation, see *British Standard.*

BS 5656: A system of rules or regulations (i.e., national standards) published in the U.K. with particular reference to escalators.

buck, door: Frame that a door is attached to.

buffer: Device used to stop a car or counterweight when it travels beyond its normal limits of travel by absorbing or dissipating its kinetic energy.

buffer, oil: Buffer that uses an oil medium (dashpot) to stop the descending car or counterweight.

buffer, reduced stroke: Oil buffer that relies on an emergency speed limiting device to reduce the striking speed of the car or counterweight so that it will have a sufficient stroke.

buffer switch: Device that prevents an elevator from operating if the oil level is below the required amount, or a mechanically activated switch that removes power from the drive machine when the oil buffer is compressed.

buffer, spring: Buffer that uses spring(s) to stop the descending car or counterweight.

buffer stroke: See *stroke, buffer*.

building code: Ordinance that regulates the construction and design of buildings and their components.

building occupancy or use: The main use for a building (e.g., residential, commercial, institutional, assembly and manufacturing).

Building Officials and Code Administrators: Publishers of the NBC, among other standards; abbreviated as BOCA.

Bulkhead, safety: See *safety bulkhead.*

bumper: Solid resilient device used in lieu of a buffer, where permitted.

burnish: Clean contacts with a mild abrasive.

busbar: Heavy, rigid conductor used to carry high currents and make a common connection between several circuits.

bushing: (1) cylindrical sleeve that acts as a bearing surface for a pin or shaft (2) grommet used for electrical insulation through a penetration.

cab: Enclosure mounted on an elevator platform in which passengers and goods are transported.

cable: More than one electrical wire enclosed in an insulating jacket. For elevators it refers to electrical conductors, not wire ropes.

cable chain: See *chain, cable.*

cable end box: Junction box used for joining power supply cables before delivery to switchboards.

cable, traveling: See *traveling cable.*

call: Signal registered at a landing (i.e., hall or corridor call) or in the car (i.e., car call) for an elevator to go to a specific floor.

call button: Button used to register a call.

callback: Unscheduled repair visit due to a reported problem.

cam: (1) an angled bevel usually used between moving and stationary objects that can be used for numerous functions; also called a vane; (2) machinery component used to convert regular rotation into an eccentric rotation or reciprocating motion in another device.

cam, retiring: See *retiring cam.*

Canadian Standards Association: Organization that publishes the CSA standards and provides certification services in Canada; abbreviated as *CSA.*

CAN/CSA B44: Safety Code for Elevators, primary standard used in Canada for the minimum requirements for the design, construction, installation, operation, testing, maintenance, alteration and repair of elevators, escalators, moving walks, and freight platform lifts.

CAN/CSA B44.1: Elevator and Escalator Electrical Equipment, joint standard with A17.5, applicable in Canada to the equipment in the scope of the B44 standard.

candela: Metric unit of luminous intensity.

canopy: Top part of the cab supported by the walls, including the ceiling.

cant: Bevel used to prevent objects from resting on top of surfaces in the hoistway.

capacitance: Property that permits the storage of electricity when a voltage is applied; units are farads.

capacitor: Electrical device used to store a charge temporarily, which consists of two conductors separated by a dielectric. Sometimes referred to as a condenser.

capacity: See *rated load.*

capacity, handling: Number of people that can theoretically be transported in a given time period.

car: Load-carrying assembly of an elevator, dumbwaiter or material lift that includes the platform, frame, cab, and door or gate.

carbon dust: Fine particulate matter created by the wear of carbon brush material.

car door: Door installed at the car entrance(s); see door.

car door interlock: See *interlock, car door.*

car door operator: Device that opens and closes a power-operated car door, and usually opens the landing door also.

car enclosure: Assembly of the walls and car top supported by the car platform.

car frame: Support framework made up of the crosshead, safety plank and stiles to which the car suspension (ropes, plunger, rope sheave, etc.), the car platform, car safeties and car guides are attached. Among the types are underslung, overslung and sub-post; also known as a sling.

car frame, overslung: See *overslung.*

car frame, underslung: See *underslung.*

car frame, sub-post: Car frame located below the platform.

car gate: Gate installed at the car entrance; see *gate.*

car gate operator: Device that opens and closes a power-operated car gate.

car operating panel: Station mounted inside the car that contains the operating controls. Abbreviated as *COP.*

car platform: Floor assembly that supports the load.

carriage: Escalator equipment located in the lower pit that guides the step chain and keeps it in tension.

carriage rollers: Rollers sometimes used to support the carriage and permit its longitudinal movement.

carriage sprocket: Sprocket used to engage the step chain in order to tension the carriage.

carriage switch: See *broken step chain switch.*

carriage tensioner: Device (e.g., springs) used to provide tension in the carriage.

carriage tracks: Tracks used to support or guide the carriage.

carriage wheels: Wheels sometimes used to support the carriage and permit its longitudinal movement.

car steady plates: Components between the stiles and the car top that prevent lateral movement.

car switch: Manually operated switch used by an attendant to control an elevator.

car switch operation: See *operation, car switch.*

car top: Top portion of the car enclosure.

car top inspection device: See *top of car operating device.*

casing: Protective sleeve placed in the jack hole to keep it from caving in.

castell key: Unique key to operate the castell lock.

castell lock: Mechanical interlock that prevents the circuit breaker or disconnect switch from closing when the key is removed.

cathode: (1) Negatively charged electrode or terminal; (2) an electrode that electrons flow away from.

cathodic protection: Method used to prevent corrosion from electrolysis.

caution: Statement indicating a potentially hazardous condition that may result in minor or moderate injury.

ceiling intersection guard: Device used to eliminate the entrapment hazard created by the intersection of a horizontal ceiling or soffit, and the inclined escalator deck or handrail.

CEN: Abbreviation, see *European Committee for Standardization.*

Cenelec: The European Committee for Electrical Standardization.

centrifugal force: Force that causes a body to move away from its center of rotation.

certified: Approval of equipment or materials by a certifying agency that is listed in a publication.

chain: Interconnected series of flexible links.

chain anchors: Devices sometimes provided to physically connect an escalator chain to a stationary part in order to prevent movement.

chain anchor switch: Switch in the safety circuit that detects if the chain anchors are in place to prevent starting of the escalator.

chain, auxiliary drive: Chain used to drive auxiliary equipment (e.g., countershaft and handrails).

chain, cable: Type of chain used on a smooth sheave.

chain, compensating: Chain used to counterbalance the weight of the suspension ropes; see compensation.

chain, drive: Chain used to transmit motion.

chain, main drive: Chain used as the prime mover of the equipment.

chain driven machine: Indirect elevator with chains connecting the motor and driving sheave.

chain fall: Type of portable hoist.

chain, roller: Type of chain used to engage a sprocket or escalator step links (rack).

chain sheave: See *sheave, chain.*

chain, step band drive: Chain used to transmit motion to the step band.

chain stretch switch: Switch used to detect excessive stretch in a chain.

chain, suspension: Chain used to support, lower and lift a dumbwaiter or material lift.

chain wheel axle, step: See *step chain axle.*

chain wheel, step: See *step chain roller.*

chain wheel track: See *step chain track.*

chairlift, stairway: See *stairway chairlift.*

chassis: Inclined elevator car frame which has supporting wheels.

check valve: Valve that prevents reverse flow.

Chinese fingers: Common term for *spool cable hanger.*

chord members: Longitudinal truss members.

choke: Inductor used to smooth the voltage in a rectified DC circuit.

circuit: Path of electrical current.

circuit breaker: Device that opens an electric circuit automatically upon an overcurrent condition and is re-settable.

circuit protective conductor: See *grounding conductor.*

circuit, safety: See *safety circuit.*

circuit, short: See *short circuit.*

circuit, suicide: See *suicide circuit.*

cladding: A covering.

cleat, step: Raised slat on escalator step treads or risers.

cleated riser: See *riser, cleated.*

clip, rope: See *rope clip.*

closer, door: Device that closes a door by gravity or mechanical means.

closer, gate: See *gate closer.*

clutch, door: Device used to couple the hoistway doors to the car door in order to open or close them together.

code: A system of regulations that are legally enforceable in a jurisdiction.

coil: Device consisting of turns of insulated wires around an iron core to create an electromagnet.

collapsible gate: See *gate, collapsible.*

collector rings: Metal rings that conduct current to or from a rotating member; also known as slip rings.

comb: Replaceable comb-like section(s) that attaches to the combplate, so that its teeth mesh with the slots in the steps or treadway.

combination mechanical lock and electric contact, hoistway door: See *mechanical lock and electric contact, combination, hoistway door.*

comb-pallet impact device: Electrical protective device that activates when either a vertical or a horizontal force of a certain magnitude acts on a moving walk combplate from a pallet striking it.

combplate: The part of an escalator and moving walk landing that the combs are attached to, under which the steps or treadway pass.

combplate lights: Light fixtures mounted in skirt panels adjacent to the combplate.

combplate stop switch: Electrical protective device that activates when a vertical force acts on the combplate from something caught between it and the steps or treadway.

comb section: See *comb.*

comb-step impact device: Electrical protective device that activates when either a vertical or a horizontal force of a certain magnitude acts on an escalator combplate from a step striking it.

comb switch: See *combplate stop switch.*

comb teeth: Projections on a comb.

common: Wire that connects circuits in parallel.

commutating field: Magnetic field created by the interpoles of a motor or generator.

commutation: Process of reversing current in an armature coil as the commutator bars pass under a brush; this converts alternating current into direct current.

commutator: A device that performs commutation; the outer elements are in contact with brushes that collect the current in the generator and the inner element distributes the current in a motor.

commutator bar: Metallic current-carrying component of the commutator; also known as a commutator segment.

commutator film: Desirable coating that forms on a commutator.

compensating chain: See *chain, compensating.*

compensating rope: See *rope, compensating.*

compensating rope sheave: Sheave that the compensating ropes pass over in the pit.

compensating rope sheave switch: Electrical protective device that activates before the compensating rope sheave reaches its limit of travel.

compensating winding: Coils connected in series with the armature winding of a DC generator or motor, which counteracts its magnetic field.

compensation: The use of ropes or chains attached between the underside of a car and its counterweight to counterbalance the weight of the suspension ropes as they pass over the drive machine.

compound generator: Generator that has a series and shunt field.

compounding: Adjustment made to the speed control system to vary the leveling speeds in the up and down directions to account for varying loading.

compounding, flat: Compounding that results in leveling speeds that are relatively the same in the up and down directions for the same load.

compounding, over: Compounding that results in a faster leveling speed in the down direction than the up direction with no load, and the opposite at full load.

compounding, under: Compounding that results in a leveling speed that is faster in the up direction than the down direction with no load, and the opposite with full load.

compound motor: See *motor, compound.*

compound roping: See *two-to-one (2:1) roping.*

concentric newel: Newel with a semi-circular shape.

condenser: Antiquated term for a capacitor.

conductance: Material property that permits current flow; the inverse of resistance; units are mhos or ohms-1.

conductor: Material that allows the flow of electricity.

conduit: Tubular pipe used as a raceway for the protection of electrical wire or cable.

constant pressure device or switch: Device that requires constant manual pressure for the device to operate.

contact: Current carrying parts of a relay or switch that completes or opens an electrical circuit.

contact, breaking: Contact that is open when the device is energized, and closed when de-energized.

contact, making: Contact that is closed when a device is energized, and opened when de-energized.

contacts, pileup: Stacked pairs of contacts, separated by insulators that are operated together.

contactor: Device that opens and closes a power circuit.

contactor, directional: Contactor arranged so that its contacts provide power for a particular direction of travel.

contact, selector: See *selector contact.*

continous pressure operation: See *operation, continous pressure.*

contract speed: See *speed, contract.*

control, AC: See *AC control.*

control, DC: See *DC control.*

control, generator field: See *DC control, generator field.*

control, static: See *static, control.*

control, SCR: See *SCR control.*

control, drive: See *control, motion.*

control, electro-hydraulic: See *electro-hydraulic control.*

control logic: The defined sequence and precedence of the operation of an elevator or escalator.

control, motion: System that controls acceleration, speed, retardation, and stopping; see AC control, DC control, electro-hydraulic control and static control.

control, operation: System that initiates the starting, stopping, and direction of motion; among the types are automatic, car switch, constant pressure, group, inspection, nonselective collective, pre-register, selective collective, and signal.

controller: (1) Device that governs the motion control or operation control systems, or both; (2) device that controls the operation of a component such as a door or motor.

controller, floor: See *selector*.

controller, motor: Part of the motion control system that includes the motor starter and power converter.

control room: Room that contains the controller, when it is not in the machine room.

control space: space that contains the controller when it is not in a control room or machine room.

control, static: See *static control.*

control valve: Valve that controls the acceleration, deceleration, speed, and stopping of hydraulic elevator.

conveyor: Horizontal, inclined or vertical acting device used to transport goods along a fixed path that has fixed or selective points of exit and entry; among the types are skip hoists, reciprocating, belt, apron, bucket, chain, electrified monorail, en masse, flight, mobile, oscillating, overland, pusher bar, screw, power and free, shuttle, slat, suspended tray, tow, trolley, vibrating, and wheel.

conveyor, passenger: See *passenger conveyor*.

cooling circuit, brake: Circuit that reduces the brake coil current after the brake has lifted in order to prevent overheating.

COP: Abbreviation, see car operating panel.

core, rope: See *rope core*.

corner post: Stiles on opposite corners of the car frame, instead of on the sides.

corridor: See *hall.*

corrosion: Electrochemical reaction that causes metal to deteriorate.

counter balanced door: See *door, counter balanced.*

counter EMF: Voltage built up in an armature that opposes the inflow of current.

countershaft: Intermediate shaft used to transmit power to the handrail drive from a main drive or idler shaft.

countershaft drive chain switch: Electrical protective device activated when the countershaft drive chain breaks or is excessively slack.

counterweight: (1) The mass that counterbalances the car; (2) any mass that counterbalances another mass.

counter weighted door: See *door, counter weighted.*

counter weighted gate: See *gate, counter weighted.*

counterweight, drum: Counterweight used on a winding drum machine; also called a machine counterweight.

counterweight filler weights: Sections of metal weights used in a counterweight.

counterweight frame: Assembly that encloses the filler weights in an assembled counterweight.

counterweight headers: Oversized weight members that extend around the guide rails in a stacked counterweight.

counterweight guard: Guard used to prevent personnel from getting under the counterweight in the pit.

counterweight rods: Rods that pass through filler weights to tie them together.

counterweight, machine: See *counterweight, drum.*

crane: Device, that includes a hoist, used to move loads horizontally and vertically; there are numerous types including gantry, semi-gantry, and overhead.

creep, rope: See *rope creep.*

crosby clip: U-bolt type rope fastening.

crosshead: (1) Top horizontal part of the car frame; (2) the traveling member of a selector.

crown wires: Outer wires of a wire rope strand.

CSA: Abbreviation, see *Canadian Standards Association.*

CSA B167: Standard used in Canada for inspection and maintenance of cranes, monorails, hoists, and trolleys.

CSA B311: Standard used in Canada for manlifts.

CSA B335: Standard used in Canada for industrial lift truck operator training.

CSA B354: Standard used in Canada for mobile scaffolds, towers, and platforms.

CSA B355: Standard used in Canada for physically disabled person lifts.

CSA B613: Standard used in Canada for private residence handicapped elevating devices.

CSA Z150: Standard used in Canada for mobile cranes.

CSA Z185: Standard used in Canada for personnel hoists.

CSA Z248: Standard used in Canada for tower cranes.

CSA Z256: Standard used in Canada for material hoists.

CSA Z271: Standard used in Canada for suspended, powered platforms.

current: The rate of flow of electricity; units are amperes.

cycle: One full period of the reversal of alternating current.

cylinder: Stationary hydraulic jack casing inside of which the plunger or piston moves.

cylinder head: Bolted cylinder top that contains the guide ring and stuffing box.

cylinder sleeve: See *sleeve, cylinder*.

damping motor: Small DC motor sometimes used to provide smooth speed changes by gradually changing the generator shunt field.

danger: Statement indicating an imminently hazardous condition that will result in death or serious injury.

dashpot: Piston device that uses a fluid (oil or air) to dampen motion (e.g., door check).

DC: Abbreviation, see *direct current*.

DC control: Type of elevator motion control that uses a DC motor to operate the driving machine; among the types are dual bridge thyristor, generator field, multivoltage, rheostatic, single bridge thyristor.

DC control, dual bridge thyristor: Type of DC control that supplies variable voltage of either polarity to the motor armature and in which current can flow in either direction.

DC control, generator field: Type of DC control in which the magnitude and direction of a generator field current is used to adjust the voltage to the motor armature.

DC control, multi-voltage: Type of DC control that impresses successively on the motor armature a number of substantially fixed voltages.

DC control, rheostatic: Type of DC control that varies the resistance in the motor armature or field circuit.

DC control, single bridge thyristor: Type of DC control that supplies the motor armature with variable voltage of fixed polarity; the field is changed to control direction and to cause regeneration.

DBG: Abbreviation, see distance between guides.

dead-end hitch: Termination and fastening point of a wire rope.

deck board: The balustrade capping component.

deck, escalator and moving walk: Transverse part of the balustrade.

deck, exterior (outer): Deck located outside of the handrails (i.e., not on the step side).

deck, high: Deck located below the handrail.

deck, interior (inner): Deck located on the step side of the handrails.

deck, low: Deck located immediately above the skirt panels or on the exterior of the balustrade in an equivalent position.

decking, balustrade: Balustrade cladding.

decking, center: The decking between escalators.

deceleration: The decrease of velocity with respect to time (negative acceleration).

de-energized: Circuit that has no electrical potential.

deflector, dust tray: Metal plate that deflects dust and debris into the dust tray.

deflector, skirt: See *skirt deflector*.

deflector sheave: See *sheave deflector*.

delta (Δ) connection: Connecting motor windings in a delta configuration.

demarcation lights, step: Green fluorescent lights located under the steps near each escalator landing.

demarcation, step: See *step demarcation*.

derailment switch: Device that detects if a counterweight has been displaced out of its guide rails, principally in an earthquake.

designated attendant: See *attendant, designated*.

designated landing: Landing that the elevator returns to when recalled by firefighters' service Phase I operation for use by emergency personnel.

dielectric: Non-conducting or insulating material.

diamond stop: See *stop diamond*.

diode: Electrical device used for rectifying or blocking current.

direct current: Electrical current that has a constant value and flows in one direction only; abbreviated as *DC*.

direct drive: Drive in which the driven part is directly connected to the driver.

direct drive machine: See *driving machine, direct*.

directional arrow: Illuminated arrow symbol that indicates the direction of travel.

directional contactor: See *contactor, directional.*

directional indicator: See *indicator, directional.*

directional limit switch: Common term for *terminal stopping device, normal.*

directional start switch: See *start switch, escalator or moving walk.*

disc brake: See *brake, disc.*

disconnected motor safety: Electrical protective device activated when an escalator or moving walk motor is disconnected from the gear reducer, if it is not connected with a continuous shaft, mechanical coupling or gearing.

disconnecting means: Device (e.g., switch) used to disconnect the power supply from electrical circuits and equipment.

disconnecting switch: Manually operated mechanical switch used to disconnect and connect the electrical supply to equipment or circuits.

dispatching: Sending a signal to the car to answer a call.

displacement switch: Device used to indicate that a counterweight has been displaced excessively by seismic forces.

diversity factor: Factor used to reduce the size of electrical service conductors based on the theory that not all the connected equipment will be operating at the same time.

door: Movable entrance component made of panels that are not perforated; among the types are counterbalanced, counterweighted, horizontally sliding, vertically sliding, multiple speed, swing, manually operated, power operated, center opening, biparting, side opening, single speed, self closing, folding, and combinations of these types; see *car door*, *hoistway door*, and *access door.*

door, access: See *access door.*

door arm: Member that the door operator uses to move the car door through linkages.

door, bi-parting: Vertically sliding door with panels that open in opposite directions from a central meeting point.

door buck: See *buck door.*

door, car: See *car door.*

door, center opening: Horizontally sliding door with panels that open in opposite directions from a central meeting point.

door close limit: Door operator contact that indicates the doors are fully closed.

door closer: See *closer, door.*

door clutch: See *clutch door.*

door, counterbalanced: Door that opens and closes vertically and the lower panels counterbalance the upper panels.

door, counterweighted: Door that opens and closes vertically and uses weights to counterbalance the open panel.

door, emergency: Door used to gain access to a blind hoistway section.

door, folding: Horizontally sliding collapsible type door.

door guide: See *gib.*

door guide rail: Tracks that guide vertically sliding doors.

door header: See *header, door.*

door, hoistway: See *hoistway door.*

door, horizontally sliding: Door with panels that slide horizontally to open and close.

door linkages: Connecting members of a door closer or operator used to move the door.

door, manually operated: Door that opens and closes by hand.

door, multiple speed: Door with two or more panels that open and close together in the same direction and the leading panels travel faster than the trailing panels.

door open limit: Door operator contact that indicates the doors are fully open.

door operator, car: See *car door operator.*

door release key, hoistway: Another term for *door unlocking device, hoistway.*

door, pass type: Vertical biparting doors in which the panels are offset.

door, power-operated: Door that is opened and closed by a car door operator (i.e., not manual).

door pre-opening: See *pre-opening.*

door reopening device: Power door device, attached to the car door or gate, that stops and re-opens a closing door when an obstruction is in the path of or close to the closing doors; among the types are mechanical, photoelectric, and proximity.

door reopening device, mechanical: See *safety edge.*

door reopening device, photoelectric: Type of door reopening device that operates when a photoelectric light beam, either visible or infrared, is blocked by an object or person. Can be either a single/dual beam (also known as a *photo eye*, *light ray*, or *safe ray*) or multiple beam type (also known as a *light curtain*).

door reopening device, proximity: Type of door reopening device that operates when an object is detected near the leading edge of the closing doors.

door, self-closing: Manual door that closes by itself when released.

door, side opening: Door that opens horizontally in one direction only.

door, single speed: Door with only one panel moving in the same direction.

door, swing: Door with hinged panels that swing horizontally to open and close.

door unlocking device, hoistway: See *unlocking device, hoistway door.*

door vane: Car door mounted cam that drives the hoistway doors.

door, vertically bi-parting: Vertically sliding door that has panels that open from a center position.

door, vertically sliding: Door with panels that slide vertically to open and close.

double button operation: See *operation, double button.*

double deck elevator: An elevator with two separate platforms and cabs, one on top of the other.

double wrap: Gearless elevator roping arrangement that increases traction by passing the suspension ropes over the drive sheave, then over a secondary sheave, and then back over the drive sheave.

dress guard: Type of skirt deflector.

drip pan: Pan attached to the underside of an escalator truss to catch excess oil and debris.

drip tray: See *drip pan.*

drive block: Device mounted on a hoistway door that the car door valve engages to move the doors.

drive chain: See *chain, drive.*

drive chain, auxiliary: See *chain, auxiliary drive.*

drive control: See *control, motion.*

drive controller: See *controller.*

drive unit: See *driving machine.*

drive sheave: See *sheave, drive.*

drive wheels: Term sometimes used for the sprockets that engage a drive chain.

driving machine: The mechanism that drives the elevator, escalator, etc.; among the types are direct, electric, geared, gearless, indirect, rack and pinion, direct hydraulic, roped hydraulic, screw, traction, winding drum, and worm.

driving machine brake: See *brake, driving machine.*

driving machine, direct: Electric driving machine in which the motor is directly connected, with or without gears, to the driving sheave, drum or shaft.

driving machine, direct hydraulic: Hydraulic machine in which the jack is directly coupled to the car.

driving machine, electric: Driving machine powered by an electric motor.

driving machine, geared: See *geared machine.*

driving machine, gearless: See *gearless machine.*

driving machine, indirect: Electric driving machine in which the motor is connected to the driveshaft, drum, sheave, or gear reducer by means of a belt or chain.

driving machine, rack and pinion: Electric driving machine in which the motor rotates a small gear mounted on top of the car that engages a stationary rack installed in the hoistway to move the car.

driving machine, roped hydraulic: Hydraulic machine in which the jack is connected to the car by wire ropes.

driving machine, screw: See *screw machine.*

driving machine, traction: See *traction machine.*

driving machine, winding drum: See *winding drum machine.*

driving machine, worm gear: See *worm gear machine.*

driving station: Drive unit area inside an escalator.

drop key: Type of door unlocking device.

dropped step support: Ramps sometimes provided to support the steps through the combs if a step wheel or roller becomes detached.

dropped step switch: Switch sometimes used to detect a dropped step situation.

drum: Cylinder on a winding drum type machine that the ropes wind on and off of.

drum brake: See *brake, drum.*

drum counterweight: See *counterweight, drum.*

duck board: Raised insulated personnel platform.

dumbwaiter: Freight handling device of limited size; among the types are electric, hand, hydraulic, power, and undercounter.

dump switch: See *selector hoistway switch.*

dust cover: Protective cover for a door track; also known as a hanger cover.

dust tray: Tray sometimes used to collect debris that falls off escalator steps on the return side.

dynamic braking: Electrically assisted stopping of a motor.

duty: (1) Rated load and speed of an elevator; (2) time and load conditions for a motor (e.g., continuous or intermittent).

earth: Main terminal used to connect the earthing and bonding system to the conductive mass of the earth.

earth leakage circuit breaker: Circuit breaker that opens the supply if current flows to earth.

earthing: Act of connecting conductive parts to earth.

earthquake protective devices: Devices used to govern the operation of an elevator during or after a seismic event.

eccentric: Disk with two round surfaces that are offset from each other.

ESCB: Abbreviation, see *elastomeric coated steel belts.*

elastomeric coated steel belts: Polyurethane coated belt with steel cords.

electrical drawing: See *wiring diagram.*

electrical print: See *wiring diagram.*

electrical interference: See *interference, electrical.*

electrical protective device: Safety device that when activated removes power to the driving machine and brake.

electric contact, car door or gate: Device that prevents operation of an elevator unless the car door or gate is in the closed position.

electric contact, hoistway door or gate: Device that prevents operation of an elevator unless the hoistway door or gate is in the closed position.

electric driving machine: See *driving machine, electric.*

electric elevator: See *elevator, electric.*

electro-hydraulic control: Type of motion control that varies the fluid flow to a hydraulicjack.

electro-hydraulic elevator: See *elevator, electro-hydraulic.*

electrolysis: Type of corrosion.

electrolyte: Solution that conducts electricity.

electromagnet: Magnet formed when current flows in a coil of wire around an iron core.

electromagnetism: Magnetism created by current flow.

electromechanical device: Mechanism that operates both electrically and mechanically (e.g., a brake that is electrically released and mechanically applied).

electromotive force: Voltage that produces current in a circuit; abbreviated as *EMF*.

electron tube: Electronic device that conducts electricity through a gas in a vacuum.

elephant ear: Term sometimes used for the ear-shaped rubber insert for a handrail entry guard.

elevator: Device that moves vertically within fixed guide rails that serves more than one fixed landing and designed to carry passengers, goods or authorized personnel.

elevator, carriage: Type of hand freight elevator.

elevator, electric: Power elevator that uses an electric driving machine.

elevator, electro-hydraulic: Direct acting hydraulic elevator that uses a motor driven pump to supply the pressurized liquid to the jack.

elevator, freight: Elevator used for carrying goods, and that only carries the operator and freight handlers.

elevator, gravity: Elevator that uses gravity to move the car.

elevator, hand: Elevator that uses manual power to move the car.

elevator, hatchway: Elevator that runs through hinged floor opening covers that open and close automatically.

elevator, hydraulic: Power elevator that uses liquid under pressure in a jack.

elevator, hydraulic, direct acting: Hydraulic elevator with the car directly attached to the piston or plunger.

elevator, hydraulic, maintained-pressure: Direct acting hydraulic elevator that has liquid under pressure, which is available at all times for use in the jack.

elevator, hydraulic, roped: Hydraulic elevator in which the car is connected to the piston or plunger by ropes.

elevator, hydraulic, water: See *water hydraulic elevator*.

elevator, inclined: Elevator that travels at least 20 degrees from the vertical.

elevator, limited use and limited application: Power passenger elevator whose use is restricted because of size, capacity, rise and speed constraints. Abbreviated as *LULA*.

elevator, machine room-less: Commonly used term for an elevator that has the driving machine installed in the hoistway (i.e., machine space) and/or has its controller installed in the hoistway or at a landing (i.e., control space) instead of a traditional machine room. Also known as a *MRL* elevator.

elevator, mine: Elevator installed in a mine shaft.

elevator, multideck: Elevator having more than one compartment on top of one another.

elevator, observation: Elevator that permits viewing the exterior while traveling.

elevator, passenger: Elevator used for carrying people.

elevator personnel: See *personnel, elevator*.

elevator, platform: Elevator that uses a platform instead of a full car.

elevator, power: Elevator that uses power, other than manual or gravity, to move the car.

elevator, private residence: Power elevator installed in a private residence.

elevator, rack and pinion: Power elevator that is supported by and uses a motor to drive a pinion on a stationary rack.

elevator, rooftop: Power elevator that operates between an exterior roof level and a landing below.

elevator, screw column: Power elevator with an uncounterweighted car that is raised and lowered by a screw thread.

elevator, service: Elevator that meets all the requirements for a passenger elevator, that is also used for carrying light freight.

elevator, shipboard: Elevator installed on a ship or drilling rig used for transporting personnel or freight.

elevator, sidewalk: Freight elevator that operates between a sidewalk and subgrade level.

elevator, special purpose personnel: Elevator installed in structures not accessible to the public used to transport authorized personnel and their equipment only.

elevator, traction: Electric elevator that uses the friction between the hoist ropes and the drive machine sheave to move the car.

elevator, used for construction: Elevator only being used temporarily for construction purposes. Different from a personnel hoist, which has no permanently installed components.

elevator, winding drum: Electric elevator that moves the car by winding the suspension ropes on and off a drum.

emergency brake: See *brake, emergency*.

emergency door: See *door, emergency.*

emergency exit: Exit used to remove passengers from a stalled elevator in an emergency situation; can be located on the top or side of the car.

emergency personnel: See *personnel, emergency.*

emergency power: See *power, emergency.*

emergency signal device: Device inside the car used to summon help; among the types are alarm bells, telephones, intercoms.

emergency stop switch: See *stop switch, emergency.*

EMF: Abbreviation, see *electromotive force.*

EN: Abbreviation, see *European Norm*, which stands for *European Standards.*

EN 115: A European standard specifically applicable to escalators.

end bell: Housing for the bearings and brush assemblies located on the ends of a motor or generator.

energized: Circuit that has electrical potential.

energy: Capacity of a body to do work by reason of its motion or configuration.

enforcing authority: See *authority having jurisdiction.*

engineer: Term used in the U.K. for a *mechanic.*

engineer surveyor: Term used in the U.K. for someone who performs a thorough examination of the equipment.

engineering test: Laboratory test performed to ensure conformance with code requirements.

entrance, elevator: Assembly used to protect hoistway openings, which include the doors, frame, gates, hardware and transoms.

eprom: Device for storing semi-permanent computer data.

equalizer, rope: See *rope equalizer.*

escalator: A continuous moving stairway used for lifting and lowering passengers.

escalator, compact: See *escalator, modular.*

escalator, conventional: An escalator with the drive machine at the upper end.

escalator, heavy duty: See *heavy duty escalator.*

escalator, modular: An escalator with one or more independent driving machines located inside the step band.

escutcheon rubber: Another term for an *elephant ear.*

European Committee for Standardization: The organization that establishes the European Standards (EN).

European Standards: Standards used in Europe; abbreviated as *EN*.

excitation current: DC current sent through a generator's field coils to produce a magnetic field.

exciter: Auxiliary power generator sometimes used to provide DC current to a hoist motor field and other high current devices, such as a door operator, which is driven by the motor generator shaft.

explosion proof enclosure: Electrical enclosure that prevents possible ignition sources (sparks, etc.) that occur inside it from being introduced to the surrounding environment.

faceplate: Front cover for a signal or operating fixture.

factor, diversity: See *diversity factor*.

factor of safety: Ratio of the ultimate strength to the maximum static working stress.

farad: Unit of capacitance.

fascia: Vertical stiff flat plate(s) used to eliminate potential shear hazards in the hoistway from an entrance door sill to the header of the door entrance below.

fastening, rope: rope fastening.

fatigue: Failure due to repeated stresses.

feeder: Circuit conductors between the service equipment and a branch overcurrent device.

fender casting: Corner piece of the ends of the skirting used on some escalators in which the handrail entry guard is fitted.

fiber, rope: See *rope fiber*.

field: Magnetic lines of force.

field coil: Coil used on a field pole.

field pole: Magnetic iron structure to which a field coil is mounted to provide a magnetic pole when the coil is energized.

field, series: See *series field*.

field, shunt: See *shunt field*.

field winding: Insulated wire wound around a laminated iron core used to produce an electromagnetic field force in motors and generators.

fillet: Concave curve at the intersection of two surfaces.

filter: An electrical device that restricts the passage of certain frequencies.

finished floor level: Level of the floor at an elevator or escalator landing.

final limit: See *terminal stopping device, final*.

fire endurance: Measure of the time that a component retains its fire resistance under certain conditions.

firefighters' service: Operation in which the elevator is taken out of service for use by the public and can operate under the exclusive control of emergency personnel.

firefighters' emergency operation: See *firefighters' service.*

fire lintel: Hinged flap installed on the top of certain vertical slide hoistway doors to provide a fire barrier when the doors are closed.

fireman's service: See *firefighters' service.*

fire rating: Measure of the time that a material can withstand exposure to fire, as determined by tests.

fire resistance: Propensity of a component to withstand fire or retain its structural integrity.

fire shutter: Fireproof rolling steel curtain that is sometimes used to provide a fire barrier at the top escalator landing.

fire stop: Incombustible material used to fill voids.

fire tab: Metallic projections that are required to maintain the fire rating of a hoistway entrance that uses a primarily non-metallic door gib and also acts as an auxiliary guide.

fishplate: Flat plate used to join guide rail sections.

fist grip: Type of rope clip with two saddles.

flange: (1) The wide top and bottom parts of an I-beam; (2) bolted ring on the top of a hydraulic cylinder; (3) bolted fitting that mated with a similar fitting used for piping connections.

floor bar: Insulated selector component with contacts that affect various operations of an elevator (slowdown, stopping, direction, etc.).

floor controller: See *selector.*

floor plate: Removable cover plate at each end of an escalator or moving walk that people walk on; used for access to internal equipment.

flywheel: (1) Mechanical device used to store rotational energy; (2) a disc sometimes provided on a motor shaft used for hand winding.

foot-candle: Unit of illumination.

foot light: See *combplate light.*

foot pound: Unit of torque, work and energy.

force: The action of one body on another that will cause acceleration of the second body unless acted on by an equal and opposite action; it is a vector quantity; among the types are static, dynamic and impact.

force, reaction: Force of equal magnitude but opposite direction to an imposed force.

fpm: Abbreviation, see *feet per minute.*

freight elevator: See *elevator, freight.*

freight loading, Class A: General Freight; no single piece of freight exceeds one-quarter of the rated load.

freight loading, Class B: Motor Vehicle Loading; used to transport motor vehicles.

freight loading, Class C: Industrial Truck (e.g., forklift) and Heavy Concentration Loading. Class C1—industrial trucks are carried; Class C2—industrial trucks are used to unload and load, but are not carried; and Class C3—load increments exceed one-quarter of the rated load.

frequency: The number of periods of a repetitive function per unit time; units are hertz or cycles per second.

fretting: Type of abrasion between wires in a wire rope due to a loss of core support and internal lubrication.

friction: Resistance to motion of two surfaces relative to each other created when the surfaces rub against each other; produces a force tangential to the contact surfaces.

friction, coefficient of: Dimensionless quantity, that is a measure of the friction potential of the surface conditions of two materials in contact with each other; classified as static (impending motion) or kinetic (in motion).

friction, low: Materials having a low coefficient of friction (e.g., Teflon).

friction-reducing material: Application (e.g., silicon) to escalator skirt panels in order to reduce the coefficient of friction.

full load current: Maximum continuous operating current.

fuse: Electrical overcurrent protective device that cannot be reset.

gate: Moveable entrance component made of perforated panels. Among the types are horizontally sliding, vertically sliding, manually operated, power operated, counterweighted, collapsible and combinations of these types; see *car gate* and *hoistway gate.*

gate closer: Device that closes a gate by gravity or mechanical means.

gate, collapsible: Horizontally sliding gate that closes upon itself (collapses) when it opens.

gate, counterweighted: Gate that opens and closes vertically and uses weights to counterbalance the open panel.

gate, horizontally sliding: Gate with panels that slide horizontally to open and close.

gate, manually operated: Gate that opens and closes by hand.

gate, power operated: Gate that is opened and closed by a car gate operator (i.e., not manual).

gate switch: Commonly used term for both a car door electric contact and a car gate electric contact.

gate, vertically sliding: Gate with panels that slide vertically to open and close.

gear: Toothed wheel designed to engage a similar component to transmit motion and torque.

gear box: Assembly of gears used for power transmission.

gear, bull: Common term used for a worm gear.

gear case: Housing for the gears.

geared machine: Traction driving machine that uses gearing to connect the motor to the drive sheave.

gear, helical: Gear with beveled teeth in a spiral around a shaft.

gearing, planetary: Gear arrangement in which a gear (planet or satellite gear) travels around the circumference of another gear (sun gear).

gear, internal: Gear with its teeth on its interior annular surface.

gearless machine: Traction driving machine in which the motor directly moves the drive sheave.

gear, planet: See *gearing, planetary.*

gear reducer: Assembly of gears that reduces the speed (rpm) and while increasing the torque.

gear, ring: Another term for a worm gear.

gear, satellite: See *gearing, planetary.*

gear, spur: Gear with radial teeth on the rim parallel to its axis.

gear, sun: See *gearing, planetary.*

gear, tandem: Geared machine with two gears driven by two worms on the same shaft.

gear, worm: See *worm gear.*

generator: Device that converts mechanical energy into electrical energy.

generator field control: See *DC control, generator field.*

generator, self-excited: Generator that supplies its own excitation current.

generator, externally excited: Generator that uses an outside source to supply its excitation current.

GFI: Abbreviation, see *ground fault interrupter.*

gib: (1) Member that moves in a sill groove to guide and retain a sliding door; (2) liner for a sliding guide shoe.

gland ring: Part of stuffing box that compresses the packing.

governor, centrifugal: Speed governor operated by weights acted on by centrifugal force.

governor drive chain switch: For governors driven with a chain, a switch in the safety circuit that opens when a break in the chain is detected.

governor jaw: See *jaw, governor.*

governor, overspeed switch: Electrical protective device that activates when the governor senses an overspeed condition.

governor rope: See *rope, governor.*

governor, speed: Continuous speed monitoring device that activates when the speed exceeds a predetermined amount to either activate a car or counterweight safety on an elevator, dumbwaiter or material lift, or to stop an escalator or moving walk.

governor tension sheave: Sheave mounted in an elevator pit to keep tension on the governor rope.

gravity elevator: See *elevator, gravity.*

grooved connector: Mechanical type coupling used for piping connections.

ground: Intentional or accidental connection between a circuit or device and the earth or some conducting body that serves in place of the earth.

grounded: Connected to the earth or some conducting body that serves in place of the earth.

ground fault interrupter: Personnel protection device that de-energizes a circuit when the current to ground exceeds a certain amount.

grounding conductor: Cable used to connect conductive parts to ground.

group: Equipment sharing the same dispatching control system.

group operation: See *operation, group.*

guard, handrail entry: See *handrail entry guard.*

guidance note: Document issued by the Health and Safety Executive in the U.K. intended to inform or advise.

guide rail: Vertical members mounted in a hoistway that guide an elevator or counterweight.

guide roller: A roller used for guiding the movement of a component.

guide, rolling: See *roller guides*.

guide shoes: (1) Devices used to guide a car or counterweight on the guide rails; (2) devices used to guide doors.

guide, sliding: Type of guide shoe that slides.

gusset plate: Triangular steel plate used for reinforcement of structural joints.

halfway box: Junction box that the fixed end of a traveling cable is attached to in the hoistway.

hall: Term used for the landing lobby or building corridor.

hall lantern: See *lantern, hall*.

hand elevator: See *elevator, hand*.

handling capacity: See *capacity, handling*.

handrail: (1) The moving handholds on an escalator or moving walk; (2) support railing.

handrail brush: Type of handrail entry guard.

handrail device, stopped: See *stopped handrail device*.

handrail drive: System that moves an escalator handrail.

handrail drive chain: Chain used to transmit power to drive the handrail.

handrail entry guard: Guard used to prevent hands and fingers from entering the openings in the newel bases that the handrails enter and exit.

handrail entry device: Electrical protective device activated when an object either gets caught between or approaches the area between a handrail and a handrail guard.

handrail entry switch: Type of handrail entry device.

handrail guard: See *handrail entry guard*.

handrail guides: Guides that an escalator handrail runs on.

handrail markers: Markings on an escalator handrail intended to give riders an indication of the direction of travel and the speed.

handrail spacers: See *handrail markers*.

handrail speed detector: See *handrail speed monitoring device*.

handrail speed monitoring device: Safety device that will stop an escalator or moving walk if it detects a continuous speed deviation in a handrail with respect to a step or treadway.

handrail tensioning device: Assembly used to maintain and adjust the tension in an escalator handrail.

hand rope: See *rope, hand.*

handwinding device: Mechanical means for manually moving the step band.

hanger cover: See *dust cover.*

hanger, door: Assembly that has rollers for horizontal movement and support of the door.

hanger track: Part of the door hanger that the rollers move in.

hardness: Property of a material to resist surface penetration.

hatch: Common term for a *hoistway.*

head: Term used for *escalator pit* in the U.K.

header, door: Horizontal structural steel frame member that supports the door hanger and the vertical struts of slide type entrances.

headroom: Vertical distance from the floor to any overhead object.

Health and Safety Executive: Body in the U.K. that oversees health and safety concerns.

heavy duty escalator: Escalator designed for public transportation environments.

helical gear: See *gear, helical.*

helper: Apprentice mechanic.

henry: Unit of inductance.

Hertz: Unit of frequency, cycles per second.

high bar: Condition in which a commutator bar projects above the others.

high mica: Condition in which mica projects above the adjacent commutator bars.

high voltage: Over 600 volts as specified by the NEC.

hinged car platform sill electric contact: Electrical protective device activated when a hinged car platform sill is not retracted enough to provide the proper clearance.

hitch plate: Termination point for a wire rope.

hoist: Lifting and lowering mechanism.

hoist machine: Common term for an electric elevator *driving machine.*

hoistway: Opening through the floors of a building that an elevator, dumbwaiter or material lift travels; commonly referred to as a shaft or hatch.

hoistway access switch: See *access switch, hoistway.*

hoistway door: Door used to protect a hoistway landing opening; see *door.*

hoistway door interlock: See *interlock, hoistway door.*

hoistway door/gate mechanical lock: See *mechanical lock, hoistway door* or *gate.*

hoistway door/gate electric contact: See *electric contact, hoistway door* or *gate.*

hoistway door combination mechanical lock and electric contact: See *mechanical lock and electric contact, combination, hoistway door.*

hoistway door unlocking device: See *unlocking device, hoistway door.*

hoistway enclosure: Fixed structures (walls, etc.) that separate the hoistway from the other parts of the building.

hoistway gate: Gate used to protect a hoistway landing opening; see *gate.*

home landing: Landing that an elevator always returns to and waits (parks) after all calls have been answered.

hook brush: Cam mounted on the selector carriage.

hook switch: Floor bar mounted switch operated by a hook brush.

horsepower: A unit for energy.

horizontally sliding door: See *door, horizontally sliding.*

horizontally sliding gate: See *gate, horizontally sliding.*

hospital service: Attendant-type service used in hospitals, in which the operation of the elevator can be controlled by someone who uses a special key.

hot: A term for *energized.*

hydraulic elevator: See *elevator, hydraulic.*

hydraulic fluid: Oil used as the working fluid in a hydraulic machine.

hydraulic machine: Driving machine, comprised of a motor, pump, valves and piping that converts electrical energy to pressurize a fluid.

hydraulic pump: See *pump, hydraulic.*

hysteresis: Resistance or lag in the change of a material's magnetism.

IBC: Abbreviation, see *International Building Code.*

ICBO: Abbreviation, see *International Conference of Building Officials.*

ICC: Abbreviation, see *International Code Council.*

ICC/ANSI A117.1: *Accessible and Useable Buildings and Facilities*, standard used in the U.S. for making buildings accessible to people with disabilities. Formerly known as *Making Buildings and Facilities Accessible to and Useable by the Physically Handicapped.*

impedance: The total opposition to current flow from a circuit's resistance and reactance.

inching: (1) Limited manual leveling by a constant pressure switch with the doors open, usually on freight elevators; (2) to move at slow speed under manual control.

inclined elevator: See *elevator, inclined.*

independent service: Manually activated automatic elevator operation that removes the car from normal service and permits operation from only inside the car.

indicator, directional: Signal light that shows the direction of travel.

indicator, position: Signal light that indicates the position of the car, located either in the car or at the landings (hall).

idler shaft: Shaft attached to an idler sheave or sprocket.

idler sheave: See *sheave, idler.*

idler sprocket: Sprocket used to guide or apply tension to a chain.

indirect driving machine: See *driving machine, indirect.*

induced current: Current created from the motion of a conductor in a magnetic field.

induction: Generation of electromotive force by varying the magnetic flux through a circuit.

inductor: Device, typically a coil, that introduces inductance into a circuit.

inductance: Property of a circuit that causes an EMF to be induced by a change in current; units are henrys.

inertia: Property of matter that resists any change in the motion of a body.

infrared: Electromagnetic radiation with wavelengths greater than visible light, but shorter than microwaves.

inspection: Mandatory examination of the equipment by a person authorized by the AHJ; usually classified as routine, periodic or acceptance.

inspection, acceptance: Examination of newly installed equipment.

inspection door: See *access door.*

inspection operation (service): Manually activated, continuous pressure automatic elevator operation that removes the car from normal service and permits limited speed operation under someone's control.

inspection outlet: Socket for a portable inspection control station.

inspection, periodic: See *inspection, routine.*

inspection, routine: Examination of existing equipment designed so that the inspector can perform it alone.

inspection transfer switch: Switch that transfers the control between inspection operation and normal operation.

inspection station: Controls used to operate the equipment under manual control.

inspection station, car top: See *top of car operating device.*

inspection unit: See *inspection station.*

insulator: Nonconductor of electricity.

insulation resistance: Electrical resistance of an insulator.

interference, electrical: Unwanted electrical signals, which produce undesirable effects in control system circuits.

interference, mechanical: A mechanical impediment.

interlock, hoistway door: Device that prevents operation unless the door is locked in the closed position, and prevents the door from being opened from the landing unless the car is in the landing zone and stopped or leveling; these functions are interdependent.

interlock, car door: Device sometimes used that prevents operation unless the door is locked in the closed position and prevents the door from being opened from inside the car unless the car is in the landing zone and stopped or leveling; these functions are interdependent.

interlocked: Arrangement in which the functioning of one part is controlled by another for safety.

interlock, mechanical: Arrangement in which components are interlocked mechanically.

internal spur gear machine: Machine with a double reduction gearing, used for heavy duty machines; the first is a worm and gear, and the second a spur gear that engages an internal gear.

International Building Code: Building code, published by the ICC, scheduled to replace the National, Standard and Uniform Building Codes; abbreviated as *IBC.*

International Code Council: Publishers of the *International Building Code.*

International Conference of Building Officials: Publishers of the *UBC*; abbreviated as *ICBO.*

Internal Union of Elevator Constructors: A union that represents workers that install, repair, maintain and service elevators, escalators and similar equipment in the U.S. and Canada; abbreviated as *IUEC.*

interpoles: Wire wound iron cores used in motors and generators.

intersection guard: See *ceiling intersection guard.*

interval: Average roundtrip time of an elevator in a group divided by the number of elevators in that group.

iron rope: See *rope, iron.*

isolation coupling: Coupling that absorbs vibrations.

isolation pad: Pad made of resilient material used to absorb vibration or noise.

isolator: See *disconnect switch.*

IUEC: Abbreviation, see *International Union of Elevator Constructors.*

jack: Hydraulic unit made up of a cylinder and a plunger or piston.

jamb, head: Top horizontal door frame member.

jamb, return: Door frame member that the door passes behind.

jamb, strike: Vertical entrance frame member that a side slide door or gate closes against.

jaws, governor: The part of the speed governor that engages the governor rope after an overspeed condition is sensed, which in turn activates the safeties.

jaws, safety: The part of the safety that engages the guide rails.

jewel: Translucent lens for a signal lamp.

joint molding: Strip used to cover the space between two panels.

joule: Metric unit of torque, work and energy.

journal: Part of a shaft or axle that is supported by a bearing.

jumper: Wires with clips used to temporarily short circuit (bypass) a device, terminals or circuits.

junction box: Enclosure for joined conductors of different raceways or cables.

keeper: Term for the mechanical latch of a door interlock.

Kellam's grip: Trade name for a type of split cable grip.

kilo: Unit prefix indicating one thousand. For example, 1 kilogram is 1000 grams.

kinetic energy: The energy a mass possesses because of its velocity; units are foot pounds or joules.

kinked link detector: Device sometimes used to detect kinked step chain links.

knockout: Stamped parts of junction boxes that can be removed for raceway or conduit connections.

labeled: Equipment or material that has a mark or label used to identify that it is certified or listed; also see *marked.*

ladder diagram: See *wiring diagram.*

landing: (1) Part of a building or structure that passengers and freight enter and exit the car; (2) stationary area at the entrance and exit areas of an escalator or moving walk.

landing plate: Fixed surface at both ends of an escalator or moving walk adjacent to the combplate.

landing, terminal: See *terminal landing.*

landing zone: Distance above and below a landing through which power opening of the car doors is permitted.

lantern, hall: Signal device at the landings that indicates the arrival of an elevator, or its direction of travel, or both.

lantern, directional: See *indicator, directional.*

lanyard: Strap used to connect a safety belt to a life line.

lateral: In a direction sideways (90 degrees) to the main direction of travel.

lay, rope: (1) Lengthwise distance that a single strand of a wire rope takes to make one complete turn around the rope; (2) construction of a wire rope's spiral; among the types are right, left, regular, and lang.

lead: Wire or conductor used as a connection.

LED: Abbreviation, see *light emitting diode.*

leveling: Slow car movement toward a landing to align the car and landing sills so that they are substantially level with each other.

leveling device: Device that will move the car toward the landing only with the doors open; among the types are one-way, two-way, maintaining, non-maintaining, automatic, selectors, inductors, photoelectric and car-top readers.

leveling zone: Distance above and below the landing through which the car can move toward the landing with the doors open.

life line: Wire rope used during construction work that runs the height of the hoistway and that has connection fittings for safety belt lanyards.

life net: Rope net used below elevator construction work to catch any workers who fall.

lift: Term used for elevator in Europe and other parts of the world.

lift, wheelchair: See *wheelchair lift.* Also known as a *platform lift.*

lift, platform: Another term for *wheelchair lift.*

light emitting diode: Diode designed to illuminate when current flows.

light ray: See *photo eye.*

light curtain: Common term for a photoelectric door reopening device that has multiple infrared emitters and receivers along the height of the door opening.

lighting, standby: lighting provided on the elevator when the normal lighting power supply fails.

limit: Mechanical or electrical device that limits the travel of moving object.

limited use and limited application elevator: See *elevator, limited use and limited application.*

limit switch: Common term for a terminal stopping device.

line side: The side of a device that the power supply is from.

lining, brake: See *brake, lining.*

link, chain: The flat metallic side bar components, which are joined by bushings to form chains.

links, step: See *step links.*

lintel: Horizontal structural member across an opening that supports the load over it.

listed: Approval of equipment or materials by a certifying agency that is listed in a publication.

live: A term for *energized.*

load: (1) The weight of an object to be lifted; (2) any device that uses power.

loaded gap: The clearance between an escalator step and the adjacent skirt panel under force.

load, rated: See rated load.

load relieving ramp: Ramp with a low friction insert that reduces the load on the step rollers at the upper turnaround.

load side: The side of a device that an electrical load is on.

load, overhauling: Negative load resulting from an overbalance between the car and counterweight.

load weighing device: Mechanism used to determine the load inside an elevator car.

lobby: See *hall.*

lobby panel: Panel located in a lobby that can have control switches and indicators (position, direction, etc.).

lobby, sky: See *sky lobby.*

locking device, hoistway door or gate: Device that secures the door or gate in the closed position and prevents it from being opened from the landing side except under certain conditions; among the types are interlocks, retiring cams, combination mechanical locks and electric contacts, and mechanical locks.

locking plate: Plate used to lock a guide rail in place.

lockout relay: Auxiliary relay that keeps a device inoperative until it is electrically or mechanically reset.

logic control: See *control logic.*

logic, relay: Uses mechanical relays to perform control functions.

logic, solid state: Uses solid state switches to perform control functions.

loom wiring: Pre-assembled wires grouped together that run parallel to each other.

loop circuit: Continuous circuit connecting elevator drive motor and generator armatures in series.

low bar: Condition in which a commutator bar is below adjacent bars or mica.

lowering valve, manual: Manually operated valve used to lower a hydraulic elevator, when it cannot be moved in the normal manner.

low step switch: See *step level device.*

lower head: Term for the lower escalator pit in the U.K.

LSD: Abbreviation commonly used to denote that the equipment has been *left shut down.*

lubricant: Material used to reduce friction.

lubrication: The act of applying lubricants.

lubrication float switch: Switch sometimes used to detect a low lubricant level in an automatic lubricator.

lubricator: Device used to apply lubricant to components, such as suspension ropes, step chains or guide rails.

lug: Type of terminal connector.

LULA: Abbreviation, see *limited use and limited application elevator.*

lux: Metric unit of illumination.

machine, chain driven: See chain driven machine.

machine, driving: See *driving machine.*

machine, geared: See *geared machine.*

machine, gearless: See *gearless machine.*

machine, hydraulic: See *hydraulic machine.*

machine room: Room that contains the driving machine and control equipment.

machine room-less elevator: see *elevator, machine room-less.*

machinery space: Space that contains the driving machine.

machine, traction: See *traction machine.*

machine, winding drum: See *winding drum machine.*

magnet, brake: See *brake magnet.*

magnetic field: Condition in a region in space, created by a magnet or current carrying conductor, in which magnetic forces exist.

magnetic flux: Total number of magnetic lines of force passing through a certain area.

magnet, permanent: Body that always produces a magnetic field.

main brake: See *brake, main drive shaft.*

main circuit breaker: Circuit breaker on the load side of the main line disconnect switch.

main contactor: Contactor controlling the main power supply.

main drive chain: See *chain, main drive.*

main drive shaft brake: See *brake, main drive shaft.*

main drive shaft: See *shaft, main drive.*

main isolator: See *main line disconnect switch.*

main line disconnect switch: Manually operated switch in the machine room that connects and disconnects the power to the drive machine and controller.

main motor: The prime mover.

main supply: The main incoming power supply.

maintained pressure hydraulic elevator: See *elevator, hydraulic, maintained pressure.*

maintenance: Process of adjustment, cleaning, examination, and lubrication and replacement of components to keep them in proper working order.

maintenance, breakdown: Not true maintenance, but repairs after a malfunction.

maintenance contract: Contract specifying the requirements for the maintenance of an elevator or escalator.

maintenance contract, comprehensive: Maintenance contract that covers normal working hours but excludes callbacks.

maintenance contract, oil and grease: Maintenance contract that requires only periodic lubrication and examination.

maintenance contract, oil, grease and parts: Maintenance contract that requires periodic lubrication and examination and also covers certain components.

maintenance contract, full coverage: Maintenance contract that covers normal working hours and includes callbacks.

maintenance contract, preventive: Maintenance contract that requires preventive maintenance.

maintenance control program: A comprehensive method to ensure that maintenance is being performed correctly. It may be required by code. Abbreviated MCP.

maintenance performance guarantee: Contract provision in which certain performance criteria (e.g., mean time between breakdowns) must be met.

maintenance, planned: See *maintenance, preventive.*

maintenance, preventive: Maintenance done at set schedules or frequencies to try to prevent malfunctions. Abbreviated *PM.*

maintenance, scheduled: See *maintenance, preventive.*

make: To close or complete (i.e., a contact closes when it makes).

manlift: Device used for vertical transportation of personnel that has a continuous belt which has handholds and steps or platforms.

manual control switch: Manually operated switch that controls the operation.

manual reset: A means of requiring personnel intervention prior to restarting the equipment.

marked: Equipment or material that has a mark or label used to identify that it is certified or listed; also see *labeled.*

material hoist: Temporary device used to raise and lower materials during construction, alterations, or demolitions; not applicable to the temporary use of a permanently installed device.

material lift: A device classified by A17.1 as an elevator that transports materials. Classifieds as Type A (no persons permitted to ride) and Type B (authorized personnel permitted to ride).

may: Indicates permissive requirements, not mandatory.

MCP: Abbreviation, see *maintenance control program*

mechanic: Skilled journeyman worker who repairs, installs, maintains and services elevator, escalators and similar equipment.

mechanical lock, hoistway door or gate: Device that prevents the hoistway door or gate from opening unless the car is in the landing zone.

mechanical lock and electric contact, combination, hoistway door: Device that prevents operation unless the door is in the closed position, and prevents the door from being opened from the landing unless the car is in the landing zone and stopped or leveling; these functions are independent; there is no positive connection between the door locking mechanism and the electric contact, therefore it only ensures that the door is closed but not locked.

mechanism: Part or compilation of parts that produces an action or effect.

megger test: Measurement of an insulation's resistance.

m-g set: See *motor-generator set.*

mho: Unit of conductance, inverse ohms (ohm^{-1}).

mica: Heat resistant material used to insulate commutator bars.

micro: Unit prefix indicating one millionth (10^{-6}); for example, 1 microfarad is 0.000001 farad.

micro drive: System that uses a main machine for starting and running, but a small auxiliary machine for leveling.

micro switch: Electrical switch that reacts to very small movement of an actuator.

milli: Unit prefix indicating one thousandth (10^{-3}); for example, 1 milliamp is 0.001 amps.

mine elevator: See *elevator, mine.*

minnie line: See *rope, tail.*

missing pallet device: Safety device that stops a moving walk if it detects a missing pallet, prior to the resulting gap emerging from the combplate.

missing step device: Safety device that stops an escalator if it detects a missing step, prior to the resulting gap emerging from the combplate.

modernization: Process of updating the equipment; depending on what work actually is performed it may be classified as an alteration.

modular escalator: See *escalator, modular.*

molding, joint: See *joint molding.*

momentary pressure device or switch: Device that requires only momentary activation for the device to operate continually.

monitoring, remote: Monitoring the status of the equipment from a remote location through electronic means.

motion control: See *control, motion.*

motor: Device that converts electrical energy to mechanical energy.

motor, auxiliary: A motor other than the prime moving motor.

motor, compound: Motor that has a series and shunt field.

motor controller: See *controller, motor.*

motor field sensing means: Electrical protective device activated when current is not flowing in the shunt field of a DC motor.

motor generator running switch: Electrical protective device that prevents power from being applied to the driving machine and brake when static control is used, unless the motor generator set is properly switched for running the elevator.

motor-generator set: Consists of an AC motor that drives a DC generator, to provide DC power for the hoist motor and control circuits; abbreviated as *m-g set.*

motor, main: See *main motor.*

motor overload: Overload relay that protects a motor.

motor room: Term sometimes used for a machine room.

motor, series: Motor with the armature connected in series with the field windings.

motor, single phase: Motor that uses single phase AC current.

motor, shunt: Motor with the armature connected in parallel with the shunt field.

motor, split: Type of single phase motor that splits the single input phase in order to run.

motor, squirrel cage: See *squirrel cage motor.*

motor stair: Antiquated term for an escalator.

motor starter: See *starter, motor.*

motor, synchronous: AC motor in which the rotor rotates at the same speed as the magnetic field (i.e., no slip).

motor, universal: Motor designed to operate on either DC or single-phase AC current within a certain voltage or frequency range.

moving walk: A power driven device that carries passengers on an uninterrupted surface that remains parallel to the direction of motion; the riding surface can be a belt or pallets.

moving stairway: See *escalator.*

MRL: Abbreviation, see *machine room-less.*

muffler: See *silencer.*

mullion: Vertical supports on glass balustrade escalators or moving walks for the skirt panels, glass panels, and handrails.

multi-deck elevator: See *elevator, multideck.*

multi-meter: Instrument that measures several electrical properties such as voltage, resistance and capacitance.

multiple speed door: See *door, multiple speed.*

multi-voltage, control: See *DC control, multi-voltage.*

NAEC: Abbreviation, see *National Association of Elevator Contractors.*

National Association of Elevator Contractors: Association of independent elevator and escalator contractors and suppliers in the U.S.

National Building Code: One of the three major building codes in the U.S.; abbreviated as *NBC*.

National Building Code of Canada: A building code used in Canada; abbreviated as *NBCC*.

National Electric Code: NFPA code for the minimum requirements of electrical installations in the U.S.; abbreviated as *NEC*.

National Elevator Industry, Inc.: Association of major elevator and escalator manufacturers in the U.S.

National Fire Protection Association: See *NFPA*.

NBC: Abbreviation, see *National Building Code.*

NBCC: Abbreviation, see *National Building Code of Canada.*

NEC: Abbreviation, see *National Electric Code* (NFPA 70).

negative: Charge resulting from having an excess of electrons.

NEII: Abbreviation, see *National Elevator Industry, Inc.*

neutral: (1) Having neither a positive nor a negative charge; (2) electrical return wire.

neutral point: Where the brushes are placed on a DC motor or generator such that they are approximately midway between the poles.

newel: Extension of an escalator or moving walk balustrade at a landing where the handrail turns.

newel base: Located under the newel, where the handrail enters and exits.

newel, concentric: Semicircular-shaped newel.

newel, elongated: Parabolic-shaped newel.

newel entry brush: See *handrail entry brush.*

newel entry switch: See *handrail entry switch.*

newel, extended: Newel whose outer end extends past the comb teeth.

newel stand: Upright mounting that supports a newel wheel.

newel wheel: A wheel used to move an escalator or moving walk handrail.

NFPA: National Fire Protection Association; U.S. organization that publishes numerous standards and codes which deal with protecting people and property from fire.

NFPA 70: See *NEC*.

noise: (1) Acoustical sounds; (2) see *interference, electrical.*

non-preformed rope: See *rope, non-preformed.*

non-reversal device: See *reversal stop device.*

non-vision wing: See *sight guard.*

normally closed contact: Contact that completes a circuit when de-energized.

normally open contact: Contact that interrupts a circuit when de-energized.

nose line, step: The top edge of an exposed escalator step.

nudging: Automatic door operation with reduced closing speed and an inoperative door re-opening device.

observation elevator: See *elevator, observation.*

Occupational Safety and Health Act: Law in the U.S. that established standards for safe working conditions and provisions for their enforcement; abbreviated as *OSHA.*

ohm: Unit of resistance.

oil buffer: See *buffer, oil.*

oil, hydraulic: Hydraulic fluid used in oil buffers and as the working fluid in a hydraulic elevator jack.

one-to-one (1:1) roping: Suspension rope arrangement in which the speed of the car, counterweight and rope are the same.

open: Condition of an electrical circuit when current cannot flow.

operating device: Device used to activate a control.

operation, automatic: Elevator operation started by momentary activation of car or hall call buttons, and that stops automatically at the landings.

operation, car switch: Elevator operation in which the control of the direction and movement of the car is directly and solely controlled by a car switch or button.

operation, car switch automatic operation: Elevator operation in which the stop is initiated by an attendant after the car slows down and stops automatically.

operation, continuous pressure: (1) Elevator operation in which buttons must be manually held to move the elevator. (2) Door operation where opening and/or closing can only occur by manually pressing a button.

operation, control: See *control, motion.*

operation, double button: See *operation, continuous pressure.*

operation, group: Type of automatic operation in which the control system coordinates more than one car.

operation, nonselective collective: Type of automatic operation in which the car responds to (collects) calls placed irrespective of the direction of travel.

operation, selective collective: Type of automatic operation in which all "up" calls are responded to when the car is traveling up and all "down" calls are responded to when the car is traveling down.

operation, pre-register: Type of elevator operation in which calls are registered in the car and automatic stops are initiated by an attendant.

operation, signal: Type of operation in which the car can only be started by a means in the car and in which stops are made automatically in response to calls.

operating devices: Devices used to control the car operation such as buttons and switches.

operating speed, down direction: Speed of a hydraulic elevator in the down direction with rated load; different from rated load, which is in the up direction.

operator: See *attendant, designated.*

operator, car door: See *car door operator.*

OSHA: Abbreviation, see *Occupational Safety and Health Act.*

out-of-phase: Alternating current of the same frequency but in which one output leads the other in time; also known as *phase difference.*

over componding: See *compounding, over.*

overcurrent: Excessive current from a ground fault, short circuit, or overload.

overcurrent device: Electrical device that automatically opens a circuit under overcurrent conditions; see *fuse and circuit breaker.*

overhauling load: See *load, overhauling.*

overhead: Structural members supporting the equipment at the top of the hoistway.

overhead machine: Driving machine located over the hoistway.

overload: (1) A load that is in excess of the rated load; (2) operation with excessive current draw.

overload relay: Relay that responds to an electrical overload condition.

overload, thermal: Type of electrical overload relay operated by current flow through heaters bending bimetallic strips to open the contacts.

overslung: Arrangement in which the suspension ropes support the car from its top.

overspeed: Condition in which the equipment exceeds its rate speed.

overspeed switch, governor: See *governor overspeed switch.*

overspeed valve: Device installed in the piping of a hydraulic elevator that stops flow through the valve when it exceeds a preset amount; also known as a rupture or seismic valve.

overtravel: The distance that an object moves past its normal limit of movement.

packing: Material used to prevent leakage in a stuffing box.

pallet: Type of treadway, similar to a flat escalator step.

pallet level device: Electrical protective device activated when a moving walk pallet is displaced downward as it enters a combplate.

parallel, connected in: Circuit arrangement in which devices are connected such that current is divided between branches.

park: See *home landing.*

parking device: Device used to open the hoistway door from the landing side when the doors are not automatically unlocked or openable by a landing button when the car is in the landing zone.

passenger conveyor: Term used for a moving walk in Europe and other parts of the world.

passenger elevator: See *elevator, passenger.*

paternoster: European term for *manlift.* Literally means "our father," and refers to "the Lord's Prayer."

performance index, step/skirt: a number between 0 and 1 that indicates the likelihood of an entrapment between a moving escalator step and stationary skirt panels

periodic inspection: See *inspection, periodic.*

periodic test: See *test, periodic.*

personnel, authorized: Individuals trained in the operation or maintenance of equipment and therefore designated by the owner to use or maintain the equipment.

personnel, elevator: Individuals trained in the construction, inspection, maintenance, repair, or testing of elevators, escalators, etc.

personnel, emergency: Individuals trained for emergency evacuation of trapped passengers or the use of emergency or standby power and firefighters' service (emergency) operation.

personnel hoist: Temporary installation used to transport workers, typically at a construction site.

personnel protective equipment: Safety gear for personnel protection; abbreviated as *PPE.*

phase: Time relationship between the waveform of an AC current and voltage.

phase difference: See *out-of-phase*.

phase loss: Abnormal condition in which one phase is not supplied to a polyphase device.

phase, single: AC current with only one phase.

phase, split: Phase difference created by two coils energized from the same source.

phase reversal relay: See *reverse phase relay*.

phase, three: AC current with three separate phases that are 120 degrees out of phase.

Phase I: Portion of firefighters' service operation that removes the elevator from normal operation and recalls it to a designated landing based on a signal from a key switch or fire alarm initiating device (smoke detectors, etc.).

Phase II: Portion of firefighters' service operation that permits the control of the elevator exclusively by emergency personnel.

phasing, single: Abnormal condition in which a polyphase device is only supplied one phase.

photoelectric: Electrical response controlled by light.

photo eye: See *door re-opening device, photoelectric*. Also known as a *light ray* or *safe ray*.

pileup relay: See *relay, pileup*.

pinion: Small gear that engages a rack.

piston: Short cylindrical member, used in a hydraulic jack, which has a sealing means that travels with it in the cylinder.

pit: (1) The part of the hoistway below the bottom landing; (2) equipment area on an escalator or moving walk located under the landing and floor plates.

pit switch: Term for a stop switch located in a pit.

plank switch: See *safety operated switch*.

platen: Steel plate that connects a hydraulic elevator bolster to the plunger.

platform, car: See *car platform*.

platform elevator: See *elevator, platform*.

platform lift: See *wheelchair lift*.

platform guard: Beveled metal plate attached to a car platform to reduce the shear potential under it; also known as an *apron*.

plugging: Braking created by reversing a motor's voltage polarity or phase sequence.

plumb: Absolute vertical.

plunger: Long cylindrical member used in a hydraulic jack; also known as a *ram*. The sealing means is provided at the cylinder head.

plunger, telescoping: Set of concentric plungers.

PM: Abbreviation, see *preventive maintenance.*

PM 34: Health and Safety Executive document titled "Safety in the Use of Escalators."

PM 45: Health and Safety Executive document entitled "Escalators: Thorough Examination and Testing."

polarity: Condition of being positive or negative with respect to a reference point, which determines the direction of current flow.

pole: (1) Moving switch contact; (2) source of a magnetic field.

pole piece: Iron or steel structure that a coil is placed on to form a generator's or motor's magnetic pole.

pole shoe: Part of the pole piece that forms the air gap between the pole piece and a rotating armature.

police circuit: Term sometimes used for the circuit that maintains the directional contactors after the brake lifts and the starting sequence finishes.

polyphase: Multiple currents with constant phase differences.

port: Connection point.

position indicator: See *indicator, position.*

positive: Charge resulting from a deficiency in electrons.

post: See *stiles.*

potential: Difference in voltage.

potential switch: Contactor with its coil in series with the safety circuit and its contacts in the power supply; if the safety circuit is opened, then power is removed from the driving machine.

pot switch: Common term for a *potential switch.*

power: Change of energy with respect to time; units are watts or horsepower.

power elevator: See *elevator, power.*

power, emergency: Legally required system that provides electrical power essential for safety to human life upon the loss of normal power.

power, regenerated: Power fed back into the electrical supply lines when the motor receives more power than it uses and therefore acts as a generator.

power, standby (legally required): Legally required system that provides power to selected loads upon the loss of normal power.

power, standby (optional): System that provides power to selected loads upon the loss of normal power.

power, temporary: Electrical power supplied during construction activities before permanent power is available.

PPE: Abbreviation, see *personnel protection equipment.*

preformed rope: See *rope, preformed.*

pre-opening: Initiation of power door opening while the car is still leveling.

pressure: Force per unit area.

pressure, relief: See *relief pressure.*

pressure, working: See *working pressure.*

preventive maintenance: See *maintenance, preventive.*

private residence: Dwelling occupied by a single family unit.

private residence elevator: See *elevator, private residence.*

pulley, diverting: See *sheave, deflector.*

pull out force: Force required to pull the governor rope from the releasing carrier.

pull strap: Strap used to close a manual vertical door or gate.

pull through force: Force required to pull the governor rope through the speed governor jaws.

pump, hydraulic: Motor driven mechanical device used to increase the pressure of a hydraulic elevator's fluid (oil) to raise the car; two main types are submersible or non-submersible.

push button: Insulated button that activates contacts when pushed.

PVC: Abbreviation, see *polyvinyl chloride*, a plastic material.

QEI-1: *Standard for the Qualification of Elevator Inspectors*, ASME standard that establishes requirements for the qualifications and duties of inspectors and their supervisors in the U.S. for the equipment in the scope of A17.1.

raceway: Protective enclosures for electrical wires or cables.

rack: (1) Toothed bar that a pinion gear engages to transmit motion. (2) an assembly of escalator step links

rack and pinion elevator: See *elevator, rack and pinion.*

radial: In a direction along a radius.

radius: Straight line extending from the center of a circle or sphere to its periphery.

rail, guide: See *guide rail.*

rail backing: Structural member used to strengthen a guide rail.

rail bracket: Member to which the guide rail is attached.

rail clip: Clamp used to attach the guide rails to the rail brackets.

rail, guide: See *guide rail.*

rail, stabilizing: Third guide rail sometimes used for dumbwaiters to absorb heavy thrust loads.

ram: See *plunger.*

rated load: The load that the equipment is designed to move at rated speed.

rated load, escalator brake: The load that the brake is required to stop and hold a moving escalator or to hold a stationary escalator.

rated speed: Speed that the equipment is designed to operate with rated load.

reactance: Opposition to current flow caused by an inductance or capacitance.

recall landing: Landing to which Phase I operation recalls the elevator; see *designated landing* and *alternate landing.*

receiver: The part of a photoelectric door re-opening device that senses the light source (infrared or visible) sent by the transmitter.

rectifier: (1) Electronic device used to convert AC to DC; (2) electrical device that allows current to pass in one direction only.

recycling operation: Restoring the relative vertical position of multiple telescopic plungers.

reduced stroke buffer: See *buffer, reduced stroke.*

regenerated powers: See *power, regenerated.*

regeneration: Process in which stored mechanical energy is fed back into the electrical power supply lines.

register: Place a call by pressing a button.

re-groove: To rehabilitate worn sheave grooves.

regulator, speed: Device used to synchronize the speed of an elevator to a prescribed pattern regardless of the load; motor and electronic types are used.

regulator, voltage: See *voltage regulator.*

rehabilitation: Process of restoring equipment that can be part of maintenance or repair.

relating device: Device used to connect multiple door panels and determine their motion relative to each other.

relay: Electromechanical device activated by a current flow or interruption that opens and closes a contact.

relay, latching: Relay that only requires momentary current to activate and remains activated by mechanical means when the current is interrupted.

relay logic: See *logic, relay.*

relay pileup: Set of stacked contact armature assemblies separated by insulators.

relay, reverse phase: See *reverse phase relay.*

relay, set/reset: Relay with two coils and mechanical latches arranged such that the relay is held in one position until the other coil is energized.

relay, stepping: Relay in which moving contacts make a series of fixed contacts in a series of consecutive steps or positions.

releasing carrier: Mechanical device that may be used to attach the governor rope to the car.

relief pressure: Pressure at which a pressure relief valve opens.

relief valve: Valve that bypasses the hydraulic pump discharge when a certain pressure is reached.

remote monitoring: See *monitoring, remote.*

reopening device, door: See *door reopening device.*

repair: Process of rehabilitation or replacement of components that is basically the same as the original.

replacement: Substitution of a component that is basically the same as the original.

residual magnetism: Magnetic force remaining in an electromagnet after the coil is de-energized.

resistance: Property of a circuit or device that opposes current flow by converting electrical energy into heat.

resistor: Device that opposes the flow of electric current; can be fixed, variable or adjustable.

restricted area: Area to which access is limited to certain personnel.

retainer, safety: See *safety retainer.*

retaining ring: Component that restrains radial movement of a rotor.

retiring cam: Retractable device used to unlock hoistway doors and gates that operate independently of the door operator.

return: Area behind a wall or enclosure that a sliding door enters when opening.

reverse phase relay: See *relay, reverse phase.*

reversible: Capable of reversing the direction of travel.

reversal stop device: Electrical protective device activated by an ascending escalator reversing its direction of travel.

reverse phase relay: Device that prevents operation of a drive motor upon reversal of the phases of the AC supply to prevent operation in the wrong direction, and may prevent operation upon a loss of one or more of the phases.

reversing switch: Switch used to reverse connections in a circuit.

rheostat: Variable resistor that can be adjusted without opening the circuit.

rheostatic, control: See *DC control, rheostatic.*

ROA: Abbreviation commonly used to denote that the equipment reported to be out of service was found *running on arrival.*

rise: Vertical distance between the top and bottom terminal landings.

riser: (1) The vertical part of a step, referred to as the back end; (2) electrical wiring section that spans vertically between floors.

riser, cleated: Step riser with cleats that are intended to mesh with the slots of the adjacent step treads.

riser, smooth: Step riser without cleats.

rod, shackle: See *shackle rod.*

roof top elevator: See *elevator, rooftop.*

roller: Small cylindrical-shaped spokeless wheel.

roller chain: See *chain, roller.*

roller guides: Guide shoes that use wheels to roll on the guide rails.

roller, step: See *step roller.*

roller, step chain: See *step chain roller.*

rolling shutter: Metal shutters that automatically close downward upon smoke detection and sprinkler operation that can be used to provide a fire barrier at the floor openings of an escalator or moving walk.

rolling shutter device: Electrical protective device activated when a rolling shutter begins to close.

rooftop elevator: See *elevator, rooftop.*

rope, aramid fiber: non-metallic rope made of aramid (e.g., Kevlar) fibers. Commonly abbreviated as *AFR.*

rope band: Steel band sometimes used instead of wire for seizing.

rope brake: See *brake, rope.*

rope clip: Type of rope fastening; among the types are U-bolt and fist grip.

rope, compensating: Rope used to counterbalance the weight of the suspension ropes; see *compensation.*

rope core: The center part of a wire rope, which supports the wire strands of the rope. The three types are fiber, wire strand and independent wire rope.

rope creep: Relative movement (slippage) between the suspension ropes and the drive sheave.

roped hydraulic elevator: See *elevator, hydraulic, roped.*

rope equalizer: Device that automatically adjusts the tension in wire ropes.

rope fall: See *block and tackle.*

rope fastening: Devices used to fasten the ends of wire ropes; among the types are tapered, wedge socket, and clip types.

rope fiber: Member that is part of a nonmetallic rope.

rope, governor: Rope used to provide continuous feedback to the speed governor and which activates the car or counterweight safety activation means after the speed governor activates.

rope, hand: Rope used to activate the controls on some antiquated elevators; also known as a *shipper rope.*

rope, iron: Soft, ductile, low strength wire ropes; usually limited to compensating and governor ropes.

rope lay: See *lay, rope.*

rope, non-preformed: Wire rope manufactured from straight strands that are then twisted.

rope, preformed: Wire rope manufactured from strands formed to fit the twist in the rope.

rope retainer: See *sheave guard.*

rope, safety: See *rope, tail.*

rope, shipper: See *rope, hand.*

rope slippage: See *slippage, rope.*

rope socket: See *socket, rope.*

rope sprocket drive: Wire rope with fixed links attached which engage slots in a grooved drive cog.

rope stretch: Elongation of a rope under load.

rope, suspension: Rope used to support, lower and raise an elevator car or counterweight.

rope, tail: Rope attached between the governor rope and the safety; also known as a *safety rope* or *minnie line.*

rope, wire: For elevators an assembly of multiple wires twisted to form strands that are in turn twisted around a core made of fiber or steel; see *rope, suspension*; *rope, compensating*; or *rope, governor.*

rope valley: See *valley, rope.*

rosette: Term for the shape that wire rope strand ends are turned into, in preparation of placing them in a tapered rope socket.

rotary switch: Switch that makes and breaks contacts as it is rotated.

rotor: Rotating element of an AC motor.

rouge: Fine red iron oxide caused by fretting that is an indication of internal wire rope degradation.

round trip time: Average time for an elevator to travel from a lobby floor to drop off and pick up passengers and return to the lobby.

rpm: Abbreviation, see *revolutions per minute.*

runby, bottom: Distance that a car or counterweight must travel past the bottom landing to reach the buffer.

runby, top: Distance a hydraulic elevator must travel above the top landing to reach the mechanical stop.

running clearance: Distance between a moving object and another fixed or moving object.

running gear: All components of an escalator or moving walk which move along its tracks (steps, step chains, etc.).

runway: Enclosure between the bottom and top landing of a wheelchair lift.

rupture valve: See *overspeed valve.*

saddle: Part of a rope clip that prevents damage to the rope.

safe edge: See *safety edge.*

safe lift: Special equipment installed on an elevator to carry loads, such as safes, which exceed the normal rated load capacity.

safe ray: See *photo eye.*

safety belt: Belt designed to limit the distance that the wearer can fall.

safety bulkhead: Plate near the bottom of a cylinder of a hydraulic elevator which has an orifice to control the loss of fluid upon a failure of the cylinder bottom.

safety, car or counterweight: Mechanical device attached to the car or counterweight frame that clamps on to the guide rails under free fall, overspeed, or slack suspension rope conditions; it only activates in the down direction; among the types are Type A (instantaneous), Type B (gradual stop type: wedge clamp, flexible guide clamp, gradual wedge clamp, etc.), and Type C (combination Type A with oil buffers).

safety circuit: Control wiring that contains relay contacts and switches related to electrical protective devices.

safety circuit switches: Switches that have contacts in the safety circuit.

safety, duplex: Two pairs of mechanical safeties.

safety edge: Common term for a mechanical door or gate re-opening device, which requires contact with an object for it to function.

safety harness: Body suit designed to limit the distance the wearer can fall.

safety mechanism switch, car: See *safety operated switch.*

safety operated switch (SOS): Electrical protective device that operates before or at the time the car safety is applied; also known as a plank switch.

safety plank: Bottom horizontal part of the car frame, to which the car safety is attached.

safety retainer: Means provided to retain a hoistway door panel if the primary guiding means fails and prevent displacement if certain forces are applied to the panel.

safety rope: See *rope, safety.*

safety test: Test of the car safety with full load in the car or counterweight safety with no load in the car at either rated or overspeed conditions.

SBCCI: Southern Building Code Congress International, publishers of *SBC.*

SBC: See *Standard Building Code.*

scavenger valve: Device that automatically recovers oil from the jack packing head.

SCR: Abbreviation, see *silicon controlled rectifier.*

SCR control: See *thyristor control.*

screw column: Vertical member having screw threads that supports a screw column elevator.

screw column elevator: See *elevator, screw column.*

screw machine: Electric driving machine in which the motor drives a nut on a screw column or rotates the screw column to move the car.

secondary: Level below the machine room where the secondary and deflector sheaves, if provided, are located.

secondary sheave: See *sheave, secondary.*

seismic switch: Signal device activated by excessive ground movement that either takes an elevator out of service at a landing or reduces its speed.

seismic valve: See *overspeed valve.*

seizing: Small diameter wire used to secure the ends of a wire rope prior to cutting or socketing to prevent unraveling of the strands.

selector: Mechanically or electrically driven device that keeps track of the car's position in the hoistway and controls some or all of the following: acceleration, deceleration, call cancellation, door operation, hall lanterns, leveling, position indicators, stopping, and travel direction; also known as a floor controller.

selector brush: Brush used to complete a circuit on a selector.

selector contact: Contact mounted on a selector.

selector hoistway switch: Two-position switch mounted in the hoistway, operated by a cam on the car, which determines the direction of travel; also known as a dump switch.

selector motor: Motor than drives a selector electrically.

selector rope, chain or tape: Rope, chain or tape that drives a selector mechanically.

selysn generator-motor: Synchronizing system in which a generator is driven by the car motion which in turn drives a selector motor at the same speed.

series, connected in: Circuit arrangement in which devices are connected in-line such that current must pass through one device before another.

series field: Motor field coils connected in series with the armature.

service brake: See *brake, service.*

service (electrical): Conductors and equipment that deliver electricity to a building.

service elevator: See *elevator, service.*

shackle, rope: See *socket, rope.*

shackle rod: Rod used to connect a rope socket to the car or counterweight.

shaft: (1) Cylindrical rotating member used to transmit mechanical motion; (2) term commonly used for hoistway.

shaft, main drive: Shaft that is the primary mover of the escalator steps or moving walk pallets.

shall: Indicates mandatory requirements.

sheathing: Protective covering.

sheave: Grooved pulley type wheel that ropes pass over.

sheave, chain: Type of sheave used for chains.

sheave, deflector: Sheave used to divert the travel of ropes.

sheave, drive: Sheave used to move the suspension ropes through traction.

sheave, governor tension: See *governor tension sheave.*

sheave guard: Device used to prevent a rope from leaving a sheave groove and to prevent inadvertent contact with the ropes on a sheave.

sheave, idler: Sheave used to guide or apply tension to ropes.

sheave, secondary: Sheave used in a double wrap roping arrangement.

sheave, traction: Another name for *drive sheave.*

sheave, traveling: Sheaves mounted on the car and counterweight when two-to-one roping is used.

sheave, U-groove: Sheave with a groove shape that is approximately semicircular.

sheave, V-groove: Sheave with a groove shape that has flat tapered sides to increase the traction.

shielded: Enclosed to prevent electrical interference.

shim: Thin material or component used as a filler or leveler between two surfaces.

shipboard elevator: See *elevator, shipboard.*

shoe, brake: See *brake shoe.*

shoe, guide: See *guide shoe.*

short circuit: (1) Faulty electrical condition caused by defective insulation; (2) any connection that bypasses the normal current path by establishing a low resistance path.

should: Indicates permissive requirements, not mandatory.

shunt: (1) Connected in parallel; (2) device used to bypass current.

shunt field: The primary magnetic field of a motor or generator.

shutoff valve: See *valve, shutoff.*

side emergency exit (electric contact) switch: Electrical protective device activated when a side emergency exit door is not closed.

side opening door: See *door, side opening.*

side plates, step: See *step side plates.*

sidewalk elevator: See *elevator, sidewalk.*

sight guard: Member mounted on a horizontal slide hoistway door to reduce the clearance between the hoistway and car doors; also known as a non-vision wing.

signal device: Device that either registers a call or provides a visual indication.

silencer: Device used to reduce the noise of hydraulic fluid flowing in piping; also called a *muffler*.

silicon-controlled rectifier: See *thyristor*.

sill: Bottom horizontal part of a door entrance.

sill guard: Beveled metal plate attached to a landing sill or a car platform to reduce the shear potential under it.

sill stop: Guide rail stop for the lower panel of a vertical biparting door used to limit the downward travel.

sill, trucking: Top part of the lower section of a vertical freight door that acts as the sill between the open landing floor and the car platform.

sine: A trigonometric function.

sine wave: Waveform expressed as the sine of a linear function of time, space or both.

single phase: See *phase, single*.

single speed door: See *door, single speed*.

single phasing: See *phasing, single*.

single wrap: See *one-to-one roping*.

skirt: See *skirt panel*.

skirt deflector: Device, typically brushes, sometimes attached to escalator skirt panels to try to deter riders from placing their feet near the skirt panels.

skirt obstruction device: Electrical protective device activated when an object becomes caught between a moving escalator step and the stationary skirt panels, normally located near the combplates; commonly called a *skirt switch*.

skirt panel: Stationary panels located immediately adjacent to the escalator steps or moving walk treadway.

skirt switch: Common term for *skirt obstruction device*.

sky lobby: Upper lobby in a high-rise building in which passengers transfer from one elevator to another to travel further upwards.

slack rope switch: Electrical protective device activated by slack in the suspension ropes of a winding drum machine.

sleeve, cylinder: Liner used in a hydraulic cylinder.

slider: Contact that moves across a conductor or winding in order to achieve a certain output.

sling: See *car frame*.

slip: Difference in rotational speed between a rotor and the magnetic field of an AC motor.

slip rings: See *collector rings.*

slippage, rope: Loss of traction of a wire rope on a sheave.

slope: Vertical rise divided by horizontal run, angle with respect to the horizontal.

smoke curtain: Ceiling-mounted vertical member at the top landing of an escalator to act as a smoke barrier.

socket, rope: Type of wire rope fastenings. Among the types are tapered and wedge; also known as a shackle.

socket, tapered rope: Type of rope socket that has a tapered cavity to secure the rosette under tension and in which a babbitt is used as a retaining means for a loss of tension.

socket, wedge rope: Type of rope socket that uses a wedge element to secure a wire rope under tension and in which retaining clips are used for a loss of tension.

soffit: Underside of a structural member, such as a beam.

solenoid: Electromechanical device operated by a coil that has a steel or iron plunger as an armature.

solenoid valve: Electrically actuated valve.

solid state: Electronic circuits using semiconductors.

solid state device: Device that controls current flow without mechanical parts.

solid state logic: See *logic*, *solid state.*

Southern Building Code Congress International: See *SBCCI.*

SOS: See *safety operated switch.*

space guard: Device mounted on swing hoistway door to reduce the clearance between the hoistway and car doors.

special purpose personnel elevator: See *elevator*, *special purpose personnel.*

specification: Detailed document that prescribes materials, dimensions, and workmanship for something to be built.

speed: Distance traveled divided by time; also see *velocity.*

speed, contract: The speed that the manufacturer of the elevator or escalator designed the equipment to operate with its rated load.

speed governor: See *governor*, *speed.*

speed, operating, down direction: See *operating speed*, *down direction.*

speed, rated: See *rated speed.*

speed reduction unit: See *gear reducer.*

speed regulator: See *regulator*, *speed.*

spider: Supporting structure typically in a hub, spoke and rim arrangement.

spike: Abnormal, very short, high amplitude distortion of voltage or frequency.

spirator: Reel type door closer used on horizontally sliding doors.

split cable grip: Strain relief type of cable support; also known as *Chinese fingers* or *Kellam grip*.

spool cable hanger: Grooved device used to support traveling cables.

spotting: Condition during slowing down in which a car will pause and even reverse direction momentarily before continuing.

spreader bracket: Bracket used to strengthen counterweight guide rails.

spring buffer: See *buffer, spring*.

sprocket: Wheel with projections designed to engage chain links.

squirrel cage motor: AC motor with windings on the rotor made up of conducting bars with their ends connected by metal rings or plates.

stairway chairlift: Device with a seat that is guided up a stairway along stairways.

standby lighting: See *lighting, standby*.

standby power: See *power, standby (legally required)* and *power, standby (optional)*.

standard: Voluntary regulations, which may be intended to be adopted as codes.

Standard Building Code: One of the three major building codes in the U.S.

Standards Council of Canada: Organization that establishes national voluntary industry standards in Canada.

star connection: See *wye (Y) connection*.

star delta connection: See *wye delta (Y-Δ)*.

starter: (1) Person stationed in a lobby who manually controls the dispatching of elevators; (2) control equipment used to start and stop motors.

starter, motor: Control equipment that starts and stops a motor.

starter switching solenoid: See *Watford starter*.

start switch, escalator or moving walk: Manually operated accessible switch used to start an escalator or moving walk.

static control: Motion control system that uses solid state devices.

static electricity: Electrical charge caused by friction.

static switch: Solid state switch.

station, mechanics: See *inspection station*.

stator: The stationary part of rotating equipment, which can include the circuitry, the frame, and so on.

steady plate: See *car steady plate*.

step band: The assembly of escalator steps and step chains.

step chain: Endless heavy duty steel chain on each side of an escalator through which the drive machine moves the steps.

step chain axle: Shaft on the step chain to which each side of the front of an escalator step is attached.

step chain drive sprocket: Sprocket used to propel the step chain.

step chain guides: Solid strip within the step chain link plates sometimes used to guide the chain laterally.

step chain guide rollers: Rollers sometimes used to guide a step chain laterally.

step chain rollers: Rollers attached to the step chain that the step chain rides on.

step chain track: Support or guide track that the step chain rollers ride on.

step links: Toothed bars that are linked together to form a rack.

step chain wheels: See *step chain rollers*.

step cleat: See *cleat, step*.

step demarcation: Method (contrasting stripping, raised tread) of assisting passengers to determine the step boundaries.

step demarcation lighting: See *demarcation lighting, step*.

step, die cast: Escalator step manufactured by die casting.

step, escalator: Step-like escalator component on which the passengers are carried.

step, fabricated: Escalator step that is assembled.

step frame: Metal framework for a fabricated step.

step lateral displacement device: Electrical protective device activated when a step is displaced excessively on a curved escalator.

step level device: Electrical protective device activated when an escalator step is displaced downward as it enters a combplate.

stepper: See *relay, stepping*.

stepping relay: See *relay, stepping*.

step riser: See *riser*.

step roller: Roller used to support each side of the back (riser) end of an escalator step; also known as a *trailing wheel*.

step side plates: Plates attached to the sides of escalator steps to reduce the running clearance between the skirt panels and the sides of the steps and to guard the hollow spaces on the sides of the steps.

step/skirt performance index: See *performance index, step/skirt.*

step upthrust device: Electrical protective device activated when an escalator step is raised at the lower transition (curve).

step wheel: See *step roller.*

step tread: See *tread, step.*

step yoke: Part of the step where the rollers are attached.

stiles: Vertical car frame components that connect the crosshead to the safety plank; also known as *posts.*

stop: Device that mechanically prevents movement.

stop button: Button used to activate a stop switch.

stop diamond: Emergency stop button design principally used on the London Underground escalators.

stopped handrail device: Safety device that stops an escalator or moving walk if the handrail stops while the escalator or moving walk is still operating.

stop switch: An electrical protective device of which there are various kinds (emergency, in-car, pit, top of car, etc.).

stop switch, emergency: (1) Accessible manually operated electrical protective device located inside the car; (2) accessible manually operated electrical protective device located on the exterior of an escalator or moving walk.

stop switch, in-car: Stop switch inside the car that is not readily accessible (requires a key to operate or access).

straight arm closer or lock: Type of mechanical door closer or lock that can only be opened from the car, except with the use of a special tool.

straight line wiring diagram: See *wiring diagram.*

strain box: Raceway box that contains devices to support vertical wiring in the hoistway.

strainer: Device that filters particles from a hydraulic fluid.

strain wire: Wire used for support in a traveling cable.

strand: (1) Metal wires twisted around each other, which in turn are twisted together to make a wire rope; (2) wire conductors that are twisted together to form a stranded wire.

strength: Ability of a material to resist failure caused by stress.

stress: Force per unit area.

stress, yield: See *yield stress*.

stretcher gear: Pair of wheels and system of weights sometimes used to tension escalator handrails.

stretch, rope: See *rope stretch*.

striker plate: Structural element attached to the bottom of a car frame or counterweight that is designed to contact the buffers.

stroke, buffer: Amount that a buffer can be compressed.

strut angle: Landing entrance components that the header is attached to, which runs vertically from the sill to a building structural element.

stuffing box: Chamber that holds packing tightly around a moving part, such as a valve stem.

sub-post car frame: See *car frame, sub-post*.

suicide circuit: Safety circuit used to cancel a generator's residual magnetism and prevent an inadvertent build up of loop current when the car is supposed to be at rest.

supervisory system: Dispatching system.

suspension chain: See *chain, suspension*.

suspension rope: See *rope, suspension*.

swing door: See *door, swing*.

switch: Device that opens and closes to control current in an electrical circuit.

switchboard: Enclosure containing the main circuit breaker, the main line disconnect switch and in many cases a means for locking out these devices.

switch gear, supply: Group of switchboards electrically connected to the main power supply and individual controllers.

tank, hydraulic: Storage reservoir for the hydraulic fluid of a hydraulic elevator.

tachometer: Instrument used to measure revolutions per unit of time, which can be converted into speed.

tandem operation: Escalators or moving walks operating in series with a common intermediate landing; the units must be electrically interlocked if bunching of passengers can occur when the unit leaving the intermediate landing stops.

tapered rope socket: See *socket, tapered rope*.

temporary power: See *power, temporary*.

tension carriage: See *carriage.*

terminal: Connecting point for a wire.

terminal block: Insulated base that terminals are mounted on.

terminal landing: Top or bottom landing served by the equipment.

terminal slow down switches: Switches used to slow down an elevator at the terminal landings.

terminal speed limiting devices, emergency: Electrical protective devices required for reduced stroke buffers to reduce the speed of an elevator at the terminal landings.

terminal stopping devices: Electrical protective devices that activate when the car approaches or passes the landing; among the types are normal, final, and emergency; commonly referred to as *limit switches.*

terminal stopping devices, normal: Activate when the car passes the terminal landing, but permits movement towards the landing; also known as *directional limit switch* or *normal limit.*

terminal stopping devices, final: Activate when the car passes the terminal landing and prevents all movement of the car; also known as a *final limit.*

terminal stopping devices, emergency: Required for static control with speeds exceeding a certain limit.

test: Mandatory operation of the equipment to verify its proper function; usually witnessed by the inspector and performed by the building owner's agent; usually classified as periodic or acceptance.

test, acceptance: Test of newly installed or altered equipment to ensure continued compliance with the relevant standards and codes.

test, periodic: Detailed test of existing equipment performed periodically (e.g., annually or every five years) to ensure continued compliance with the relevant standards and codes.

test, safety: See *safety test.*

three phase: See *phase, three.*

thermistor: Electronic device in which a change in temperature causes a change in resistance.

threshold plate: Term sometimes used for a combplate, especially on moving walks.

throw: The number of make-break operations that can be made with a single pole of a switch or relay.

thyristor: Rectifier that conducts in only one direction and once triggered continues to conduct until an external circuit is interrupted; also known as an *SCR.*

thyristor control: See *DC control, single bridge thyristor and DC control, dual bridge thyristor.*

tie down: Mechanical arrangement to prevent equipment movement.

time lag: Time interval between two events, such as a cause and effect.

toe guard: See *sill guard.*

tolerance: Permissible variation of a quantity from a specified value.

top-of-car operating device: Device located on top of the car that removes the elevator from normal service and only permits its operation from the device.

torque: Rotational force.

track: Guideway.

traction: Friction developed between the suspension ropes and the drive sheave.

traction elevator: See *elevator, traction.*

traction machine: Direct drive machine that moves the car through friction between the suspension ropes and the drive sheave.

traction sheave: See *sheave, traction.*

traction steel: Grade of steel that suspension ropes are made of for use on a traction elevator.

trailing wheel: See *step roller.*

transformer: Electrical device used to increase (step up) or decrease (step down) an AC voltage, or to isolate a circuit from its power source.

transmitter: The part of a photoelectric door re-opening device that emits the light source (infrared or visible).

transom: Panel sometimes used to close the opening above a hoistway entrance.

transverse: In a lateral direction.

travel: Distance the equipment moves along the path of motion between the terminal landings.

traveling cable: Flexible cable that electrically connects an elevator, dumbwaiter or material lift to a fixed point.

traveling nut: Nut that moves along a screw as the screw turns.

traveling sheave: See *sheave, traveling.*

treadplate: See *combplate.*

tread, step: Top horizontal surface of an escalator step or moving walk treadway that passengers stand on.

tread section, step: Removable step tread section.

treadway: Moving walk component on which passengers are carried; among the types are pallet, belt and belt-pallet.

trickle charge: Continuous low rate of charge used to keep a battery fully charged.

trigger: To activate or trip.

trip: Term used for *activate*.

trucking sill: See *sill, trucking*.

truck zone: Distance above a landing that the car can move toward the landing with the doors open.

truss: Escalator support structure assembly.

turn around: Section of an escalator where the steps change from the exposed side to the return side.

two-to-one (2:1) roping: Suspension rope arrangement in which the car's speed is half the rope's speed; the ropes start at a dead ended hitch in the overhead, down under the car, up over the drive sheave, down to a counterweight sheave and back up to a dead ended hitch in the overhead.

type test: Laboratory test conducted to verify code compliance in which a certificate is issued.

oil buffer: See *buffer, oil*.

UBC: See *Uniform Building Code*.

U-bolt rope clip: Rope clip in which only one end has a saddle.

U-groove: Semicircular shaped sheave groove.

under compounding: See *compounding, under*.

undercutting: Removing mica so that it is below the surface of the commutator bars.

underslung: Arrangement in which the suspension ropes support the car from its under side.

underspeed switch: Switch in the safety circuit that activates when the speed drops below a predetermined limit.

understep lighting: See *demarcation lights, step*.

UL: Abbreviation, see *Underwriters Laboratories*.

unloading ramp: See *load relieving ramp*.

unlocking device, hoistway door: See *hoistway door unlocking device*.

unlocking zone: Distance above or below the landing that the car can be and the doors are permitted to be unlocked.

Underwriters Laboratories: An independent U.S. testing and certification organization.

Uniform Building Code: One of the three major building codes in the U.S.

unlocking device, hoistway door: Device used to open a locked hoistway door, with the car not at the landing, through the use of a special tool. There are several types—drop key, lunr key, T-key.

upper head: Term for *upper escalator pit* in the U.K.

upthrust angle: See *upthrust track*.

upthrust pin: Lug or pin sometimes provided on the step to engage the upthrust track.

upthrust tab: Tab sometimes provided on the step to engage the upthrust track.

upthrust rollers: Hanger roller that limits the vertical upper movement of a door.

upthrust device, step: See *step upthrust device*.

upthrust track: (1) Track used to prevent upward displacement of escalator steps in the return (underside) side; (2) track commonly used to activate a step upthrust device.

U-rail: U-shaped guide rail used for dumbwaiters.

valley, rope: Where adjacent strands of a wire rope contact.

valley break: Outside wire strand break that extends from one valley to the next.

valve: Device used to control the flow of fluid through a piping system.

valve, control: See *control valve*.

valve, manual lowering: See *manual lowering valve*.

valve, shutoff: Valve used to isolate the hydraulic jack from the rest of the system.

valve, relief: See *relief valve*.

valve, solenoid: See *solenoid valve*.

vane: See *cam*.

vane, door: See *door vane*.

variable resistance control: See *DC control, multi-voltage*.

variable voltage AC (VVAC) control: See *AC control, variable voltage*.

variable voltage/variable frequency (VVVF) control: See *AC control, variable-voltage/variable-frequency*.

vector: Line segment that has both a magnitude and direction.

velocity: The rate of change of distance traveled with respect to time; commonly used interchangeably with speed; however, velocity is a vector quantity (i.e., it has both magnitude and direction), but speed is a scalar (i.e., it only has a magnitude).

V-groove: V-shaped traction sheave groove.

vertically bi-parting door: See *door, vertically bi-parting.*

vertically sliding door: See *door, vertically sliding.*

vertically sliding gate: See *gate, vertically sliding.*

viscosity: Fluid property that measures a resistance to flow.

vision panel: Small window in a car or hoistway door.

Volt: Unit of measure of electrical potential difference.

voltage drop: Voltage difference across a device or circuit.

voltage regulator: Device that maintains a constant voltage output.

voltmeter: Instrument used for measuring voltage.

volt-ohmmeter: Instrument used for measuring voltage and resistance.

V-ring: Commutator assembly component used to keep the bars together.

VVAC: Abbreviation, see *variable voltage alternating current.*

VVVF: Abbreviation, see *variable voltage variable frequency.*

Ward-Leonard control: A term used for *generator field control.*

warning: Statement indicating a potentially hazardous condition that could result in death or serious injury.

water hydraulic elevator: Hydraulic elevator that uses water pressure to move the car.

Watford starter: Solenoid actuated accelerating rheostat that shorts out resistance in steps.

watt: A unit of energy.

web: Thin connecting member between the flanges of an I-beam.

wedge guard: See *ceiling intersection guard.*

wedge rope socket: See *socket, wedge rope.*

weight: Resultant force of attraction on a mass due to a gravitational field.

weights, test: Metal ballast of a known weight used for testing of elevators or escalators.

well: Term used for *hoistway* in Europe.

wellway: Part of the building in which an escalator truss is installed.

wheelchair lift: Device intended for use by the mobility-impaired; does not penetrate a floor and is not provided with a full enclosure; has a limited vertical travel, speed and platform area.

wheel, newel: See *newel wheel.*

wheel, trailing: See *step roller.*

winding: Conducting coil.

winding drum elevator: See *elevator, winding drum.*

winding drum machine: Geared drive machine in which the suspension ropes are fastened to a drum and wind on and off the drum.

winding, field: See *field winding.*

winding, primary: Transformer winding connected to the power supply.

winding, secondary: Transformer winding connected to the load.

winding, starting: Winding used to produce the torque needed to start a motor.

wipe: Sliding or rubbing motion between two contact surfaces.

wire: Long thin metal rod with a circular cross section.

wire crown: See *crown, wire.*

wiring diagram: Schematic drawing showing the electrical control and signal circuits; also known as a straight line or ladder diagram, or electrical prints or drawings.

wiring diagram, field: Electrical drawings showing the wiring sizes and connection details.

wiring loom: See *loom, wiring.*

work: The product of a displacement and the component of the force vector in the direction of the displacement that caused it.

working pressure: Measured pressure at the hydraulic drive machine when either lifting the rated load at rated speed, or leveling up with the maximum load for freight Class C2.

worm: Spiral grooved shaft.

worm gear: Gear that engages a rotating worm.

worm gear machine: Direct drive machine in which the motor connects to the drive sheave or drum through worm gearing.

worm reduction gear: See *gearbox.*

wye (Y) connection: Connecting the motor windings in a Y configuration; also known as a *star connection.*

wye-delta (Y-Δ): Term used to describe an electrical motor start-run winding configuration.

yield stress: Stress in tension that produces a permanent deformation of 0.2 percent.

yoke, step: See *step, yoke*.

zone, landing: See *landing zone*.

zone, unlocking: See *unlocking zone*.

About the Authors

The unique aspects that the authors bring to this book are their varied and multifaceted experience related to elevator and escalator accidents.

Jim Filippone is a mechanical engineer, who started his career in the design and construction of nuclear power plants. Three Mile Island subtlety convinced Jim that a change in industries was in order. He joined the Port Authority of NY & NJ several years later, and started his elevator and escalator career.

He became deeply involved with inspections, maintenance evaluations, testing, code compliance, accident investigations, and specification and contract development/review. This has included jurisdiction over approximately 900 elevators and 500 escalators and moving walks. It is reported that this represents the second largest grouping of escalators for one owner in the USA and one of the largest for elevators. This equipment is installed at three major airports, the World Trade Center, bus and train terminals, seaports, and a wide variety of industrial/commercial facilities.

The challenges of this diverse operating environment was supplemented by the necessity for assuming the role of equipment owner, building management, lessor, inspector and consultant as the conditions and need arose.

Jim is licensed in New Jersey and QEI certified an elevator/escalator inspector. He is a licensed professional engineer in New York and New Jersey. He earned a BS degree in Mechanical Engineering (BSME) from Manhattan College and an MS degree in Management (MSM) from Polytechnic University.

Jim has been deeply involved with development of the A17.1 Safety Code for Elevators and Escalators and the A17.2 Inspectors' Manual for Elevators and Escalators, serving on the following A17 Code Committees:

Main (Standards)- 1995 to present (member) &1993-1995 (alternate)

National Interest Review- 1991 to 1995 (member)

Inspections- 1989 to present (member), Vice Chair 2006-2012, Chair 2012-2015

Maintenance, Repair and Replacement- 1996 to present (member)

Escalator and Moving Walk: 2002-present (corresponding/contributing member)
National Interest Review Committee: Member 1991 to 1995
Editorial, 1996 to present (member)
He is also a NYC Elevator Code Committee member

Joel D. Feldman, Esq. is an attorney who received his J.D. in 1981 from Villanova University School of Law. He is a shareholder and managing partner of the Philadelphia law firm of Anapol, Schwartz, Cohan, Feldman & Smalley, P.C. He has served as an associate editor of the Philadelphia County Reporter, which publishes trial court opinions in Philadelphia. He is admitted to the Bar in Pennsylvania and New Jersey, and is an active member of the Philadelphia and American Trial Lawyers' Association.

He is the author of a number of articles pertinent to litigation, including "Protective Orders in Product Liability Cases," Vol. 4, No. 1, The Brief, American Bar Association, Fall, 1984.

He is a member of the Philadelphia Bar Association's Mid-Sized Law Firm Management Committee, and has been active in various organizations pertinent to the preservation of historical structures in the Commonwealth of Pennsylvania.

His product liability practice has included successfully representing victims injured by faulty machines, products, tools, construction equipment, automobiles, consumer products, leisure and sport equipment, as well as elevators and escalators. His litigation experience involving escalators and elevators has included cases against elevator and escalator manufacturers, owners, and maintenance companies.

He is a frequent lecturer in Pennsylvania and New Jersey, as moderator and faculty member, continuing legal education courses involving aspects of litigation including deposition techniques, use of expert witnesses, accident reconstruction, highway design, governmental immunity, liquor liability and ethics.

His nonlegal interests include historical preservation, snow skiing, rock climbing and gardening.

He lives in Springfield, Pennsylvania with his wife Dianne L. Anderson, and his children, Casey and Brett, to whom this book is dedicated.

He can be reached at jfeldman@anapolschwartz.com

Ronald D. Schloss, executive director, SEEC, LLC (seec@att.net), is an elevator consultant and electrical engineer with a life-long dedication to the vertical transportation industry. All of his 50-plus working years, except for military obligations, have been in the elevator industry. This is ironic because his first 17 years were isolated in a small southern Illinois coal-mining town. The area was devoid of elevators and escalators, except for those elevators that carried the miners several hundred feet below the surface and down into the tunneled world of coal mining. His father, Moxie "Max" Schloss, first introduced him to elevators. After a career as a professional boxer, bouncer and bartender Max worked the remaining years in elevator maintenance and eventually got Ron into the International Union of Elevator Constructors (IUEC) after Ron returned from his 2 year tour in the Far East Theater in the US Army. Ron was an installer for Otis, and a maintenance technician, engineer and manager for Westinghouse Electric Corporation's Elevator Division that later became Schindler Elevator Corporation. Ron left the corporate world in 1996 and founded SEEC, LLC.

Ron has published numerous books and articles for the vertical transportation industry, some of which can be obtained through Elevator World magazine and McGraw-Hill Publishing Company.

He is a member of the American Society of Mechanical Engineers, National Association of Elevator Contractors, and International Association of Elevator Consultants.

Ron is serving as a member on the following ASME A17 Code Committees:

National Interest Review, 1997 to present Inspectors' Manual, 1993 to present
Maintenance, Repair and Replacement, 1996 to present

David Cooper, BSc(Hons), MSc, MPhil, CEng, FRSA, FIET, FCIBSE has over 30 years of experience in the lift and escalator industry. He is the Managing Director of U.K. based consulting engineers LECS (U.K.) Ltd. He holds a Master of Philosophy Research Degree following a five-year investigation into accidents on escalators, a Masters Degree in Lift Engineering and a Bachelor of Science degree, Higher National Certificate and Continuing Education Certificate in lift and escalator engineering. He is a Fellow of the Chartered Institute of Building Services Engineers (CIBSE) and a Past President of the Lifts Group. He is also a Liveryman in the Worshipful Company of Engineers. He has appeared on a number of TV and radio programs with respect to lifts and escalators. He has co-authored a number of books including *The Elevator & Escalator Micropedia* (1997) and was the lead author of CIBSE Guide D (2000, 2005 and 2010 editions). David has been a regular columnist in the U.K. trade journal *Elevation* since 1994 and has had articles published in other journals including *Elevator World*, *Elevatori*, *Elevator Kai*, *Lift Report* and *Revista del Asenscori*. He is also the founder and principal of the Lift Academy which provides educational support for apprentices and trainees in the industry and also a trustee of the Lift & Escalator Industry Charity which supports families with financial assistance in the event of an industry member being injured at work. He has been a member of 480 Elevator and Escalator Accident Reconstruction and Litigation the British Standards Institute committee for lifts and escalators (MHE/4) since 1990.

Joseph L. Stabler began his career in the elevator industry in 1975 before graduating from the Basic Institute of Technology in Electronic Engineering Technology (1977). Thereafter, he co-founded Custom Home Elevators of St. Louis where he served as president, owner/manager, and principal sales engineer of commercial and residential vertical and incline platform lifts, dumbwaiters, and residential elevator systems. Joe subsequently sold his company interest in 1979 to pursue and earn his journeyman mechanic's certificate through the International Union of Elevator Constructors (1984) where he worked as an elevator constructor, service technician, adjuster and field engineer for two multinational manufacturers. He subsequently earned his QEI certificate from NAESA (1991-Present) and then founded Stabler Associates, Inc. (1992), an independent elevator and escalator consulting firm where he serves as the President/CEO. In 1995, Joe was appointed by the Governor of Missouri to codify and promulgate rules for the Missouri Elevator Safety Act and serve as a "Special Inspector" on the Elevator Safety Board (1995-2003). Further, Joe has earned and holds numerous certificates and licenses for elevator/escalator inspection including an additional QEI certificate from Lift Technologies International (1997-2008); Missouri State Licensed Elevator Inspector (2000-2003); and, Electrical Contractor's License (2005-Present). He has been directly involved in design, construction, inspection, modernization, planning, repair, review, service and testing of approximately 6,000 conveyance systems. Joe is also a member of the American Society of Mechanical Engineers (2009-Present) and serves on the following committees: ASME A17 National Interest Review Committee (1996-Present); Maintenance, Repair & Replacement Committee [(Alternate R. Schloss) 2007-Present]; Escalator & Moving Walk Committee (2009-Present); Inspection Committee [(Alternate R. Schloss) 2011-Present]. Joe has also given presentations on post-accident investigation and equipment inspection to the Society of Forensic Engineers and Scientists (1998) and NAVTP (2003), respectively; performed or reviewed over 700 accident investigations; and given approximately 325 depositions and testified as an expert witness in 18 trials throughout the United States on subjects regarding contracts, warranties, design defects, construction, repair, maintenance, modernization, and industry customs and practices regarding various short range vertical, horizontal and inclined conveyance and transportation systems. In 2004, Joe became Co-Owner, Assistant Vice President, Chief Director of Operations and Technical Support of Custom Home Elevators for new product sales, field engineering, construction, service, repair, troubleshooting and testing of residential elevators, incline platform lifts, vertical platform lifts, incline chairlifts, and dumbwaiters.

Gabriel F. Zambrano, Esq. attended the University of Miami for undergraduate studies and received his J.D. from Boston University in 1993. He is a career litigator and Trial Lawyer based out of South Florida.

He handles personal injury cases and catastrophic injury cases on a daily basis. This includes injuries from motor vehicle crashes, trucking and commercial vehicle crashes, as well as elevators and other vertical transportation devices. His professional background includes handling select product liability cases which include mass tort and pharmaceutical device cases resulting in disability or death.

He is a member of the Executive Committee for the **National Trial Lawyers**, the **National Trial Lawyers Top 100**, **American Association for Justice**, and hold an AV rating by his professional peers trough the Martindale-Hubell © Peer Review Rating system. He lives in Fort Lauderdale, FL, with his wife and four children.

His nonlegal interest include, stand up paddle boarding, surfing, mountain biking, rollerblading, running and being a volunteer recreational youth soccer coach for the City of Fort Lauderdale, FL.

He can be reached at gabe@gabrielfzambrano.com , gabe@florida.law and https://www.linkedin.com/in/gabrielfzambrano

Index

E

M

R

Slips and Falls: A New Approach to Friction Measurements, Second Edition

By Fred M. Johnson, Ph.D.

Slips and Falls: A New Approach to Friction Measurements, Second Edition is an explanation of the physics topic of friction and its relation to slips and falls. As well as slipping phenomena, other important and relevant friction related concepts and applications are presented to clearly guide you through this complex topic. This book explains the use of equipment such as tribometers in measuring friction in falls and their level of accuracy. It explains other measuring techniques used and assumptions that come up when working with friction in fall cases, and shows which ones are erroneous and which are valid.

This book also discusses other aspects that apply to the physics of friction in slip and fall accidents, and gives you a back-to-basics understanding of the physics of falls. It is a great companion volume to *Slips, Trips, Missteps and Their Consequences*. It is an essential book and a call to action for any professional currently involved in the investigation, research and litigation of slip and fall incidents.

Topics Include:

- Introduction of Friction
- Pedestrian slip and fall
- Friction parameters
- Adhesion
- Forces and energy
- Traction demand
- Human gait
- Coefficients of friction
- Heel strike
- Push-off
- Slip hazards
- Measurement methodology
- Measurement technology
- Measurement techniques
- Lab facilities for friction measurement

Produce Code: 6648 • ISBN: 978-1-936360-71-0
Pages: 144 • Softbound • 6"×9"

Construction Accident Reconstruction, Second Edition

By Jon R. Abele, Esq. and Calvin Zemsky, PE

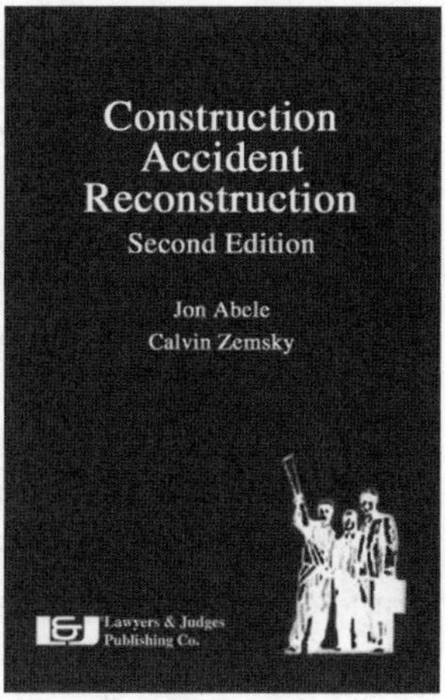

Litigation relating to construction site accidents appear on the court dockets of every judicial district throughout the country. The number of lawsuits filed because of accidents has grown year after year. Until now there has been no single place for a person to obtain the information of what a forensic engineer does when reconstructing an accident. This book, now in its second edition, fills that void. It has been updated and expanded throughout by Jon Abele, Esq. It also allows attorneys to learn the basics of forensic engineering while providing guidance to accident reconstructionists on how to conduct an investigation into a construction worksite accident.

Construction Accident Reconstruction will introduce attorneys and engineers to the proper methods of investigating an accident case of this type. It is presented in a straightforward, yet lively manner that should inform and also challenge the reader to think about accident reconstruction in a new way so that they can better represent the workers injured on the construction site. This book presents the statistics of fatal and non-fatal accidents to acquaint the reader with the magnitude of the number of people who are seriously injured in the construction industry every year. Jobsite injuries are preventable, yet millions of workers suffer injuries when the proper preventative measures are not used. Failure to follow safety standards leads to lawsuits when workers are injured.

Produce Code: 1035 • ISBN: 978-0-913875-65-0
Pages: 329 • Softbound • 6"×9"

Electrical Injuries:
Medical and Bioengineering Aspects, Second Edition

Edited by Raymond M. Fish, Ph.D., M.D., and Leslie A. Geddes, Ph.D.

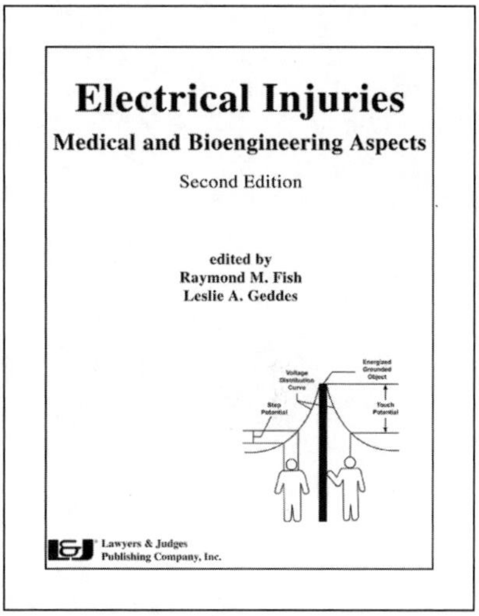

Since the first edition of this book, new information about many aspects of electrical and blast injuries has become available. As a result, a variety of topics have been added and updated in this second edition. You will be pleased with the results. This book explains electrical and blast injuries in a useful way to physicians and other medical personnel, military personnel, patients and their families, educators, engineers, attorneys, and other professionals.

Divided into six sections for ease of use and navigation, this book covers clinical management, bioengineering, body system injuries, electrical sources, accident reconstruction, and much more! Understanding electrical injuries and explosions (electrical or bombing-related) is complex and a multi-disciplinary perspective is required. Information from both medicine and engineering is relevant to the understanding of such injuries. This new edition offers you this approach.

Topics include:

- Basic concepts needed to understand electrical injury
- The let-go phenomenon
- Initial priorities: accident scene and emergency department
- Subtle diagnostic and prognostic factors in electrical trauma
- Treatment of specific injuries
- Patient disposition: indications for monitoring
- Electrical injuries by body system
- Psychological effects of electrical accidents
- Forensic perspectives in electrical fatality cases
- Accident reconstruction in electrical injury cases
- Understanding the information in medical record

Produce Code: 6087 • ISBN: 978-1-933264-63-9
Pages: 616 • Casebound • 8.5"×11"